Home Town News

Home Town News

William Allen White and the *Emporia Gazette*

SALLY FOREMAN GRIFFITH

THE JOHNS HOPKINS UNIVERSITY PRESS

BALTIMORE

Originally published in 1989 in a hardcover edition by Oxford University Press.
Published by arrangement with Oxford University Press.

Johns Hopkins Paperbacks edition, 1991

The Johns Hopkins University Press
701 West 40th Street
Baltimore, Maryland 21211

The paper used in this book meets the minimum requirements of American National Standard for Information Sci-
ences—Permanence of Paper for Printed Library Materials,
ANSI Z39.48–1984.

Library of Congress Cataloging-in-Publication Data
Griffith, Sally Foreman.
Home town news : William Allen White and the Emporia gazette /
Sally Foreman Griffith. — Johns Hopkins paperbacks ed.
p. cm.
Reprint. Originally published: New York : Oxford University Press, 1989.
Includes bibliographical references and index.
ISBN 0–8018–4210–7
1. White, William Allen, 1868–1944. 2. Journalists—United
States—Biography. 3. Emporia gazette (Emporia, Kan. : 1899)
4. Emporia (Kan.)—Social life and customs. I. Title.
[PN4874.W52G75 1991]
818'.5209—dc20
[B] 90–21686 CIP

To my parents,
Mary Anne Foreman
James Bradshaw Griffith

Acknowledgments

This work has been shaped by the many communities of which I have been a part. I am indebted to those institutions that have provided essential financial support at various stages of the work's development: Johns Hopkins University and the Smithsonian Institution provided graduate fellowships, and Villanova University a faculty summer research grant. Other institutions have ensured access to the materials essential to historical research. The librarians in the Manuscript Division of the Library of Congress, the Kansas Collection of the Kenneth Spencer Research Library at the University of Kansas, the Lilly Library at Indiana University, and Special Collections of the William Allen White Memorial Library at Emporia State University and at Grinnell College and Villanova University were gracious and helpful. The staff of the Lyon County Historical Museum in Emporia greeted me with professional assistance and genuine friendship during my visits to Emporia. None of this work would have been possible without the support of the White family, Mrs. William L. White and Mr. and Mrs. Paul David Walker, who allowed me access to materials in their possession and generous permission to quote widely from William Allen White's writings. At Oxford University Press in New York, Sheldon Meyer was consistently encouraging and Gilda Abramowitz's editing was admirably alert and sensitive.

The weekly seminars of the history department at Johns Hopkins University when I was a graduate student created a challenging yet congenial environment in which to develop as a historian. No doubt, many of my ideas were shaped there in exchanges that I have long since forgotten. All of the Hopkins history faculty contributed to my education to some extent, but my teachers, Louis Galambos, John Higham, Vernon Lidtke, and Kenneth Lynn, contributed most through their knowledge and their commitment to the collective scholarly enterprise.

This work evolved through countless retellings of White's story, in informal conversations and at scholarly conferences. Each telling before a different audience added to my understanding, but I have benefited most from the responses of those who read part or all of the work at different stages in its long development: James L. Baughman, James Bergquist, John Milton Cooper, the late Catherine L. Covert, Elizabeth L. Eisenstein, David Glassberg, Richard L. McCormick, William S. Pretzer, James K. Pringle,

Richard A. Schwarzlose, Kate Torrey, June Underwood, Joseph F. Wall, and Bernard A. Weisberger. During my tenure at the National Museum of American History as a Smithsonian graduate fellow, Elizabeth Harris and Stanley Nelson of the Division of Graphic Arts shared with me their expertise in the world of "practical printers," and Carl Scheele, now retired from the Division of Community Life, offered his sage perspective on American culture. Portions of Chapter 9 appeared previously in somewhat different form in *Mass Media Between the Wars: Perceptions of Cultural Tension, 1918–1941,* Catherine L. Covert and John D. Stevens, eds. (Syracuse, N.Y.: Syracuse University Press, 1984), pp. 141–55.

Whatever insights I have into small-town life are the product of my singular good fortune in having been born and reared in Lusk, Wyoming. My parents taught me, among many other things, the importance of community participation. During my years of working after school at the *Lusk Herald,* the staff demonstrated to me the best values of community journalism in action. Jane and Gerald Bardo, in particular, continue to provide a shining example of how life can be deepened and enriched through commitment to a community.

S.F.G.

Contents

Home Town News

Introduction

William Allen White arrived in Emporia, Kansas, in the early evening of Saturday, June 1, 1895. He had just bought the *Emporia Gazette,* borrowing all of the $3,000 he had paid for the down-at-the-heels little newspaper. He had $1.25 in his pocket. As he stepped down from the train he had taken from Kansas City, he faced a decision. Nearly fifty years later he would relive the moment with particular relish:

> I still can remember with what joy I rode across Kansas into the sunset and through the long twilight. . . . This also I remember: when I stepped off the train at Emporia it was into a considerable crowd of idlers who in that day came to the station to see the two plug trains come in from Kansas City. The announcement had been made that I had bought the Gazette. . . . I knew many of the faces that greeted me. I had a moment's indecision: Should I lug my heavy baggage uptown to the boarding house where I was expected, and establish a reputation as a frugal, thrifty young publisher, or should I establish my credit in the community by going in a hack? The hack was a quarter. I decided, as a credit-strengthening act, to take the hack. . . . I never regretted it. . . . A good front is rather to be chosen than great riches.[1]

Evoking Benjamin Franklin's account of his arrival in eighteenth-century Philadelphia with only a Dutch dollar and a copper shilling in his pocket, White's story is an origin myth that has been often related as the beginning of his ascent to fame. Like Franklin or a Horatio Alger character, he went on from this moment to make a successful career. By the time of his death, in 1944, he was nationally known, and widely beloved, as an author, political leader, and social commentator.[2]

This story of White's arrival in Emporia is more than a steppingstone to his eventual renown, however. It vividly illustrates that the small-town newspaperman was a public personage in nineteenth-century America. He played a major role in his community, and he performed it in a public setting, very much as an actor performs a role onstage. Emporia was a face-to-face community in 1895, its population just over eight thousand. The small town was a world that paid close attention to the behavior of its citizens. In a simple society with few formal institutions, members of the community needed personal knowledge of one another, and behavior bespoke character.[3]

Moreover, the proprietor of the local newspaper wielded special powers.

He determined which events and people were deemed "newsworthy," and, in the days before systematic polling techniques, he defined "public opinion." He also performed roles within his community far beyond the obvious function of recording the news. As a businessman in his own right, the newspaperman was a leading member of the local business community and was expected to play a prominent role in promoting the town's economic development. He was a moving force behind nearly every public community activity, whether it be a civic celebration or a fund-raising drive. He was invariably an activist in his political party, and both he and his newspaper served as the principal means of political communication. He maintained wide networks of journalistic, political, and economic connections that were necessary for conducting business in the nineteenth century. He was a spokesman for his community and was often called upon to act as mediator, both among local groups and between his community and the outside world. These functions were performed informally, but they were the result of the newspaperman's control of the preeminent medium of communication in nineteenth-century America.

White's memory of his arrival also underlines that he was quite conscious that he *was* playing a role, and that he relished the opportunity to manage appearances that such performances offered. He knew this small-town world intimately, for he had been born in Emporia twenty-seven years before and had grown up in El Dorado, not far away. When he stepped down from the train that day, he knew instinctively that all eyes in Emporia would be on him. He also knew journalism, for he had spent ten years working for newspapers in nearly every possible capacity, from printer's devil to political columnist. And he knew that what was *not* made public was as important as what was. About his arrival, he commented, "If the crowd had known that when I paid the hackman I had just a dollar left (a fact which was nobody's business) the opinion of the town would have been divided about me. As it was, no question arose in the mind of the town about my financial ability." As editor of the *Gazette*, White skillfully managed the newspaper's image of himself and, most important, of his community. He worked behind the scenes to stage public events, and then reported them in his newspaper without acknowledging his role. Like Franklin, he realized that one gained more credit by refusing to take public credit. But he also hoped to create the impression that these events were a spontaneous expression of Emporia's community spirit.

White also understood, as Franklin had, that his public actions had economic implications, for the judgments of his neighbors would determine his access to financial resources. Both men knew that journalism was a business and that the small-town newspaperman who hoped to prosper was perforce a businessman. But where Franklin hoped to acquire a useful reputation for thrift by carrying his own newsprint through the streets of Philadelphia, White understood that his credit rating would benefit more from an appearance of prosperity than one of frugality.[4]

This moment of arrival not only launches this account of White's career as editor and publisher of the *Emporia Gazette,* it introduces this book's purpose and approach: to understand the role of journalism in American culture by examining its actual practice in a single community at a specific historical moment. In form, it is a biography of William Allen White, but it uses his career as a window, or perhaps I should say a prism, to observe the communication process as a complex interaction among communicator, audience, and medium, involving many different facets, including the psychological, social, cultural, economic, technological, and political.[5]

Journalism eludes established disciplinary boundaries. A major means of expressing ideas, it has throughout American history been intimately tied to politics. Yet it is also a business that both instigates and adapts to economic and technological change. The small-town newspaper, moveover, has played an integral role in the development of communities in America, acting as their promoter, interpreter, and watchdog. The difficulty in placing newspapers in standard academic categories may help explain why historians have paid relatively little attention to journalism as an object of research, even as newspapers form one of their most popular sources of information. Nonetheless, its eclectic nature makes journalism an excellent subject for interdisciplinary research. To do justice to this diversity, this study has applied the perspectives of a wide range of scholarly disciplines, including communication studies, anthropology, and sociology, and economic, political, intellectual, and community history and the history of technology.[6]

One might wonder how much can be learned about the practice of small-town journalism from the study of such an atypical figure. White's career as editor and publisher of the *Emporia Gazette* was chosen for several reasons, the first practical. Although in aggregate numbers far more Americans at the turn of the century read smaller local newspapers than read metropolitan dailies, journalism historians have focused almost exclusively upon the latter. One reason is that few records exist for most small-town newspapers or their publishers. William Allen White, on the other hand, left voluminous collections of his papers at the Library of Congress and elsewhere. These contain much of the *Gazette's* business correspondence, particularly for the years 1899 through 1916. This correspondence provides abundant material for a study of the day-to-day business of a small-town newspaper: selling advertising, promoting circulation, cultivating correspondents, and buying type, paper, and printing machinery. We are consequently able to observe how different aspects of the industrialization and modernization processes—such as the mechanization of production, the increasing dominance of large national corporations in the production and distribution of goods, the rise of the advertising industry, and the advent of rural free delivery—acted and interacted to change both journalism and community life.[7]

White's letters also reveal the many roles he performed in Emporia, roles that were typical and, indeed, expected of small-town editors in White's day, and to a great extent even today. White played each of these roles well in Emporia. By the 1920s, he had also become a figure on a larger national stage, transforming his typical performance into an archetypal one—that of the Small-Town Editor—well suited to the nostalgia of a newly urbanized society. By following the progress of his career, first locally and then nationally, we see enacted central themes of his vocation.

One of the most important roles that White was expected to perform as a small-town newspaperman was that of "boosting" his community in every way possible. Boosterism, that favorite butt of urban satirists, has emerged as a central theme of this book because of the sheer dominance of its assumptions and rhetoric in the *Gazette* and in White's writings. It became clear that his relentless preaching and organizing on behalf of Emporia was more than simple puffery. The assumptions behind his words and actions embody a world view—assembled from such disparate sources as Puritan theology, classical republican ideology, Hamiltonian political economy, and Emersonian idealism—that permeated popular thought about community and economic growth in nineteenth-century America. While it can hardly be called a philosophy, this world view merits the title of "booster ethos."[8]

Although a number of historians, most notably Daniel Boorstin and Lewis Atherton, have described aspects of boosterism in nineteenth-century America, there has as yet been no effort to delineate fully and systematically its arguments and assumptions or to assess its place in American culture. The booster ethos addressed the need in newly created towns for both economic growth and social order. It offered a vision that fused economic and moral values in the belief that a town's prosperity rested upon its spiritual condition. Though frequently expressed in hardheaded terms of practicality and economic success, boosterism was essentially idealistic in that it assumed that spiritual qualities controlled material ones. One might say that boosters raised practicality to the level of an ideal.[9]

Economic growth, however, was the nineteenth-century town's reason for being, and the booster ethos assumed that the interests of local businesses were identical with those of the community as a whole. Consequently, prosperous businessmen were also the community's natural leaders. Although such assumptions clearly provided a rationalization for the dominance of an economic elite, they entailed obligations as well. Boorstin notes the new connotations of the term "businessman" in nineteenth-century America: he is not "simply a man engaged in mercantile transaction," but "a peculiarly American type of community maker and community leader." According to the booster ethos, a businessman was not in business for himself, but for his entire community.[10]

This conception mitigated the potential for conflict within small communities based upon an economic system that, at least in theory, pitted men against each other in the pursuit of profits. The booster ethos sought to channel individual competitive energies toward the interests of the community as a whole, arguing that the fortunes of each were tied to the prosperity of all. Harmony within the community was therefore a means to both economic growth and social cohesion.

White's role as a leading booster significantly shaped his practice of journalism. Boosterism's demand for economic growth directed the content and tone of his newspaper; its demand for harmony limited its ability to accept expressions of conflict, narrowing public access to different points of view; and its emphasis on business leadership affected its definition of the visible community. In sum, the booster ethos helped substantially to sustain the local authority of businessmen in small-town America.

White also performed other roles that sometimes reinforced and sometimes counteracted his role as booster. The newspaperman, for example, was almost invariably a political leader. In the nineteenth century, most small-town newspapers devoted much of their attention to politics. Indeed, many were wedded to politics because they depended for their survival upon the financial support of political parties or factions. In return for material aid, newspapers were expected to promote their parties' policies and a vision of the community that reflected partisan interests. As White would discover to his chagrin, the demands of politics and boosterism could conflict.

By the end of the nineteenth century, however, changes in America's economy had begun to erode this relationship between newspapers and political parties. The small-town newspaperman had become an increasingly prosperous businessman in his own right, as the rise of advertising as a major industry provided new revenues for his paper as well as for urban papers and magazines. Moreover, these newspapers aided the process of economic change by acting as go-betweens in the formation of an alliance between local retailers and producers of brand-name goods against the enemies of both, urban department stores and mail-order houses. Most important, through advertisements and proconsumption publicity the newspaper introduced its readers to the brand-name products of the national corporations.

Historians have observed the emergence at the start of the twentieth century of a new political system in which the power of partisan political organizations had declined, to be replaced in part by the influence of special-interest organizations. This study traces an important link in that shift. As other sources of income freed journalists like White from dependence on political patronage, they began to openly challenge the prevailing political order. They justified this bid for independent political power by claiming to represent "the people" through their accustomed role as spokesmen for public opinion. In Kansas, journalists were prominent leaders of a new insurgent coalition within the Republican party that around 1905 sparked the beginning of progressivism in Kansas.[11]

"Progressivism," that slippery cluster of causes, ideas, and institutions, is a prominent part of this story, because it was a major part of William Allen White's life and identity. This study traces the interaction of personal, political, and economic factors in White's gradual transformation from conservative to progressive Republican. Above all, by placing White's changing political activities and ideas in the context of his roles as aspiring community leader and successful small businessman, it captures the sense of progressivism, not as a single coherent intellectual system but as a set of flexible yet powerful arguments for reform. White's career offers insight into the mechanisms whereby a disparate and often contradictory set of causes emerged and assumed at least the appearance of a united progressive movement.[12]

In promoting a variety of reform causes in Emporia, in Kansas, and throughout the nation, White developed his own brand of progressivism by adapting the booster ethos to changing times. He shaped a vision of the small town as a progressive ideal in which shared "social sympathy" provided the cohesion necessary for true democracy. He also argued that the small-town newspaper fostered this feeling of community through its reporting of the homely news of everyday life. This vision remains today a central tenet of the philosophy of community journalism.

If White can best be understood as a performer of many roles as a small-town newspaperman, his career must also be placed in the specific context of his audience, his community. Unlike today's journalist, who rarely hears from his readers but receives most of his responses from professional colleagues, White was surrounded by his audience. He was never at a loss to know how his work was received, for he faced the reviews of his previous day's effort each morning as he pursued his business up and down Commercial Street. He chatted about current events with passers-by and stopped at all the stores and offices to gather news, solicit advertising, and in general feel the pulse of public opinion. His office was open to all who cared to stop in and talk.

By closely examining White's activities in Emporia, this book observes concretely the relationship between the newspaperman and his audience. It applies tools of community studies to learn about Emporia itself, drawing upon a wide variety of local sources to examine the connection between "actual" events and their depiction in the *Gazette*. A study of a newspaper in the context of its community has added significance because of the central place of the press in what historian Thomas Bender has called "public culture," the common arena in which society's many groups have met and struggled to make dominant their particular definition of reality.[13]

It has been the goal of this work to pay attention to the texture of life as White and his fellow Emporians experienced it, to capture some of the richness and ambiguity of life in small-town America at the turn of the twentieth century. By staying close to concrete experience it also provides insight into the specific causes and effects of historical change that are commonly obscured through sweeping generalizations about "industrialization." It has listened closely to the words used by White himself and paid close attention to the connections between his rhetoric and the specific goals that he hoped to accomplish. We thereby gain insight into the precise relationship between expressed ideas and goals, or how one "does things with words."

Similarly, the book has been structured largely as a narrative in order to focus attention upon human experience as a continuing process of adapting to unique situations. In keeping with these intentions, discussions of historical theory and method have been kept in the background, although historiographical implications have been touched upon in the footnotes. Theory has not been ignored, and has frequently informed interpretations of specific events. But too often when theoretical analysis is placed in the foreground in historical writing, the complexity of human experience is lost, reduced to logical abstractions or ideal types. Concepts borrowed from social science theory, such as the contrast between "traditional" and "modern" societies, "genteel" versus "commercial" culture, or "inner-directed" versus "other-directed" personalities, may offer insight when carefully applied as analytical tools. But too often they become convenient labels with which to categorize rather than understand experience. Assuming that such distinctions refer to inherently contradictory or mutually exclusive tendencies prevents the realization that these characteristics often coexist, happily or uneasily, within the same person or culture.[14]

The structure of this book mirrors its intention to combine conventional biographical narrative with analysis of White's many roles. Part I describes his life before his arrival in Emporia and his first years as the new editor of the *Gazette*. Part II describes the many strands of change in White's career after 1900 by focusing on specific roles: Chapter 3 on his management of the *Gazette*'s expansion; Chapter 4 on his emergence as a progressive; Chapter 5 on his leadership of reform in Emporia and Kansas; Chapter 6 on his interpretation of progressivism for his national audience; and Chapter 7 on his elaboration of the role of community journalism. These chapters build upon each other to disclose the complex intertwining of factors in the development of White's career. Finally, Part III carries the themes established in Parts I and II through the 1910s and 1920s. The Epilogue comments on White's national reputation in the 1930s and 1940s. Despite his growing national fame, White would continue as official editor and publisher of the *Gazette* and remain involved in community affairs until his death in 1944. By the 1920s, however, he was also participating in a larger, more cosmopolitan national community. He delegated most of the *Gazette*'s management in order to pursue his book and magazine writing and political activities. For the *Gazette,* as in many other aspects of American culture, the 1920s mark the end of an era, and for that reason this study concludes there.

From his youth on, White was ambitious, as he put it in his *Autobiography,* "to be somebody." He became a national figure by deftly performing each of his many roles as small-town newspaperman, drawing upon the strengths of each in pursuing the others. *Home Town News* follows the career of this remarkable man, from aspiring small-town editor to America's beloved archetypal Small-Town Editor.

PART I

The New Man

1

The Education of a "Somebody"

> There is another man in town they call Pap. He wears a stove pipe hat and carries a cane, and weighs (since the event) eight hundred pounds. He talks of sending the "young man" down on "Warnut" to take charge of the branch store.[1]

Thus did the *Emporia News* take notice of the birth of a son to Mary Hatten and Allen White on February 10, 1868. To a modern reader this birth announcement seems strangely lacking—it mentions no names, reports none of the vital statistics, and overlooks the child's mother entirely. Yet it is a revealing introduction to the world into which William Allen White, the son in question, had been born and in which he would grow to manhood. The men and women in this world would be young Will's models of how to act and what to believe.

The United States had just begun the most dramatic stage of its transformation from an agrarian to an industrial society. By 1900 the American economy would be dominated by giant national corporations, its people increasingly clustered in large cities. But in 1868 most Americans lived on farms or in small towns like Emporia, a community of five hundred inhabited by small-scale businessmen, artisans, and farmers. This world was founded on personal, face-to-face relationships. In such a world, personal identity was in many ways a public product. Just as the *News* could indicate the man, Dr. Allen White, merely by describing his customary attire, the individual self was defined by how one looked and behaved to others. Identity was the product of countless encounters with and judgments by friends, acquaintances, and neighbors. It was far from the world of autonomous, self-willed individuals posited by some social theorists and historians as characteristic of nineteenth-century America.[2]

In such a world people learned the really important local news by word of mouth. Because the *News,* a weekly paper, came out several days after the birth in the White family, the facts would already have been widely known. Consequently, the paper provided commentary instead. It jocularly underlined the meaning of the event for the community: "Doc" White, in becoming a father, had moved to a new stage in life—hence the reference to his even greater than usual "weigh[t]" under new responsibilities and his solemn plans for the future.

The small-town newspaper in the nineteenth cenutry followed few of the norms of today's ostensibly objective journalism. Its purpose was less to mirror reality than to create a vision of the community that embodied the economic and political goals of its proprietors and backers. Such goals determined not only how the paper reported specific events, but the very definition of what was newsworthy. For example, that the *News* completely ignored Mary White's part in the birth illustrates that the public it portrayed was dominated—and for the most part peopled—by men. Politics and local economic development, the main concerns of small-town newspapers, were considered part of the purely masculine sphere. As young Will White would quickly learn, politics was a central feature of men's lives and identities. Boys fought fistfights on behalf of their father's party's presidential candidate; voting for the first time was a key rite of passage to male adulthood; and political discussion was a major form of masculine entertainment.[3]

The newspaper was also a central tool of town building in nineteenth-century America. Emporia had been founded in 1857 by leaders of the anti-slavery forces in the struggle to determine whether Kansas would enter the Union as a slave or free state. Its founders hoped to accommodate the influx of Northern settlers and make money by selling town lots. They launched the Emporia *News* a few months later, and, like other such enterprises, it sought to create an image of its community that promoted its economic growth. Nearly all of the copies of the first issue of the *News* were mailed east to prospective emigrants, and it portrayed Emporia as founded upon the bedrock of free-soil ideals of enterprise and progress. These were reinforced by the town charter's ban on gambling and alcohol. The very name of the new town reflected its founders' intention to plant a commercial city, for the first Emporia had been a great trading city-state in the western Mediterranean.[4]

In short order the fledgling community acquired the economic and civic institutions that were considered essential to the success of midwestern towns in the nineteenth century. It captured the coveted status of county seat from nearby Americus in 1860 and secured the Kansas State Normal School, the teachers' academy, in 1863. Soon after young White's birth the railroads arrived and Emporia became a crossroads of the Santa Fe and the Missouri, Kansas, and Texas, or "Katy," railroads. In 1882 Kansas Presbyterians would locate their college there, naming it the College of Emporia. With these institutions, and with the prosperity of the farms and ranches in its hinterland, Emporia quickly became a flourishing commercial center for Lyon County and east central Kansas.[5]

The *News* was first edited by nineteen-year-old Preston B. Plumb, an investor in the company that founded the town. Plumb quickly became the unquestioned leader of the fledgling community. He was of a breed familiar in those days of expansion, a man who lavished his time and fortune on "his" new town. Although undeniably motivated by self-interest—he owned one-fifth of the town lots and stood to benefit from the increase in value that would accompany growth—Plumb wanted more than money. He aspired not simply to wealth, but to public respect, to becoming what was known as a "leading citizen." Such standing required a reputation for public service and strong ties of personal loyalty developed by helping one's friends and neighbors. Plumb formed many lasting bonds when he led the company of Emporians who defended the Union during the Civil War. As the town grew after the war, ties of financial obligation reinforced those of friendship. When the Emporia National Bank was chartered in 1872, Plumb became its president, and his former captain, L. T. Heritage, became cashier.[6]

Like Plumb, Allen White aspired to be a leading citizen. As a young boy William Allen White would absorb from his father a sense of the necessity of leading an active public life, not merely because of civic duty but because such contributions defined and reaffirmed one's identity. Though unquestionably a man of strong character, the senior White craved public recognition and delighted in contact with others. His son recalled, "I know that one of his hidden vanities was to be the first man on the subscription paper with the largest donation." Whenever Allen White stopped to chat on Main Street "he drew a crowd around him by some kind of spiritual gravity." He was "an addict to hospitality" who "knew his greatest joy as a host." In fact, he habitually brought out-of-town acquaintances home to dinner, even though he knew it meant recriminations afterward from his wife, who resented the extra work.[7]

As his son remembered him late in his own life, Allen White was a paradox, a gregarious, self-deprecatory man who nonetheless was not afraid to hold unpopular opinions. He was a Democrat in a fiercely Republican section of Kansas, and he advocated a negotiated peace in a civil war in which most of his male neighbors were fighting. Yet his good humor, his civic spirit, and his generosity won him acceptance and respect. Although he had a medical degree, White could barely make a living practicing medicine, because he rarely collected his fees. So he alternated medicine with business, and was far more successful financially at keeping a store and speculating in real estate.[8]

Despite or perhaps because he was short and fat (one account described him as "five feet by 240 pounds"), Dr. White was concerned about the impression he made. His hat and cane, which his son said he carried to lend an air of dignity, were so much a part of his public image that the *News* could use them alone to signify him. He was meticulous about his appearance, in summer sporting a white Panama hat and immaculate white nankeen linen suits. Indeed, judging from William Allen White's frequent detailed descriptions of the dress of the men in his childhood and youth, such concern was common. It was a way to establish one's public image.[9]

Nonetheless, Emporia frustrated White's ambition for local eminence, perhaps because of his political deviance, perhaps because of Plumb's preeminence. Soon after their son's birth, the Whites moved to El Dorado, a town southwest of Emporia on the Walnut River, or "Warnut," as the birth notice had put it. It had been founded only a few years before and provided Allen White with greater scope for his energies and ambitions. A longtime El Dorado resident recalled him as "the strong central figure" in the town during the 1870s. "He was enthusiastically interested in the growth and progress of the town and hardly a night passed that he did not have some private or public meeting of the people to discuss something of importance." Another said that he was jokingly called the "Boss of the El Dorado Ring. . . . because we acknowledged him to be our leader."[10]

Allen White promoted his adopted community in every conceivable way. He put up a substantial building for his new drugstore and invested in local real estate. He raised a fund to underwrite the founding of a newspaper and persuaded an Emporia friend, Thomas Benton Murdock, to edit it. He led a campaign to secure the county seat for El Dorado. Although he never went to church himself, he helped to build every church in El Dorado and to pay the minister in at least three of them. He served often on the city council and took a term as street commissioner to make sure that Main Street was paved.[11]

He also loved politics, and took pains to bring up his son to follow after him. He took young Will with him as he traveled the county putting together a Democratic organization, and later took him along on trips to state political meetings. Though he sought political positions, serving often in town offices, his son depicted him as being more comfortable working behind the scenes. Later in life, William realized that his father "was in some ways an exceptional man who sought real leadership and tried to keep it anonymous; who loved power but always pretended he had none. . . ." William Allen White learned from his father that in nineteenth-century politics, holding office was only one way, and often an inferior one, of achieving political power.[12]

Will grew up with the security of knowing that "my father was somebody" and that his family was of the "ruling class" of their status-conscious little world. Such an awareness imparted a sense of confidence but also an instinctive awareness that in a small town status depended on being recognized by others. It was the product of a reciprocal relationship between a "somebody" and his public. Growing up as an active participant in a world formed of dense networks of personal connections, White would become perceptive at assessing "public opinion" through the reactions of his neighbors on the street. He would not always obey its dictates, but he never failed to understand its language.[13]

Allen White died in 1882. He was mayor of El Dorado, and the entire town turned out for the funeral, filling the yard of the White house and the streets beyond. His son, who was then fourteen years old, later admitted, "I was not without my pride, looking back as we made the turn half a mile from home and headed for the East Cemetery, to see the long line of carriages and wagons and carts still moving into the procession on Main Street." The turnout was indeed an impressive public demonstration that Allen White had succeeded in his ambition to become El Dorado's leading citizen. His son would be driven by the ambition to be "somebody," as his father had been.[14]

As portrayed by her son, Mary Hatten White was the antithesis of her husband in nearly every conceivable aspect of personality and belief. Where he was emotionally reserved, she was sentimental and given to emotional outbursts. He avoided quarrels; she was fierce and relentless in argument. He loved jokes of all kinds; she had no sense of humor whatsoever. He was a skeptic in matters of religion, more at home with the spirit of classical humanism; Mary, born to Irish Catholic parents but converted to Congregationalism as an orphaned teenager, was intensely religious. According to her son, she was obsessed with questions of social status and public opinion, while her huband was indifferent to what others thought. Finally, she had as a student at Knox College seen Abraham Lincoln debate Stephen Douglas and had fallen "madly, platonically, but eternally in love" with Lincoln. She was a staunch Republican.[15]

If his father introduced young Will to the masculine world of politics, his mother shared with him the supposedly more feminine world of literature. Long after he could read to himself, Mary White read to her son every evening, although her husband complained bitterly that she was spoiling him and hampering his development. Together they read the nineteenth-century classics: Scott, Cooper, George Eliot, George Sand, Tennyson, Trollope, and above all Dickens, whom both mother and son adored. Allen White, on the other hand, urged his son to read Plutarch, with less success.[16]

It is impossible to know whether this opposition between the two was as absolute as their son recalled, but their differences did frequently lead to heated arguments, often in their child's presence. William Allen White would come to believe that his parents represented temperamental poles and that he had inherited equally from both. As a child he longed for harmony in his household, and as an adult he would struggle to balance the demands of ambitions and traits bequeathed by both parents. The strong differences between his parents also engendered early in young Will a sense of moral relativism—as he put it, "a certain lack of conviction which comes from seeing both sides well presented by those you love and knowing full well there are two sides to everything. . . ." Many times as an adult he would seek the moral certainty that his upbringing had denied him, and he often fell under the influence of those who appeared sure of what they wanted and believed.[17]

Despite these conflicts, William Allen White recalled his childhood in nearly idyllic terms. He had the run of the town and the surrounding countryside with its dense woodlands and open prairies, and his *Autobiography* is lyrically nostalgic about the freedom of a frontier boyhood. He was the beloved only child of aging parents, for Mary was in her late thirties and Allen in his late forties when he was born. A brother, born several years after him, died at two or three. White's only recollection regarding his brother was a feeling of intense jealousy, and his departure from the scene seems to have made him doubly grateful for the privileges accorded an only child.[18]

After her husband's death, Mary White took in boarders to supplement the income from his real estate investments. This brought into the house-

hold two new adults who to the fourteen-year-old represented a more cosmopolitan vision of culture. The local newspaperman, Thomas Benton Murdock, and his wife, Marie Antoinette Murdock, were a strikingly handsome
and highly cultured couple who clearly enthralled the impressionable youth.
An eccentric aesthete who affected exquisite negligees, Mrs. Murdock taught
dramatic elocution, read the latest books and magazines, and wrote literary
reviews for her husband's newspaper. According to White, she was one of
the first to recognize the literary breakthrough represented by *The Story of
a Country Town,* the novel by fellow Kansan E. W. Howe.[19]

Virginia-born "Bent" Murdock was similarly cultivated and assured. He
read widely, wrote well, and dressed impeccably, importing his suits from
Brooks Brothers. A journalist, who as a young *Gazette* reporter knew Murdock a quarter of a century later, recalled: "He was always faultlessly
dressed, his collar flowing out to points and his cravat neatly tied, and he
invariably wore a flower in his lapel." Murdock had been a close friend of
Allen White and quickly became a surrogate father to young Will, who
"grafted [Murdock] into the wound that death had left when my father
went, and gave him a son's affection and respect which I never withheld."[20]

Murdock seemed to be a paragon of genteel respectability. But he was
more: the Republican boss of the county, the representative "of the benevolent . . . plutocracy that was governing our land." As young White would
learn, Murdock knew how to use his connections and railroad money to
ensure the election of his candidates. Cultural historians of the nineteenth
century like to place at opposite poles attributes of the "genteel tradition"
and of the less elevated worlds of "practical" politics and business. But men
like Murdock and Allen White easily employed both styles, with no inkling
that they were incompatible. "Genteel culture" was not something ab-
stracted from the rest of life, but simply one of several available ways of
behaving.

By his late teens White was of medium height, slightly over five feet seven
inches. Like his father, he was destined to be fat, and even then was considered "chunky," but beneath the gathering layer of fat were powerful
muscles, the product of an active childhood. His features were amiable but
undistinguished: sandy brown hair, light brown eyes, and a wide round
face that during adolescence was marked by acne. But he was not shy. Like
his father, he loved anything that brought him in touch with people. He
eagerly organized social events for his clique of friends, who called themselves the "Spring Chicken Club" but to whom Murdock referred as the
"Trundle Bed Trash." White loved clothes, and until he learned more
moderate tastes favored gaudy outfits in the latest fashions. Above all, he
was ambitious, with "a deep-seated desire to be somebody, sometime."[21]

In 1884 White graduated from high school and enrolled in the College of
Emporia, the Presbyterian school that had opened only the year before.
Classes met in upper rooms in a building on Commercial Street, in the
heart of Emporia's bustling business district. Emporia, now a thriving town

of six thousand, and Kansas generally were booming in the mid-1880s, as settlers took advantage of easy credit to establish farms and businesses.[22]

Though little impressed by the dry classical curriculum, White was drawn deeper into the heady world of Gilded Age genteel culture during his year and a half at Emporia. A fellow student named Vernon Kellogg was one who introduced him to its treasures. The son of a prominent Emporia railroad attorney and Republican politician, he brought White home to "the first house full of books that I had ever seen—bookcases around the wall, books on the table." White formed a close attachment to Kellogg, which on White's side was heavy with hero worship. He became Kellogg's "willing slave" and eager errand boy, a role he would repeat with other friends throughout his life.[23]

Kellogg also introduced White to the town library, where he first read Emerson's essays. He recalled in his *Autobiography* that as he read "Self-Reliance," "my spirit expanded as though I had heard the trumpet call of life." A diary he kept during this year gives little suggestion of such immediate transformation, however. He wrote, "I like [the essay] as far as I've gone very much but find it *very* deep." On the other hand, he expressed unguarded enthusiasm for Dickens, whom he described as "one of the greatest . . . geniuses this world has ever produced." At the library he also read the *Atlantic Monthly* for the first time, and there he encountered William Dean Howells. White read *A Modern Instance* and E. W. Howe's *Story of a Country Town* in the spring of 1885, and, though aware that these pioneer realists departed from his beloved Dickens, he "someway felt that I had made a great discovery." A year and a half later he would make his "first literary pilgrimage," to Atchison, Kansas, to meet Howe, who published a newspaper, the *Globe,* even as he was building a reputation as a man of letters.[24]

By the end of his first year, uneasy that his mother had to take in boarders to pay for his schooling, White decided to find a job that would teach him a useful skill. The only opening in El Dorado was at the *Butler County Democrat.* Perhaps encouraged by the knowledge that his literary heroes Howells, Howe, and Mark Twain had started as printers, he set out to learn that trade. It was also a common steppingstone to a career in politics. He recalled, "There was a flavor in those days about the printing office. Printers were supposed to graduate into editors, editors into statesmen, statesmen into leading citizens, and so rise to empyrean heights in the state and nation."[25]

Actually, he had first gotten a taste of journalism a few years before, when he was thirteen. His father had invested money to launch the Democratic newspaper and, believing that a job would build his son's character, sent him to be printer's devil there. After a few weary days, the boy discovered that it was his father, not the editor, who was paying his wages, and left the job in disgust. He could have had few illusions even then about the financial independence of the press.[26]

White's seven months at the *Democrat* provided a fuller initiation into the world of country journalism and the printer's trade. Physically, it was not an impressive enterprise, housed in smoke- and ink-blackened rooms on the second floor of a brick building off Main Street. The shop had several small foot-powered presses for job printing but lacked a newspaper press. The daily paper was printed on the flatbed cylinder press of its competitor, Bent Murdock's *Republican*. Two of its four pages came from Kansas City "ready printed" with world and national news on the front and fiction and humorous items on the back. The inside pages were filled with editorials, local items, and a little advertising. Other small newspapers of the day reversed the order, using preprinted "patent insides." In either case, the original contents focused on political controversies and events as seen through the editor's partisan lens.[27]

The *Democrat*'s editor, T. P. Fulton, was a perfect specimen of the freewheeling nineteenth-century partisan journalist. Like Murdock and Allen White, he dressed with distinction, in a cutaway Prince Albert coat with a flower at the lapel and gray trousers. Fulton was a hotheaded southern Ohioan, whose "vitriolic pen" and sense of honor drew him into assorted libel suits and gun duels with his opponents. His paper was a shambles financially, and to keep afloat "he intrigued diabolically" for the city and county printing. He solicited advertising, according to White, in "the manner of editors of the day . . . half blackmailer and half mendicant." He kept no books, rarely made collections, and paid his printers only sporadically. When Fulton—free railroad pass in hand—went to Washington to pursue a postmastership from the new Cleveland administration, his men distributed the office receipts among themselves in retaliation.[28]

From the perspective of the mid–twentieth century, Fulton would be transformed in White's memory into a symbol of a bygone age of independent journalism: "The newspaper business in that far day was not a manufacturing enterprise. It was an artistic adventure. The editor, to all intents and purposes, owned the simple tools of his art. . . ." Nostalgia distorted this portrait, however, for even the simple technology of the mid–nineteenth-century print shop was beyond the financial means of most journalists. Their independence was commonly circumscribed by their need for outside money, such as Dr. White's, to set themselves up, and for public sinecures like the county printing or the postmastership to keep going.[29]

In his first days at the *Democrat* White inhabited the artisan world of the print shop, learning every step in a printing process that had changed little from the days of Benjamin Franklin. Type was set, or composed, by hand, as the compositor selected with one hand individual pieces of type, or sorts, from a compartmentalized case. He then placed them in a holder, or stick, held in his other hand. When his stick was full, he transferred this composed type, or matter, to a long, shallow tray known as a "galley." He made copies from the galleys to check for errors, and then arranged the corrected matter in pages and locked them in an iron frame, called a "chase," to make a form. The pressman locked the form on the press, prepared the paper and ink, adjusted the press, and printed the forms. On a job press, an impression was made on the paper by pressing a platen against the forms; the power was supplied by hand or foot. But with "country" presses, the paper traveled around a cylinder that pressed it against a type form locked into a flat bed; hence, they were known as "flatbed" presses. The power was supplied by either turning a crank or harnessing the power of the new town water system. After the matter was printed, the printer's devil cleaned off the ink and the compositors redistributed the sorts into their proper compartments.[30]

Here, too, far from the editor's pretensions of gentility, the printers observed their own craft traditions and taught the child of the small-town elite a new set of codes. They subjected White to the time-honored initiatory hazing. He joined his colleagues in a riotous after-hours party, though he refused to drink the beer that flowed freely despite Kansas prohibition. When the town marshal, in on the gag, appeared in the shop the next morning and threatened to arrest White for having been drunk and disorderly, he was mortified even though he knew he was innocent. The episode taught him "a great lesson—that it is far more shameful to be caught than to be guilty." In the end he was forced to provide an alcoholic "treat," and, just as Benjamin Franklin had done in the eighteenth century, he learned the wisdom of going along with popular custom.[31]

When editor Fulton was away, White wrote the "locals," short items about the activities of El Dorado residents. This meant going to the streets to gather the news, and from the first he loved the work. It gave him an excuse to mingle with people and endowed him with special status: "I was a 'person' on the street," he recalled. But when he wrote an item criticizing the town's standing poker game, he was immediately yanked back to his duties at the type case.[32]

By January 1886 White had gained sufficient proficiency as a compositor to pass as a "sub" at the Emporia *News* when he returned to the College of Emporia. Soon thereafter he was promoted to street reporter, and rarely returned to the type case, but his experience had given him hands-on knowledge of all the steps of the printing process and enabled him to claim the status of "practical printer."

Thereafter, White was seldom without a full- or part-time newspaper job. He worked during school vacations for Murdock's *Republican* and, after he transferred to the University of Kansas in the fall of 1886, the Lawrence *Journal* and *Tribune* and a host of student publications. He also worked occasionally as a stringer for the Associated Press and several newspapers in the region. In addition to reporting and writing editorials, he learned the business side of journalism by managing carriers and handling subscriptions, advertising, and job printing.[33]

He quickly learned that his new career brought special powers and privileges. Journalists, he discovered, had the peculiar ability to define who among their neighbors were most worthy of attention: "I could wave my wand and bathe them in valuable publicity; or I could withhold the baton and keep them in outer darkness." Newspapers in effect determined who was counted a "public figure" and whether the result would be esteem or notoriety. When public reputation was so crucial to one's identity, newspaper coverage was a source of general concern.[34]

On the other hand, young White also learned that his audience had ways of trying to limit this power. A brash teenager, he tried to make his news items snappy and humorous in the fashion of his favorite humorists, Mark Twain and Bill Nye, and he gained a reputation as a "smart aleck." The objects of his creativity were not always amused, and a few responded to slights to their honor with violence or threats of violence. His first lesson in "the perils and penalties of indiscretion" came after he ridiculed an itinerant corset saleswoman. Rawhide whip in hand, she stalked him while he haunted the alleys and collected the news through back doors. After two and a half days, she gave up and left town. Through a number of such adventures in his early reporting career, White learned that a reporter who liked to speak his mind must be willing to face the consequences.[35]

The newspaper's need for financial survival also dictated that certain community members be given special consideration. For example, Murdock was an indulgent editor who, with a few significant exceptions, overlooked White's rambunctiousness as a reporter: "He liked to hear the paper talked about. He liked to have a stir and rumpus going on. So he never pulled the rein on me as I roamed about the town seeking whom I might bedevil, provided he was not a good advertister, a political ally, or someone connected with the county printing." The printing, White emphasized, "was our reason for being." It provided "five or six thousand dollars a year, was chiefly profit . . . almost our only profit."[36]

As a cub reporter, White reveled in the special treatment accorded "gentlemen of the press."

> I rode free to the railroad stations and to public ceremonies in the new varnished hacks that rattled about the streets. I had passes on the railroads. At the eating houses I was a favored guest. . . . The opera house opened its door for me when I flashed my old printer's rule. . . . When junketing excursions of councilmen started on big drunks, to view municipal improvements in other towns on the taxpayers' money, reporters were taken along and treated as young princes. . . .

Such privileges were in keeping with the press's power. They were also consistent with the ethos of reciprocity that permeated Gilded Age culture: if your friends did favors for you, you did them favors in return. White did not question this assumption, so deeply embedded in all aspects of his world. It was simply how things were done; informal ties of friendship and loyalty were the channels through which flowed much of America's political and business life in the nineteenth century.[37]

His initiation into the political applications of the principle of reciprocity came under Bent Murdock's tutelage. He observed firsthand how his boss translated the trappings of power into political influence: "It was his job to see that the county convention was packed with Republicans who would nominate for the legislature Mr. Murdock's friends, who in turn would vote as he suggested, on . . . matters pertaining to railroad rates, corporation laws, the control of insurance and banks." It was taken for granted that, as part of his job as reporter for Murdock, White would help his boss pack the convention with his "friends." "It was my business . . . to round up voters at the caucuses where the delegates were named." There he distributed to Murdock's allies lavish supplies of alcohol and cigars—those tradition-honored sealers and signifiers of masculine friendship—provided by the Santa Fe Railroad.[38]

Meanwhile, White had immediately plunged into student life at the University of Kansas. His academic record was undistinguished, and he never graduated because he could not pass the required mathematics courses, but he excelled at the unofficial curriculum whereby students gained practical political experience. He "craved social leadership," and found plenty of avenues to pursue it in fraternities, student publications, and social life. He again gained prominence from being a journalist when his impudent, "bumptious" newspaper articles quickly made him a "figure" on campus. In Lawrence he formed many friendships that would prove invaluable in years to come. As before, White made himself errand boy to friends whom he idolized, including Frederick Funston, who would later emerge a national military hero by battling Philippine rebels. For his friends, White was "a pointer dog who retrieved beautifully," he remarked later.[39]

He gained further practical political experience in the local wards of Lawrence. In the summers of 1888 and 1889 he worked for Oscar E. Learnard, owner of both the Republican *Journal* and the ostensibly Democratic *Tribune*. Learnard was "an old-fashioned, black radical Republican—radical in the sense that he would go any length for his party." His papers were supported by his job printing shop, which "did all the commercial printing for a railroad," most likely the Santa Fe. When the time came to pick the county Republican ticket and delegates to the state convention, White, "being on the paper, took a hand." There he learned to stack a nominating convention in advance, a skill he often was to employ in later years.[40]

Under his father's influence, White had been an ardent Democrat as a boy. But since Allen White's death the people who had meant most to him had all been Republicans. In a society in which one was either one thing or the other—if only to avoid being a despised mugwump—he felt he had to make a choice. His social science professor, James H. Canfield, advised him that to have an effect in Kansas one had to be a Republican. Canfield had remained an independent, and he told White, "I have got nowhere politically." Backed by this advice, influenced by his friends—all of whom were Republicans—and aware that it would please his mother, White in 1888 "crossed the Rubicon and became a Republican."[41]

Even as he gained political experience, White continued to drink deeply from the fountains of genteel culture at Lawrence. He spent more time reading current literature in the college library than he did in classwork. A literature professor persuaded him to read the *Nation*. Aided by his free passes as a gentleman of the press, he developed a passion for the theater, opera, and concert music. He discovered James Whitcomb Riley's "poetry of common things" and began to publish his own imitations in local newspapers. These experiences whetted his ambitions for literary distinction as well as success in journalism and politics.[42]

One might speculate that White was trying to please both parents by inhabiting two worlds simultaneously: the world of business and politics for his father and that of the arts for his mother. Yet he seems to have had far less sense that these were separate and opposing arenas than we, accustomed to thinking of the genteel and the practical as warring cultures, do today. In White's youth, when occupational categories were less clearly defined, men comonly performed a wider range of roles without sensing conflicts among them. He saw around him E. W. Howe and other exemplars of the successful combination of careers. Eugene Ware, a Kansas attorney and politician whom Roosevelt would appoint U.S. Pension Commissioner and whose "Rhymes of Ironquill" was widely read, represented a "realizable ideal" to White. Prominent Kansas politicians George R. Peck and John J. Ingalls were also known and respected as men of letters.[43]

Late in 1889, Bent Murdock offered White a job managing his newspaper, and White decided to leave the university without a degree. During the next five years of his employment as a journalist, he would gain a widening reputation among newspapermen in the region. Kansas newspapers reprinted his articles and verses, and some eventually appeared in the Kansas City papers.

It is a mistake, however, to read too much of White's later fame into these reprintings, for they were part of the customary newspaper exchange system. In the nineteenth century newspapers of similar political outlook traded subscriptions with one another and borrowed much of their contents from their counterparts. This informal syndicate created an ideal forum through which young talent could become known to the wider journalistic fraternity. A well-written piece even in a lowly country newspaper was quickly picked up by newspapers throughout the network—particularly if it pungently expressed a widely shared sentiment. The budding journalist received no pay for his work, but he acquired that even more important value, public recognition. The exchange system was the typical means by which a young journalist advanced his career, and White was by no means the only reporter being reprinted.

Murdock had hired White because he had been elected to the state senate and would often be away on political business. He left White in charge of the paper's day-to-day management, which included the business as well as editorial direction of the paper. Under Murdock the *Republican* was perpetually in shaky financial condition. According to White, he rarely paid even the interest on his mortgages, but survived "because he represented the powers in the state, and because the private cars of the rich and great stopped at the El Dorado station to take him on. . . ."[44]

White, on the other hand, worked to make the newspaper solvent. In the fall of 1890 he distributed copies of *Home Magazine* to his country subscribers and offered them a year's subscription free if they could "strike a balance with us on the old account and pay for the Republican a year in advance, ($1.00)." He also searched out opportunities for himself in the burgeoning field of newspaper syndication. In July 1890 he offered to write dialect verses for the American Press Association's special holiday pages: "I should of course make the verses in touch with the sentiment of the day of publication and your artist might spice them up a good bit."[45]

As these efforts testify, White was aware of new opportunities in the wider world of publishing created by the advent of cheap magazines and newspaper syndicates. Changes in production and distribution were gradually shifting the economic base of journalism from the political patronage upon which Murdock depended to revenues from mass circulation and advertising. Young White might not have perceived all this, but he was developing shrewd business skills that would be essential in making the transition to the new system.

Another indication of changes afoot was the stirring of agrarian revolt in 1889 and 1890, just as White began his career in journalism. Kansas suffered from a severe drought and an economic collapse that brought an abrupt halt to the boom of the mid-1880s. In those days of easy credit, many farmers had bought land at inflated prices, and now they were hard pressed to keep up their mortgages. This economic distress fanned long-smoldering coals of agrarian discontent and found potent new social and political expressions in the Farmers' Alliance movement and the People's party. As these movements quickly gained strength in Kansas they challenged the dominance of the Republican party. In the 1890 elections Kansas Republicans suffered heavy losses. Some, such as U.S. Senator P. B. Plumb—who owned large interests in Colorado silver mines—hoped to preempt Populist support by advocating inflation through the free coinage of silver. But others, including White, refused to give any quarter to Populist "demagoguery" and insisted on the gold standard as the bedrock of "sound economics."[46]

With the zeal of a new convert to Republicanism, White looked upon the Populists as "ragged nobodies," "the dregs of Butler County society," and ridiculed them in colorful, contemptuous editorials. He had become, he recalled, "a full-fledged Republican with some enthusiasm—if not for my faith, at least for my friends!" With a group of college friends, he formed a Young Republican organization whose stated purpose was to aid in the regeneration of the party. But, as White commented wryly later, "Youth pretends that it is organizing to reform the world. As a matter of fact, it is organizing politically to get jobs."[47]

After the convention, White wrote his first short story, "The Regeneration of Colonel Hucks," and published it in the *Republican*. Drawing upon the longstanding ties between Republicanism and the Union cause, it told the story of an old soldier who flirted with Populism but returned at last to the bosom of the Grand Old Party. Its blatantly sentimental appeal made a great hit with party regulars. Senator Plumb, who said it brought tears to his eyes, directed the state committee to set it in stereotype plates and send it to every Republican paper in the state. It was picked up by party organizations in nearby states and in Kansas City by both the Republican *Journal* and the independent *Star*. Before long both papers offered White jobs writing editorials. Charles Sumner Gleed, an attorney for the Santa Fe, was managing the Kansas City *Journal* for the railroad; he knew White because both were "alumni" of the Lawrence *Journal*. "Thinking I should be happier writing for the Republican organ than for a mugwump Independent newspaper," White chose to work for the *Journal*. So, in the fall of 1891, White, twenty-three years old, left familiar El Dorado for the foreign world of a big city. He left with Bent Murdock's warning ringing in his ears: "They'll tie you up there like a mule to the treadmill, and you'll grow old and gray in the city, a hired man, a nobody."[48]

With over a hundred thousand people, Kansas City was the largest city White had ever seen. This center of commerce, manufacturing, and transportation for the Missouri Valley was beginning to feel the pinch of hard times when White arrived, but the small-town boy did not realize that until later, awed as he was by the urban wonders of its tall buildings, cable cars, and telephones. During his four years in Kansas City White became well acquainted with all the amenities of urban civilization in the late nineteenth century. He learned to dress with taste, to appreciate good food, and to enjoy the finest drama and music of his day.[49]

He also quickly became aware of the drawbacks of being a hireling journalist in an impersonal urban world. In the pathetic figure of Colonel Robert T. Van Horn, ostensibly editor in chief of the *Journal*, White saw for the first time the vulnerability of partisan journalism in a changing economy. A once-powerful publisher who had helped to build Kansas City, Van Horn had been reduced to the flimsiest of figureheads by the revolution in urban journalism in the 1880s. His *Journal*, a classic party newspaper, had been unable to compete with the *Star*, a new "penny" newspaper. Founded by real estate developer William Rockhill Nelson, the *Star* was part of a second generation of cheap, mass-circulation papers, such as Joseph Pulitzer's St. Louis *Post-Dispatch*, that came of age in the rising midwestern cities of the Gilded Age. The *Journal* had gone into receivership and fallen into the hands of the Santa Fe, which kept Van Horn on as a pitiable retainer.[50]

Through his work on the *Journal*, White's political education advanced to the level of state and regional politics. In March 1892 he became the paper's Topeka correspondent, and from that vantage he observed the inner workings and came to know the leaders of all three political parties. He also formed a close attachment with another father surrogate, Republican boss Cyrus A. Leland.

Like Murdock, Leland had been a friend of Allen White's when he was an attorney in El Dorado. In fact, Leland had witnessed Dr. White's will.

By the early 1890s he had become a powerful figure in the inner circles of the Kansas Republican party. As White reported the 1892 Republican convention for the *Journal,* he watched Leland lose the "main event"—the gubernatorial nomination for his candidate—but nonetheless stay in the battle until he had gained every other place on the ticket for his slate. White and Leland were the last to leave the hall, side by side. White recalled, "I gave my heart to a man who would stay in the game, protect his ante, and play his cards, even after he had lost his major stake. I was a Leland man after that." White was attracted to Leland's personal qualities of tenacity and certainty of purpose as well as to his obvious political prowess.[51]

White's literary world also widened during his years in Kansas City. While still in El Dorado he had met a young Fort Scott poet named Albert Bigelow Paine, and the two decided to publish a book of poems together. *Rhymes by Two Friends* finally emerged from a Fort Scott printer in 1893, with an introduction by Eugene Ware. In Kansas City, White joined the Western Artists and Authors Society, an organization of about one hundred midwesterners—"newspaper poets, newspaper artists, painters of china dishes, writers of unplayed plays. . . ." He promoted his literary reputation by reading his dialect poetry—after the manner of James Whitcomb Riley—in nearby towns. He also published essays on politics and literature in *Agora,* a magazine published in Topeka. He sent copies of his work to established regional authors such as Hamlin Garland, who commended it but advised, "get closer to Kansas and farther from Indiana in your dialect."[52]

Despite some local success, White's ambitions to break into the literary big time of the Eastern "genteel" magazines met with disappointment. He wrote his friend Paine in early 1893: "I am trying with all my might and main to sell something to Harper or Century or Cosmopolitan or Scribners but I cant cut it."[53]

In the fall of 1891 he met a fellow society member, Sallie Lindsay, who had published several stories in a Chicago newspaper. A romance blossomed as they read Kipling aloud together, and they were married on April 27, 1893. Sallie became the guiding spirit not only of his literary career, but of his life. She was always his foremost editor, and her imprint is visible on every piece of fiction and every important piece of journalism that he published. Although Sallie fully subsumed her life to her husband's career, she was far from a passive figure in its development. In many ways she should be considered a full, if less public, partner in the firm of William Allen White, Ltd.

By all accounts, Sallie exerted a strong personal influence over her husband. Some Emporians were even of the opinion that she "wore the pants" in the White household. She was a shrewd judge of character and, according to their son, often acted to steady White, who tended to react impulsively and regret it later. One can only speculate about other possible influences. Sallie had been born in Kentucky to a once-prominent planter family, now impoverished by the Civil War, and she seems to have brought to her relationship with White some of the values of the old South. Cer-

*William Allen White in
1899 (William Allen White
Memorial Library, Em-
poria State University)*

*Sallie Lindsay White in
1895 (William Allen White
Memorial Library, Em-
poria State University)*

tainly she delighted in displays of hospitality as much as her husband, and the White household would be famous for its constant stream of guests. White's letters to his wife also reveal a sensitivity to questions of "honor" that may have been responses to her values. Yet White's own upbringing had already prepared him to accept communal judgments as the basis of identity, an orientation that has been defined as central to southern conceptions of honor. Sallie's expectations may have simply reinforced the lessons of his childhood and youth.[54]

In September 1892 White quit his job at the *Journal* in protest at the mishandling of a major reporting scoop, and quickly found a job at the *Star*. There he had his first experience of a nonpartisan, though most decidedly not nonpolitical, newspaper. He wrote political and "minion" editorials—light commentary on the arts and the passing scene—and a column on Kansas affairs. The *Star's* publisher, William Rockhill Nelson, sent White to investigate urban problems such as utility rates, slums, election frauds, and stockyard conditions. White's research did not make him a muckraker, but it did introduce him to issues that would come to dominate political debate in the new century. Early in 1894 the *Star* launched a Sunday edition, for which White wrote features and short stories. Many of the stories were later collected in a book, *The Real Issue*. Based upon the land and people of Kansas, they were an awkward blending of harsh realism and sentimental pathos.[55]

By 1894 the attractions of city life had long faded for White. He quickly grew to resent the restrictions that came with being a "hireling" journalist. He bristled at the blue penciling of a difficult Sunday editor, and was increasingly irked by the knowledge that his allegiance to Leland was only barely tolerated by his mugwump boss. He feared ending up like aging colleagues at the paper who had worked their entire lives for others. While he was working in Kansas City, his contemporaries in Kansas, rising young men in Republican circles, were already beginning to take charge of their own country newspapers. White recalled,

> Charley Scott had bought the Iola Register. Arthur Capper was establishing himself in the Topeka Capital. Victor Murdock was coming back from his reportorial job in Chicago to run the Wichita Eagle. Henry Allen, a reporter on Bristow's Journal, was buying the Manhattan Nationalist, and [Joseph Bristow] himself had bought the Salina Republican. . . . I was eager to join the goodly company of my peers in politics.[56]

He had already begun to think about buying a small newspaper. He considered buying the Fort Scott *Monitor* early in 1893, but found it beyond his means. Then his small savings were lost in the Panic of 1893, and it was not until late 1894 that White again began to look in earnest. This time he sought a newspaper in a college town, which he hoped would have a higher level of culture. In his *Autobiography*, White recalled that he and Sallie agreed that they needed the support of a "considerable dependable minority of intelligent people." Sallie must have contributed substantially to this resolve, since Fort Scott, where White first attempted to buy a paper, had no college.[57]

They finally settled upon Emporia, his birthplace and the home of both the College of Emporia and the Kansas State Normal School; the smaller of its two Republican newspapers, the *Gazette,* was for sale. He negotiated with its editor, W. Y. Morgan, whom he had known in Lawrence, and agreed to pay $3,000, though Morgan later admitted that "every newspaper-man in Kansas knew it was not worth $2,000." The *Gazette* published daily and weekly editions, but its daily circulation was under five hundred. Having no savings, White offered his mother's property in El Dorado as security and drew upon his extensive network of friends and contacts in negotiating for loans in the capital-tight economy. Cy Leland helped persuade E. N. Morrill, his recently successful candidate for governor, to lend $1,000. The estate of P. B. Plumb, who had died in 1891, lent $1,000, and Plumb's brother George $250. P. B. Plumb had been a friend of Allen White's and a close political ally of Bent Murdock's, and his son Amos had been a fraternity brother of White's. The rest was covered by transferring to White's name a note that Morgan had carried with the Emporia National Bank. A college friend vouched for White with the bank's president, Calvin Hood, who had also known his father. At the age of twenty-seven, White thus became the proprietor of his own newspaper, primarily owing to his reputation and contacts. His ability to do this testified that he had mastered the rules of politics and business in the Gilded Age.[58]

As he, in one of his favorite phrases, "crossed the Rubicon" and became his own boss, White proclaimed his emergence into full, autonomous adulthood. Nonetheless, looking back over the evidence of his childhood and youth, one sees a pattern of contradictions. White was intensely sensitive to "public opinion," even as he admired the integrity of men who seemed purely self-possessed. His *Autobiography* assigns the first characteristic to his mother, the second to his father; yet many of his descriptions of his father suggest his strong need for community approbation as well. White also repeatedly depicts himself as desperately eager to please his friends, particularly those who seemed most self-assured. White's purchase of the *Gazette* points to a desire for independence, but he admitted that his goal was to "join the company" of his generation in Kansas politics. He reveled in the masculine world of business and politics, yet he was forever dependent upon the ministrations of strong-minded women. His mother had kept house for him for most of his college and early work years; she "tagged along" on his wedding trip; and she followed him to Emporia, where she resided next door to the Whites until her death. He rarely made a political, literary, or business decision without consulting his wife.

The contradictions between these characteristics may be only superficial, however, the result of the tendency to set individual and community at opposite poles. White was intensely ambitious for personal achievement. He wanted to become a "leading citizen" as his father had been, a power in politics as Bent Murdock and Cy Leland were, and a distinguished man of letters like E. W. Howe and William Dean Howells. These ambitions could be fulfilled only in a public context, for they demanded the ratification of an audience. To become a somebody required an audience. To gain the status of leading citizen, one had to commit oneself to a community. He had chosen Emporia.

By 1895 White had worked as a printer, a business manager, a reporter, and a practical political organizer. His editorials and fiction were bringing a widening reputation among newspaper readers throughout Kansas. As the new editor of the *Emporia Gazette,* however, he would have to start over again, to make himself known to every Emporian as a man to be reckoned with.

2

The New Editor

The day after he arrived in Emporia to take possession of the *Gazette* was Sunday, and William Allen White walked to the newspaper office to survey his new possession. It was located on the second floor of a building over-looking Sixth Avenue near its crossing with Commercial Street, at the heart of Emporia's business district. The entire enterprise occupied a room twenty-five by sixty feet, with one corner partitioned off to serve as the news room and business office. The rest held the print shop, containing only a cylinder newspaper press, six cases of type, and several composing stones.[1]

That afternoon White wrote his first editorial as his own boss.

ENTIRELY PERSONAL

To the gentle reader who may, through the coming years during which we are spared to one another, follow the course of this paper, a word of personal address from the new editor of the *Gazette* is due. In the first place, the new editor hopes to live here until he is the old editor, until some of the visions which rise before him as he dreams shall have come true. He hopes always to sign "from Emporia" after his name when he is abroad, and he trusts that he may so endear himself to the people that they will be as proud of the first words of the signature as he is of the last words. He expects to perform all the kind offices of the country editor in this community for a generation to come. It is likely that he will write the wedding notices of the boys and girls in the schools; that he will announce the birth of the children who will some day honor Emporia, and that he will say the final words over those of middle age who read these lines.

His relations with the people of this town and country are to be close and personal. He hopes that they may be kindly and just. The new editor of the *Gazette* is a young man now, full of high purposes and high ideals. But he needs the close touch of older hands. His endeavor will be to make a paper for the best people of the city. But to do that he must have their help. They must counsel with him, be his friends, often show him what their sentiment is. On them rests the responsibility somewhat. The "other fellows" will be around. They will give advice. They will attempt to show what the public sentiment is. They will try to work their schemes, which might dishonor the town. If the best people stay away from the editor's office, if they neglect to stand by the editor, they must not blame him for mistakes. An editor is not all wise. He judges only by what he sees and hears. Public sentiment is the only sentiment that prevails. Good sentiment, so long as it does not assert it-

William Allen White in the first Gazette *office in 1896*
(William Allen White Memorial Library,
Emporia State University)

self, so long as it is a silent majority, is only private sentiment. If the good, honest, upright, God-fearing, law-abiding people of any community desire to be reflected to the world, they must see that their private opinion is public opinion. They must stand by the editors who believe as they do.

It is a plain business proposition. The new editor of the *Gazette* desires to make a clean, honest local paper. He is a Republican and will support Republican nominees first, last, and all the time. There will be no bolting, no sulking, no "holier than thou" business about his politics—but politics is so little. Not one man in ten cares for politics more than two weeks in a year. In this paper, while the politics will be straight, it will not be obtrusive. It will be confined to the editorial page—where the gentle reader may venture at his peril. The main thing is to have this paper represent the average thought of the best people of Emporia and Lyon County in all their varied interests. The editor will do his best. He has no axes to grind. He is not running the paper for a political pull. If he could get an office he wouldn't have it. He is in the newspaper business as he would be in the drygoods business—to make an honest living and to leave an honest name behind. If the good people care for a fair, honest home paper, that will stand for the best that is in the town—here it is.

In the meantime, I shall hustle advertising, job work and subscriptions, and write editorials and "telegraph" twelve hours a day in spite of my ideals. The path of glory is barred hog-tight for the man who does not labor while he waits.[2]

At twenty-seven, William A. White was known among Kansas journalists and politicians as a "coming young man," but few among his new audience in Emporia knew or much cared about that. To build the *Gazette* into a successful newspaper, he would have to make it an integral part of Emporia's daily life. Knowing with the advantage of hindsight that he did prosper, one is tempted to view White's rise in Emporia as both inevitable and immediate. In fact, it took years for White and the *Gazette* to become firmly established in Emporia. More than a decade later, he warned a protégé starting out on his own, "It takes a long time to pry any one away from an old established paper." His advice came from experience.[3]

In a small town where people rarely distinguished between the person and his business, success required not only putting out a good newspaper, but establishing a strong reputation. White's task would be to assure Emporians that he was one of them: that he spoke their language, shared their way of thinking, and could be trusted to pursue the town's best interests as well as his own. Any newcomer would have had to do the same, and his behavior as he met his neighbors and colleagues would have been carefully observed for signs of his intentions. When the newcomer was the proprietor of such an important public institution as a newspaper, townspeople could be expected to scrutinize him with particular concern. At the same time, this position provided ample opportunity to demonstrate his virtues. White assembled his first editions of the *Gazette* with the same acute awareness of the impression he was creating that he had manifested in his arrival in Emporia.

The town that William Allen White addressed in his salutatory editorial was, like many in its time, riven with factionalism. Competing factions, united more by shared interests and personal loyalty than by ideology, had emerged after the Civil War, as Emporia grew from village to town, heightening competition for the limited number of positions of prestige and power in the community. Though various groups of Democrats and Populists clamored for their share of power, the two most powerful factions were both Republican. Each was headquartered in one of the town's two major banks. The Emporia National represented P. B. Plumb's interests. The First National, chartered in 1872, was headed by men who had arrived in Emporia after the Civil War and who challenged Plumb's hegemony. Its president was attorney Harrison C. Cross; its vice-president, cattleman William Martindale, had been one of the founders of Madison, a town south of Emporia that had lost out in the race for preeminence in the area. Martindale was the effective head of the "First National crowd." White later characterized him as "a cowboy turned cattleman, rough, parsimonious, unschooled, and sometimes uncouth . . . loyal to his associates, suspicious, and sometimes not very nice in his attitude toward his enemies. . . ."[4]

During the Gilded Age, ownership of a bank was a useful tool in securing the bonds of personal obligation that underlay political life. In the days before effective outside regulation, bank loans were as much an assurance of loyalty as a sound financial investment. As he became involved in Emporia politics, White's convention strategies often went awry because his delegates turned out to be borrowers at Martindale's bank. In Emporia, friendships and social contacts also followed factional lines.[5]

Factional leaders also used their banks' financial resources to underwrite other institutions that reflected and reinforced their power. In the 1880s, for example, members of the First National group established a new horse-drawn street railway, a gaslight company, a first-class hotel, and a magnificent theater, the Whitley Opera House. In secret, they also funded the establishment in 1882 of a daily newspaper, the *Emporia Republican,* to compete with the *News* and present *their* vision of community. It was edited by Charles V. Eskridge, a real estate developer who had served as state legislator, senator, and lieutenant governor. In 1863 he had significantly aided Emporia's development by winning the location there of the Normal School. The *Republican* was launched with what one journalist later described as "a great flourish of trumpets" and a year later moved into its own grand three-story brick building, crowned by a soaring gilded American eagle above the cornice.[6]

The new paper dealt a damaging blow to the financial fortunes of the faltering *News,* which finally sold out to the *Republican* in 1890. Meanwhile, agrarian protest expressed itself in two new papers. The *Tidings,* a Populist newspaper, moved to Emporia from northern Lyon County in 1891 and changed its name to the *Times* in 1895. In 1890 J. R. Graham, a ne'er-do-well printer who had previously worked with both the *News* and the *Republican,* started his own paper, the *Gazette.* It was ostensibly independent but was dedicated to the free-silver cause. After a few years he sold it to William Y. Morgan, a young Republican party activist backed by the Emporia National Bank. The transition made the *Gazette* the new organ for that faction.[7]

Since Plumb's sudden death in 1891 the Emporia National crowd had been led by Calvin Hood. He had arrived relatively late on the Emporia scene, in 1871, but had quickly allied himself with Plumb when the two formed a partnership to cash in on the lucrative boom in trading Texas cattle. In quick succession Hood became director and then vice-president of the Emporia National Bank. Over the years he served his apprenticeship as Plumb's henchman and go-between in matters political as well as economic.

In 1883, for example, he had persuaded then-governor John P. St. John not to contest Plumb's senate seat by tendering a $3,000 "contribution" to St. John's next gubernatorial campaign.[8]

Hood was an epitome of the small-town gentry in those last days of the Gilded Age, a man for whom the display of both wealth and civic pride testified to his preeminent status. He was a man of taste, who brought works of art home from his frequent trips to New York, supported the library and the theater, and maintained the finest carriage in town. According to White, Hood's name was always first on the subscription list for every worthy project. Finally, White recalled, "he was generous to his friends and ruthless to his enemies." As he gained his bearings in Emporia, the new editor quickly realized that he was destined to be Hood's man, and therefore Martindale's enemy.[9]

"Entirely Personal" was White's first opportunity to express himself in print to his new audience, and he used it to assure Emporians of his commitment to his home. New publishers customarily took the occasion to unveil their finest rhetorical wares and delineate the high ideals upon which their journal would be based. In contrast, White's first independent editorial effort was remarkable for its simplicity and emphasis upon everyday life. His first concern was to proclaim his intention of becoming a permanent part of Emporia, "to live here until he is the old editor." He would in coming years recommend this approach to young journalists. " 'We have come to stay' was not imbedded in the foundation of this business idly. It is the one thing that you must make your people feel. . . ."[10]

In promising "to perform all the kind offices of a country editor" for a generation to come, he affirmed his lifelong commitment to his community. At the same time, this statement likened his position to that of the ministry, endowing him and his new role with the authority and benevolence associated with a beloved elderly parson. As he depicted it, the country newspaper solemnized the major turning points of life in the secular realm just as the church did in the spiritual, by recording in print the weddings, births, and deaths in the community.

White dramatized the fusion of his identity with that of his new town even more vividly by uniting his name and his town's in his wish "to sign 'from Emporia' after his name when he is abroad." This statement has been misinterpreted by those who knew White only in his later years of national fame and who insisted that White had little in common with his small-town environment. Biographer Walter Johnson argued that, from the beginning, White possessed a "city perspective" distinct from that of his neighbors and that this statement "suggests that even this early White planned to spend a great deal of time away from Emporia." Newspaper writer Lewis Gannett commented in the 1920s that "you aren't 'from Emporia' when you're in it."[11]

This interpretation is mistaken on several points. It reads history backward, by reading White's behavior in the 1890s in the light of much later events. More important, it ignores the fact that in the nineteenth century even the poorest journalists traveled often and widely, supplied with free railroad passes. T. B. Murdock and T. P. Fulton, White's first bosses, were frequently out of town on political or other business. While "abroad" they often acted as semiofficial spokesmen for their towns, for they often served as mediators in communication between the local sphere and the outside world.

With this first editorial White established a tradition that his name did not appear in the *Gazette,* although there would be occasional exceptions to the norm. This policy was unusual at a time when journalists were often blatantly self-aggrandizing, but it did not mean that the newspaper would be devoid of the editor's personality. It was only the editor's *name* that was banned. White consistently referred to himself in print as "the *Gazette* editor," or even "the *Gazette.*" Just as the newcomer's name had been symbolically linked with his town in the words "from Emporia," White's public image was to become inseparable from that of his newspaper.

By requesting the counsel of the "best people" and "the close touch of older hands," White demonstrated his willingness to defer to his seniors, but he also underlined his newspaper's power to define public opinion. If the good citizens of Emporia wanted their sentiment to prevail, they must "stand by the editors who believe as they do." This statement assumes a reciprocal relationship between the newspaper and its community: that the paper's duty is to accurately reflect the "best sentiment," and that the public's duty is to support the paper, financially as well as morally, for doing so. This assumption underlay much of White's thinking about the role of the newspaper.

White downplayed the political role of his newspaper by raising it only in the next-to-last paragraph. Even then, he minimized its importance at the same time that he vowed orthodoxy. He seemed to be appealing to both partisan readers and a wider audience, in a sense seeking a balance between the Kansas City *Journal* and the *Star.* He implicitly criticized the latter kind of independent paper for its "holier than thou" pretensions. At the same time, by acknowledging politics as "so little," he noted his intention of transcending the limitations of a partisan readership by emphasizing the general-interest news that the *Star* featured. Similarly, White disclaimed any desire for political office, for his early political experience had taught him that "he who seeks honors loses power." Nonetheless, he referred only to actual officeholding when he disclaimed interest in "political pull," for the *Gazette* would always be an essential tool in his political strategies.[12]

When White referred to the *Gazette* as "a plain business proposition" and equated journalism with a "drygoods business," he also seemed to be deemphasizing politics. Like any other Emporia merchant, he would prosper by offering a decent product, "a fair, honest home paper." He would purvey news rather than political opinion. At the same time, he differentiated himself from impractical reform types: he would succeed through hard work "in spite of my ideals." It is tempting to interpret White's manifesto as a proclamation of a new, more "objective" definition of news, but it would be misleading. This rhetorical opposition between a "party paper" and one that addresses the entire "public" was a longstanding tradition in journalism, as newcomers struggled to characterize their predecessors as the "kept organs" of special interest and themselves as the agents of the people. Seen in this context, White was here contrasting the *Gazette* with a party paper—by implication, the *Republican*. The juxtaposition suggested that the *Republican* was not a true business, making its living by meeting the real needs of the populace, but was a party hack. In years to come White would frequently contrast "business" and "politics," invariably posing the former as virtuous, the latter as corrupt.[13]

At the same time, however, this rhetorical tactic did evoke the vision of a unified community that would become central to White's hopes for Emporia. For White, the search for a harmonious community would answer a multitude of needs, economic, psychological, political, and intellectual. By proposing to downplay politics and "represent the average thought of the best people," he hoped to address a broader audience than his Emporia National backers. Nevertheless, until he found other sources of income for the *Gazette*, it would remain Calvin Hood's faithful ally.

The first issues of the *Gazette* under White's editorship embodied the themes of his first editorial and gave promise that it would be a lively, entertaining paper. The front page of the four-page newspaper attempted to balance political orthodoxy with human interest. The right half was devoted to national and state news, with a heavy political emphasis, including articles critical of the free-silver movement within the Republican party and of Populist management of state institutions. The left half was wholly given over to local items. Except for stories on commencement at the College of Emporia and an ice-cream social, news of the day appeared in locals, short paragraphs without headlines, packed together densely to save space. The extreme left-hand column was headed "Personal Mention" and contained even briefer notes on Emporians' travels, visits, and illnesses.

Many of the news stories on the right-hand side of the page were prefaced with the words "By the Gazette's Leased Wire." This signaled that the news had been obtained directly by telegraph and set in type at the *Gazette* office. Such news was much timelier than the so-called telegraphic plate news that generally ran in small-town papers—including the *Republican*. This news had been wired to central points like Kansas City, set in type there, reproduced by making stereotyped plates from the type, and then shipped by rail to outlying newspapers. The next day, White, never shy about publicizing the virtues of his paper, called attention to his *real* telegraph news.

> The dispatches which appeared in the Gazette last night came over the Postal Union and cost the editor a neat little sum of money. If the people of Emporia want them they can have them. But they must pay for them. The merchants of this town have talked about having a paper with bonafide dispatches. If they will pay for such a paper, a reasonable amount, they can have it.[14]

Many of the local news items commented on the passing scene in ways that conveyed the same sense of affability found in White's editorial. He assured his colleagues on Commercial Street that he was "one of the guys":

> The new editor met 215 strange men this morning and didn't hear a man swear. It may be that Emporia is a terribly good town, but the chances are the fellows were just sizing the new man up to see how he would take a "damn" or two. On the dead quiet it may be said that the new man needn't be feared. He has heard men swear before. Let 'er rip. Don't wear your Sunday manners around the new man.[15]

White also demonstrated both his geniality and community spirit by feigning an avid interest in the fate of the local baseball team, the Maroons. Although he had little interest in sports, the team was on a losing streak when he arrived in Emporia, and boosting it might have seemed a good way to show his faith in the town. In fact, White explicitly tied the team's success to the spirit of folks back home. "The Maroons are all right. . . . When a ball team has a crowd of clever fellows here at home, such as the Maroons have, ready to back them against the world, they just can't have a very bad run of luck." When the Maroons finally triumphed, the *Gazette* exulted, "We have always contended that the Maroons are all right."[16]

By criticizing other communities, White further demonstrated his loyalty to Emporia. Regarding a young man who stole a horse and wagon in nearby Osage City, the *Gazette* commented: "The young man gives as his excuse for the crime that he had drank a quart of alcohol and didn't know what he was about. However that is such a common thing at Osage City that it wont excuse him." This comment also indicated his support of prohibition and contempt for those communities that flouted the law. The next day the *Gazette* reported the shocking story, highlighted by four decks of headlines, of the drunken jag in the streets of Atchison of a sixteen-year-old named Lola. This spectacle was possible, it said, because of the town's "devotion to whiskey as a political issue" and because "Atchison Killed Equal Suffrage."[17]

More significant, White served notice that he would be an ardent booster of Emporia. As the publisher of a local newspaper, White would be expected to be an active proponent of schemes to improve his town. At the same time, in the highly mobile society of nineteenth-century America, boosterism provided a commonly understood routine through which any newcomer could demonstrate his commitment to his new town. By busying himself with projects for civic betterment, he showed his abilities without appearing overly assertive, for his efforts were for the good of all. In his second issue White urged the improvement of Maplewood cemetery, using a common booster technique of invidious comparison to nearby—and competing—communities. "If the Emporia cemetery only had water it could be one of the most beautiful in the West. Lawrence and Topeka have beautiful resting places for the dead. Emporia, which is ahead of these towns in other shades of refinement, should not be behind them in this important matter."

The following week he returned to this theme: "Emporia is getting big enough to have a few respectable looking public buildings, and a public park. . . . A town like Emporia has to go a good deal on her looks."[18]

Such comments reflected an important tenet of boosterism: to prosper, businessmen must make their town attractive to customers and new residents. A corollary of this belief was revealed in another item in the latter issue:

> The best fiddler in the world was in Kansas City the other night, and no one went to hear him. What Kansas City likes is the lady who can kick the back of her head with her shoe heels. Kansas City is a great old jay. It is surprising that Emporia people should think that they can get bargains there. Our dry goods merchants and hardware men and shoe men and furniture men make 5 per cent lower prices than Kansas City merchants do.

The newspaper's booster role was to foster a sense of reciprocal obligation between commerce and the larger community: businessmen must improve the town and townspeople must in turn buy at home.

At the same time, White repeatedly appealed to the "business" values he had upheld in his first editorial. When he eliminated the practice of giving complimentary subscriptions he invoked sound business practices: "The new management desires to put the *Gazette* upon a cash basis. . . . It is only business. And we are all here for business." In these comments White connected "business" with qualities on the one hand of reciprocity and loyalty, on the other of rationality and efficiency, revealing a fundamental contradiction in the booster ethos. Nonetheless, although newspapers often couched their arguments in terms of impersonal economic interests, such as lower prices, their ultimate appeal was to the higher good of the community economy.[19]

Though the *Gazette* would pay most attention to Emporia's businessmen and Republican politicians, White's search for a broader audience meant that he included other Emporians. A regular column, "Railroad News," published items on the work activities and personal lives of the many Santa Fe and Katy employees and their families living in Emporia. The locals gave particular attention to younger Emporians and their latest fads: "Ben McCandless has a new bicycle which he says will be a good one when he gets it broke to ride." Young women made increasing appearances: "The town horses are gradually becoming used to the female bicyclist with bloomers. Country horses and men are about the only animals that are skittish and shy to the side of the road." In fact, gentle allusions to the "war between men and women" provided human interest, with the focus most often upon the foibles of the "weaker sex":

> Sunday is a great relief day for Emporia men. The women don't wear sailor hats and shirt waists on Sunday and a man can tell whether he is flirting with his own wife or not.

> Our society editor is very fly. She talks about the "refreshments matching the decorations." What she really means is that pink lemonade was served. But you have to write that round about way in society doings. Of course the men

all make fun of gush, but you bet, if the society reporter tells the cold chilly truth about [a] woman's social function, she has the paper stopped in a minute. Laugh at the gush; it will be your turn next.

Some one ought to start a shop where the girl's pneumatic sleeve punctures could be repaired.

A woman in a Dutch bonnet and French bloomers was one of the Emporia sights last night.[20]

Sallie White soon joined her husband in Emporia and began to write for the *Gazette*, and she may have been responsible for some of the paper's irreverence. We know that she wrote one such item that backfired. She reported that John Martin, a local Democrat, had paid his son Charley a dollar to call him Uncle instead of Papa when they were on a trip to Kansas City. She prefaced the story with a Kipling quatrain:

> This is the sorrowful story
> Told as the twilight fails
> And the monkeys walk together
> Holding their neighbours' tails.

When the newspaper came out, a printer had accidentally tacked the Kipling lines onto the wrong story, the solemn announcement of the engagement of the daughter of a prominent local family. White recalled that "on the whole it was good medicine for the Gazette. It had never made such a deep and widespread impression on the town as that which came in that item."[21]

Occasionally the paper poked fun at men:

There is a man in town who only belongs to one lodge. He ought to be kept on exhibition in the city museum.

A couple of small boys were playing "injun" this morning in front of the *Gazette* office, and a man who brought in a notice saying he was a most worshipful squeeggee of something or other, told the little boys they should not give their valuable hours of youth to such frivolous sports.[22]

These comments were probably oblique jabs at the old guard in Emporia, including *Republican* editor Eskridge himself, who was a founder and devoted member of the local Masonic lodge. White also flouted custom in his treatment of the Grand Army of the Republic. Each week the two local posts were accustomed to receiving free lengthy announcements of their regular meetings. When White condensed these announcements to save space, the outraged G.A.R. threatened to boycott the *Gazette*. Eskridge blasted White in the *Republican* for insulting the men who had saved the Union, but White replied that he was merely trying to provide room in the paper for "real news." He was trying to redefine the prevailing definition of news to include a broader segment of Emporia society.[23]

Such wit and irreverence attracted attention to the new editor and his newspaper. It differentiated the *Gazette* from the *Republican*, which was undeniably more sober and narrower in its definition of newsworthiness. Some Emporians were shocked by what they viewed as the new paper's "sensationalism"; a few claimed that they would not have it in their homes. White welcomed the attention, however, as he had when he was a cub reporter. He even capitalized upon it, with advertisements on local billboards and theater programs that read: "All right! Cuss the Gazette, but read it!"[24]

Eskridge seemed to have been waiting for an excuse to challenge the newcomer to an old-fashioned newspaper war. When White's purchase of the *Gazette* had been announced, Eskridge reported the news, adding only the terse comment "Next." The *Republican* was slightly more welcoming upon White's arrival: "Mr. Morgan and the editor of this paper always got along amicably and we trust the same feeling may prevail during the editorial life of his successor." But it continued more ominously: "At least, it will not be our fault if the serenity heretofore existing does not continue." For his part, White professed concern only for maintaining "gentlemanly" relations with his neighbors. In his second issue he expressed the happiness of "the *Gazette*" that the city council had decided to entertain bids in choosing the city printer, but disclaimed a desire for it if it meant a fight. Vowing to "make a fair business bid at fair business prices," he promised to abide by the council's decision. "The little old city printing isn't worth as much as the good will of any honest man in the Council."[25]

Relations soon became strained. Eskridge reminded his readers, "The *Republican* does not brag and glow about itself, nor does it assume to know more than its readers. We let its appearance, matter and make-up speak for it. It is not so egotistical as to imagine it can fool anybody." For his part, White missed no opportunity to point out the superiority of his paper: "The *Gazette* is the only paper in Emporia that receives telegraphic dispatches by wire. Absolutely the only paper." Reporting that the city council was considering an anticigarette ordinance, he jabbed, "The *Gazette* is the only paper in Emporia that knew this fight was going on."[26]

Open warfare came when the city council, after much maneuvering, voted four to three to award the next year's printing contract to the *Gazette*. White predicted, "There will be a roar no doubt from the old man." Indeed, Eskridge charged that a rotten "combination" had been at work, because he had proposed to do the city advertising for free, while White planned to charge $300 to $500 for the same work. White defended his supporters, Messrs. Hornbarger, Thomas, Jones, and Evans. Noting the Welsh surnames of the last three, he appealed to the sentiments of the large Welshborn population in the area. "How do the Welsh people of Emporia like the insinuation that their representatives in the city council are thieves. Still they have had to endure the same thing from the same source for years."[27]

As the conflict mounted, a citizen named R. B. Evans, aided by a law firm closely allied with the Martindale faction, obtained an injunction against the agreement. This injunction was partially dissolved a few days later, but one of White's backers, J. G. Hornbarger, switched his vote to the *Republican* several weeks later. White responded to the loss by claiming the moral victory: "[The editor] does not propose to pay attention to the men who insist on being his enemies." He reaffirmed that his paper was above petty factionalism: "In the meantime, if you want the news unfettered by cliques, or gangs, or crowds, if you want a square manly paper with no quarrels, no sneers at women, with no abuse and no petty meanness in it, now is the time to subscribe to the *Gazette*."[28]

Although bickering between the two papers would continue for years, a truce of sorts was finally reached the following spring. In April 1896, White and Eskridge agreed that the *Republican* would be named the official city paper but the *Gazette* would receive a copy of the council proceedings in time to publish it the same day. In return, they agreed to split the printing fees equally. Such agreements were fairly common; the *Republican* and the *News* had made an identical one in 1886. It is not clear whether this one was made public, but in June 1897 the city council heard the report of a committee "in regard to the contract with the Emporia *Republican* and *Gazette* for doing the city printing for the coming year."[29]

At the end of his first year, White was still in business but had by no means triumphed. Because no business correspondence before 1899 has survived, it is hard to say exactly what the *Gazette*'s financial condition was. Within a few days of taking over the newspaper, he had announced that business was so good that he was expanding the paper to six pages. He promised, "As long as subscription and advertising hold out to burn, the six pages will continue." By the fall, however, the paper had returned to four pages, which it would remain through the rest of the decade. It had also dropped its telegraphic "specials" and used stereotyped news just as the *Republican* did.[30]

Publicly, the new editor was upbeat. On the first anniversary of assuming the editorship, he reported that the *Gazette* had three hundred new subscribers (which would have brought its circulation to around nine hundred), had paid off $214 in notes, and had invested $600 in a job press. "This office is a paying institution. It is here to stay. If you want to get on the bandwagon, bring your work here." One must take most statements of circulation in this period with a grain of salt, however, particularly those made in such a context. In 1901, when the *Gazette* had a circulation of around fifteen hundred, White claimed that it was three times as large as it had been in 1897.[31]

Forty years later, White gave a very different account of his situation in the summer of 1896: "I had bought my small paper and was $3000 in debt. I had not paid a dime on it except the interest during the year of the mortgage. The Saturday night payroll became a looming red curse Thursday morning. Monday morning and every Monday morning found me in the red at the bank."[32] Still later, in his *Autobiography*, White recalled a growing overdraft at the bank during his first year at the *Gazette*: "once in a while Major Hood at the bank would call me in and remonstrate. Twice that summer [1895], we had to give our note for fifty or a hundred dollars to cover the deepening overdraft."[33]

As he remembered the situation, their financial worries were alleviated when, "in the winter or early spring of 1896," he received several "offers" to publish a book of his short stories. He recalled that a $500 advance from Way and Williams was "slapped on one of the mortgages," and "seemed to cheer the old Major up." Nonetheless, White seems at the distance of nearly half a century to have condensed a considerable period of time in his account. He and Sallie White did indeed select and polish his stories and mail them to Way and Williams in March of 1896. They chose the firm, a new enterprise dedicated to fine book publishing along the lines of William Morris's Kelmscott Press, because it was located in Chicago and they felt a certain loyalty as fellow westerners. But over five months later, *after* the publication of "What's the Matter with Kansas?", they were still waiting for Way and Williams to decide whether to publish the book. Without financial records or fuller correspondence from this period, we cannot know absolutely which of the above self-characterizations was closest to the truth as represented by his bank balance, but it is fair to conclude that in the summer of 1896 White's financial status was still somewhat shaky.[34]

Despite White's hopes of broadening his audience, politics repeatedly intruded into the *Gazette*. White was an irredeemably political man, and the mid-nineties were intensely political times. The Populist rebellion had gathered strength in Kansas as elsewhere in the South and Midwest, and in 1895 a coalition of Populists and Democrats swept the Lyon County courthouse.

As the 1896 presidential election neared, the political temperature of the *Gazette* rose. In the summer of 1896, White and other Republicans gathered around the ticker in the local telegraph office to follow the Democratic National Convention. When the dramatic news of William Jennings Bryan's nomination came in, marking the victory of prosilver forces within the Democratic party, one of the group cried out: "Marat, Marat, Marat has won!" White had been raised on Carlyle's and Dickens's accounts of the French Revolution, and he characterized the farmers' demands for reform of government and the economy as the first wave of revolution. To White and his Republican colleagues, Bryan was "an incarnation of demagogy, the apotheosis of riot, destruction, and carnage." Given his perspective, it is not surprising that the *Gazette* was patently biased in its coverage of Populism, however this might undermine his attempts to enlarge his audience. Throughout the summer and fall of 1896 his editorials raged against the Populist menace.[35]

White did try to mix human interest with his politics. In June 1896 he covered the Republican National Convention in St. Louis for the *Gazette* and the Kansas City *World*. His reports, sarcastically entitled "Among the Jays," were more in the tradition of Mark Twain's travel letters than political correspondence. White described St. Louis, the largest city he had ever seen, through small-town eyes that were at once naïve and shrewd. He complained about the smells of the city, and about the ugliness of city women: "They have a constitutional cross look which is generic." He praised the city's restaurants and open-air markets. Above all he ridiculed conventioneers in general and Kansans in particular. Like an American abroad, White was sensitive about the image made by his compatriots: "Kansas is the scruff of the earth. No one cares what she thinks. . . . The Kansas visitors wear a sunflower badge. . . . You can see St. Louis people pointing at the sunflower and tittering." He may have been made all the more sensitive by the adverse national publicity that Kansas was receiving because of its strong Populist movement.[36]

All White's efforts to downplay politics in the *Gazette* threatened to come to nought with the publication on August 15, 1896, of his editorial "What's the Matter with Kansas?" The outlines of the story have been often repeated: On a blisteringly hot August day in 1896, White was stopped on the street and harangued by a crowd of Populists, angry at his treatment of their party in the *Gazette*. Unable, as he often was, to defend himself in impromptu speech, he returned to his office and vented his frustration in an editorial. Before it appeared he took a train to Colorado to spend a week with Sallie, who had gone to the mountains because she was ill.

WHAT'S THE MATTER WITH KANSAS?

Today the Kansas Department of Agriculture sent out a statement which indicates that Kansas has gained less than two thousand people in the past year. There are about two hundred and twenty-five thousand families in this state, and there were ten thousand babies born in Kansas, and yet so many people have left the state that the natural increase is cut down to less than two thousand net.

This has been going on for eight years.

If there had been a high brick wall around the state eight years ago, and not a soul had been admitted or permitted to leave, Kansas would be a half million souls better off than she is today. And yet the nation has increased in population. In five years ten million people have been added to the national population, yet instead of gaining a share of this—say, half a million—Kansas has apparently been a plague spot and, in the very garden of the world, has lost population by ten thousands every year.

Not only has she lost population, but she has lost money. Every moneyed man in the state who could get out without loss has gone. Every month in every community sees someone who has a little money pack up and leave the state. This has been going on for eight years. Money has been drained out all the time. In towns where ten years ago there were three or four or half a dozen money-lending concerns, stimulating industry by furnishing capital, there is now none, or one or two that are looking after the interests and principal already outstanding.

No one brings any money into Kansas any more. What community knows over one or two men who have moved in with more than $5,000 in the past three years? And what community cannot count half a score of men in that time who have left, taking all the money they could scrape together?

Yet the nation has grown rich; other states have increased in population and wealth—other neighboring states. Missouri has gained over two million, while Kansas has been losing half a million. Nebraska has gained in wealth and population while Kansas has gone downhill. Colorado has gained every way, while Kansas has lost every way since 1888.

What's the matter with Kansas?

There is no substantial city in the state. Every big town save one has lost in population. Yet Kansas City, Omaha, Lincoln, St. Louis, Denver, Colorado Springs, Sedalia, the cities of the Dakotas, St. Paul and Minneapolis and Des Moines—all cities and towns in the West—have steadily grown.

Take up the government blue book and you will see that Kansas is virtually off the map. Two or three little scrubby consular places in yellow-fever-stricken communities that do not aggregate ten thousand dollars a year is all the recognition that Kansas has. Nebraska draws about one hundred thousand dollars; little old North Dakota draws about fifty thousand dollars; Oklahoma doubles Kansas; Missouri leaves her a thousand miles behind; Colorado is almost seven times greater than Kansas—the whole west is ahead of Kansas.

Take it by any standard you please, Kansas is not in it.

Go east and you hear them laugh at Kansas; go west and they sneer at her; go south and they "cuss" her; go north and they have forgotten her. Go into any crowd of intelligent people gathered anywhere on the globe, and you will find the Kansas man on the defensive. The newspaper columns and magazines once devoted to praise of her, to boastful facts and startling figures concerning her resources, are now filled with cartoons, jibes and Pefferian speeches. Kansas just naturally isn't in it. She has traded places with Arkansas and Timbuctoo.

What's the matter with Kansas?

We all know; yet here we are at it again. We have an old mossback Jacksonian who snorts and howls because there is a bathtub in the State House; we are running that old jay for Governor. We have another shabby, wild-eyed, rattle-brained fanatic who has said openly in a dozen speeches that "the rights of the user are paramount to the rights of the owner"; we are running him for Chief Justice, so that capital will come tumbling over itself to get into the state. We have raked the old ash heap of failure in the state and found an old human hoop skirt who has failed as a businessman, who has failed as an editor, who has failed as a preacher, and we are going to run him for Congressman-at-Large. He will help the looks of the Kansas delegation at Washington. Then we have discovered a kid without a law practice and have decided to run him for Attorney General. Then, for fear some hint that the state had become respectable might percolate through the civilized portions of the nation, we have decided to send three or four harpies out lecturing, telling the people that Kansas is raising hell and letting the corn go to weed.

Oh, this is a state to be proud of! We are a people who can hold up our heads! What we need is not more money, but less capital, fewer white shirts and brains, fewer men with business judgment, and more of those fellows who boast that they are "just ordinary clodhoppers, but they know more in a minute about finance than John Sherman"; we need more men who are "posted," who can bellow about the crime of '73, who hate prosperity, and who think, because a man believes in national honor, he is a tool of Wall Street. We have had a few of them—some hundred fifty thousand—but we need more.

We need several thousand gibbering idiots to scream about the "Great Red Dragon" of Lombard Street. We don't need population, we don't need wealth, we don't need well-dressed men on the streets, we don't need cities on the fertile prairies; you bet we don't! What we are after is the money power. Because we have become poorer and ornerier and meaner than a spavined, distempered mule, we, the people of Kansas, propose to kick; we don't care to build up, we wish to tear down.

"There are two ideas of government," said our noble Bryan at Chicago. "There are those who believe that if you legislate to make the well-to-do prosperous, this prosperity will leak through on those below. The Democratic idea has been that if you legislate to make the masses prosperous their prosperity will find its way up and through every class and rest upon them."

That's the stuff! Give the prosperous man the dickens! Legislate the thriftless man into ease, whack the stuffing out of the creditors and tell the debtors who borrowed the money five years ago when money "per capita" was greater than it is now, that the contraction of currency gives him a right to repudiate.

Whoop it up for the ragged trousers; put the lazy, greasy fizzle, who can't pay his debts, on the altar, and bow down and worship him. Let the state ideal be high. What we need is not the respect of our fellow men, but the chance to get something for nothing.

Oh, yes, Kansas is a great state. Here are people fleeing from it by the score every day, capital going out of the state by the hundreds of dollars; and every industry but farming paralyzed, and that crippled, because its products have to go across the ocean before they can find a laboring man at work who can afford to buy them. Let's don't stop this year. Let's drive all the decent, self-respecting men out of the state. Let's keep the old clodhoppers who know it all. Let's encourage the man who is "posted." He can talk, and what we need is not mill hands to eat our meat, nor factory hands to eat our wheat, nor cities to oppress the farmer by consuming his butter and eggs and chickens and produce. What Kansas needs is men who can talk, who have large leisure to argue the currency question while their wives wait at home for that nickel's worth of bluing.

What's the matter with Kansas?

Nothing under the shining sun. She is losing her wealth, population and standing. She has got her statesmen, and the money power is afraid of her. Kansas is all right. She has started in to raise hell, as Mrs. Lease advised, and she seems to have an over-production. But that doesn't matter. Kansas never did believe in diversified crops. Kansas is all right. There is absolutely nothing wrong with Kansas. "Every prospect pleases and only man is vile."[37]

Pulling out all the stops, White made particularly effective use of two classic party-press rhetorical tactics: vituperation and name-calling. He marshaled his considerable skills to brand the Populist leadership as rubes, failures, and political hacks acting out their resentment of the more able. The Populist candidate for governor he characterized "an old mossback Jacksonian" who feared modern plumbing. The candidate for chief justice was "another shabby, wild-eyed rattle-brained fanatic." The candidate for Congress was "an old human hoop skirt who has failed as a businessman, who has failed as an editor, who has failed as a preacher." Finally, female Alliance lecturers became "harpies."

The editorial embodied in particularly colorful and pungent language the standard assumptions of boosterism. Primary among these was the insistence that a community must make itself attractive to outside capital if it wanted to prosper. White's biographer Everett Rich pointed out, quoting from an editorial White wrote after the election, that "its thesis in so far as it had a thesis was 'that if Kansas fought the money power, the money power would fight back.'" Ignoring the long-term agricultural depression, White blamed Kansas's economic ills on its bad image abroad. No doubt his recent experiences in St. Louis had made him particularly sensitive on this point.[38]

The "money power" was quick to appreciate the editorial's value. It was picked up by the newspaper exchange network while White was still in Colorado. Paul Morton, a vice-president of the Santa Fe Railroad, saw it and passed it along to Herman Kohlsaat, the antisilver Republican publisher of the Chicago *Times-Herald* and the *Evening Post*. Morton wrote White:

> Have just talked with Leland about you. Your article . . . has created a great sensation in Chicago—Col. Purdy of the Rock Island—Lyman J. Gage, Pres. 1st Natl. Bk Chicago and many prominent men, are greatly taken with it. I shall see that it is read as a campaign document. It was edited yesterday by the State Comm. for the patent inside sheets of the West.[39]

Through the efforts of Morton and other businessmen as well as Mark Hanna's well-oiled Republican party machine, the nation was blanketed with millions of copies of "What's the Matter with Kansas?" Republican newspapers throughout the country reprinted it, the Republican National Committee distributed a million copies during the campaign, and the *Gazette* sent out reprints in response to requests from around the country. White later expressed his surprise that "my wail of woe had stirred a popular chord." It may well have, but the refrain had caught the public's ear through the medium of a sophisticated arrangement and a large, expensive, well-tuned orchestra.[40]

The consensus among White's biographers has been that "What's the Matter with Kansas?" made his career. This assessment overlooks the fact that, for White as a Kansan and a small-town journalist, the fame brought by the editorial was a very mixed blessing.[41]

There is no doubt that the editorial brought White to the attention of national Republican leaders and of Republican journalists around the country. But White's was not the first editorial to be thus widely reprinted, nor the last. As Everett Rich noted, such attention did not guarantee lasting fame: had he failed to fulfill expectations, "he would have disappeared as quickly from the national arena as did Arthur Guy Empey." The publicity did provide the boost needed to get his literary career off the ground, and Way and Williams at last decided to publish his short stories. They appeared as *The Real Issue* in December 1896. White, ever the shrewd promoter, exploited his political reputation to advance his literary career. When he was invited to present a toast, "What's the Matter with Kansas?", at a Republican victory dinner in Ohio, he wrote his publisher: "it means that in the next 40 days we can sell Ohio a gold brick in the shape of 500 books if we go at it right."[42]

Back in Emporia, however, the editorial probably hurt more than it helped his efforts to establish himself as a leading citizen. His intemperate attacks on fellow Kansans damaged his efforts to present himself as genial and fair-minded and the *Gazette* as an unbiased observer of community life. Populists, after all, controlled the county courthouse and in 1897 would also win city hall. The *Gazette's* foreman, Jack McGinley, left in charge of the paper while his boss was in Colorado, had hesitated to publish the editorial, convinced that it would disgrace Emporia and Kansas and bring the *Gazette's* ruin. He reluctantly gave it to Laura French, one of the compositors, to set in type. She was a passionate Populist and many years later recalled that she had "boiled with indignation" as she set it.[43]

The local Populist paper, the *Times,* responded to the editorial with character attacks of its own. It introduced the charge, to become common among his enemies, that White was emotionally unstable.

> There was a two column editorial in the Gazette Saturday evening which were any body in the habit of considering seriously anything that occurs in that eccentric sheet would demand a severe rebuke. Of all the giddy, disgusting nonsense that has thus far emanated from the befuddled intellect of the man who writes for that paper this last attempt to slander the state and its people is clearly entitled to take the lead. No man who is well balanced would demean and deride the good name of his town and state in any such style.

The criticism of disloyalty seems to have been telling, for a year later the *Times* was still referring to White as "the erstwhile slanderer of Kansas, her people and institutions. . . ." In private, an Emporia woman, Anna Watson Randolph, cut the editorial out of the *Gazette* and saved it in an envelope on which she wrote: "I should think that a man who wrote such a vile thing as this would feel the *Shame* of it *always.*"[44]

White had run afoul of the inherent conflict between party journalism and boosterism, between the need to attack one's political opponents and the booster imperative never to give one's community bad press in the outside world. In part White's sin had been inadvertent, for the editorial was written primarily for local eyes. Without the intervention of national capitalists like Morton, it probably would have circulated only in the immediate area. Nonetheless, the episode reflected the dangers in trying to serve both political masters and the local community.

Even before his political thinking changed after 1900, White was chagrined by the editorial's continued fame. Though he never rejected the publicity it brought, he sought to minimize the damage done by its criticism of his home state and rhetorical excesses. He advertised *The Real Issue* in the *Gazette* as "stand up for Kansas" stories and urged Emporians to send it to "your eastern kin." The toast he delivered in Ohio insisted that Kansas was "all right" and, while continuing to lambaste the Populists, asserted that Kansas Populists were no worse than those anywhere else. A few years later he dismissed the editorial as a mistake: "It was written because I was mad, and I could not do it again, or anything like it." When Doubleday &

McClure tried to include the editorial in a 1899 reprint of *The Real Issue,* he was furious: "For Heavens Sake let the dead past bury its dead." Perhaps it is most accurate to say that "What's the Matter with Kansas?" left White with a national reputation to live up to and a local one to live down.[45]

The most significant outcome of the 1896 election, from the standpoint of the *Gazette*'s future in Emporia, was the political patronage that McKinley's victory brought. In recognition for his early support, McKinley appointed White's mentor Cyrus Leland the U.S. Pension Agent for a large district including Kansas, Missouri, Nebraska, and the Indian Territory and serving more than a hundred thousand pensioners. Leland in turn awarded White the contract for all of the agency's printing. No records of payments to the *Gazette* survive, but the job work entailed must have been substantial, for the agency was second in the nation in total disbursements. White later recalled that the printing had brought him profits of around a thousand dollars a year.[46]

The editorial also gave White a reputation as a spokesman for the Midwest among national magazines seeking to address this new audience. Genteel magazines that had earlier rejected his fiction now solicited his nonfiction reporting on the region. Walter Hines Page asked White to contribute to an *Atlantic* series on American communities by writing "a composite photograph" of life in eastern Kansas towns, combining "sociological facts" with "human interest." For a *Scribner's* series on "The Conduct of Great Businesses" he wrote "The Business of a Wheat Farm." In the *Forum* he discussed "Kansas: Its Present and Its Future." The popular new mass-circulation magazine *McClure's* reprinted two of the more sentimental stories from *The Real Issue* and a year later commissioned a story on the Omaha Exposition.[47]

White used these opportunities to reach a national audience to make up for the damage he had done to Kansas's reputation. His *Forum* article, for example, reassured eastern investors that Populism was only a temporary aberration caused by the underdevelopment of the Kansas economy. He predicted that it would disappear as soon as economic growth and diversification increased employment and resolved the problem of high transportation costs. And he reported encouraging signs that this was already happening: "Nearly every Kansas newspaper contains references to the establishment of small industries, by local capital, all over the State. . . . Kansas is finding herself,—just as the Middle States found themselves a generation ago."[48]

Back in Emporia, White was busy preparing the evidence that he cited in his magazine articles. He had long urged that Emporians get busy and attract new manufacturing enterprises. In 1896 he predicted that Emporia "must eventually be the town of Kansas," but warned that it would not happen "if one crowd pulls against the other." In response to those who scoffed at the idea, he said, "What Emporia needs more than any thing else is a few first class funerals. . . . The fellows who set down on the wrinkled tails of their shiney coats and sniff when a man talks about Emporia's prosperity, would aid the town materially by annexing themselves for legislative purposes to the cemetery. There is going to be a big town in central Kansas in twenty years."[49]

In February 1897 he and a group of similarly ambitious young Emporians founded the Business Men's Association to ensure that Emporia would be that town. By the end of the month the group was already boasting the acquisition of a canning factory for Emporia. With White among the leaders were O. M. Wilhite, J. E. Evans, and Robert L. Jones. Like White, Evans and Wilhite had come to Emporia in the 1890s and worked hard to establish their businesses. "Mit" Wilhite, proprietor of the Mit-Way restaurant, had recently installed a telephone line so his diners could follow local baseball games. Jerry Evans had worked his way up from bookkeeper in an Abilene lumber store and recently opened a store in Emporia in partnership with one of his former employers. As a member of the city council in 1895, he had been White's staunchest ally in the battle for the printing. White had become friends with Robert Jones when he boarded with his family while an Emporia College student. Now an attorney and abstracter, Jones was active in politics as a Populist.[50]

Meanwhile, White lectured in the *Gazette* about the need for industrial growth. An April 1897 editorial proclaimed "The Shame of Kansas":

> We are great boosters in Kansas about the crops we raise. . . . Yet, with all these resources, there are not enough laboring men in Kansas to put out a good-sized prairie fire. All the truck that Kansas raises . . . is dumped raw into a box car and shipped out of the state—often a thousand miles—before it finds a lot of men at work who will turn it into the finished product. Then in about ninety days after the Kansas corn has left the siding, a smooth fellow in a high collar and a dollar and a half necktie and a corrugated vest, and patent leather shoes . . . chases across the state selling corn syrup [made] in Ohio to the jobbers, or corn starch made in Oswego, N. Y., to the wholesale grocers. He wears these slick clothes to celebrate the return of the Kansas corn to the men who raised it.[51]

At the same time, he worked behind the scenes to attract new industries. In 1899 he wrote the McCormick Harvester Company: "My friend, Mr. Davis . . . tells me that you are thinking of establishing a branch house and he suggested that it is possible that we might be able to get you here. I have purposely said nothing about it in my paper because I was so anxious to get you, that I did not wish any other town to know that you contemplated establishing a branch house." Aware that they would expect financial "encouragement" in choosing a site, White urged them to write him frankly and to tell him "in confidence" what they wanted. "I assure you that I shall do what I can. I have been fairly successful in the business of bringing things to Emporia, having got the Creamery here. . . ."[52]

Through activities such as these, White was beginning by 1899 to make his presence felt in Emporia as someone who could get things done on behalf of the town. Such a reputation was far more important for his standing in the local community than any national literary or political fame. Yet his widening connections outside Emporia were not irrelevant: they frequently proved useful in getting things done. One of the most important of White's connections was his relationship with the Santa Fe Railroad, whose vice-president Paul Morton had been so pleased with "What's the Matter with Kansas?" In the closing years of the 1890s and the early years of the new century, White frequently acted as an unofficial public relations officer for the railroad, passing along valuable information and suggesting ways to improve the Santa Fe's public image. For example, he suggested that a transferred employee, John Lucas, be returned to Emporia: "His standing with the business men of this town was excellent. . . . I am not writing this at Mr. Lucas' suggestion, but I am writing it because [some]times Mr. Paul Morton or Mr. W. J. Black ask me to do things for the road here." In turn, he asked for favors, as when he recommended that Calvin Hood be named a director. He noted that "his appointment would please Emporia, where he is what the newspapers call 'A Leading Citizen.' "[53]

White's ability to get things done was proven once and for all when he masterminded a mammoth street fair in Emporia in 1899. Not only did his organization of the fair mark a turning point in his rise as a community leader, but it embodied organizational tactics and booster themes of reciprocity, harmony, and participation that he would employ throughout his career.

White got the idea for a street fair from his literary-journalist model, E. W. Howe: "Ed Howe had been doing the same thing in Atchison for a year or two and, copy-catting him, I went into the street fair business in Emporia." In fact, street fairs seem to have been in vogue, for on July 10 the *Gazette* reprinted a two-page illustrated feature article on "modern street fairs," demonstrating how attractive booths and parades had been mounted in many other communities. Some towns, such as Keokuk, Iowa, had staged their first street fairs the year before to celebrate their nation's smashing victory in the Spanish-American War. There were even professional street fair promoters.[54]

Emporians needed diversion in 1899, for the town was reeling from the aftershocks of the failure of the First National Bank. Around noon on November 16, 1898, townspeople were stunned to see a small piece of paper posted on the front door announcing that the bank had been closed by order of the state bank examiner. Little more than an hour later, word came that the bank's president, Charles S. Cross, had gone to his farm northwest of town and fired a single revolver shot through his temple. Cross had inherited the bank's presidency from his father; with it he had also inherited a short-fall of around sixty thousand dollars, which he had juggled the books to hide. Earlier in the year the bank examiner, C. S. Jobes, had become suspicious and begun to press Cross to rectify the bank's finances. In a suicide note, Cross assumed complete responsibility for the bank's condition.[55]

Factional tensions, never far beneath the surface in Emporia, emerged into open conflict as Emporians and financial officials attempted to order the bank's tangled affairs and distribute its assets. Immediately after the closing the *Republican* attacked the action as premature, based only on "a slight deficiency" in the legal reserve. It termed examiner C. S. Jobes a "bank wrecker," responsible not only for unnecessarily destroying a bank through his "arbitrary exercise of authority," but for Cross's death. Jobes, it turned out, was a Kansas City banker and a close political associate of Cyrus Leland.[56]

Another Leland ally, Mort Albaugh, was named receiver of the bankrupt bank. He found its assets riddled with worthless investments made to Martindale's political cronies. Among them was some thirty-two thousand dollars in notes and accumulated overdrafts owed by the *Emporia Republican*. Refusing to hold Cross fully responsible for the failure, Albaugh pressed for Martindale's criminal prosecution. Meanwhile, controversy raged over liquidation of the bank's assets, particularly the sale of Cross's Sunny Slope Farm, which was widely known for its prize-winning purebred Hereford stock. The first arrangement, made between the receivers and Calvin Hood, was attacked for being far beneath the farm's value, and depositors succeeded in having it annulled.[57]

Although White steadfastly defended Hood's and Leland's interests, he seemed to realize that it was a propitious moment to preach harmony in Emporia. A public drive to mount a gala celebration was just the thing. In late June the Young Men's Business Association announced its intention of organizing a fall carnival. The first step was to raise a subscription to underwrite the event, which would also serve to assess the community's willingness to support it. To add an element of tension, the association vowed to call off the affair if they could not raise $1,000 in pledges within eleven days. White was named chairman of the committee to raise the subscription. It was one of the few times his name would be explicitly mentioned in the *Gazette* in connection with the event.[58]

The *Gazette* had already begun to point out the need for such an undertaking. An article on plans for the upcoming fourth of July did not hide its disapproval of the dearth of public activities: "Emporia always did like things quiet. . . . The G. A. R. people have made no special arrangements for the day. . . . There will probably be good rates on the Santa Fe and a large crowd will go to Kansas City to spend their money and have a good time."[59] White's criticism of the G.A.R. here was framed in booster terms: they neglected to promote civic activities that would attract business.

From the outset, the *Gazette* was fully committed to the project. Every issue preceding the deadline carried front-page stories, boldly outlined in stars, urging Emporians to lend their support. Each day it published the growing list of subscribers and the amounts pledged. The paper hammered away at the importance of fighting off the usual summer doldrums, which hurt business: "Here it is, gentlemen. It's up to you. Are we going to rust out this summer and fall, or are we going to Keep Something Going On?"[60]

The *Gazette* hailed the success of the initial fund-raising drive as evidence that a new, harmonious civic spirit was abroad in Emporia. A look at the list of contributors, however, reveals that the fair was most strongly supported by a coalition of the Hood faction with the younger generation of Emporia businessmen. The largest sum, one hundred dollars, was pledged by the Young Men's Business Association itself. Following that, with fifty dollars apiece, were Hood's Emporia National Bank, the *Gazette,* and G. W. Newman and Co., a prosperous dry-goods concern. Newman had founded his store in 1868 with the backing of a timely note from P. B. Plumb, and he remained allied with the Emporia National Bank thereafter. Newman's brother Frederick was president of the Citizen's National Bank, which in political matters operated within the orbit of the larger Emporia National. Fred Newman was also married to Calvin Hood's daughter.[61]

Among the next level, of twenty-five-dollar contributors, were the Citizen's National Bank and the Emporia Savings Bank; young businessmen A. O. Rorabaugh, Mit Wilhite, and J. W. Lostutter; impresario H. C. Whitley; the law firm of Lambert & Huggins; postmaster F. W. Ewing; and W. T. Soden & Son. Of these last three, Lambert and Ewing were leaders of the Emporia National faction. Soden, a wealthy miller, was vice-president of the Emporia National Bank. Continuing down the list, there appeared the names of nearly every other business and most of the professional men in Emporia, for amounts of fifteen dollars, ten dollars, and less. Included were the *Emporia Times* and *Emporia Democrat,* a recent arrival upon the scene, each at ten dollars. Conspicuous by their absence were names such as the *Emporia Republican,* William Martindale, and C. V. Eskridge.[62]

The subscription goal had no doubt been reached by a certain amount of arm twisting on Commercial Street, of which we have no record. White, did, however, solicit in writing a contribution from the Armour company, which ran a packing plant in Emporia. His arguments reflect the booster basis of his appeal: "It strikes me it would be a very wise thing for Armours to help us out a little; just whatever their share would be if they were a local concern. . . . It will remove whatever slight impression there may be, that Armours are outsiders, if they take an active, substantial interest in the concerns of the town."[63]

White's correspondence also documents his intense involvement in every aspect of the fair. From the very beginning, he wrote dozens of letters on its behalf—to professional promoters and entertainers, to colleagues, and to literally everyone and anyone he knew—for advice, funds, and, especially, favors. In order to make the fair a success, White called in many political debts and incurred further personal obligations. For example, he wrote Cyrus Leland, enclosing an article that Leland had wanted published, and asking a favor in return:

> I am promoting a street fair here in Emporia; it is my scheme, I have raised the money by subscription; the people look to me for its success or failure and I am out after attractions for it. I want some Indians to give a "corn dance" . . . I would like to have the Indians from the Potowatomie; but I am not particular where they come from just so they are Indians and can do a "corn dance."

Leland, who as pension agent was part of the Interior Department, put White in touch with the Indian agent for the Potawatomi reservation—and White got his corn dance. He asked former governor E. N. Morrill's help in securing the Soldiers' Home Band: "Anything you can do for this will be a personal favor to me, as I personally stand for this fair and my reputation will fall with its fall, or rise with its success."[64]

Ever since he first heard Pat Gilmore's band in Kansas City, White had had a passion for band music, and he went all out to bring a large number of bands to the fair. He recruited amateur bands from throughout the region, offering to pay their train fare and expenses. Above all, he sought to obtain the sixty-piece Marshall's Band of Topeka, widely regarded as the best band in the state. He wrote its leader:

> One of the features of the festival will be a state band contest, and the biggest feature of the band contest we wish to be Marshall's Band. . . . I want to make a Band carnival here as good as anything Ed Howe can get up in Atchison, and we are willing to pay for it. . . . Of course you understand that Marshall's Band would not have to contest for the prize unless it wanted to. We could make the capital prize your figure for coming and guarantee you the prize, or we could make a straight contract to give you so much money to come here and play. . . .[65]

He advertised for midway entertainers and screened the respondents to make sure they provided "a clean, respectable Midway." He secured a slide program, a black "jubilee" chorus, and the first automobile west of the Missouri River. To find an automobile, White called upon his acquaintances at *McClure's*, which had just published an article by Ray Stannard Baker about the marvelous new machines. He asked their help in interesting a Chicago manufacturer in bringing a machine to Emporia.

> Our flower parade will attract ten thousand people from a rich and prosperous section of Kansas, where they spend thousands of dollars every year on fancy traps, dog carts and all sorts of red wheeled rigs . . . and I really believe if I could get this automobile man, to send a trap or a dog cart for exhibition here, it would bring him trade.

Baker suggested several names—and White got his automobile.[66]

Such a diverse and sumptuous array of treasures from the outside world would certainly indicate Emporia's wealth and power, somewhat as captured trophies were carried in the triumphs of ancient conquerors to attest their prowess. Yet, in order to represent the community's new "wide awake" spirit, the fair also needed active local participation. White envisioned the fair as including practically everyone in Lyon County in one way or another—each, in fact, according to his allotted role in the community. Merchants would display their wares in booths lining both sides of Commercial Street; farmers' produce would fill stands running down the middle of the street. Church women were marshaled to provide meals for the multitude; society women would impress visitors with their beauty and taste in the grand flower parade that was to be the crowning event of the fair. White used the *Gazette* to promote the activities of each group according to this vision.

Like many aspects of the fair, the flower parade had a predecessor in the Atchison Corn Festival. In early September the *Gazette* began to encourage the efforts of prominent Emporia women to organize the event: "The women are taking hold of the flower parade with a boom in the last few days. . . ." A few days later it quoted an item from the Topeka *Capital* (probably itself prompted by the earlier *Gazette* notice): "The women of Emporia are taking hold of the flower parade in earnest. This ensures its success. It is the hard work of the women that makes a success of the Atchison floral feature." By means of this repeated journalistic self-reflection the *Gazette* kept the parade and other events constantly before the public.[67]

The next day a front-page story detailed plans for the parade and lauded the work of its organizers, particularly Mrs. J. M. Steele, wife of the assistant cashier of the Emporia National Bank. The story concluded with a booster litany:

> The prettiest parade Emporia has ever seen will occur. It is but one feature of the three day's Fair. This Fair is going to be clean, decent and gentlemanly. It is known all over Kansas as the biggest entertainment in Central Kansas. It has made Emporia known all over the state for a wide awake, hustling community.
> Keep up the good work.
> Talk for the Fair.
> Work for the Fair.
> It is the first sign of revival of life in Emporia. Wake up.[68]

White particularly wanted the full participation of farmers from Emporia's hinterlands, to symbolize the happy partnership of agriculture and commerce and to demonstrate to visitors the productivity of the region's land. In the newspaper, in letters, and, presumably, in person, he pressed farmers to come to the fair. The *Gazette* urged, "Bring In Your Pumpkins":

> The Emporia Street Fair will combine all the features of the old fashioned county fair with the best features of the new street fair. In the middle of Commercial Street a row of booths will run in which the best products of Lyon county farms will run. . . . Decorate your wagon for the farmer's day parade. Remember the Fair will give $25 to the township making the best showing. Come in by townships with decorated wagons—cover them with corn and other grains, or fruit and vegetables. . . . Everything will be clean and decent. There will be no gamblers in town.[69]

A week later, in a front-page box headed "The Rivalry Growing," the paper reported the competition among sections of the county to have the best display. Its main evidence was an item from a northern Lyon County weekly, the Allen *Journal:* "All North Lyon county towns should be represented at the Street Fair, which will be the best advertisement North Lyon county has ever had, as thousands of strangers are expected in Emporia during these festivities. . . ." An editorial in that issue warned that the fair

> will be a flat failure if the country people don't do their share. They must bring in the products of the farm. It is only fair. It takes two to make a bargain. If the town people put up $1,500 to help the show, the country people should bring in their part. . . . the town people . . . have paid for all the outer and visible forms of the show, the bands, the booths, the attractions, the prizes; but the inward and spiritual grace of this show must come from the farms. . . . Let's all pull together in this matter, the business man on the farm, the business man in the store. Lyon county is a bully good county—let's prove it to the world.[70]

The response to this varied appeal to boosterism, reciprocity, and competitive instincts, with a touch of theology thrown in, still seems to have been insufficient, for White took direct action. He wrote to a Lyon County farmer who was a Republican candidate for county office:

> The people of Emporia are very much afraid that we are not going to have enough products for our street fair, and our committee, which represents the best business men in town, has asked me as a special favor, to ask you if you will not go out with your buggy, Monday and Tuesday, and solicit people to bring in stuff. Make this a personal appeal. . . . Lay special stress upon the fact that this fair is to advertise Lyon County to all outside. . . . Do this for me and as you know I will do the same for you.[71]

Similarly, when church women were slow in organizing to provide meals, the *Gazette* chided: "What are they thinking of?"

> Railroad men . . . estimate that 10,000 people will be here. These people must be fed. . . . The town must turn in and help. If these people have to go hungry, they will hate Emporia forever.
> It is up to the people of Emporia.
> It is up to the women of Emporia. . . .
> What are the women of this town thinking of?
> Do they know that these excursion trains running to town are absolutely the first excursion trains that have run to Emporia for fifteen years? Don't they realize that the Santa Fe railroad, which is no fool, is back of these excursions and wouldn't get them up if there wasn't an awful jam coming to Emporia?[72]

Since the fair would ultimately be judged as a success or failure according to the size of the crowds it attracted, one of the most crucial factors in its organization was ensuring adequate and cheap transportation to Emporia. This depended on the railroads, and here White's contacts most clearly came into play. Despite the implication above that the special trains had been the Santa Fe's idea, they were the result of White's prodding. In August he had written to W. J. Black, general passenger and ticket agent for Santa Fe at Topeka. He began,

> This letter is the beginning of a great deal of trouble for you. Hereafter until September 27th, you will never look at a letter with the "Emporia Gazette" in the corner, without heaving a deep sigh. As you probably know, I am doing what I can, in a feeble way to promote a street fair.

He then launched into a series of requests—for free or reduced tickets for his multitude of attractions and for special excursion trains and rates for visitors—that was breathtaking in its audacity. He concluded: "In a measure, my reputation in this town will rise or fall with the success or failure of that fair. It is of deep personal interest to me, and whatever you can do to help us, I shall feel you have done in a measure to help me, and shall feel obligated accordingly."[73]

True to his word, White wrote frequently to the Santa Fe. He pushed for a special excursion train from Marion, Kansas: "We have hired the Marion band and they have circulated a paper and claim to have one hundred people who have signed it agreeing to come here to our fair on Friday. . . . At any rate, send a lot of bills down there, and wire your agent to have Ed Hoch give the thing a push in his paper, and that will help a great deal." He arranged for the appearance of a giant "King Corn" statue that Santa Fe had created for the Atchison Corn Festival. He even went straight to the top, to ask Paul Morton for his help:

> The money for the fair is raised by private subscription among merchants of the town; most of the soliciting I have done myself and have secured all of the attractions, and I feel a great personal interest in the fair for I am its "daddy". Emporia has not been a very wide awake town during the last four or five years, and is just now waking up. . . . I know this is asking a good deal of you, Mr. Morton, but I am asking it for the town and if we can wake up the town, it will help the road.[74]

Finally, White called on his colleagues on other Kansas newspapers to help him boost the fair. Such "puffs" were commonly expected reciprocal favors among friends, but, as shown by the above quotations, they would subsequently be cited as evidence of the state of "public opinion" elsewhere. In late August he wrote the editor of the nearby Americus *Greeting* and asked him to mention that the Americus band would be at the fair and that there would be a booth for Americus people. He urged the editor of the Allen *Journal* to "make a good feature in your paper about the Automobile, which will be the first Automobile that has ever crossed the Missouri river, and the only one that will be shown in Kansas this year." He suggested promotional copy to the editor of the Madison *Star,* beginning, "Madison people generally are talking about the Emporia street fair, and if we can get a special train one or two days there is no doubt but that Madison could fill a couple of cars." Then, when the requested items appeared, he reprinted them in the *Gazette,* with the preface "Still the country towns around Emporia talk Street Fair." He quoted the Hartford *Times:*

> There is no use talking about it, Emporia is improving. . . . some force is at work there to make them more public spirited. They have chipped in and

Commercial Street during the street fair, 1899
(Lyon County Historical Museum)

G. W. Newman & Co. booth during the street fair; Newman in booth at left
(Lyon County Historical Museum)

paid for a free Street Fair for next week, a kind of a "sett 'em up" to the county. This fair will be the first indication of life and public spirit that the town has had in years.[75]

The weekend of September 27 came, and sure enough, thousands of visitors crowded Commercial Street and the side streets, so densely that movement was often impossible. A contemporary chronicler of Emporia said that the automobile was the main drawing card. It was on show all three days, and its owner, Edward F. Brown of Brown Brothers Manufacturing Company in Chicago, obligingly provided rides for those daring enough to take them. The *Gazette* reported that the automobile had been pictured in *McClure's Magazine* and that its owner and his family were guests of Mr. and Mrs. W. A. White.[76]

During the fair, the *Gazette* was filled with anecdotes about every aspect of the great event, taking time out only for a column of news about the New York celebration of Admiral Dewey's return. It commented: "There is lots of noise in New York today, but there is more genuine home made fun in Emporia than anywhere else on earth." The paper had liberal praise for everyone connected with the event, particularly the railroads: "But for the Santa Fe this Fair would have been as idle as a painted ship upon a painted ocean."[77]

The fair climaxed on Saturday with the flower parade. Marshall's band led off down Commercial Street, followed by the automobile, carrying an odd but appropriate set of riders: E. W. Stanley, the Republican governor of Kansas; the Potawatomi Indian chief who had been imported to do a corn dance; and William Allen White. Behind them came the buggies, carriages, and traps of Emporia society, covered with rainbows of handmade paper flowers. First was "a Roman chariot beautifully decorated in pampas grass and red poppies and drawn by two oxen," driven by a local beauty, Maude Baker, who "made a striking appearance in her Roman costume." To add to this triumphal theme, fair organizers had persuaded a group of young black boys to pose as "Filipinos," dressed only in loincloths and carrying stalks of corn made to look like spears. But the boys' mothers had discovered the plan and descended upon the children, covering them with capes and hustling them home, to the amusement of the onlooking fairgoers. Closing out the mile-long procession was a carriage driven by Colonel H. C. Whitley, dressed as Uncle Sam and accompanied by children on decorated bicycles. The *Gazette* proclaimed the flower parade

> without doubt the most beautiful spectacle ever witnessed in Emporia. It was the first time the women have ever attempted anything of the sort and to say that they made a grand success of it is putting the thing mildly. Everyone from out of town declared the parade was wonderfully fine, and congratulated the Emporia people.[78]

The entire street fair was an unquestionable success. In its aftermath came a debate over what it signified. The *Gazette,* for its part, handed out laurels all around. One article printed the names of all involved in organiz-

Mrs. G. W. Newman's carriage in the flower parade
(Lyon County Historical Museum)

ing the fair, each paragraph with the response "To them honor is due." "It was everybody's show. Every business man on Commercial Street save two contributed money, and every man helped as much as he could." Finally, it lauded the executive committee: A. G. Lakin, E. E. Fawcett, Jerry Evans, Mit Wilhite, "and a disreputable fellow whose name is barred from the *Gazette*." The first four men "have done more for Emporia . . . than have any other group of men in five years."[79]

Few Emporians were fooled by this ruse. In the fair's aftermath, Mit Wilhite started a subscription to buy White a new desk. The *Gazette* protested (in White's absence) that "the four other members of the committee deserve a desk if Mr. White does," and urged Emporians to "pass up the subscription paper and go to rooting for a convention hall." Nonetheless, the fair went down in local memory as "Will White's Street Fair." It marked his arrival as an important community leader in the eyes of his townsmen. White admitted as much in his *Autobiography:*

> I took my first long step forward in public affairs by putting on a street fair. . . . People knew that I was responsible for the show. . . . And Emporia also began to realize that the editor of the Gazette was not one of them damn, long-haired literary fellows. . . . That first street fair, which made the merchants a lot of money, did more for me in the town than "What's the Matter with Kansas?" did for Mark Hanna.[80]

White probably had several reasons for refusing credit for his and his newspaper's part in the fair. He may have, like his father, "sought real leadership and tried to keep it anonymous . . . loved power but always pretended he had none. . . ." His political experience had taught him that real power was exercised behind the scenes. But he seemed to have a genuine hope in addition that through the *Gazette's* efforts Emporia would leave its notorious factionalism behind and achieve a new harmony. Perhaps in his new home he could be the peacemaker that as a child he had tried to be in his family. By continually asserting in the *Gazette* that the fair had been created solely by the new spirit of the town, White seemed to hope to make it so. He summed up these hopes in an editorial, "The Meaning of the Fair," that perfectly represents the booster blending of commerce and spirit:

> Never before in the history of Emporia was there such a crowd as gathered here last week. It was a peaceful crowd, and it conducted itself decently and in order. There were no fakirs to rob the people of their money, and so the merchants had a good steady trade. For the first time in the history of the town six excursion trains dumped their multitudes into the streets. These people came from a territory within a circle of a radius of one hundred miles from Emporia. This is Emporia's commercial territory. . . . The real meaning of the fair was not a festival, and had its serious side. Emporia has changed. It has not come in a night this change—from the country village, to the energetic, enterprising town; but it has been a matter of slow, steady perseverance. The manifestation last week, was the only sudden thing about it. The old town of cliques and factions and rings and gangs and crowds is gone; the new town of energy, and unity of spirit and ambition for Emporia has replaced it. This is what the Fair means. This is its promise; the promise of a better town, of an awakened industry, of new prosperity. . . . To no one man, nor to one set of men, does the success of this Fair or any portion of it belong. It was the people's Fair; every one helped. It was the small efforts of every one that made the great Fair so creditable. Every one did his part; no one shirked. Emporia was at her best.[81]

White and his colleagues in the Young Men's Business Association believed that this unity and energy would rejuvenate the town's economy. They hoped that economic growth would resolve the conflicts of the preceding decade. But accompanying and sustaining the economic rationale was a genuine search for a sense of community. The street fair, in which all Emporians had seemed to participate harmoniously under the natural leadership of businessmen, in which order and decency reigned and no one "shirked," provided a model of what civic life should be. In the coming years, White, the *Gazette,* and other young businessmen would continue to pursue this ideal through a wide range of political, economic, and cultural endeavors.

After four years in Emporia, White was no longer the "new man." He was well launched toward his ambition of becoming a leading citizen of Emporia. He had demonstrated in a particularly dramatic and concrete way that he could get things done and act effectively as spokesman for his community. Yet even as he was showing his ability to fill the booster role expected of a small-town newspaperman, he was reshaping it. In coming years, the small-town economy would face increasing change, and in helping local merchants respond the small-town newspaper would assume added importance. Increased revenues from circulation and advertising would make it less dependent upon its traditional patrons, political parties and local factions. Changes such as these would both enable and require the *Gazette* to broaden its appeal and further emphasize the booster search for a harmonious community.

PART II

The Old Order Changeth

3

A Practical Printer

In 1901 William Allen White wrote the president of a projected new rail-road to propose "a practical business scheme" that he thought would make them both some money. "I am a practical printer and have made the News-paper business a financial success and I know how to run a printing office." Though this scheme failed to materialize, White was right. As much as he was an aspiring writer, politician, and community leader, he was a shrewd businessman. During his first decade as proprietor of the *Gazette*, White turned a second-rate newspaper with an antiquated print shop into a flour-ishing enterprise that employed the latest printing technologies to expand readership and increase advertising revenues. He accomplished this trans-formation through a carefully planned program of gradually acquiring new printing machinery, expanding circulation, and attracting new advertising contracts.[1]

The *Gazette*'s growth and prosperity were common to the experience of small-town newspapers at the turn of the twentieth century. Although its expansion was sometimes aided by White's ability to invest income from his outside writing, in most cases it was funded by reinvesting the newspaper's profits. Above all, the fundamental causes for the *Gazette*'s success were not unique to White but the result of developments in the wider society that transformed the economic base of small-town journalism in this period. Foremost among these were the introduction of rural free delivery and the rise of the national advertising industry. Many of the newspapers published by White's colleagues in Kansas during this period became at least as pros-perous as the *Gazette*.[2]

A newspaper is the result of a manufacturing process, and its contents at any particular period are shaped by the state of the technology used to pro-duce it. Consequently, White's improvements in the *Gazette*'s circulation and contents were closely linked to changes in its print shop. Expanding circulation required similar growth in the capacity of his machinery, both to accommodate larger press runs and to make it possible to include more and timelier news. Increased circulation, in turn, was essential if White was to take advantage of new advertising revenues. Although changes in the *Gazette*'s technology, contents, and advertising were closely intertwined, for purposes of clarity this chapter will discuss each in turn. In the end, being a practical newspaperman in the early twentieth century meant that White presided over the transformation of the practice of journalism as he had learned it in the late nineteenth century.

The *Gazette* as White found it in 1895 was limited to four pages more by the condition of its print shop than by the amount of available news or advertising. The newspaper was printed on a flatbed cylinder press that the *Emporia News* had purchased new in 1883. It could make at best about 1,350 impressions an hour and was powered by pressure generated by the city waterworks system. When the river ran low the foreman had to call in one of the town's unskilled black laborers as an alternative energy source. Once printed, the newspapers were hand-folded by the boys who delivered them. A few cases of type, assorted hand tools, and two imposing stones completed the newspaper's capital inventory.[3]

The *Gazette*'s staff included the foreman, a journeyman job printer, an apprentice, four journeyman compositors, and two reporters. To cut labor costs, White switched soon after his arrival to "girl" compositors, who were paid far less than their male counterparts. Not surprisingly, male printers had resisted the entry of women into their shops; not only were they an alien element in a masculine world, but they generally depressed wages. During his days as a printer's devil, White had sat with the other printers "discussing matters of the craft: the secret of glue making, how to mold rollers, how to cast slugs, and how to stop the encroachment of women compositors in the back rooms of the printing offices." But now he was the boss, and it seemed an expedient way to cut labor costs.[4]

Job printing was a primary means of economic support for small newspapers, and White hoped it would help meet expenses until he got his newspaper on its feet. Consequently, his first step in building the *Gazette* was to acquire a job printing press. Years later he recommended a similar policy to Charles Vernon, a former employee trying to build his own newspaper: "Keep pounding away and make the job printing end pay for the news end for two or three years." The lucrative contract from Cyrus Leland for the pension-office printing was a substantial aid in this direction. It brought so much work that by 1902 it occupied one printer nearly full time. The first addition to the print shop for which direct record survives was a second job press purchased in 1899.[5]

Job printing would continue over the years to be essential to the *Gazette*'s financial well-being, despite the newspaper's increasing income from other sources. Although no direct records of income have been preserved, it is clear from White's correspondence that job printing long remained a source of concern and occupied a great deal of his and his staff's time, in making bids, ordering special engravings, paper, and ink, and securing payments. When visiting his colleagues, White always checked into their job business. In 1904 he complained to Sallie that one publisher did "much more job work than we do." But a year later he exulted, "We are doing a whaling lot of job work in the office. There never has been such a run since we came here of first class high priced work."[6]

Job printing was often a political plum given by the prevailing party or faction to the newspaper it supported. In addition to the big prizes, such as the position as state printer or the pension printing contract, many smaller jobs handed out from time to time were also tied to politics. For example, in 1900 White wrote to Secretary of State George Clark, asking for the printing of an amendment in Lyon County. He reminded Clark, "I believe the *Gazette* is the only paper in the county that has supported the republican ticket from top to bottom, or any considerable portion of it."[7]

Job printing contracts could be tied to nonpolitical connections as well, based on the principle of reciprocity. For example, White wrote to the head of a large wholesale concern that had recently moved to Emporia, enclosing a clipping from the *Gazette* in which he had "boosted" it. He continued,

> If at any time I can add to this in any way, and encourage the Emporia merchants to trade with you let me know, and it will be given without money and without price. I believe in standing up for Emporia things. In the mean time, if you have any job work to do, bring it to the *Gazette* office, and I will duplicate the prices you are getting in Lawrence, and give you just as good work.[8]

The growing amount of job work done by the *Gazette* consequently reflected its owner's widening community ties. Over the years his shop performed a wide variety of jobs: business cards, stationery and statements, wedding invitations, calling cards and social stationery, convention badges and programs, programs for dances and theatrical performances, pamphlets, directories, newsletters, business and college catalogues, school annuals and books.[9]

As it grew in volume, this job printing strained the shop's production capacities and required further investment. In 1901 White had to send type composition work to the Topeka *Mail and Breeze,* which owned a linotype. By late 1905 a larger job press had become necessary, and White bought a secondhand Optimus "pony" press for book and catalogue work. The acquisition of other printing machinery coincided with specific contracts. For example, in 1906 White told his machinery supplier that he needed a power stitcher but had waited "to see how the county printing was going. The election went all right [i.e., the Republicans won], and now we are in the market for a stitcher."[10]

White's first major step in modernizing the *Gazette*—and in publicly dramatizing the prosperity of his business—was to construct his own building. In September 1899, amidst the clamor over the street fair, a notice appeared in the *Gazette* calling for bids for the stonework on a 25- by 80-foot building. It was to include a concrete-floored basement for the presses and a front "all in iron and glass." The site at 513 Merchant Street was one block west of Commercial Street and immediately north of a lot that had been purchased in the early 1890s for a post office building. Though the project had been put on hold by the depression, White judged that it was only a matter of time until it was built. When that happened, the *Gazette* would be ideally located to mail its newspapers and printing. The new post office was,

POST OFFICE AND EMPORIA GAZETTE BUILDING
EMPORIA. KANSAS.

Emporia Post Office (left) *and* Emporia Gazette *building* (center) *on Merchant Street (Lyon County History Museum)*

in fact, completed in early 1903. When White's new red brick building was finished in March 1900, he installed a new eight-horsepower gas engine in the basement, for the presses.[11]

As White strove in succeeding years to build the *Gazette*'s circulation, he encountered successive bottlenecks created by the printing capacities of his shop. The first of these was caused by the composition of type by hand, which limited the size of the newspaper and the timeliness of its contents. Beginning with the first successful commercial use of Otto Mergenthaler's "Line-o'-type" machine in 1886, large urban dailies had begun to break this bottleneck—and, not coincidentally, to cut labor costs. Operated from a keyboard, this machine used an intricate system of chutes, belts, and levers to mechanically assemble tiny molds for each letter to form a line the width of the newspaper column. It then used molten lead to cast a slug, or solid line of type, from the molds. A skilled operator could set approximately five times the output of an experienced hand compositor. By the 1890s most large dailies had at least one machine, and often many more. In Kansas eight newspapers, located in the largest cities, owned a total of twenty-two machines in 1897. Small and medium-sized papers like the *Gazette* did not enter the market until after the turn of the century, but then they did so with a vengeance: between 1900 and 1905 the number of typesetting machines used by Kansas newspapers tripled, to seventy-three.[12]

In October 1902 White proposed to the Mergenthaler Linotype Company:

"I would like to figure with you for a machine. . . ." Power for it was a major stumbling block, for Emporia had electric current only for street lights. There was also the question of payment for the $3,400 machine. White was reluctant to become more indebted to local banks, but Mergenthaler solved the problem by providing the credit itself. The deal was finally closed in early December.[13]

The next major concern in introducing the linotype successfully was labor—not labor resistance, as occurred in urban print shops, but finding skilled operators. The introduction of typesetting machines in urban newspapers left thousands of compositors unemployed, but it is not clear whether any of the *Gazette*'s compositors were laid off immediately because of the machine. Much of the *Gazette* continued to be composed by hand, and one young male compositor, John Schottler, remained long after the introduction of the linotype. The long-term effect, however, was the departure of women from the *Gazette* print shop.[14]

To attract skilled linotype operators White had to pay significantly higher wages than he had for hand composition. By 1901 wages for compositors were a flat five dollars a week; when he hired his first operator, in January 1903, he offered fifteen dollars a week for a guaranteed output of five thousand ems per hour. Eight months later he offered the same wages for only four thousand ems per hour, and still later he offered sixteen dollars for a night operator. Nor were such wages necessarily sufficient. At the end of 1902 White advertised for an operator in the *Inland Printer,* a Chicago trade journal. Although he received a number of responses, nobody replied after hearing about the wages. When, finally, he received an inquiry from one Julius Melton, he assured him that he planned to introduce a profit-sharing system and offered to provide free transportation to Emporia. "I merely mention it to indicate that you are not going against a cold deal."[15]

In introducing the linotype, White for the first time went beyond his own mechanical experience. He later wrote, "When I bought the paper I was a fairly good printer. . . . When the linotype came, I was an outsider." He admitted to the Mergenthaler people, "I have looked over your circulars and have done my best to understand them, and considering my limited knowledge of machinery, I suppose I am doing fairly well." He consequently relied increasingly upon the expertise of his young foreman, Walter E. Hughes. Hughes had come to the *Gazette* as an apprentice in 1893 and become foreman in 1900. He quickly became White's most trusted employee and over the years assumed responsibility for the business as well as the mechanical side of the *Gazette*. Before the new linotype arrived White sent Hughes to the factory to learn about the complicated new machine so that he would be able to evaluate the performance of the new operators.[16]

Acquiring expensive and complex machinery like the linotype made White aware of his increasing dependence upon skilled employees. To ensure their loyalty and stability, as well as to attract skilled workers, White initiated more paternalistic labor policies. He did establish a profit-sharing plan. Details about how it worked in the early years are not available, but by

1920 it consisted of a bonus granted to the paper's full-time employees at the end of each year, based on a percentage of the profits apportioned according to length of employment. In 1906 he introduced a voluntary sickness, accident, and life insurance program that similarly encouraged permanence by rewarding workers according to their years of service. Each Christmas he honored all his staff with a festive dinner at which he distributed gifts and holiday turkeys.[17]

White continued to expand the *Gazette*'s use of the linotype as finances and composition needs warranted. To make fuller use of his investment in the linotype, White soon hired another operator to take a second shift on the machine. He also quickly began planning to acquire a second linotype. In April 1904 he told the Mergenthaler Company, "I hope to get this machine paid for this spring and then get one of your new double-barrelled machines that will do everything but sweep out the office and hold a mirror in front of the stenographer." But in the fall he learned through a former employee of a used machine for sale and bought it for $1,900, paying another $200 to have it upgraded. In 1905 he acquired a three-magazine Model 8 linotype to set advertising copy, display type, and job work, and he bought a fourth machine in 1907.[18]

Introducing the linotype increased the size of the paper and made possible changes in content, which spurred increases in circulation to around two thousand by the end of 1903. But here White encountered another technological bottleneck posed by the capacity of his aging press. As circulation rose, the time required to print the paper lengthened. The longer it took to print the paper, the earlier the first run had to begin and the later the last run was likely to be finished. This time element was particularly important because White was trying to increase the circulation to outlying areas of the county that were reached by mail, via train. The paper had to meet strict train schedules to ensure delivery the next day. Because of this mechanical logjam, the rate of increase in the circulation in 1904 and 1905 slowed from that of 1903. To continue expanding his rural market, he would have to acquire a more modern press.[19]

White was aware of the problem, but was held back by the high cost of a new press. To cut total printing time, he had in 1902 purchased an automatic folding machine that took up papers directly from the press. He considered buying a new press as early as 1903, but hesitated to increase his indebtedness. Nor was he sure what kind of press to acquire. By the turn of the century technological innovations that had long been available to large urban newspapers were being applied to smaller presses designed for "country" papers. One possibility was a rotary press that used curved metal plates that had been stereotyped, or molded from type forms. White considered such a press, but was concerned that the stereotyping process would be too complex for "a fair good country pressman" to handle.[20]

He also considered the Cox Duplex Press, first invented in 1889, which avoided the cost and nuisance of stereotyping by an ingenious arrangement of several flatbeds and traveling cylinders. Paper was automatically fed from a roll in a continuous sheet, or web, and an entire four-, six-, or eight-page paper could be printed at a single stroke. White had evidently decided in favor of a Duplex by mid-1904, when he told a friend that all his money was going into a fund for a new Duplex press that would cost $6,500.[21]

There matters remained for a year and a half. By September he had put the press on indefinite hold because of a shortage of funds. White may also have had second thoughts about the Duplex's practicability, for he was warned against the press by several colleagues. In the fall of 1905 he wrote to a Pennsylvania newspaper that used the Duplex to ask about its performance. He explained, "I have a circulation of about 2,400, and have a territory that may be reached with a quick press that will run me into four thousand; forty-five hundred will probably be my limit for ten years. What would you say about the ability of your press to handle that?"[22]

Meanwhile, the old Cottrell press was showing signs of its age. Breakdowns were common, and in the best of times the press produced a half-printed sheet because of its severely worn rollers. The breakthrough finally came in mid-1905, when the *Saturday Evening Post* decided to publish a series of White's stories on small-town life. Sallie White was delighted: "I can see our noses out of water now can't you? . . . it means the press and Europe."[23]

White signed a contract for a new Cox Duplex around January 1906. The change-over took some time and created many disruptions. The basement had to be enlarged to accommodate the new press. New types of paper and ink had to be ordered. White hired a new pressman, but the complex new machinery nevertheless took time to master. The first newspapers finally emerged from the new press on June 2.[24]

White's first mention in the *Gazette* of his newspaper's technological advance was strikingly ambivalent:

THE OLD PRESS.

The Gazette's old press is going to the depot today. . . . [It] has lived a good and useful life in Emporia, and should go to some press heaven. It has recorded much Emporia history that is important. Men and women have been born and married through its cylinder, and it has grumbled along carrying its daily load of joys and sorrows, and for the most part has been a hard-working old press, though of late it has been a little watery-eyed and rickety. But it is a good old press and everyone around the office is sorry to see the old press go, but everyone would scream if he thought it was coming back! Probably that would be the way with most of us after we are gone![25]

Several months later, the *Gazette* was more wholeheartedly enthusiastic about progress, publishing a three-column photograph of the press. It used the occasion to publicize recent advances in circulation.

Four months and a half the Gazette has been running on the Duplex press that gets the paper out on time and puts it in the hands of the reader by sundown. During that time the Gazette has gained one hundred subscribers a month, due largely to the fact that the paper comes out early, that it is well printed and that it uses a larger paper than formerly. . . .

It has enabled the Gazette to extend its circulation into every part of Lyon county. It has put the paper in the hands of all the neighborhoods adjoining Emporia before supper time and it is covering Lyon county with Gazettes like a blanket. . . . It is the best business venture the Gazette ever made, and will put this paper all over this congressional district within a year.[26]

Technological change had ended the simple print shop of White's youth, but it was his primary tool in expanding his market. Modernization was necessary to expand the *Gazette*'s circulation, but there also had to be a potential demand for increased circulation. Fortunately for White, the advent of free daily mail delivery to rural residents at the turn of the twentieth century widened the potential readership of the *Gazette* and other small-town newspapers throughout America. Rural free delivery, or RFD, had long been sought by farm organizations, but had been blocked by concern about its cost and opposition from rural merchants, who feared that farmers would come to town less often and would buy more of their goods from mail-order houses. Nonetheless, rural delivery finally began to be instituted nationally in the mid-1890s, and first came to rural Lyon County in 1900, when five routes were established. More routes were added in following years. RFD offered a special benefit for publishers like White, for their newspapers were delivered postage-free within their counties.[27]

To take advantage of this new potential audience and to attract a wider readership inside Emporia, White continually sought to improve the contents of the *Gazette* along with its printing technology. Within the limits set by his machinery at any particular point, he attempted to make the paper ever "newsier." This meant not only improving national news but expanding local coverage. It also compelled White to further downplay partisan interests and feature general-interest topics that would appeal to a wider audience. The booster emphasis on a unified, harmonious community was reinforced by direct economic incentives.

Attracting new rural readers meant including the kind of news they found most interesting. White learned this lesson most vividly early in 1900, when he hired Rose Edington, a professional canvasser for country newspapers, to solicit subscriptions for the *Gazette* in rural Lyon County. After she began work, she told him that she would have to recruit more country correspondents before she could hope to increase subscriptions: "You run a good paper, but it is in bad shape to commence a canvass on because you have scarcely anything but Emporia news." She lectured him on the principles of attracting rural readers:

I am aware that you [are] a writer of considerable note and may labor under the impression that this correspondence must be something with brains to it. No, that isn't necessary at all. Most anyone writes good enough, and if it is only "Jim Jones butchered yesterday" and "Mrs. Smith had a quilting and Mrs. Brown and Black were there," Jones, Smith, Brown and Black will take the paper and the general public can skip such items if they don't want to read them. . . .

"Put people's names in your paper," she promised, "and they will step up to the counter and pay you for it."[28]

Accordingly, White stepped up his efforts to recruit country correspondents. Although they were not paid for their weekly letters, correspondents did receive free stationery, stamps, and subscriptions to the paper. In 1901 White also began offering as an incentive subscriptions to the *Saturday Evening Post,* and several years later he offered a choice of the *Post, McClure's,* or *Ladies' Home Journal.* Occasionally he gave special rewards to particularly faithful correspondents: in 1904 he presented Mr. and Mrs. John A. Sims with tickets and round-trip train fare to the World's Fair in St. Louis, in recognition of Mrs. Sims's nine years as a contributor to the *Gazette.*[29]

Beyond increasing country news, White courted rural readers by trying harder to curb his polemical tongue and make his news coverage more evenhanded. In a conciliatory editorial in August 1900, he admitted that four years earlier, "some way the *Gazette* made the opposition mad." He continued to defend the gold standard, which he credited with the return of prosperity, but he also proposed reconciliation.

> Now that everything is lovely and the altitude of the goose is unquestioned, friends and brethren, neighbors and fellow citizens, don't you think it is time to come in to the *Gazette* office and apologize; also get a clean, newsy paper, that never abuses candidates on any ticket . . . that says kind words about friends and foes alike; that prints all the news all the time and shields no one or fights no one or abuses no one.[30]

Promoting harmony was not only part of the booster ethos; increasingly, it was necessary for expansion.

To increase local circulation, White also stepped up his efforts to gather local news. He began to hire extra part-time reporters from the local colleges. He devoted the *Gazette*'s third page, previously a dumping ground for patent medicine advertising and stale boiler-plate humor, to irreverent and spicy local human-interest items. He called attention to the change on the front page: "A *Gazette* advertiser kicked because he was put on the third page yesterday. Today an item is put on that page which may cause a shooting." In addition to the usual locals, such as "Miss Reed, from Hartford, is the guest of Mrs. W. A. Parker," the third page contained "scandalous" items like these: "There is a married man who is in business on Commercial street who is calling too much on a Constitution street woman and the result is talk." "Because a woman sent to a neighbor's to borrow some little baby clothes to use for a pattern in making some clothes for a poor woman's baby, one of the worst scandals in town started."[31]

Similarly to expand local circulation, White launched special eight-page Saturday editions of the *Gazette* in 1900. Modeled after the Sunday editions of urban newspapers, and particularly after the Topeka *Mail,* the largest weekly in Kansas, these editions were crammed with local human-interest news, features, and, most strikingly, illustrations.[32]

These Saturday editions illustrated the human-interest formula that would come to dominate the *Gazette* in subsequent years. Although they featured many aspects of Emporia and Lyon County society, paying unprecedented attention to its women and children, the chief actors on the community's stage were the town's businessmen. Each edition typically featured several photographs on the front page, highlighting local people and Republican state political figures. Illustrated series of articles reported on local landmarks, such as one that toured the "great homes" of Emporia. It began with the G. W. Newman and Calvin Hood residences. There was often a "mystery photograph" of a well-known local figure photographed from behind, with clues to his identity in the caption. One week it was "The Town Business Woman": "This is a picture of a keeper of a profit shop. In that shop, its handsome, plucky owner has made a neat little fortune in the last fifteen years." The further information that she had come from Ireland and married "a sawed-off little German" would have told nearly everyone that this was milliner Maggie Byrnes Ballweg. The same issue reported on a baby show in the rural Lyon County community of Admire and proposed, "Why Not a Baby Parade?" with the next flower parade. A circus managed by fourteen-year-old Billy Gibson was praised for its "side splitting comedies," "thrilling acrobatic feats and juggling," and reasonable admission cost of two cents. The Saturday *Gazette* also published a regular book review column, "Home Made Book Notes," and illustrated articles on the latest fashions.[33]

The many illustrations in the Saturday edition marked its most dramatic departure from the weekday *Gazette*. Given the state of the technology of photographic reproduction in printing at the time, illustrations were a problem for small-town publishers. They could not make the necessary halftone engravings themselves and had to send photographs or drawings to out-of-town engravers and hope they would return in time for the next edition. Too, the engravings were expensive. For example, illustrations for the first Saturday issues cost White around five dollars a week, the equivalent of a full week's salary for one of his compositors. There were, however, several ways to cut the cost of illustrations. One was to borrow engravings, or cuts, from other newspapers. White quickly followed this route and wrote to colleagues far and wide asking to borrow cuts that he had seen in their papers. He also purchased illustrations more cheaply in stereotyped form from the houses that sold boiler plate to country publishers. For example, in April White asked the American Press Association to send him "six columns of your best fashion plates" for his new Saturday edition.[34]

After about eight months of these eight-page editions, White evidently decided that they were not worth the considerable extra work that he had put into them, and they were quietly discontinued. Thereafter few issues of the *Gazette* were as heavily illustrated, although photographs appeared occasionally.

In 1900 White used a great deal of stereotyped plate for news and illustrations in the *Gazette*. He bought stereotyped national and regional news from the A. N. Kellogg Newspaper Union. He also regularly ordered from Kellogg special holiday-page plates, which lent greater visual variety to his newspaper than was possible with the few typefaces and the scanty supply of decorative borders on hand. But the major advantage of plate was that it filled more space more cheaply than could be done each day by hand composition alone. Without a linotype to speed type composition, a newspaper could fill out its pages only with plate, and White regularly purchased from Kellogg dozens of columns of "short miscellany" plate for filler. He also used a plate service offered by the Kansas secretary of state, and occasionally exchanged advertising space for plate.[35]

On the other hand, a major drawback of plate material was that, being mass-produced, it could not reproduce local news. Nor was plate news as timely as the AP wire copy would have been. In May 1901 White complained to Kellogg about the quality of its news: "You have apparently been giving me the evening report of the day before dated ahead. The report Tuesday contains news that could have been sent out at four o'clock Monday evening and was not at all satisfactory. Please change this, give me the morning report or nothing."[36]

The linotype was consequently essential to both increase the *Gazette*'s size and improve its contents. When the first linotype debuted in March 1903, the *Gazette* immediately expanded to eight pages. White advised a colleague a year later that "a [linotype] machine would be a good thing for you, if you could afford it. You could double the size of your paper without any trouble. . . ." Shortly after signing the contract with Mergenthaler for his first linotype, White also applied for membership in the Associated Press. He wrote his friend Frank MacLennan, "Here is another Rubicon: I am going to make the jump." He applied for the "pony" service, which was shorter than the regular service for larger newspapers. It cost one hundred dollars a month, but he gambled that increased subscriptions would pay for it.[37]

Improved technology opened the way for improved content, which translated into increased circulation, which, in an upward spiral, would eventually require further technological improvement. As soon as the linotype was in place, White launched a campaign to increase his circulation, hiring solicitors to canvass in Emporia and Lyon County and offering special premiums to new subscribers. The response was gratifying; by July 1903 circulation within Emporia had increased by 300, to nearly 1,300, and total circulation had reached 1,750. White was confident that by fall it would hit 2,000—as much as he could accommodate with his old printing press. A similar intensive campaign accompanied the introduction of the new press in 1906 and brought the *Gazette*'s circulation to 3,000, where it remained for the rest of the decade.[38]

Between major circulation campaigns, White promoted his newspaper in other ways. He collaborated with fellow publishers in "clubbing" arrangements whereby several subscriptions could be ordered together at discount rates. Reflecting the diversity of the *Gazette*'s readership, such publications ranged from newspapers like the Kansas City *Journal* and *Star* and the Topeka *Capital* to the *North Lyon County Journal,* and from periodicals like *Cosmopolitan* to the *Live Stock Indicator* and *American Farmer.* He also offered special clubbing rates to induce subscribers to pay in advance; he obtained these special rates in exchange for advertising the periodicals. White arranged to have his newspapers sold in Emporia's train depots and on the trains. To encourage the newspaper-reading habit, he sent the *Gazette* free to county schools and gave complimentary subscriptions to newlyweds.[39]

White also schemed to take full advantage of the expansion of rural free delivery. In the summer of 1905 he devised a plan to improve the delivery of the *Gazette* in the northern part of the county, for which train delivery was roundabout and quite slow. He hired a number of county youths, who commuted to Emporia to attend school, to carry newspapers to the rural post offices, whence they would be delivered as regular mail. This required the consent of the postmaster general, which White received with the backing of his congressman.[40]

In his first decade as proprietor of the *Gazette,* White had transformed the printing of his newspaper, increased its circulation, and upgraded its contents. These changes required substantial capital investment and increased labor costs, while making the management of the whole enterprise far more complex. Why were such changes desirable, or feasible? The complete answer lies in the other major source of revenue for newspapers—advertising. During precisely those years in which White struggled to modernize his print shop, advertising was playing an ever larger role in the economics of newspaper publishing.

In the last decades of the nineteenth century and the first of the twentieth, advertising in America grew from a small, marginal activity into a multi-million-dollar industry that transformed the economic base of newspaper publishing. Newspapers had always carried advertising, and mass-circulation periodicals had derived substantial income from advertising since the days of the first penny papers. But it was not until the beginning of the twentieth century that advertising became the major source of income for all newspapers, large and small. This development has been largely overlooked in journalism history, because of its emphasis upon urban dailies. Moreover, treatments of advertising during this period have focused upon the rise of the mass national magazines. But White's correspondence and the *Gazette* itself demonstrate the dramatic effects of the growth of advertising upon a single newspaper.[41]

At the national level, manufacturers in certain high-volume consumer-goods industries turned to advertising as part of their effort to achieve greater control over the distribution of their products. Not only did advertising help increase the demand for the greater output of goods they were capable of making with new mass-production processes, it produced product differentiation by fostering name recognition for their brands, which weakened wholesale jobbers' and retailers' control over distribution. Further, it was a weapon in the ongoing struggle of manufacturers with the large urban department stores and mail-order houses that had acquired increasing power over distribution.[42]

The advertising agent was a crucial link in the emergence of a national advertising industry. At first he was merely a space jobber, who guided advertisers through the uncharted wilderness of thousands of American newspapers of widely varying quality. In the beginning, agencies often bought blocks of space in newspapers and resold them in smaller lots to advertisers. Agents typically received a commission from the publishers of 20 to 25 percent of the cost of the advertising space, but their greatest profits came from the difference between the newspapers' stated advertising prices and what publishers, often desperate for cash, would settle for, particularly for a large, long-term contract.

Nineteenth-century advertising agents capitalized upon the instability and decentralization of the American newspaper industry. They benefited from both advertisers' lack of information about newspapers and publishers' generally impecunious condition. In addition, a number of agencies began as adjuncts of type foundries or printing supply houses and made handsome profits by bartering advertising for news ink and type. Country publishers, perennially short of cash, welcomed the chance to gain a new "dress" of type in exchange for advertising, and the agencies kept the difference between costs of the supplies and retail prices for type and advertising as charged to advertisers. In fact, barter of all sorts was common in small newspapers well into the twentieth century. William Allen White customarily acquired through advertising "swaps" type, ink, and office equipment, as well as a sewing machine, bicycles, buggies, books, and a variety of other goods for his own use.[43]

The *Gazette,* like countless other small-town newspapers, began to receive its share of the increasing expenditures of the national, or, as White customarily put it, "foreign," advertiser around the turn of the century. At first, as with most nineteenth-century papers, most of this advertising came from the makers of patent medicines. Small in size and featuring a high ratio of price to weight and hence easily transportable, proprietary medicines were one of the first nationally marketed products. They were also some of the heaviest consumers of advertising in both urban and rural newspapers. The *Gazette* contained high proportions of ads for patent medicines throughout the 1890s and the early years of the new century. Patent advertising pioneered the cultivation of brand-name identification, as well as the manipulation of emotions to sell products. A four-column ad in 1901 for Lydia Pinkham's Vegetable Compound, uncommonly large for the *Gazette* at the time, featured a drawing in which a fashionably dressed woman shrank beneath a male doctor's intent gaze. A testimonial in another Pinkham's ad reinforced this recurring theme of the difficult relations between women and the predominantly male medical profession. Mrs. Sophie Binns, president of her local Young People's Temperance Union, reported that the Vegetable Compound had cured her of "Congestion and Inflammation of the Ovaries," for which her doctor had "recommended an operation which I would not hear of."[44]

In the early 1900s, all of the major patent medicines advertised in the *Gazette* at one time or another.[45] Like most of its counterparts, the *Gazette* rarely turned down advertisements of this type, although it reserved the right to reject or modify ads it considered obscene. White turned down an ad placed by the Dauchy & Co. agency for the Marvel Company because it was "objectionable," and his bookkeeper wrote the C. H. Fuller agency that "we could not handle some of the copy at any price, unless it is modified." They did not state explicitly what made copy objectionable, but it seems that overt sexual references and advertisements for contraceptives or abortifacients were included in this category. When a rejected advertiser asked for an explanation, the bookkeeper replied, "We do not like the looks of the ad." One advertising account that was rejected was for Madam Dean's French Female Pills.[46]

Gradually, advertisements for other nationally marketed products began appearing in the *Gazette*. Though they brought needed revenues, such advertisers were not always easy to deal with. In 1899 White wrote the Royal Baking Powder Company in high spirits:

> [T]he last strike is now driven. I am ready to sign a contract with you. . . . This comes at the end of a correspondence running over three years. I desire to congratulate myself and you on the end of this controversy [and upon] finishing this letter will go out and take a drink. Trusting that you will do the same, I remain. . . .[47]

Such amity did not continue. Six months later he wrote in response to a Royal complaint about the position of an ad:

> We would be very pleased if you would settle with us for what you are willing to admit we have performed correctly, and cancel the contract. Your business is a constant annoyance to us. . . . Send us a check for anything you think is reasonable, and let us saw this matter off, and for heavens sake don't ever write to us again.[48]

However welcome, then, increased brand-name advertising brought major headaches. Although a few agencies seem to have had traveling agents, the vast majority of the business was conducted by mail, with concomitant delays, mix-ups, and misunderstandings. As advertising volume rose, White spent an increasing amount of time on advertising correspondence: negotiating contracts, placating advertisers, and pursuing payments that were often tardy and sometimes never forthcoming. Eventually White created the position of foreign advertising bookkeeper to handle the day-to-day details of the new advertising arrangements.[49]

By far the major source of contention between White and his foreign advertisers was rates. They were ostensibly based upon circulation, but in the nineteenth century, when publishers habitually claimed inflated circulations, it was no easy matter to know what a newspaper's actual circulation was. Newspaper directories prepared by various agencies contained most of their accumulated information, but they still relied upon the statements of publishers themselves. The accuracy of their information was further compromised by the fact that they also contained advertisements by newspapers, which were usually paid for by exchanging advertising space.[50]

This was an especially acute problem for White. His paper had made dramatic gains in circulation since 1895, but it was difficult to convince advertisers of this when directories such as Rowell's continued to rank the *Gazette* as under one thousand circulation, along with the faltering *Republican*. In 1901 White raised the matter with the Lord & Thomas agency, which published its own directory. He sent copies of the *Gazette* and the *Republican* and challenged:

> You can see at once by comparing the two papers which paper is the popular paper of the town. I send you herewith a sworn statement of our actual circulation. I do not like to be put in the light of questioning the affidavits of any body, but neither do I like to be put in the position of playing second fiddle to a paper that has less than one third the circulation of the Gazette.[51]

White frequently sent out sworn circulation statements, but, as the above indicates, these were of limited value when other publishers were less scrupulous. Ultimately, the answer for White and the combined advertising and publishing industries was professional self-regulation. At first, some directories gave special recognition to publishers who met certification requirements; White proudly pointed to the fact that the *Gazette* was on the Rowell "Roll of Honor," a listing accorded newspapers that backed their sworn statements with receipts from paper companies. In addition, White welcomed an advertiser's request to have his circulation records audited by the Association of American Advertisers: "nothing would please me better than to give them the fullest access to our accounts . . . as I desire very much to have the exact circulation known and guaranteed by the Association." Later, like other progressive businessmen seeking legitimacy through government regulation, White would back his circulation figures with post office statements. By the end of the Progressive Era, circulation figures for the entire industry were regulated by the Audit Bureau of Circulations, an industry successor to the AAA.[52]

Nevertheless, in the early days advertisers and agents seemed interested less in quantifying advertising's effectiveness than in getting newspaper space as cheaply as possible. Consequently, the process of making a contract was a drawn-out affair, as each side made offers and counteroffers until a compromise could be reached. In 1899 White wrote to an agent,

> I do not wish to seem arbitrary in this matter but the rate I quoted you I am getting from all the best advertisers in the country. . . . The rate I asked you was $24.00 gross, with a 25% commission, or $18.09 net. The rate you offer is $12.00. I realize that the Swamp root business is good business and will stay year in and year out, and therefore will make this concession: If you wish

I will split the difference between us, and make it $15.00 net. I trust you can see the wisdom of using my medium at this rate.[53]

At times, when White received particularly outrageous offers, his temper overcame his business sense. In 1899 he wrote the N. W. Ayer & Son agency:

I have a proposition from you for practically 1300 inches in my daily, and 650 inches in my weekly, for which you offer me $40.00. You will confer a great favor on me if you will not send me any postal cards, circular letters, reminders, amended propositions, or anything else on this business, until you are ready to talk at a rate of $130.00 less the usual commission. For heavens sake let this be the last of this correspondence. I will not think of advertising at any other rate.[54]

By the late 1890s White's opening figure for advertising in the daily was usually five cents an inch, or one dollar an inch per month for ads running without change. But he frequently settled for three cents or less. Gradually, over the following decade, his prices rose, to six to eight cents an inch, or a dollar and a quarter an inch per month by 1904, and, by 1910, to ten cents an inch for contracts of over two thousand inches per year. As the *Gazette* became more established and the advertising business more rationalized, haggling over prices gave way to more hard and fast rates, based on clear-cut criteria such as the newspaper's circulation, the size of the contract, and whether special placement was requested.[55]

Initially, after a contract was agreed upon, the agent or advertiser forwarded copy to the newspaper, which set it in type. This inevitably resulted in significant variations across newspapers, as typefaces and compositors' abilities varied. Eventually advertisers who wanted greater uniformity sent electrotypes, or electros, plates that had been mass-produced through an electroplating process. When mounted on wood blocks, they could be easily fitted into the page forms. Publishers preferred them because they eliminated the need to set type, and generally gave further advertising discounts for them. When larger newspapers introduced into their shops foundries to cast the curved stereotyped forms used on high-speed rotary presses, advertisers began to send them papier-mâché molds, or mats, from which plates could be cast, thereby saving the expenses of making and sending electrotyped cuts. But the *Gazette* would not have this capability until the 1920s.[56]

A few agencies were beginning to expand their services to include designing as well as placing advertising. Instead of merely sending out an advertisement to run for months at a time, they planned a series of ads. They also paid greater attention to the placement of advertisements, requiring publishers to run specified ads in particular positions on designated days. Such complicated demands further challenged the organizational abilities of small print shops like the *Gazette*.

By the early twentieth century, the advertising industry had developed to the point where its leaders became more sensitive about its "respectability." This concern was most clearly manifested in changing attitudes toward patent medicine advertising. By 1904 patents faced increasing public criticism in magazines such as *Ladies' Home Journal* and *Collier's,* and the Pure Food and Drug Act of 1906 attempted to protect the public by requiring accurate labeling on patent bottles. Advertising agencies like N. W. Ayer had begun to weed out some of the most objectionable patent medicine accounts by 1900, while continuing to carry others. In part this new selectivity was the result of distaste for the patents' excessive curative claims, but it is also clear that such discrimination was made possible by increased revenues from other, more reputable, sources.[57]

Similarly, as the *Gazette*'s total advertising revenues increased, it became not only possible to begin to cut out patent medicines, but profitable to do so, because it improved the "tone" of the whole newspaper. Indeed, this was one reason why White had long rejected overtly sexual ads: when a prospective advertiser questioned his rates, he sent a copy of the paper, "in which you will see we have no cheap advertising. . . ." Nonetheless, White did not come immediately to realize the benefits of selectivity, nor was he in the vanguard of the antipatent movement, as some have credited him with being. Even after the *Ladies' Home Journal* renewed its longstanding campaign against patent medicines in 1903, the *Gazette* continued to carry and to solicit their advertising. In 1904, during a campaign to bring in new advertising contracts, White solicited business from medicines such as Wine of Cardui, Liquozone, Kilmer's Swamp Root, Dr. Green's Nervura, and Munyon's Remedies, all of which were shortly to fall victim to the muckrakers.[58]

In June 1904 White signed an advertising contract that was to attain a peculiar kind of fame. This contract, with one Frank J. Cheney, maker of Hall's Catarrh Cure, contained the "red clause," soon to be made notorious by muckrakers Samuel Hopkins Adams and Mark Sullivan. It stipulated, in red ink, that "It is mutually agreed that this Contract is void, if any law is enacted by your State restricting or prohibiting the manufacture or sale of proprietary medicines." This was Cheney's clumsy effort to blackmail newspaper publishers into lobbying against antipatent legislation. In 1905 Mark Sullivan, investigating the patent industry for *Ladies' Home Journal,* obtained a copy of the minutes of a meeting of the Proprietary Association of America, in which Cheney touted the efficacy of his clause. Seeking further evidence about use of the clause, Sullivan eventually turned to White, probably through their mutual connections at *McClure's Magazine.* Also at *McClure's* at this time was Samuel Hopkins Adams, who happened to be preparing a series on patent medicines for *Collier's.* It was Adams who wrote to White asking to see his contract with Cheney. The offending document was subsequently published twice in the *Collier's* campaign: in Adams's lead article, "The Nostrum Evil," and a month later in Sullivan's exposure of the red clause, "The Patent-Medicine Conspiracy Against the Freedom of the Press."[59]

It is not clear when White himself became aware of the implications of the red clause. Lydia Pinkham's advertisers had used a similar clause since the 1890s, and according to Adams, Cheney had devised his plan "some years" previously. White had had several contracts with Cheney before the

1904 agreement, and there is no evidence that he ever questioned or complained about the clause. There was, however, some disagreement about prices and the position in which the advertisement was running in the *Gazette*. It will also be noted that White *had* signed the contract, and it was still in force a year later, when his bookkeeper Mae Austin wrote *Collier's* to ask for its return.[60]

Even though White was not an early crusading antipatent editor, he was quick to respond to the revelations of this latest round of exposés. In 1906 he published the results of chemical analyses of products such as Liquozone and called attention to the *Collier's* reports. The *Gazette* had accepted advertising for Liquozone and other patents through August 1905, but in September he directed his staff to cut patent medicine advertising.[61]

It was not always easy, however, to know which products to cut and which to leave in. The easiest targets were those products that were being singled out by the magazines, and as their contracts ran out advertisers such as Lydia Pinkham's and Peruna were told that their advertising was now "objectionable" and no longer welcome. Other medicines, such as Herpicide and Pepsin Syrup, were accepted. When rejected advertisers protested, some attempt was made to formulate an explicit policy. To the advertisers of "D. D. D.," the bookkeeper explained, "You promise impossible things and we do not believe in that." Mae Austin admonished the Chamberlain Medicine Company, "we believe your remedies contain dangerous drugs and we believe that it can be shown that selling them is injurious."[62]

White eventually settled on a distinction based on both restraint in curative claims and the medicine's capacity to cause actual harm. He carefully differentiated between products that were taken internally and those that were applied externally. For example, he rejected an advertising contract for a "Hair Health" product when he discovered that it was a tonic. He told another agency he was "perfectly willing to take Cuticura soap but not the Cuticura medicines." In subsequent years, White extended his policy of protecting readers from unscrupulous advertisers by rejecting ads for mining schemes and for stocks not listed by the New York or Chicago Board of Trade.[63]

On the other hand, he made no attempt to police more psychologically sophisticated advertisements. Such failure to curb advertisers' appeals to consumer emotions may well have encouraged the chemical companies' shift from products that claimed to cure to those that promised social acceptance.[64]

This policy of excluding many patent medicines may have hurt the *Gazette* financially in the short run, but in the long run it probably helped make the paper more attractive to the growing numbers of other advertisers of brand-name products. White could justify increased advertising rates on the basis that because advertisers did "not have to compete with a lot of large Patent Medicine advertisements," their space was "worth more than the average Newspaper which accepts every sort of advertisement." He

could also argue for a rudimentary form of market segmentation, as he did
to the agency handling the lucrative Postum account:

> . . . it seems to me that our newspaper is peculiarly fitted for your purpose.
> We run no patent medicine advertising, no beer advertising, no cigarette ad-
> vertising. We give you a paper that has a circulation in a rural community
> where there are more buyers of your product per capita than in any other sec-
> tion of the country. . . . Considering that you don't have to snuggle up to
> fake mining propositions and patent medicines, it seems to me that your ad-
> vertising is worth more.

Similarly, he pointed out to the makers of Coca-Cola that their advertising
"would not have to compete with trash. Your only competitors would be
high-class local advertising and the best line of foreigns—food-stuff, furniture, hardware, farm material and cigars."[65]

Indeed, producers of the new nationally branded foods wanted to make
their products seem as wholesome and familiar as they could. They responded to public fears about poisoned patents and adulterated food by
cultivating reputations for cleanliness and predictability. For example, Royal
Baking Powder ran on the *Gazette*'s front page a blind "reader" ad (an ad
set in regular news type, with a headline, and without clear identification
as advertising) warning against baking powders that contained alum. The
article named a number of products "in which chemists have found alum,"
including most of Royal's major competitors. When another such reader,
"How Cheap Baking Powder is Made," ran several years later, Calumet
Baking Powder, one of the "cheap" competitors, complained bitterly. Since
Calumet had recently also become a *Gazette* advertiser, the paper was compelled to stop running such advertising. By 1908 White had banned this
sort of advertising as a general policy.[66]

Royal's display advertising nonetheless continued to mine this rich vein,
warning that "Alum in food will change Health's ruddy glow into pinched
paleness by drying up the rich red blood which nature provides. . . . There
is only one sure way to guard your health against alum and its injurious effects—Buy only an absolutely pure Grape Cream of Tartar Baking Powder—
buy by the name—Say plainly ROYAL BAKING POWDER." Another advertiser,
Lee Foods, followed up revelations about impure foods with reassurances
that

> There is absolute protection for you in buying food products of your grocer.
> See that each label bears the mark that means pure, wholesome, delicious
> foods. All goods bearing this [Lee] Trade Mark are packed under an Iron
> Clad contract specifying the best that nature produces, and human skill com-
> bined with modern methods can prepare.

Brands thus promised to point the way out of the dangerous jungle of adulterated foods.[67]

In the first decade of the twentieth century, the trademarks of a great
many of the new nationally advertised brands began to appear in the *Gazette*. In addition to those named above were Nabisco's Uneeda Biscuit,

Hires Root Beer, Arbuckle's Coffee, Quaker Oats, Scotch Oats, Jell-O, D-Zerta Pudding, and Shredded Wheat among the foods; and Gold Dust Washing Powder, Cottolene, Jap Rose Soap, Kodak, and the Standard Oil Wickless Stove among other goods. Advertisements for these products sought to endow them with reassuring qualities of familiarity, effectiveness, and wholesomeness; missing were appeals to the "therapeutic" ideals perceived by some recent cultural historians.[68]

Many of these advertising contracts came to the *Gazette* as a result of White's active campaigns to improve his newspaper. After each technological expansion, he redoubled his efforts to attract more brand-name advertising. In his solicitations he featured his newspaper's growing circulation figures, but he also emphasized the special qualities of his medium. In 1899 he wrote: "I can give you a sworn statement of circulation of 1300 bonafide copies, going in the richest farming community in the west. It circulates among republicans; people who are prosperous, contented and have money, and is therefore a preferred list."[69]

After the introduction of the linotype in 1903, the *Gazette* again pursued new advertising accounts. He wrote dozens of letters like the following:

> We notice that you are placing the advertising of the "Shredded Wheat Biscuit" in a great many of the Kansas papers. Why is it you don't try the *Gazette?* We can furnish you an affidavit of over eighteen hundred copies daily and we are still in the midst of a vigorous circulation campaign. We have the only Associated Press Report within fifty miles from here.[70]

As this letter indicates, White was quick to notice advertising appearing in other Kansas newspapers. He often wrote to other publishers to find out where they got their accounts and to the agencies to point out that his medium was superior to some that they were using. And he was quick to seize upon possible advertising prospects:

> I understand you are going to devote some time and money to educating the public into a new attitude toward a new price that has been imposed by the raw cotton markets; the Emporia Gazette is a member of the associated press and a paper of some standing and circulation in Kansas. Any advertising that you would be glad to send us in a regular legitimate way, either in the shape of locals or display advertising in the line above mentioned, we would be very glad to have, and would give it the best possible place and position.[71]

White's experiment in publishing an eight-page Saturday paper had been aimed as much at increasing advertising as circulation. White touted it to Procter & Collier, agents for Procter & Gamble: "It is eight pages, all home print, all devoted to local news. The society page contains their [women's] special features of a local nature." Although he abandoned this effort, it became clear that he would have to find ways to honor advertisers' demands for prominent placement in sections targeted to particular audiences. For example, the Curtis Publishing Company ordered an ad to be inserted in the "boy's department," and a woman's magazine asked for one on the woman's page. In the latter case the *Gazette* assured the magazine that "every Friday, we have a women's club column that is of interest to the women and is read by the women in the town." In addition, advertisers increasingly requested a preferred position "top of column and next to pure reading matter," to achieve greater visibility. In a four-page paper there was a limit to the number of preferred positions that White could give, particularly because he refused to run display advertising on the front page. This problem was solved when the new linotype enabled expansion to an eight-page paper in 1903, increasing the number of preferred positions.[72]

Local advertising was as vital to the *Gazette*'s prosperity as foreign advertising. During the first decade of the new century, advertising by local businesses in the *Gazette* also increased, reflecting changes in the economy comparable to the emergence of the national brand manufacturers. At the local level, however, increased advertising was as much a defensive as an expansive strategy. Continued improvements in transportation and, particularly, the advent of free rural mail delivery threatened to erode the natural geographical monopolies that had protected rural and small-town retailers. Even as the farm economy entered its "golden age" after 1900, smaller merchants saw the farmers' dollars increasingly bypassing them on their way to mail-order merchants, and those of their own small-town neighbors going to urban department stores. Gradually, the more enterprising adopted more aggressive marketing practices in an effort to hold on to their local customers and attract rural shoppers. They improved the appearance of their shopwindows and floor displays, stocked the brand-name goods their customers saw in newspapers and magazines, held frequent special sales, and began to advertise more aggressively on their own account.

In this, as in the emergence of brands, the local newspaper was an important mediator. In fact, the small-town publisher was often responsible for educating small retailers about advertising's potential. Further, he acted as a matchmaker between retailers and large manufacturers, helping to initiate an alliance of both against their common enemies—mail-order houses and large department stores. Historians have seen this partnership as an obvious response to economic conditions, but the merchants were slow to perceive this at the time, and it took years of cajoling from local editors and the successful examples of a few more daring retailers to persuade most of them of advertising's efficacy.[73]

In the nineteenth century, advertising had played a decidedly minor role in local retail trade in small towns like Emporia. Consumers could choose among competing stores, but in accordance with the tenets of booster cooperation, overt price competition was discouraged. Each merchant instead attempted to secure business through his personal reputation for honesty and quality. Patronage was also determined by personal or group loyalty; in Emporia, the Welsh immigrant community wielded disproportionate influence over retail trade because of its strong ethnic solidarity.[74]

Advertising made little sense in such a personalized economy. Merchants occasionally placed small display advertisements or a few locals—one or two lines set in regular type and interspersed with news items—to announce the arrival of new merchandise. Professional men commonly ran standing business cards, more as a means of supporting the newspaper than of gaining trade. Few believed that advertising "paid," and besides, a man with a solid reputation in his community shouldn't need to advertise.

To persuade local merchants to advertise, White had to reverse such long-standing attitudes. His strongest arguments ultimately came from "foreign" sources: enterprising young merchants who introduced urban retailing techniques, and incentives offered by the national brand manufacturers.

White found one such young merchant in A. O. Rorabaugh, who opened a dry goods store in Emporia in 1896. Three years later, after Rorabaugh moved his store into a new building, the *Gazette* praised him as a model of the new businessman: "Mr. Rorabaugh is a young, energetic man who learned his business in Topeka and now gives his attention to every detail of his Emporia business. . . ." Always a consistent advertiser in the *Gazette*, Rorabaugh in 1901 embarked upon an even more ambitious advertising program. He negotiated with White to buy a large amount of space at a special rate. A month later, the *Gazette* again lauded Rorabaugh's enterprise and gave special attention to his exemplary use of advertising:

> Five years ago A. O. Rorabaugh . . . opened a store on Commercial street and began advertising in the *Gazette*. He is today one of the largest dealers in retail dry goods in the west, and all because he studies his trade, saves his money, buys carefully and advertises wisely. He has spent over $2,000 with the *Gazette* since he came here and that is a fairly good sum for a country advertiser in a country town. He will tell you that he has got every penny of it back.[75]

A year later the *Gazette* again offered Rorabaugh as an object lesson in modern marketing techniques:

> The "advertising-doesn't-pay" merchant would have had his theory badly damaged if he had been in Rorabaugh's store early this morning. Monday the store advertised a special sale of sofa pillows. They were on display in one of the big windows and nearly filled it. The sale was advertised for today. . . . This morning in spite of the rain the crowd came before the clerks. The first pillow was sold at 7:30 and the last one at 10 o'clock. It took all the clerks in the store to wait on the crowd and one person was kept busy answering the orders by telephone.[76]

The other ally in the *Gazette*'s campaign to increase local advertising was the national brand advertiser. At first, foreign advertisers, particularly the makers of patent medicines, used the prospect of advertising to induce orders, thus enabling them to go over the heads of wholesale jobbers. Such collaboration was achieved in several ways. A manufacturer might agree with a retailer to place an advertisement, with the latter's name inserted at the bottom, in return for an order. Or he might make his initial contact with the local newspaper, requesting information about the stores most likely to stock their products. Or he might even ask the publisher to act as his agent to persuade a local druggist to order his product, in exchange for an advertising contract. For example, in 1904 Mae Austin reported to the Mahin Advertising Agency that she had been unable to find a druggist to accept its proposition regarding the Elmo Chemical Company because everyone felt that the seventy-dollar minimum order was too large. She had more luck in arranging a deal between the makers of Dr. Lowler Malt & Meat and "one of the principal druggists in town," who promised to order a case, "providing that an advertisement is run in the *Gazette* with his name attached to it. . . ." In succeeding years other manufacturers, of products ranging from sheet music to wire fences to ostrich feathers, employed this approach, particularly when they were trying to break into a strange market. The local newspaper was clearly considered a major source of information about its business community.[77]

The development with the greatest long-range implications for the future of retail distribution was the introduction of the "co-operative system" through which local grocers coordinated their orders and advertising with the promotional plans of the advertising agencies. In 1903 the Mahin Advertising Agency announced its new program. Bookkeeper Mae Austin replied, "We are ready to go to work on this thing and we would like to know what kind of foods we are supposed to ask the grocers to handle, as we cannot get them to take hold until they know what they are supposed to buy." Less than a month later she returned a signed contract "for the Mahin Co-operative Introduction System" and two signed grocers' agreements and asked for more agreement forms.[78]

The full flowering of such "cooperation" between national manufacturer and local retailer would await later decades. But by the end of the first decade of the twentieth century it had already begun, illustrated by an increase in the amount of brand-name advertising done by local retailers themselves. Although this alliance, fostered by the local newspaperman, may have bolstered the economic fortunes of small retailers, it represented an important loss in his independence. Hereafter, his function would be increasingly diminished to that of stocking products on the basis of what was most heavily advertised rather than what he judged to be of highest quality.[79]

Ultimately, these combined inducements persuaded Emporia's merchants that "advertising paid." White began to make long-term advertising contracts with other local businessmen, giving them discounts according to space purchased, much as he did with national advertisers. As early as 1901 the *Gazette* exulted that the paper was so "full of good bargains that there is little room for news." And in 1906 a front-page box warned, "Step Lively": there was so much advertising that it was straining the capacity of the office to handle it. "So hereafter the *Gazette* cannot agree to take advertising later than 12 o'clock."[80]

This increase in local advertising represented more than a simple economic arrangement: it marked a partnership between newspaper and small retailer in promoting the local commercial economy. In entering into this collaboration, White had to sacrifice advertising contracts that conflicted with it. For example, he had often solicited advertising from a large Kansas City department store, Emery, Bird & Thayer, citing the very conditions that threatened local merchants:

> As you probably know, the shopping train leaves here every morning for Kansas City, and I believe advertising in the *Gazette* would pay more than in any other town in Kansas. This is particularly true of the Holiday season, when hundreds of people go to Kansas City to see foot ball games, and various theatrical attractions and do their shopping on the side.

Two years later, he urged the department store to increase its business still further, noting that "this territory is yours by geographical location. . . . I note that you are doing business with the 'Atchison Champion,' a paper that has not half the circulation of the 'Gazette,' and in a town which does not furnish Kansas City as much trade as Emporia furnishes."[81]

The *Gazette* continued to advertise the store through 1902, but stopped abruptly in January 1903, when it announced to its agent, "We cannot accept the Emery, Bird Thayer Dry Goods Co. advertising at any rate." It seems that Emporia merchants, whom White had finally persuaded of advertising's efficacy, had taken him at his word: they pressured him to drop their competitors' advertising. Similarly, White dropped advertising for all mail-order firms. He explained, "Our local merchants kick at the advertising of the Mead Cycle Co. because it [is] a mail order concern. If you can get any advertising whose product sells through the local dealers or has an agent here, send it on and I shall be glad to run it."[82]

Clearly, the newspaper's growing circulation was a weapon in the struggle of Emporia merchants to hold on to the farmer's dollar. Shortly before installing his new Duplex press, White wrote his principal local advertisers about the tremendous increase in circulation that it would bring. Noting that the *Gazette* already went into 95 percent of Emporia houses, he predicted, "With the new press we expect to go into the rural routes out of Emporia and cover them equally as well." He justified an increase in his advertising rates by arguing that the press would bring a more than comparable expansion of their trade area.

> I believe that when I get out among the farmers with the Daily it will supply every newspaper demand of theirs, and the Kansas City papers will lose 50 to 75 per cent of their circulation, as they have in Emporia since the *Gazette* began taking the Associated Press report. This means that the farmers will read Emporia advertisements and not Kansas City advertisements, and they will not send as much money away from the town as has been going from the town. I firmly believe that I can offer a real weapon with which to combat the mail order houses. . . .[83]

Changing economic fortunes had shifted the relative position of newspaper publisher and merchant. Where in the nineteenth century the small-town newspaperman had been, in White's word, a "mendicant" at the hands of prosperous merchants, he was now, at a time of rapidly changing systems of production and distribution, an essential ally. He provided an answer to the threat that large-scale retailers posed to the small-town economy. Moreover, the newspaperman prospered as never before. White later recalled that between 1895 and 1915 his gross income from advertising increased twentyfold.[84]

Nonetheless, newspapermen like White were equivocal allies. As mediators between national manufacturers and local merchants, they helped engineer the increased dependence of the latter upon the former. And as their newspapers carried increasing amounts of foreign advertising and national news, they introduced local readers to cosmopolitan trends and fashions even as they sought to defend the local economy. On the one hand, the newspaper promoted the autonomy and unity of the small-town community; on the other, it exposed local readers to a larger national economy that was increasingly dominated by giant industrial corporations.

To secure the increased advertising available in the early twentieth century, White had labored hard to increase the *Gazette*'s circulation. This had in turn necessitated improving his paper's contents to attract a larger audience and modernizing his print shop to handle the enlarged demands upon it. Gradually, he became a substantial businessman and manufacturer in his own right, with increasing fixed costs and payroll expenses. His business acumen enabled the *Gazette* to outstrip all other newspapers in Emporia, which were unable to respond to the demands of growth. Where a number of small papers had existed in Emporia in the nineteenth century, reflecting a variety of points of view, the *Gazette* emerged in the twentieth as the dominant public voice. White's increasing prosperity gave him greater independence from his political patrons, and would make possible his emergence as a champion of reform.

4

The Making of a Progressive

During the first half of the first decade of the twentieth century, William Allen White became a progressive. Borrowing from the biblical motif of the prodigal son, he would later characterize the change in terms of a near-religious conversion from conservative to reform Republicanism. Nonetheless, the transition was more a matter of identity than of ideology. It can best be understood as the gradual elaboration of a new self-definition in response to a series of moral challenges and political and economic opportunities. These changes were sometimes very subtle, for he abandoned few of his former roles and rarely altered his ideas substantially. But, to make sense of his experiences, White gradually reordered the priorities among the many roles he performed as small-town newspaperman. He pieced together a new configuration of roles and beliefs, which together formed a new identity as moral champion of his community. White's emergence as a progressive is closely linked to his career as editor of the *Gazette,* for his newspaper was his chief tool in crusading for moral and economic righteousness. Moreover, its prosperity made possible his political independence.[1]

After 1900, White's ambitions for greater autonomy and recognition brought tensions among the obligations of his diverse roles as prospering businessman, rising community leader, aspiring man of letters, and faithful Republican partisan. He had learned well the lessons of practical politics, and he had served the Hanna organization as publicist and grass-roots organizer. In turn, he had been rewarded with the patronage and public reputation that had assured his journalistic career. Yet, as local resentment of "What's the Matter with Kansas?" had taught him, partisan loyalty could have its drawbacks: it undercut his efforts to expand the *Gazette*'s circulation and ran counter to his role as local booster. Moreover, as White sought greater political influence, he became aware that his factional allegiances blocked his own coming of age as a leader. Over the next five years White gradually loosened his ties to the conservative faction led nationally by Mark Hanna, regionally by Cyrus Leland, and locally by Calvin Hood, and cast his lot with a new coalition of ambitious young Kansas Republican politicians who identified themselves with the dynamic new president, Theodore Roosevelt.

Although this transformation was gradual, it was not without trauma, for it required cutting personal bonds of long standing and questioning long-held assumptions. White's quite genuine anguish when he found himself torn between his loyalty to Cyrus Leland and his idolization of Theodore Roosevelt is vivid evidence of the extent to which his sense of identity was bound up in his political alliances and personal affiliations. Before emerging as a full-fledged reformer, White faced a period of intense intellectual confusion and emotional conflict, during which he suffered a debilitating nervous breakdown. Although in the absence of more explicit evidence we cannot offer a definitive diagnosis of his breakdown, it is clear that White was plagued by frustrations and disappointments on many fronts. In order to resolve these conflicts, he gradually pieced together a new progressive identity that justified his renunciation of old political allegiances and cast him in a leading role as protector of his local community.

Paradoxically, the transition was sustained both by White's growing personal attachment to Theodore Roosevelt and by Roosevelt's vision of a politics that placed public welfare above factional or personal loyalties. Roosevelt's rhetoric of masculine honor and righteousness appealed to White's unfulfilled longing for certainty and integrity. At the same time, it provided a moral language with which White could justify his emergence as a political and community leader, explain his break with former political mentors, and resolve the personal tensions engendered by his ambitions. By fiercely attacking immorality at home and business exploitation abroad, he demonstrated his new progressive identity.

In describing White's life it is misleading to make sharp distinctions between the public and the private man, for his sense of self was indistinguishable from his actions and his standing in the eyes of others. Nor did he develop a personal philosophy, in the sense of a set of logically ordered principles that determined his actions. Rather, he generally expressed his ideas as means to specific public ends, and his statements varied according to the rhetorical demands of the moment. Nonetheless, for purposes of analysis, this chapter will focus on White's personal development. The next chapter will restore the individual to his community by exploring more fully the public issues in Emporia in which his new identity was manifested.

The first steps in White's personal journey began soon after his street fair triumph, as he embarked upon a series of ambitious projects to promote his own and his town's interests. In January 1900 he hired Rose Edington to expand the Gazette's rural circulation. In April he inaugurated the paper's enlarged Saturday editions. In May he launched a campaign to bring a new railroad to Emporia. In December he demonstrated his aspirations to community leadership by founding a men's discussion group, called the Current Club. In the summer of 1900, too, his personal life seemed complete with the birth of a son, named William Lindsay White.

White's writing career also flourished with the new century. His second book of short stories, In the Court of Boyville, a collection of "boy stories" that he had written at the behest of S. S. McClure, had been released late in 1899. He was busy with other commissions, including more serious stories for *Scribner's* and profiles of political leaders for *McClure's*. With the sudden ascent of his friend Theodore Roosevelt to the presidency in the fall of 1901, White's success seemed assured. He happened to be in Washington at the time of McKinley's assassination, and a few days later the proud announcement appeared in the *Gazette*, breaking the ban on mentioning the editor's name: "W. A. White lunched with the President's family a day or two ago. He says they had oyster soup, broiled chicken, mashed potatoes, string beans (boiled with salt pork in the old fashioned way) and baked apples. That sounds like it might have been served in Emporia."[2]

Yet by the end of 1901 White was suffering from a severe nervous breakdown. In his *Autobiography* he recalled that he suffered from "nervous exhaustion" around Christmastime, and in mid-January he was seized by "a queer kind of sickness" that left him completely unable to write or conduct even routine business. Rest seemed clearly in order. Yet the source of his problem lay not in overwork, but in his very environment. On January 21, White wrote to E. W. Howe asking him to mention in his Atchison *Globe* that he was taking a vacation, "as I do not want it to appear in the 'Gazette'." He said that his doctor had ordered him to "get away from the work and the town and go and loaf." Leaving their son with Mary White, he and Sallie went first to Colorado and then to California, finally settling into a beach house on Catalina Island. There Sallie handled all business correspondence; at mid-March she predicted to the *Gazette* staff that her husband might be unable to work for another six months. By April, however, he had begun to mend, and he was able to return to Emporia the following month.[3]

Why this sudden and complete collapse, when things seemed to be going so well? White and previous biographers have given several explanations for his breakdown, including overwork and a threatened libel suit over his profile of Thomas Platt in the December 1901 *McClure's*. Neither is wholly convincing, however, particularly because White seemed to welcome the publicity provided by the Platt controversy. His surviving correspondence yields too little explicit evidence about his state of mind to justify a psychiatric diagnosis, but for our purposes it is rich in details about the kinds of tensions he was feeling at the time. White's ambitions had led him to overextend himself, and he was encountering increasing conflicts among the various roles that he aspired to play.[4]

One nagging issue was that White's writing career, although prolific, was not moving in the direction that he most desired. Since his first discovery of E. W. Howe and William Dean Howells, White had aspired to write a great realistic novel. After the success of *The Real Issue* he had set out to write a long story of western life, which he described to his first publisher, Chauncey Williams, as "the Great American novel" and "the biggest job that I have tackled yet." He later discussed the project with Frank Doubleday, then head of Doubleday & McClure. In 1900, and again in 1901, Doubleday inquired after the book, insisting, "I believe the psychological moment has arrived when a book of the kind you told me about would have the greatest success." He urged White to send it to him, but White, though he had devoted many hours to the project, was unable to pull the novel together. Ultimately, in 1905, he would admit to Doubleday, "I do not seem able to write a novel. . . . I have tried time and again but I can not seem to do it."[5]

On top of this frustration of his literary ambitions, White faced a major upheaval in his political universe in the fall of 1901. Cyrus Leland's post as pension officer would come up for renewal early in 1902. McKinley had promised to reappoint Leland, but when Roosevelt suddenly became President, the opposing Republican faction in Kansas, calling themselves "Boss Busters," launched a major assault on Leland as a "machine politician." Roosevelt may have been predisposed against Leland because of the latter's close ties to his rival Mark Hanna, but he explained to White that he could not oppose a senator's nomination without good cause. He did not consider Leland worth fighting for, he told White, because "if a fight comes I want to be dead sure my man is white—not, perchance gray."[6]

White was torn between two strong personal loyalties. One day these conflicting allegiances would represent to him the "old" and the "new" Republicanism. But in the fall of 1901 the situation did not seem so much an ideological turning point as an excruciatingly painful double bind. On the one hand, White had been Leland's devoted admirer and protégé ever since they had left the 1892 Republican state convention together. White's efforts on Leland's behalf had always been generously rewarded; indeed, he owed a large part of his newspaper's prosperity to Leland's patronage. In addition, he admired the older man's consummate political skill and respected his fierce loyalty to his friends.

Yet White was also strongly drawn to Roosevelt's charismatic personality. Nearly fifty years later, White would recall his first meeting with Roosevelt in 1897 in the ecstatic tones of first love:

> I had never known such a man as he, and never shall again. He overcame me. And in the hour or two we spent that day . . . he poured into my heart such visions, such ideals, such hopes, such a new attitude toward life and patriotism and the meaning of things, as I had never dreamed men had. . . . After that I was his man.[7]

He was stunned to hear Roosevelt's scorn for McKinley and Hanna and for "the order which I had upheld, to which I was committed, to which I had commended my soul." Roosevelt seemed to represent a new model of politics as a quest for transcendent ideals rather than a game to be won for one's friends. Its chivalric echoes evoked in White a longing for moral conviction that had been thwarted by the divisiveness of his childhood and the cynicism of Gilded Age politics. It redefined masculine honor in terms of struggle and sacrifice, as opposed to Gilded Age values of loyalty and reciprocity.[8]

Nonetheless, it would be some time before White was free to follow

*William Allen White and Theodore Roosevelt in front of
the White home in 1913 (William Allen White Memorial
Library, Emporia State University)*

Roosevelt. For nearly five years after that first meeting he had managed
to juggle his conflicting loyalties, but now it seemed he had to choose. He
resisted that choice, ardently defending Leland to Roosevelt. Leland had
done nothing illegal, he argued, but had only played politics by the accepted rules.[9]

White was also well aware that Leland's opponents in Kansas, the "Boss
Busters," were motivated purely by factional interests. During the contro-
versy, he revealed weariness with such political intrigue in a letter to
Charles S. Gleed, who was opposing Leland.

I picked up the "Journal" this morning and found an article endorsing Richard Kerens [a Missouri Republican] and snorted with disgust. Then I began to laugh, just as I started to ask myself, how Charley Gleed who draws the line on Leland, can stomach Kerens. It occurred to me that perhaps Gleed thought, how can Will White who draws the line on Kerens, stomach Leland. And then I laughed and laughed and laughed and laughed, at the funny things one meets in a day's journey in politics, when he has not got a gun.[10]

All the same, White could not bring himself to question Roosevelt's motives. The same day that he wrote to Gleed, he published an editorial lauding the new president:

Roosevelt is taking the country back to the days of the high integrity of the fathers. . . . The influence of Roosevelt, for clean politics, for high civic ideals, for political virtue will be and is now inestimable. It is breeding patriotism. . . . He has exalted the nation.[11]

When it became clear that Leland was beaten, White tried to gloss over his conflicts by reaffirming his loyalty to the Republican party. Publicly, he greeted Roosevelt's decision with equanimity, treating it as one of the risks of the game. He wrote in the *Gazette,* "This ends the fight. Leland and his friends accept it good naturedly. They are not 'Injuns.' They will go ahead as good Republicans working for their party and sustaining its officers. . . ." Shortly before his breakdown in January, White reiterated his devotion in an editorial, "On Being a Republican." Arguing that Republicans stood for "decency," he continued to stress the primacy of party loyalty, regardless of who was nominated: "Yet the best sort of Republican doesn't bolt the ticket. He takes his medicine like a little man. . . . This thing of being a Republican means a great deal. It means as much to civilization as it does to belong to a church. . . ."[12]

This awkward effort to fuse politics as game and politics as exalted principle suggests a struggle to reconcile the contradictory demands of loyalty and righteousness in his own mind. Further adding to his psychological unease was frustration that his strenuous efforts on Emporia's behalf were not being properly recognized or rewarded. Early in 1901, stung by insinuations that he was promoting a new railroad only to gain revenues from printing its legal notices, White had retorted angrily in the *Gazette.* He protested, "it is disheartening to write for a town, talk for a town, boom a town, and then without cause or warning, to have to stand up in that town and prove that you are not a liar and a cheat and a robber and a traitor to the town."[13]

White's dissatisfaction with his situation in Emporia is also suggested by the fact that, despite his much-publicized refusals to leave Emporia for lucrative eastern jobs, he did consider making just such a move at the time of his breakdown. He sought the advice of Postmaster General Charles Emory Smith concerning S. S. McClure's proposal that he come east to edit a political magazine: "You know more about politics than I do, and you know more about the publishing business on a large scale. Would you mind telling me in confidence, what you think of this scheme?"[14]

That this frustration was prominent in his mind at the time of his break-down is strongly indicated by an uncharacteristically bitter letter that he wrote to wealthy Emporia businessman George Newman shortly before he left town. The letter reveals White's resentment that he was not being properly appreciated by his fellow townspeople, and it also clearly demon-strates his assumption that a newspaper's boosterism should be recipro-cated by local financial and personal support.

> For a year you have ignored the Emporia Weekly "Gazette." It is a town in-stitution and its editor does what it can to help the town. When you want a man blistered, good and hard, for a fire sale, you come to me and ask me to do it. . . . When there is a railroad committee to form, I serve on it. . . . And when I have a good, square, honest Republican advertising medium like the Emporia Weekly "Gazette," I think it is only a matter of common, ordinary decency that you patronize it, and when you have enough money to blow it to spend it in out of town papers, as you did last week. . . . You have not shown a single favor to the "Gazette". . . . You have had your semi-annual circulars printed else where. . . . It isn't the matter of the money, I am not hard up and the "Gazette" is making money right along, but I like to have the moral support of George W. Newman in the Emporia Weekly "Gazette." You have never asked a favor of me of any sort, that you didn't get it freely and without the slightest hesitation. It seems to me, that in asking this favor of you, I am not over stepping the bounds of propriety nor the limits of a reasonable expectation.[15]

Such statements, together with his comment to Howe, quoted above, that "I have got to get away from the work and the town," suggest his frustra-tion with the slow realization of his ambitions for power and influence.

Yet White would not resolve these conflicts by abandoning his town for the city, as many other Americans were doing. Rather, he would return to Emporia, where a fierce controversy was raging over efforts to disbar a local physician, William Meffert. White's leadership in that battle marked his assumption of a new role as defender of his community's honor. His actions, and particularly his use of the rhetoric of righteousness as he claimed to speak for the will of "the people" of Emporia, established the pattern for his new reform identity.

We have few clues to White's state of mind when he returned. In April he had written for the *Gazette* lighthearted essays on tourist life in Cali-fornia. Journalists customarily wrote such travel letters to the folks back home, but the insistent good cheer of these pieces suggests that they were also intended to counter rumors that he had gone mad, spread by his fac-tional enemies. His health, however, would continue to be precarious, and for several years he was plagued by a variety of ailments, such as insomnia, that suggest continuing tensions.[16]

When the Whites arrived at the Emporia station on May 26, 1902, they were greeted by a crowd of well-wishers and the town's brass band—that quintessential display of community pride in turn-of-the-century America— playing "See, the Conquering Hero Comes." The *Gazette* did not mention this reception in its only notice of their return: "Mr. White has regained his health." But other newspapers did, and a few days later President Roosevelt congratulated him: "They tell me you were received with a brass band on your return to Emporia." Still, the Whites' welcome, however it might have impressed Emporians and Roosevelt, had not been spontaneous. White reported in his *Autobiography* that, to counter the rumors of White's mental illness, Calvin Hood had hired the band and "rounded up a congregation of my friends."[17]

White found a bitter local controversy also awaiting him. During the Whites' absence, a respected young Emporia grocer named Stephen Conklin had committed suicide after attempting to kill his former wife, Cora, and her mother. The couple's recent divorce had been caused by Cora's repeated sexual infidelity. Since then, Stephen had grown increasingly despondent, and while seriously ill he became obsessed with the idea of reconciliation with Cora. As the *Gazette* commented grimly, "In this he failed." Cora and her mother recovered from their wounds, but the wounds to the town's sense of order were not so easily healed.[18]

Emporians seeking an explanation for this tragedy found one ready at hand in William Meffert, a local physician with a scandalous reputation. In 1899 he had been charged with performing an illegal abortion, but the charges were dropped when a material witness—his patient—fled the state. What was more, he affronted local propriety by living "openly" in a boardinghouse run by his divorced wife, Delta Meffert. He was also reputed frequently to have exercised his considerable personal charms upon unsuspecting female patients, to their moral and social peril. Soon after Stephen Conklin's death, rumors spread that he had accused Meffert of bringing about his former wife's "ruin" by seducing her while she was under the influence of medication, thereby inflaming the passions that had led to their divorce. According to an article in the Topeka *Capital*, "respectable citizens" in Emporia became "indignant that such a person was allowed to practice in town," and threats of tar and feathers and even lynching were "freely indulged in on the street." In late April, a group of "prominent citizens" met at Mit Wilhite's restaurant to consider what should be done.[19]

The men discussed Meffert's "well known doings" and soon realized that he could not be prosecuted legally without the witnesses implicating themselves. "At this point," the *Capital* related, "some were in favor of taking the law in their own hands, but better councils prevailed." Rather, the meeting decided to bring the case before the State Board of Medical Registration and Examination, by petitioning it to revoke "the professional Lothario's" license. This board had been established in Kansas only the previous year, to regulate the practice of medicine by licensing physicians.

Among the qualifications named in the legislation was a proscription of "grossly immoral conduct." A committee set about to gather evidence of such conduct on Meffert's part.[20]

During White's absence the *Gazette* carried no hint of the controversy until it reprinted the *Capital* article on May 19. It ran the full-column story without comment, except that "the following special from Emporia" had appeared on the front page of the Sunday *Capital* under the headline "No Room for Meffert." The "special" had most likely been written by one of the *Gazette*'s reporters, for they often worked as stringers for outside papers; by reprinting an article from another newspaper the *Gazette* could report the case without seeming to take sides.

When White returned, he immediately threw the *Gazette* fully behind the forces arrayed against Meffert. Three days after his return, the *Gazette* published an article describing further charges of illegal abortions performed by Meffert brought before the state medical board. The story also revealed that Emporians were not unanimous in their abhorrence of Meffert and hinted that Emporians were dividing along familiar factional lines. "Of course the town has taken sides. But the main champion of Dr. Meffert is Wm. Martindale who went to Topeka and saw members of the board in Dr. Meffert's behalf."[21]

Several days later the *Gazette* reported that the state attorney general, after hearing additional charges made by the "citizen's committee" against Meffert, had told them, "you may depend upon me using all my power to rid the state of this fellow." He also said to Dr. Henry W. Robey, a member of the medical board, "If you decide to oust him, there will be no appeal to me from your decision." Two days later the *Gazette* published Meffert's response, the first time that his side had been presented there. He pointed out that the attorney general's comments, if correctly reported, put him "in the questionable position of endeavoring to prejudice and bias a tribunal in advance. He asked, "I sincerely submit to you and your readers, is this fair? Is it consonant with the boasted advance in civilization? Does it not savor a trifle of the spirit of the dark ages and its legitimate descendant, mob law?"[22]

With these remarks, Meffert served notice that his defense would stand upon technical legal considerations of due process. These were antithetical to the notions of community morality upheld by his persecutors. It would be law against honor.

When the case came before the state board, Meffert's attorney challenged the board's constitutional right to revoke his license. The *Gazette,* on the other hand, assumed that the board's only function was to represent the will of the community. It suggested that the hearings be moved to Emporia, so the "board will be able to judge what feeling there is in the town for or against the doctor." In reporting the hearings, the *Gazette* faithfully recorded testimony both for and against the defendant, but it invariably presented the case as one of "respectable citizens" seeking to protect their community from a moral threat. It also depicted Meffert's legal counsel as morally suspect. For example, the coverage of the hearing preliminaries emphasized the legalistic, technical character of defense arguments and also played up slights made to the fair name of Emporia by Meffert's Topeka-based attorneys. In response to an affidavit that noted that the "conservative" elements had decided to drive Meffert out legally instead of taking more immediate action, attorney A. L. Redden was said to have sneered, "If this . . . is representative of the conservative feeling, God help the people of this little hamlet. As to the Conklin murder, I know nothing of it. I presume it is one of those scandals which this town seems to revel in." The *Gazette* characterized these remarks as "his cauterizing of the newspapers and the people of Emporia."[23]

The first round of the battle went to "the people of Emporia" when the medical board revoked Meffert's license. In reporting the story the *Gazette* saluted the verdict as a victory of morality over law:

> The case which terminated thus was a hard fought one and the *Gazette* feels that the weakness of the legal case against Meffert might have been strengthened by what the board may have regarded as the moral force of [the] case against him. In no court of law could the verdict have been obtained but then as every one knows there is often complaining against the technicalities of courts of law which often seem to hamper equity and justice. It is more than likely that the presence of the Emporia delegation . . . in their grand lodge clothes had more to do with the decision of the board than any other one factor. The board seemed in its questions yesterday to be seeking for the moral sentiment of the community.[24]

Nonetheless, legal technicalities prevailed in round two, when Meffert immediately obtained a court injunction against enforcement of the board's decision until the constitutionality of the regulatory legislation could be tested. For the next five years the matter would continue to be mooted within the courts and on the streets of Emporia. Within the legal system, Meffert argued that he had a "vested right" in his license that could be revoked only by a court of law. When the board's decision was upheld in district court, he appealed to the State Supreme Court; failing there, he appealed to the U.S. Supreme Court. According to the *Gazette* and White's later accounts, Meffert also adopted an "extralegal" strategy back in Emporia: blackmail. He obtained affidavits charging many of his opponents, including Calvin Hood and his chief factional lieutenant, Isaac Lambert, with various immoralities and threatened to circulate the information unless they stopped pushing the case.[25]

The strategy was effective. In his *Autobiography* White recalled an emotion-laden visit from Hood and Lambert soon after Meffert made his threats:

> . . . the little Major sat down beside me, put his warm, hard, bony hand on my knee—a favorite gesture of his in the technique of his seduction of adversaries—cleared his throat, and spoke in the softest, most self-deprecatory voice.
> "Now, Will, here's a little matter in which you can help our friend." He nodded to his companion, and went on: "Our good friend, the doctor . . . has

told us that if we could just persuade you to drop the fight and let his appeal to the Supreme Court go unopposed, he would be glad to forget this affidavit!" . . . It was the hardest thing I have ever done. . . . "Oh, Major, I just—I just can't! I mustn't do it!" I looked at my dear friend. His face was distorted with fear and pain, but I shook my head. I did not dare trust myself to further language. I was tempted of the devil.[26]

White thus dramatically portrayed the moment as a turning point, a choice between personal loyalty—the "devil"—and higher forms of honor. Although it is doubtful that the break with Hood came as suddenly as he recalled forty years later, White did take charge of the anti-Meffert forces in the fall of 1902. It was a perfect moment for his debut in a local leadership role distinct from Hood. By taking up the banner of moral purity let drop by Hood and his friends, White could assert his independence while defending the moral integrity of his community.

For the next two years, he was unrelenting in pursuing the case against Meffert. As he had done in promoting his street fair, he called into play his network of friends and the publicity afforded by his newspaper. He headed a "citizens' committee" that employed an attorney to assist the state, and constantly pressured public officials to persist in their prosecution of the case.[27]

Just as he had in the street fair, he also insisted that he was only representing the will of the people of Emporia. He assured Dr. Robey, a member of the medical board, that "the people of Emporia" were even more determined to eliminate Meffert after his blackmailing attempts:

They are angry clear through. They have implicit faith in you and your board, and we who believe that Meffert should go are strengthening this faith. I write to you today that you may know the situation fully and fairly and that you may not be deluded, by some one who fears further blackmail, into thinking the people of Emporia have cooled down in this case. . . . The whole town of Emporia is with you.[28]

As we will see in the next chapter, Emporians were far from united in opposition to Meffert. But White was finding that the rhetoric of community unity, so crucial to the booster ethos, could also have its uses in promoting moral reforms.

White's efforts brought him into behind-the-scenes conflict with Hood, who pressured Governor Bailey, a Leland man, to remove Dr. Robey from the medical board. White applied counterpressure, drawing a rhetorical contrast between morality and politics in asserting to Bailey that while he was "willing to 'play politics' where ever the game is legitimate . . . here in this Emporia case is not the place to play politics."

A big moral issue is at stake. The people of this town have a festering sore in this doctor Meffert. . . . Now Willis J. Bailey, I will do anything on earth for Ike Lambert but this one thing. . . . But the minute Ike ties up with that Doctor, I and Jerry Evans and Charley Harris and Mit Wilhite and the fellows who try to do things down here have to fight the combination. . . . The people of this town, who are your friends and Leland's friends politically, will absolutely cut loose from the whole business if Robey is taken off that board just now.[29]

Meanwhile, White mobilized the expression of outrage by these very Emporians. He wrote Sallie White about spending one afternoon "writing letters on three different kinds of type writers, and each kind spaced differently, for business men in town here to Governor Bailey demanding the reappointment of Dr. Robey." He had composed eight different two-page letters for his colleagues, including those mentioned in his letter to Bailey. "It was as hard mental work to keep from duplicating ideas and expressions as I ever did in a given time."[30]

With every victory in court against Meffert, White and the *Gazette* became ever more vehement in their assertions that the anti-Meffert cause represented "righteousness." After the Kansas supreme court's decision against Meffert in April 1903, White warned Meffert not to practice illegally. Law-abiding Emporians had waited patiently for justice to be done through the courts, but "now that the end is near they are in no mood to witness any trifling with their righteous wrath."[31]

The U.S. Supreme Court finally sustained the state court's decision in November 1904. White claimed in his *Autobiography* that "I tried to eliminate bitterness, and thought I had done it." But the *Gazette*'s front-page story was far from impartial. It closed with a warning of an impending reckoning:

> The members of the committee who have had Meffert's case in hand have thought it wise to give the fellow the benefit of every court before prosecutions begin. . . . But they have been keeping tab on him and are now ready to swear out warrants against him. . . . The committee is determined that the moral cancer shall be removed from Emporia.[32]

Not surprisingly, Meffert's friends did not agree that White had avoided bitterness. Two days later, as he left his office for home, White saw Delta Meffert standing in a doorway just down the street. His account of what followed appeared in the next day's paper:

> . . . as the Gazette man started to pass, Mrs. Meffert pulled from her cloak a small but effective-looking whip. The editor of the paper side-stepped and did what every true gent would do; ran forty yards like a whitehead back to the office by the back door.
>
> That calm dispassionate communion which a man holds with a situation in the sixteenth part of a second convinced the man in question that when a lady challenges a gent to an athletic contest of any kind, he cannot win a sparring match with any grace, nor be the victor in a wrestling match with a lady with any credit at all; but that a foot-race is the one event in the sporting calendar in which any gent may vie his prowess with any lady. And how he did run! Shooting the chutes, leaping the gap, or looping the loop are clumsy dilatory tactics, compared with the way that fat old codger hiked the hike around to the back door of his office.[33]

White treated the matter lightly in the *Gazette*, and in his *Autobiography* recalled that "that episode and the uproarious ending I gave it, strengthened me in the town." But he was not so sure of this at the time. The Democratic Emporia *Times* version sided with Delta Meffert, who was reported as saying to White, "I am still a lady and but for that would shoot you, but as it is will whip you." According to the *Times*, White was spared a whipping only by the intervention of a passer-by. Other political opponents around the state reported that White had actually been whipped, and implied that it had been just retribution for abusing a lady. When this version appeared in the eastern press, White was more than a little upset. He circulated his own account and wrote scores of letters to prominent eastern editors, politicians, and others whose good opinion he valued. In explaining the situation, he implied that the attack had been prompted by efforts to enforce prohibition: "I have been making a fight for enforcement of law here at home for two weeks since the election. . . ." He claimed that men had threatened him with violence but had been too cowardly to carry out their threats. The false news story, he said, had been circulated by political enemies as revenge for his coverage of embezzlement charges against the state treasurer. And he insisted emphatically that Delta Meffert had not touched him.[34]

The episode clearly touched a sensitive nerve for White. Understanding the meaning of this sensitivity opens to us a further dimension of his thinking. As we have seen, he later interpreted his break with Hood as a choice of righteous principle over personal loyalty. But we must be wary of seeing this as simply a movement toward greater individualism in moral decision-making. White's fear that Delta Meffert's attack would be misinterpreted suggests that he was still intensely concerned with public perception of his actions. It also reveals that his own thinking was still influenced by traditional definitions of honor that assumed that the community's judgment was the source of ultimate value and meaning.

As a young reporter, White had encountered questions of honor when dealing with angry citizens bent on revenge for some insult. His accounts of these episodes in his *Autobiography* were humorous, but they also emphasized that he had not lacked for physical courage in defending himself. He knew that according to the "gentleman's code of honor" it was shameful to be hit by a woman. This was why it was so crucial to White that it be known that Mrs. Meffert had not touched him. Looking back some twenty years later at his reasoning in the split second after Delta Meffert pulled out the rawhide, White recalled that he considered letting her strike him, "in a fine martyrdom which would exalt my cause." Then he realized that "the merry laugh of the multitude would unhalo the martyrdom," and began to run. Thus, his handling of the story in the *Gazette*, however jocular, nonetheless conveyed the important message that his response to Mrs. Meffert's attack had been true to the "gent's" code: he had not fought back against a "lady," but neither had he allowed her to hit him.

White's sensitivity to questions of honor is also strikingly revealed in a letter he wrote to Sallie in April 1903, in the midst of the Meffert contro-versy. He wrote in great distress because it appeared that Calvin Hood would succeed in gaining a state appointment for his own son over the poor farmer to whom White had promised it. The terms in which White de-scribed the situation and his feelings reveal much about how he fused questions of private principle with those of public reputation.

> The thing that has depressed me today and made me sick at heart—is the probable appointment of Henry Hood and the turning down of Pete Peter-son. . . . He has taken my word in simple faith as a gentleman should—and I seem to be betraying him. . . . I am utterly heart broken, and unless I fight Hood I can not save my good name. . . . It is really a grave matter with us dearie for by this seeming perfidy will [we] be judged here in this community. It has seemed to me that I should go to the Major, tell him frankly my posi-tion, beg him for my sake to withdraw Harry's name from a candidacy that he does not need and tell him when he refuses that I am bound in honor to fight Harry and that I cant do it with my notes in his bank. Pay up everything and then in a simple dignified way protest against the appointment of Harry Hood. I would get the entire county central committee with me, and more than nine tenths of the cattle men of Kansas, and more I could put the blocks to Leland and Bailey. . . . Dearest this sounds crazy but I must do something.[35]

Perhaps, as she often did, Sallie dissuaded him from taking such a rash and potentially disastrous step. At any rate, he did not follow through with this plan for a dramatic public break with his former patrons. But the fact that, in the safety of correspondence with his wife, he fantasized taking such a step indicates his yearning to declare political independence and to secure public influence, even when he was aware that the moment had not quite come. His realization that such a move would require cutting the umbilical cord of credit at Hood's bank by paying all his notes reveals two things: such financial bonds still existed as late as 1903, and he had begun to expect that one day he would be free of them. In fact, he was at this very moment introducing his first linotype machine, and this same letter to Sallie re-ported advances in the *Gazette*'s circulation.

Nevertheless, although his most private letters revealed increasing aliena-tion from Leland and Hood, publicly he continued to support their inter-ests and to run political errands for them. In both financial and political terms, then, it was a transitional moment for White.[36]

At this point the Meffert controversy seemed to have ended, with the triumph of righteousness and the establishment of White's reputation as a crusader. In his *Autobiography* he concluded that the horsewhipping de-nouement "advertised the victory over the doctor all over Kansas and even across the country. . . . And I established a reputation for competent and determined righteousness. . . ."[37] Unfortunately for the cause of moral reform in Emporia, the case did not end there, for Meffert refused either to stop practicing medicine or to leave town, and the "citizens' committee" could not do anything about it. Meffert would be granted a new license in 1907 and continue to practice medicine in Emporia until his death in 1921.

Ultimately, White's battle against Meffert was more successful in fostering the development of his new crusading identity than in ridding the community of its "moral leper."[38]

White would transfer the rhetoric and tactics first practiced in the struggle against Meffert to the arena of moral, political, and economic reform. Nonetheless, he came late to reform politics. He emerged publicly as a reform leader only in response to three further experiences. First, he had a close brush with public disgrace after he flirted with illegal speculation. Second, a new reform coalition among young Kansas Republicans demonstrated that it was a viable alternative to the established factions. Third, the Gazette's very success created disillusionment with the trusts that dominated the national Republican party.

Despite his devotion to Theodore Roosevelt, White continued after 1902 to work closely with powerful economic institutions that were allied with his faction. He was as likely to employ the rhetoric of righteousness in the interests of factional politics as for local moral reform. For example, in the fall of 1903 he warned Roosevelt not to appoint Topeka attorney Charles Blood Smith to a federal judgeship, as Kansas senator Joseph Burton, a factional opponent, had requested, because Smith was merely a tool "of the Missouri Pacific Union Pacific railroad combine." Despite the progressive ring of the words, it is significant that Smith was also strongly opposed by the Leland faction. These men were by no means antirailroad; they merely opposed those railroads that were allied with their factional enemies.[39]

Until 1905, White continued to work closely with the Santa Fe. He acted as an informal public relations consultant for the railroad, suggesting ways it could become more responsive to public opinion and head off rising public disaffection. At times this mediating role influenced what appeared—or did not appear—in the Gazette. After a railroad accident in 1903, for example, White wrote to a Santa Fe attorney, "One of our reporters stumbled onto a piece of information . . . which you should have. Of course I did not print it." He explained that an Emporia woman who had been injured in the wreck had told his reporter that a farmer living near the site had said that the bridge had been rickety "and that he had been expecting this accident every day for a month." He continued:

> If that farmer is talking that way you should know it. He wouldn't be a nice man to meet on the witness stand in a damage suit. The sooner you or Mr. Chamberlain has a talk with him the better. . . . This Mrs. White [the Emporia woman] is a neighbor of mine and if I can be of any service to you with her, let me know. I stand ready to do all I can for you.[40]

In 1902, as protests mounted against rate discrimination, White advised the railroad about how to cultivate public opinion:

> I see some changes are being made in the carload rate to Topeka. When you were here you spoke about similar changes being contemplated for Emporia. . . . I think it would be better for the Santa Fe, if these changes should

seem to come as the result of a local request. If you will give me a pointer when to begin, I will set the wheel in motion to have the business men of Emporia make a strong request for this rate and then when it comes, it will bring considerable gratitude with it.[41]

He suggested specific actions the railroad could take to prepare for an impending strike: "If there is going to be a strike . . . the more thoroughly the company's side is known, the more surely the company may be of having public sentiment with them." In return, White used his contacts to boost economic development. In 1903 he sought the Santa Fe's aid for local farmers hoping to diversify their production, reminding them that it could mean new business all around. He also took full advantage of the railroad's willingness to trade rides for advertising in the *Gazette*. In this way he obtained numerous tickets and free passes for himself, his family, his employees, and his friends.[42]

White also hoped that such powerful connections would one day help make his personal fortune. As the Whites returned to Emporia from California in 1902, it seemed that these ambitions were about to be fulfilled. Traveling through the Pacific Northwest, they met several prominent politicians and Union Pacific railroad officials, including "the general superintendent of the [Oregon Short Line] railroad" and "one of the best practical fruit men in Idaho." These men urged the Whites to join them in a project to grow fruit on land to be irrigated under the Newlands Act, and before returning to Emporia they made the initial payment on 160 acres of federal desert land.[43]

Indeed, the Northwest seemed to offer opportunities to White as both investor and journalist. After his return to Emporia he contracted with the *Saturday Evening Post* to write a series of articles on what promised to be a major gold rush in Idaho. In September 1902, he packed into the rugged Thunder Mountain region with a group of New York mining experts and promoters, to whom he had been introduced by his important new friends. He wrote four articles for the *Post* full of Rooseveltian praise for the strenuous life in the wilderness and enthusiasm for the fortunes that could be reaped from exploiting its minerals—judiciously tempered by caveats that such investments were risky.[44]

The following summer, White was summoned to Chicago by the mining group's leader, H. L. Hollister—whom White had described in his articles as "a capitalist from New York"—to confer about a plan to benefit further from the opportunities of the Pacific Northwest. In Chicago, White met Hollister's partner Lewis C. Van Riper, a New York speculator. Van Riper treated White to a glimpse of the high life, taking one whole day to drive the publisher around the city in his new automobile. White ate it all up. He wrote ecstatically to his wife, wishing she could have seen him "riding all one blessed day in a big red double seated brass mounted buzz wagon— just to keep cool! . . . we transacted all our business in the buzz wagon while the yeomanry on the side walk and in little old donkey carriages and barouches were properly awed by the presence of the gentry!" The deal that they concluded was this: White was to receive blocks of stock, worth $250,000 at face value, in corporations Van Riper and Hollister were setting up to mine gold in Idaho and grow fruit on desert land. In return, White would provide promotional services, to "advertise the land and power deeds, write circulars, help them put an immigration paper on its feet and do that sort of work also helping with advertising agencies." He added ingenuously, "They of course know nothing of these things—are perfectly ignorant of how to act in the matter."[45]

White did proceed to promote the projects. He wrote glowing letters to prospective investors and mobilized personal and political contacts on the projects' behalf. When Roosevelt named Francis E. Leupp commissioner of Indian affairs, White wrote a colleague in the mining business that he was "my very good personal friend. I have known him a good many years and have been entertained at his house in Washington, so that I will get action there." He also devoted his writing talents to boosting the projects, as in articles in the *Saturday Evening Post* on the wonders being wrought by irrigation in the Northwest. He then forwarded responses to these articles directly to the Twin Falls Land and Irrigation Company, with whose mastermind, Ira B. Perrine, he worked closely on both the mining and irrigation deals.[46]

Then, early in 1905, Roosevelt's Public Land Commission disclosed extensive fraudulent use of land entries by timber corporations, and White realized that he and his colleagues had used the same method in entering their claims. It began to dawn on him that he had gotten involved in an operation that was at best legally questionable. He later recalled that "suddenly my hair rose in amazement and genuine fear when I found they were sending men to the penitentiary for doing exactly what I had done."[47]

He sought the advice of college fraternity brother William E. Borah, by then a prominent Idaho attorney. As White later told Theodore Roosevelt: "Clear as a bell came back the answer, and when I had followed his advice I first dropped the entire matter, and second made a record which would have convicted me before the law, but which would have persuaded any fair-minded man that I was morally blameless." He wrote Perrine in March 1905 that he was "abandoning the whole matter and leaving them free to do as they please with the land." In words that seemed intended for eyes in addition to Perrine's, White explained that he was taking this step "because upon investigation, I found that while we had entered our plans in full intention to obey the law strictly, my own ignorance of the law, led me into a place where my memory will not be sure as to whether or nor I did or did not technically invalidate any title in the Keefe and Hunt land . . . and I would not bear to have even a technical violation of the law on my mind."[48]

Despite this shock, White was not at first completely disillusioned with his colleagues in speculation, for he wrote to Lewis Van Riper several months later offering to write an article for his *United States Mining Journal* in exchange for ten thousand dollars' worth of shares in one of Riper's Idaho mines. According to the *Autobiography*, the moment of truth came when this article appeared. The editors had "distorted my viewpoint, . . . inserted puffs for certain mining enterprises that I did not believe in, and otherwise again mixed me up in scandalous proceedings." White asserted that these experiences, combined with developments in state politics, finally opened his eyes to the economic corruption of the nation's political and economic system.

> The fact that from the private car I had walked straight to the threshold of the penitentiary also disturbed me deeply. . . . I was amazed and ashamed— ashamed that I should have been such a sucker, and ashamed of my profession when I read the article in that mining paper. . . . That men of wealth, if not of standing, could do such things, soured me on wealth, made me suspicious of the whole system which was institutionalized in the prestige and power of wealth. I narrowly escaped disgrace.[49]

The experiences left White with a distaste for both financial speculation and legal manipulation, particularly when practiced by outsiders more powerful and crafty than he. As his income grew, White would invest it primarily in Emporia real estate, which, though also essentially speculative, he could keep an eye on. His reform novels later depicted the greed of industrialists, but in each case the original economic sin involved financial speculation and legal manipulation. The most immediate outcome, perhaps, was to sour his relations with the railroad executives who had gotten him involved in the mess to begin with.

White's fear of public disgrace illustrates the complex relationship among rhetoric, roles, and identity in White's development. He had assumed the mantle of righteousness in the Meffert case from mixed motives, in part to assuage his anxieties and in part because it justified his break with Hood. Yet, once assumed, the role would have to be played consistently or he would run the risk of accusations of hypocrisy. White's subsequent account of his short fling with illicit speculation recalled both outrage at his colleagues' duplicity and fear for his own reputation. Realizing the contrast between his private ambitions and his public image seems to have aroused feelings of shame more than guilt, fear of public rejection more than self-recrimination.[50]

He recalled that his fears were all the greater because of his recent leadership of the anti-Meffert campaign. Too, he had expressed self-righteous outrage in 1904 when his political enemy Joseph Burton was indicted for taking a bribe. Burton had headed the "Boss Busters," the self-styled reformers who had unseated Leland in 1901. His career was now ruined by the discrepancy between public rhetoric and private behavior. The Boss Busters had resurfaced early in 1903, led by Burton and Marion newspaper publisher Edward W. Hoch, who was disgruntled that a back-room deal had robbed him of the lucrative post of state printer.[51]

Burton's departure from the political scene triggered a major realignment among Kansas Republicans, in which young men who, like White, had learned politics under Cyrus Leland now moved away from him and joined with others, like Hoch and Walter R. Stubbs, who had previously been allied with Burton against Leland. In response, veteran politicians such as Leland, Chester Long, and Charles Curtis forgot their factional differences and regrouped as "stalwart" Republicans. The resulting political ferment in Kansas, a curious mixture of moral principle, economic interests, and old-fashioned factional maneuvering, marked the birth of the progressive movement in that state.[52] The *Gazette*'s economic development in this same period provided one final impetus to White's emergence as a crusader in the state as well as local arena. Paradoxically, as his newspaper prospered and became more independent of party patronage, White grew more aware of differences between the interests of local businessmen and the large corporations that increasingly dominated national economic life. Frustration with the treatment his own business received from "the trusts" was the last straw in White's disillusionment with the status quo.

White became more aware of the railroads' inadequate service and high rates as his own business grew more complicated. His improvements to the *Gazette* print shop introduced sophisticated machinery that required constant maintenance and parts and supplies that had to be transported by rail. Increasing job work and newspaper circulation also meant greater demand for paper and ink, which had to be purchased from wholesalers in Kansas City and shipped by rail. Delays in their arrival could be very costly. Newsprint was ordinarily purchased by the carload and delivered several times a year. At times when the newspaper was growing in size and circulation, it became harder to judge how much newsprint to order, and the *Gazette* often ran out or came very close to it before the new shipment arrived. When this happened, emergency shipments had to be ordered to tide the printers over until the carload arrived, and no matter who caused the delay, the *Gazette* had to pay a much higher rate for the paper. On some occasions the *Gazette* bookkeeper protested: "Owing to the fact that you get all of our business, and three car loads of paper a year, we think you ought to give us our rate. We think it is only fair, and that you are doing us a great unjustice." But her protests were to no avail.[53]

White also felt directly the increases in railroad rates because the *Gazette* was responsible for paying a newsprint shipment's freight costs upon arrival. He had to come up with cash at short notice, which was not always easy. He reported to Sallie in 1904, "We got in another car-load of paper and had to dig up $145 for freight. That is why I am gray and wan and pale today." This arrangement occasionally created controversy: in 1903, for example, a shipment of newsprint remained unloaded at a siding in the Emporia railroad yard for over a week while the paper wholesalers, the railroad, and the newspaper wrangled over the proper charges, and the print shop watched its supply dwindle.[54]

Even though White dealt through a wholesale house, his relations with the great paper producers were a major source of resentment that reshaped his attitudes toward the economic system. The consolidation of much of the newsprint industry into the International Paper Company in 1898 succeeded not only in halting the downward trend in prices that had occurred during the depression but eventually in raising prices. IPC also introduced a new payment system that penalized purchasers. In 1903 and 1904, because of poor service and underweight shipments, White became increasingly antagonistic toward the paper "trusts." In August 1903 the *Gazette* received 618 pounds less paper than it had ordered and been charged for. When another shipment a year later was almost a thousand pounds underweight, White decided he had had enough. Summoning his most righteous language, he demanded satisfaction from the wholesaler:

> I am willing to get you an affidavit of the weigh master and of the drayman. This is the second time that this trouble has occurred, and if you do not allow this, we will have to cancel the contract with you and put our business in another place. If the paper trusts want to go ahead and make trouble, they can do it. I believe I can make just as much trouble for the paper trusts as the paper trusts can make for me.[55]

Nonetheless, no redress was made and shortages continued to occur: six months later Mae Austin complained that they had been shorted on the past two shipments. "It seems queer that the shortage is always on the same side. We think we have put up with this as long as we ought to." But there seemed to be little they or their wholesaler could do.[56]

In 1905 the *Gazette* became known around Kansas as a reform journal. White's resentment of the "trusts" was channeled into statewide reform movements that reflected widening dissatisfaction among small businessmen. He criticized railroad interference in political affairs—interference that he had once viewed as part of the game—but he also roundly attacked their rates. In June 1905, he attacked in the *Gazette* the high rates for newsprint between Kansas City and Emporia:

> The rate from Kansas City to Emporia, a distance of one hundred miles, is four cents more than the rate from Appleton, Wis., to Kansas City, a distance of 600 miles. How do you get over, around or about that iniquity? . . . here is a practical abuse . . . which costs a paper like the Gazette more than its taxes to the county. It is a dirty shame, and if the newspapers don't adjust this matter, they are rabbits.[57]

In large part, White also responded to changes in middle-class opinion in shifting from railroad ally to critic. As ever, he was acutely sensitive to his audience's reactions. Over twenty years later, pondering his conversion, he recalled "the changed attitude I saw in the eyes of my fellow passengers on the railroads when I flashed my [railroad] passes."

> In the eighties and nineties their eye said: "Behold, the badge of the excellent person." But after Roosevelt had come to the White House and was ringing the changes against the plutocracy, the eyes of my fellow passengers glared this message: "Oh look at the grafter; observe the dirty crook. We are paying his way."

Hence, he admitted, came his first "reform editorial," against the free railroad pass.[58]

White's new identity as a crusader for reform was thus shaped by the combined force of many changes in his political and economic environment. Ultimately, however, it is not sufficient to describe it as only a calculated response to new conditions. Simply put, White came to perceive previously acceptable behavior as corrupt. When, in early 1907, the usual railroad lobbying sent conservative Republican Charles Curtis to the U.S. Senate, White was outraged by actions that he had once considered part of the game. His new crusading identity was sealed in the white heat of his anger. As he sought to persuade his friends to join an opposition movement, his language assumed what can only be described as the intensity of a recent religious convert. These letters suggest that the Curtis nomination finally crystallized the reorientation of White's identity that had been taking place over time. This new organization restored order and meaning to his mental universe after the confusion and frustration of the previous years. At that moment, White knew who he had been, who he was, and what he must do. He wrote his good friend Henry Allen immediately after Curtis's nomination:

> . . . it seems to me that it is your duty and that of every man who does not wish to compromise with wrong in this situation to unite to fight for those things which will take power out of the hands of men whose object it is merely to win the game for themselves or their friends, and put it into the hands of the people. I believe that so long as politics is played under the present rules of the present game, Mort and Jim and Dave and Cy will win. . . .
>
> Now, it seems to me that you should join the hell raisers. . . . It will cost us all some money—but has God been good enough to you and me for us to give something to help our state rise above a disgrace like that which has come upon it? You and I both know that if we had our deserts we would be in far different stations from those we occupy today. Then why shouldn't we show our gratitude to the power outside ourselves that has guided us away from the consequences of our own weaknesses and errors to return to that power something that will help the current move onward.[59]

By mid-decade, White had significantly redefined both his sense of himself and his public duties. Although he eliminated none of his former roles, he changed the priorities among them. He still considered himself a "practical" politician, and he continued to work hard in the interests of a group of political allies. But now he considered practical politics as means to certain moral ends, at the heart of which was defending the will of "the people." His new identity was centered upon his role as the champion of his community against both moral corruption from within and economic exploitation from without. This heightened emphasis upon the whole community rather than party or faction was made possible by the *Gazette*'s increased economic independence from patronage; it was made necessary by the need for a growing local readership in the interest of his advertisers. The next two chapters will discuss how White expressed his vision of community in terms that extended and elaborated tenets of the nineteenth-century booster ethos.

5

Booster Progressivism

William Allen White did not become a reformer as an isolated individual, but as a citizen of Emporia and the publisher of the *Gazette*. Although he was part of a widening national network of reformers, he continued to make his livelihood, live most of his days, and gain much of his sense of identity and accomplishment within his home town. For White, being a progressive was a matter as much of concrete public actions as of ideology. His new identity was not merely reflected by, but was embodied in, a series of reform movements that he spearheaded in Emporia.

No one person creates a social movement. White was a member of a shifting coalition of Emporians interested in a range of causes such as moral reform, civic improvement, economic regulation, and municipal re-organization. All of these concerns have been identified with a national wave of reforms that is commonly labeled progressivism, and, surveying the history of Emporia in the first decades of the twentieth century, one senses a spirit of civic activism that is in keeping with the national ethos. Yet if one looks more closely at each cause, it becomes harder to detect a single unifying concern among them all. No one of the simple explanations favored by historians suits all cases. Certainly, Emporia did not experience industrialization, rapid urban growth, or an influx of immigrants in this period. It was not dominated either by a displaced gentry or by a centralizing professional class. Rather, Emporians sought a variety of reforms for a wide range of reasons.

Championing reform had enabled White to claim a leadership role, and it may well have fulfilled similar personal aspirations for others. Some Emporians were determined to impress their visions of morality upon the community. Some middle-class women wanted a greater role in public affairs. Some local businessmen sought government protection against the dominance of national corporations. Some perennial boosters simply wanted Emporia to have whatever was most up-to-date, most "progressive," in urban amenities.

What gives the period unity was not motivation but rhetoric: all the campaigns in Emporia turned for inspiration and justification to the booster ethos. Boosterism balanced economic growth with social order through a set of ethical injunctions that defined morality in middle-class terms and made it inseparable from, and essential to, business success. Ideally, the citizen would advance self and community by placing public duties above immediate personal interests. This voluntary self-discipline relied upon the virtue of a community's people. At the same time, continued prosperity required economic growth, which depended in turn upon the initiative of a community's businessmen. Neither virtue nor enterprise could be ignored without peril. Reformers would point to dangers to both in justifying their campaigns.

At first glance, the reform agenda in Emporia seems to depart from nineteenth-century boosterism, particularly as manifested in White's own "What's the Matter with Kansas?" After 1900 White and other reformers would give priority to the need for local self-determination over the need to attract outside capital. Yet they were not so much repudiating their booster faith as attempting to preserve its spirit while adapting it to changed conditions. Though they remained committed to progress, they became aware that the interests of national corporate capitalism and small-town businesses were not always the same.

In promoting each cause, whether it be moral reform or improved public services, White employed the techniques and rhetoric of community mobilization that he had perfected with the street fair and his campaign against William Meffert. He kept each issue constantly before the public through the *Gazette* while working behind the scenes, tapping personal connections to reinforce his public statements. He preached the need for unity in the face of outsiders, putting dissenters in the position of disloyalty to their town. Above all, he strove to create an urgent sense that the town's very future rested on the outcome of the present campaign.

Taken together, White's arguments and those of other reformers suggest that Emporia was undergoing a crisis. Much of this sense of urgency, however, may be attributable to the nature of reform rhetoric. After all, to promote change one must prove a need for it, in the form of some present danger. On the other hand, to be effective rhetoric must address commonly held beliefs and arouse anxieties among at least some of the prospective followers of a movement. This interaction of language, psychology, and economic interests makes it difficult to isolate a single element as the "real" cause of any social movement.

Like many American towns and cities in the early twentieth century, Emporia was changing rapidly. Physically, it was taking on the appearance of a modern city, with newly paved streets and sidewalks, street lights, and an expanded sewage system. Emporians acquired improved public utilities, and their city government modernized its services. At home, as the increasing volume of advertising in the *Gazette* testified, the daily lives of many Emporians were being transformed by the products of the growing mass-production national economy. They became owners of laborsaving appliances and consumers of commercially prepared foods, and they enjoyed new ways of filling the leisure time thus created. Meanwhile, Emporia businessmen were trying to adapt to the power of the new national economy, and above all to retain a sense of control over their own livelihoods.

Some may have felt uneasy about the increase in material comfort and decrease in individual agency related to this transition to a nationally centralized, consumer-oriented economy. If so, boosterism provided a way to assuage that anxiety. It gave assurances that civic virtue and material progress were compatible. And it prescribed civic activism as a way to protect one's community and demonstrate one's continued commitment to the common good.

Not all Emporians greeted these campaigns with equal enthusiasm. Their varying responses reflected real economic and cultural differences within the community and suggested that the business elite was most receptive to the arguments of the booster ethos. In the end, many of the movements produced more conflict than permanent reform. Nonetheless, the reformers seem to have been willing to risk disharmony in order to pursue higher ideals that they believed would benefit the whole community. If their campaigns sometimes failed to attain these ideals completely, they at least served to dramatize their own dedication to them.

As the twentieth century dawned, William Allen White was engaged in projects that were perfectly in keeping with nineteenth-century boosterism. One was the most traditional of booster endeavors: bringing a new railroad to Emporia. He also helped found a new civic organization designed to keep Emporians apprised of the latest social trends. And he consistently used the *Gazette* to preach the virtues of the booster ethos.

Despite the return of prosperity in the late 1890s, the railroads continued to be a source of concern to many Emporians. In 1899 federal courts annulled the state regulatory board that the Populists had created, and railroads moved quickly to raise their rates. Emporia coal and lumber dealers and Lyon County cattlemen were among the first groups in Kansas to organize in protest. Some local businessmen, smarting under railroad rates and service that gave an edge to competitors in other towns, had long advocated state regulation. A few, such as lumberman John S. Watson, had been active Populists. Others, such as cattleman George Plumb, the late senator's younger brother, pressed within the Republican party for railroad legislation and currency reforms. Many, particularly the owners of large farms or ranches in the area, were allied with William Martindale in local and state politics.[1]

In response to these protests, White at first tried to mediate between the railroads and local businessmen. In the *Gazette* he emphasized that the lumbermen were "business men" and should be treated with respect. Employing the rhetorical opposition of business and politics that he often used against the Populists, he warned, "Isn't it wiser to talk business with business men than to talk politics with Populists?" But he also published the railroad's justifications for its increases.[2]

Nonetheless, White hoped that such conflicts could be resolved through further economic growth, particularly increased competition. Hearing rumors in the spring of 1900 that promoters for a new railroad were thinking of coming through the area, he wrote to point out Emporia's many advantages: "There are several sites for division shops and a depot near town which could be bought dirt cheap. If you could come down here quietly in the next ten days I think we could find something that would make it profitable to you." When the response was positive, he promised to rouse the community to action.[3]

Soon the *Gazette* proclaimed, "Get together for Emporia," announcing a public meeting to plan "ways and means to bring the new Stilwell road to Emporia—with divisions and shops if possible." It insisted that the town's future was riding on the outcome:

> This is positively the last call. If Emporia lets this chance slip by, the town will always be what it is now, a bully old town—but never will it become anything like a city. There must be no fumbles or bobbles with this proposition. There should be neither cliques, factions nor rings in connection with the committee that has the matter in charge. . . . This is a town affair and its success or failure means life or death to Emporia. Every business man should attend the meeting.[4]

To gain the railroad, White trotted out all the traditional booster rhetoric: the insistence that this issue marked a turning point in the town's history, the assumption of business leadership, the emphasis upon the interdependence of economic interests within the community, and the demand for complete public unity.

In pursuing this opportunity White worked closely with fellow members of what he called the "Town Strategy Board," Mit Wilhite, Jerry Evans, and Robert Jones, whom White described as "fellows who like to help get things for the town." All had been founders of the Business Men's Association and had helped White organize the street fair.[5]

Unity was the keynote of the public meeting, which was chaired by Evans as president of the Business Men's Association. Eighteen Emporia men were appointed to negotiate with the railroad planners. Among them, in addition to White, Wilhite, Evans, and Jones, were prominent businessmen such as Howard Dunlap, W. T. Soden, George W. Newman, and O. B. Hardcastle, and Populist leaders John Watson and L. R. Wright. The major factional leaders were absent. By November an election was scheduled to approve $140,000 in county and city bonds.[6]

The *Gazette* was, as always, tireless in promoting the bond issue. Throughout December it kept the measure before the public with news items and reprints from other papers. In both editorial and news columns White argued that the new railroad would solve Emporia's economic problems. He insisted that high freight rates were caused by lack of competition: "Lyon county pays tribute in freight rates, clothing, furniture, groceries and feed enough to pay the interest on bonds for all the railroads in the county." All residents of the area would benefit:

> The railroad proposition means in short: More roads, more jobs, more jobs, more consumers of butter and eggs and hog meat and steer meat and milk and chicken and garden truck. . . . It is a question of whether Lyon county

shall go forward or stagnate. . . . The question is this: Shall we let strangers move into Lyon county or shall we stay here and rot out.[7]

Promoters called their new railroad the "Kansas City, Mexico and Orient," because they envisioned it as connecting the Midwest to America's newly acquired Pacific empire via the west coast of Mexico. A special sixteen-page Christmas issue depicted the railroad as a direct link between Lyon County and the Far East.

It will be the shortest American line to Asia, to the Philippines, to Oceania, where the great markets are. The shortest line makes the rate. If that line comes through Lyon county, Lyon county farmers will get the profit. . . . Here is a great and growing market within our reach. . . . Here is the opportunity of a century before the people of Lyon county. What are they going to do about it?

Overall, White identified the question with growth and progress: "The town's future lies in the balance. . . . Shall it grow with the growing West or shall we let the old cat die?" When the bond issue passed, White projected that Emporia's population would be fifteen thousand by 1905. "Emporia will be a school and a dinner bucket town."[8]

The following spring, with the railroad promising to begin work in Emporia any moment, White concocted a scheme for a grand Fourth of July celebration to publicize Emporia and the railroad. Emphasizing his credentials as publicist and organizer, he wrote about his idea to A. E. Stilwell, the Orient's president:

I handle the "Associated Press" report for this part of Kansas. I can get up a story . . . which will make an advertisement of the Orient Railroad all over the Western States on the morning of the 5th of July, and we can have a day here in Emporia, so important, that however how much the Roads may dislike the Orient Road, they will have to run special trains into the town accommodating the crowd. I promoted a Street Fair here in Emporia that loaded down all kinds of trains. I can promote this 4th of July celebration if you will help me, in such a matter that your road and Emporia will get a great deal of first rate advertising out of it. You do not have to lay a single rail or drive a single spike *after the 5th*, but by putting up a good bluff on the 4th, you can do the business. Will you help me?

Stilwell's reply, as reprinted in the *Gazette*, was "Go ahead . . . hire all the brass bands in the state."[9]

White planned to combine the driving of the railroad's first spike with the laying of cornerstones for a new Lyon County courthouse and a Carnegie Library being built at the College of Emporia. Together, these public ceremonies would dramatize Emporia's central location, with railroad connections emanating to all points of the globe: "the spokes on the hub of the universe, which will center in Emporia, Kansas, U.S.A." He even tried to induce newly inaugurated vice-president Theodore Roosevelt to speak, arguing that the driving of the first spike would be "the first palpable and tangible result that American supremacy in the Philippines has given American industry."[10]

Although White liked to portray Emporians as united behind the project, not all were as enthusiastic as he, particularly those who would be required to pay the highest costs of progress. Second Avenue residents vehemently opposed the plan to make their street the railroad right-of-way. Their neighborhood, just "below" the tracks that already ran along Third Avenue, was made up largely of working-class homes and was focused around the town's Catholic church, parochial school, and hospital, run by the Sisters of Charity. Protests soon appeared in the *Gazette*—under belittling headlines such as "The First Roar" and "Roar No. 2." The latter correspondent complained that he had been an early supporter of the proposition, only to find the "reward is to have the railroad under our very noses, and get a first taste of fire and brimstone." "If this is the first of Emporia's boom," he concluded wryly, "I pity the last of it." As the prospect of grade work within the city limits loomed, and Robert Jones set to work obtaining the rights-of-way for the Orient, protestors held public meetings and sent petitions to the city council.[11]

White tried to quell this opposition by undercutting it in the *Gazette* and at times denying it access to his newspaper. He advised the local Catholic priest, who was leading the protest, that because most Emporians wanted the railroad, it would be foolish to alienate them.

> Now if the Second Avenue people do anything, they must do it by encouraging public sentiment at this side rather than by antagonizing it. . . . Your letter was earnest, and it would arouse this force of public sentiment in a degree that would hurt your cause, more than it would help it. So I believe that I am helping your cause by returning this letter herewith.

Not completely insensitive to these complaints, he had tried to mediate them behind the scenes. He explained the situation to an Orient official and suggested an alternate route. Since this required crossing Santa Fe tracks, he offered to help there, too. "I have some acquaintances and I believe some friendships with a number of the highest officials of the Santa Fe, notably: President Ripley and Mr. Paul Morton and one or two others less important." When these efforts were unavailing, he sought to silence the opposition.[12]

When work began on the Second Avenue grade early in June, attorney John Madden, representing the Second Avenue residents, obtained a temporary restraining order to halt construction. At this point the conflict took a humorous turn. It was the custom in celebrations of this kind to hold an open ballot to select the "most popular" young lady to represent her community, in this case by throwing the first shovelful of dirt in the dedication ceremony. When Madden threatened to slap an injunction on whoever began work, "whether that person is a pretty young woman or a rough section hand," Emporians responded by electing his daughter May. The affair was resolved when District Judge Dennis Madden, John Madden's brother and law partner, dissolved the restraining order. The celebration came off successfully, with the Orient vice-president driving a golden spike to symbolically launch construction on the new "transcontinental" railroad—and Miss May Madden throwing the first shovelful of dirt.[13]

Despite White's great expectations for the Orient, it never reached Emporia. Hopes for construction revived periodically, and White and other boosters remained faithful to the project. Second Avenue residents remained adamant in their opposition. In 1910 White would warn that they were again trying to overturn the railroad's right-of-way. "I believe if I were you I should consult Mr. Stilwell and tell him that your franchise through Emporia is in some danger and that it would be reenforced if a little work of some kind might be done upon it from time to time."[14]

Meanwhile, even as White promoted Emporia in true booster fashion, other projects employed approaches that would be more prevalent in the twentieth century. In December 1900, he, Normal School president Albert R. Taylor, and First Congregational Church pastor Frank G. Ward invited some thirty fellow male Emporians to meet once a month "for the purpose of investigating and discussing current sociological and economic problems." Known as the Current Club, it was an informal, home-grown precursor of nationally affiliated organizations of community leaders like the Rotarians. The group suggests the twentieth-century tendency toward increasing unity among economic and professional elites that would be reflected at the national level in the National Civic Federation. More immediately significant to Emporians was the fact that the club bridged old political and factional divisions and brought together some of Emporia's most prominent and intelligent men in a setting that emphasized enlightened civic improvement. In coming years the group would in fact serve as a staging ground for many such projects. The first members included the presidents of both local colleges and the three remaining banks—Calvin Hood of Emporia National, Frederick Newman of Citizen's National, and Howard Dunlap of the Emporia Savings Bank. Emporia's pioneer generation was represented by L. T. Heritage and J. M. Steele. Prominent Populists John Madden and L. R. Wright, a cattleman who had just been elected to the state senate, were also included. There were even several attorneys connected with the Martindale camp, though none of the major figures of that faction were invited. About two-thirds of the members were professionals of one sort or another, and most of the rest were in finance rather than retail business.[15]

Through projects such as founding the Current Club and promoting the Orient railroad, White fulfilled his responsibility to promote Emporia's growth. Moreover, he regularly used the *Gazette* as a pulpit to preach the virtues that were also considered essential to community success. In editorials and news stories he frequently chided Emporians who failed to meet standards of "respectable" behavior, and his statements reflect the assumption that private morality and public prosperity were inseparable. His sermons prescribed proper behavior not only for men as businessmen, but for women as homemakers.

The booster ethos posited the nuclear family—defined in terms of father as breadwinner and head of the household and mother as caretaker of the home and nurturer of the children—as the fundamental unit of the community. Such was the division of roles that had been devised by urban middle-class Americans in the mid-nineteenth century to counter the destabilizing effects of commercial and early industrial capitalism. For White as for many other Americans, this arrangement ensured harmony and prosperity in the community as well as in the household. Women were essential, as housekeepers and mothers, in this domestic corollary of boosterism. A competent housewife was believed to be the key to her husband's—and hence the community's—prosperity, for her thrift could amass the capital with which a small business grew. She was also responsible for inculcating in the next generation the qualities of character that would ensure the community's future prosperity and stability.[16]

Seen in this context, White's praise of good housewives and criticism of slovenly ones in the *Gazette* were not simply an indulgence of personal prejudice; he was fulfilling his booster responsibility to promote the welfare of the community. In 1900 the *Gazette* published in one of the special Saturday editions a photograph of sturdy-looking Mary Suhl, winner of a bread-baking contest. The accompanying article, entitled "A Sensible Girl," enumerated her virtues and suggested their importance to a prosperous community:

> She is just a plain American girl who "helps around home," never gads the streets, isn't afraid of hard work, and can put her hands in the dishwater when she has to. . . . The *Gazette* warns the boys of this town to make up to the Mary Suhl kind of girl. . . . She is of fast colors and twenty years from now she will be a good, substantial woman who will help a man save, and be his partner in everything.

The article predicted great things for Mary and the lucky young man she would marry: "you just watch their smoke, watch them accumulate collateral, and see their credit rise at the bank." Elsewhere the *Gazette* often implied that a wife's lack of frugality, rather than her husband's low wages, was responsible for her family's difficulties in making ends meet.[17]

White regularly attributed social problems to moral failings, which in turn he often blamed on laxity in parental education. He especially criticized mothers who allowed their daughters to "gad" about the streets, where they might mix with who knew what sorts of men, instead of keeping them at home, where they could learn useful domestic skills. In 1900 a young El Dorado woman named Jessie Morrison was tried for the murder of a romantic rival, and in the *Gazette* White repeatedly hammered in the lesson of the story. Pointing to Morrison's testimony that on the day of the murder she had gone "downtown," leaving her mother doing the family washing, he concluded that "a woman who is heartless enough to do that is heartless enough to work herself up to a 'state' and slash her rival with a razor." But much worse, Morrison was not an isolated case:

> In Emporia there are a hundred Jessie Morrisons. They are gadding up and down Commercial street every day, pestering young men who are at work. Their mothers wheedle money out of their fathers to overdress the little hussies—to dress 'em like princesses instead of like daughters of men getting from $40 to $75 a month for hard work. . . . They are taught by authors of silly novels that every time their pulses quicken at the sight of a he creature it is a Sacred Thing, and that they must live for Love or die. Jessie Morrison has this idea, and her mother never had a plain talk with her and told her the facts in the case.

A number of such girls in a community, he suggested, would go a long way to undermining both its moral and its economic order.[18]

White's debut in the *Saturday Evening Post* in 1901 was an editorial reprinted from the *Gazette* that made a similar link between private virtue and public order. "The Sheriff or the Chaperon" attributed a rise in crime to parents' neglect of their responsibility to supervise the young. "If parents persist in shunning the parlor as a place forbidden to them, if mothers turn their daughters over to the newspapers and billboards and theatres and novels for spiritual refreshment and confidence, if fathers let their sons get their education and moral ideals from the street, then the world must not complain at the sight of its tax bills." A year later, with the Meffert controversy, White would move from merely preaching private morality to mobilizing the community to enforce it.[19]

The Meffert controversy was as instrumental in sparking a general reform consciousness among middle-class Emporians as it was in launching White's personal career as a crusader for righteousness. Indeed, Emporia businessmen started the campaign to cleanse Emporia of Meffert's influence while White was away in California. It was led by men, such as Mit Wilhite, who were White's colleagues in boosting Emporia's economy. The affair raised the issue of civic virtue to immediate public awareness, for by flouting conventional morality Meffert seemed to strike at the heart of the community's social order.

In late April 1902 a group of Emporia's "prominent citizens" gathered at Mit Wilhite's restaurant to discuss how to handle the uproar against Meffert following Stephen Conklin's suicide. Although it was not an official body, the group constituted itself into a sort of shadow government, chaired by Mayor H. B. Morse, in keeping with traditions of extralegal community action. Indeed, the Topeka *Capital* described the meeting as "a sort of vigilance committee," whose goal was to drive "the obnoxious person out of town."[20]

The men were in an awkward position. Meffert clearly flouted their basic moral values, and the immediate reaction of some was to use traditional means of restoring communal order: ritual violence against the offender.

As the *Capital* noted, there had been talk on the streets of tar and feathers and even lynching. But, considering themselves modern businessmen, the group at the Mit-Way could not contemplate such lawless actions, more appropriate to the backward South than to the civilized Midwest. The *Gazette* always deplored lynchings in such terms. Yet there could be no thought of simply tolerating Meffert's deviance. The men were caught in the contradiction of the small town's position midway between country and city, between provincial repression and cosmopolitan anomie.

Their answer was to take the matter to the new state medical licensing board. The widening role of such administrative bodies, acting in partnership with increasingly influential professional organizations like the American Medical Association, is generally considered to reflect the centralization and bureaucratization of power in the early twentieth century. Meffert's enemies in Emporia, however, saw the board only as a new tool through which they could peacefully rid the community of a troublesome influence and protect the authority of their moral standards. Ironically, however, by pursuing the issue through the medical board and the courts, they unwittingly contributed to the rise of new professional and bureaucratic elites that would in time undermine the authority of their local code.

The town fathers had every confidence that questions of morality, rather than points of law or professional expertise, would determine their case. Their evidence of Meffert's "gross immorality" consequently consisted of court records from the dismissed 1899 abortion case, statements regarding other illegal operations, and petitions from local physicians, teachers, ministers, and "prominent citizens" testifying to the man's infamous behavior and immoral reputation. Several affidavits from married women charged that he had made improper advances toward them; several men testified that they had witnessed a meeting in an open field in rural Lyon County between Meffert and an unchaperoned woman.

At basis, Meffert's crime seems to have been that he endangered the chastity of Emporia's women. The ministers' petition against him asserted their conviction that Meffert "was a man of immoral character," whose "practice of medicine was a menace to the reputation of any woman who might call on him for professional services" and whose "presence was a menace to the morals of the community." The article on the movement against Meffert in the *Capital* concluded, "The young doctor . . . is credited with being a hypnotist and with using this power to obtain his desires with patients, as some of his alleged victims before associating with him were young ladies of not only irreproachable character but also of education and years that should have made them thoroughly capable of taking care of themselves." Hypnotic power seemed the only way to explain this man's attractiveness to women. In violating his trust as a physician, he seemed to be introducing corruption into the very heart of the community's moral universe: the purity of its women and the sanctity of its homes.[21]

Seen another way, however, Meffert was the center of a group of women and men who, if they were not bohemians, at least failed to live according to "respectable" middle-class standards of behavior. When the controversy began, Meffert was living "openly" in the boardinghouse run by his ex-wife, Delta, but he had been connected romantically with several other single women. One, who was also living in the boardinghouse, had been fired from her teaching job because of her reputed connection with Meffert. She stayed there, she said, because "things were unpleasant at her home."[22]

Statements made before the state medical board suggest that there were significant class differences between Meffert's opponents and his supporters. The former were drawn almost exclusively from the business and professional leadership of Emporia. Of the sixty-seven people who testified or signed petitions against Meffert, nearly half (thirty-three) were listed in city directories as having professional occupations, and over a third (twenty-three) were proprietors of substantial local businesses. Three others were salaried managers, while only two were skilled laborers. Significantly, Meffert's opposition was overwhelmingly dominated by men, who traditionally were responsible for redressing questions of honor. Only four women were publicly named in all the petitions against Meffert: one was a physician, and three married women testified that Meffert had behaved improperly toward them when they sought his medical services.[23]

On the other hand, Meffert's defenders were women, laborers, and small shopkeepers, representing a less powerful group than his attackers. The *Gazette* noted that "several hundred" of Meffert's patients had signed a petition in his support, but it printed only the names of twenty-one of the "best known" of them. In addition, twenty-nine persons testified or signed affidavits attesting to Meffert's good character and reputation. Of the fifty persons thus named, twenty-two were women. Four could be identified as widows, two were farmer's wives, and four were married to railroad employees. Three were single and employed in clerical or service jobs, and only one—Sallie Martindale, wife of factional chieftain William Martindale—could be considered of the Emporia elite. Several of the women had lived in Delta Meffert's boardinghouse. Among his male defenders, only one, a dentist, was in a professional occupation. Six were proprietors of small shops, and six were independent artisans. One was a farmer, three were white-collar employees, and five were semiskilled or unskilled laborers.[24]

Some who testified for Meffert seemed aware that differences in class and standards of respectability were involved in the dispute. According to the *Gazette,* George Goddard, a Santa Fe employee, asserted that "though the best people of town were against the Doctor . . . some of them are only gossip mongers, trying to kick a man when he is down." Others, who had boarded or visited at Mrs. Meffert's establishment, defended the propriety of the residence as well as the doctor's behavior. Meda Stine, a bookkeeper in the Emporia telephone office, insisted that in her year as a resident of the boardinghouse, "she has seen numerous women there whose names are familiar in Emporia and that the doctor's conduct toward these women was above reproach."[25]

Such statements seemed to be defending not only Meffert but a way of life. Lurking behind the stated issues of Meffert's actions were questions about boardinghouse life and, especially, the legitimacy of women's living alone. One of White's employees, Laura French, was such a woman, and her treatment of the controversy in her 1929 history of Emporia suggests the strength of divisions over the case: "Much bitter feeling was engendered in this matter, and half the town and county were lined up either for or against Meffert."[26]

As the issue dragged through the courts, Meffert's allies remained loyal. In the spring of 1903 he was rumored to have gathered the signatures of three hundred Emporians pledging to switch their subscriptions from the *Gazette* to the *Republican* if the latter's new owner would support Meffert. According to White, several of his friends discovered the plan and put a stop to it. Many Emporians continued to call on Meffert for medical services, despite the *Gazette*'s warnings of legal retribution. In June 1903, when the Kansas Supreme Court denied Meffert a rehearing, White's increasingly vituperative rhetoric embraced the doctor's supporters: "to Dr. Meffert and all his nefarious gang Emporia can have but one word—GO!" When the U.S. Supreme Court finally ruled against Meffert in 1904, the *Gazette*'s front-page story threatened harassment against not only Meffert but his patrons: "Every one at whose house he had been calling may be brought into court, and the cases against him will be tried so long as he stays here. The committee is determined that the moral cancer shall be removed from Emporia." Most likely, not a few Emporians relished the image of White's unceremonious retreat before Delta Meffert's whip.[27]

The Meffert controversy drew a sense of urgency from middle-class concerns about the public implications of private immorality. While Emporians awaited the outcome of that battle in the Supreme Court, attention shifted to other fronts in the war against private corruption: drives against drink and prostitution. Through this widening of concerns, the reform coalition broadened to include middle-class women, who insisted upon the need to ensure the virtue of the town's young men as well as its women. They took on the town's Democratic mayor, who, they claimed, failed to enforce adequately the laws against vice. Republican political leaders, sensing the opportunity to harness this sentiment to their goal of regaining local political power, welcomed the reformers into their organization. Although it was not completely successful in ridding the town of illicit alcohol, the crusade did enable Republicans to wrest control of city hall from the allied Democrats and Populists.

The fusion of public and private in boosterism offered a rationale for an expanded role for women in the local community. As improved public utilities, commercially prepared foods, and household appliances lightened the domestic duties of middle-class women in the early twentieth century, White faced a quandary based upon his conflicting roles as a newspaperman. As a traditional booster, he celebrated the contribution of women in the home, through their domestic production. Frugality was to be prized, self-indulgence discouraged. But as a newspaper publisher, he could hardly oppose spending for new laborsaving products, since he benefited from the increased advertising they brought. He resolved the dilemma by arguing that women *who could afford them* should take advantage of these amenities, but then should devote their leisure to public needs. As women's domestic responsibilities were lightened, he redefined the public realm to create a new place for them as guardians of noncommercial civic virtues.[28]

In May 1900, "A Town Improvement Club," a front-page article in the *Gazette,* marked the birth of this new approach. White began with a tactic common in booster rhetoric, an invidious comparison between Emporia and the small towns of Colorado, where many middle-class Emporians vacationed during the hot summer months. He praised Colorado's "well kept lawns, beautifully parked streets, clean roads, alleys that are as wholesome as streets and an air of prosperity." In contrast, Emporia was characterized by "weeds in the street, unmowed lawns, dirty alleys, papers blowing on every breeze, parkings harrowed up by the town-herd, and the general air of a picnic ground the day after." He wondered that the contrast did not move Emporians to "spruce up." "But she doesn't. She just slomishs around in her old wrapper and looks like a past due note." His imagery thus fusing slovenliness with insolvency, he pursued the implication of his use of the feminine gender, by arguing that women should assume responsibility for Emporia's public spaces.

> The town needs to be dressed down, trounced, licked, tanned, switched, spanked good and hard. It's no one's business. That sort of business is never transacted. The women, who should really do whatever spanking is done around a house, should get after old Emporia and make her dress up, make her wash her neck and ears and comb her hair.
>
> There are a dozen women's clubs in this town studying by the year subjects which range in vital importance from Egyptian art to the architecture of the renaissance—mostly flub-dubbery. If these women would buckle in and help clean up Emporia as the Colorado women do the Colorado towns! . . . But the Colorado women aren't wasting much brain tissue on the pedigree of Greek gods and the ladies of the French court who were no better than they should be, and so the people now on earth in Colorado live amid pleasant surroundings. . . .
>
> Why should not the hand that rocks the cradle reach back out of the misty past, and spank Emporia into some sort of sense of municipal beauty?[29]

Whether or not they were prompted by this chiding, the assorted women's study clubs of Emporia did assume just such responsibility for public "business" and organized a City Federation of Women's Clubs in 1901. This was part of a nationwide shift in emphasis in women's clubs from cultural self-improvement to united civic action. At the national level, General Federation of Women's Clubs leaders defended their activism in terms similar to White's, arguing that cities had become extended households, in which women's special attributes were sorely needed.[30]

The Emporia federation's leadership and activities reflected its position as partners to the town's businessmen. The first president was Jennie Kellogg, an attorney in practice with her husband, Lyman Beecher Kellogg; the vice-president was Margaret Evans, wife of Jerry Evans; and the secretary was Belle Harris, wife of G.A.R. leader Charles Harris. In August 1901 the *Gazette* reported that the federation had set out trash cans along Commercial Street and lauded their efforts: "The women hope to make Emporia a clean town, while the men make it a live one." The following month the Ladies' Parliament Club opened a free public rest room to accommodate farm wives and children visiting town—a move that combined concern for the well-being of their rural sisters with encouragement of their shopping trips to Emporia. The federation also experimented with a day nursery and lobbied the city board of health to step up enforcement of ordinances regarding sanitation, weeds, and sidewalks. By 1904, however, the federation had adopted a more assertive role in city politics by entering the time-honored debate over local enforcement of prohibition.[31]

Emporia had ostensibly been dry since its founding, and Kansas since statewide prohibition passed in 1881, but enforcement varied according to the administration in power. White's parents had supported the prohibition cause in the 1870s, and although he took an occasional drink as a young man, he permanently abjured alcohol at Sallie Lindsay's demand during their courtship. From 1901 on he served on the Executive Committee and later as vice-president of the Kansas State Temperance Union. Nonetheless, in 1901 he criticized an Emporia Law and Order League rally on booster grounds: "What joints do the temperance people propose to close in Emporia. The *Gazette* contends that there are no joints in this town. The dispatches sent out saying that the people of Emporia are going to rise to put down the Rum Fiend in this town, hurt the town more than whisky is hurting it."[32]

After Democrat John Martin was elected mayor in 1903, however, White took up the league's charges. Early in 1904 he claimed that the prohibition law was not being enforced and argued that laws should be either enforced or taken off the books: "The violation of law breeds mobs and mobs anarchy." He also depicted the league's drive for enforcement as a booster effort to improve the town, rather than to defame its image. "This is a cleaner town than most towns but it can do better. For some time the Gazette has pointed out the fact that there are too many tin-horn gamblers and too many loafing ladies in Emporia. They should take the hint from the law and order league and hike."[33]

During national election campaigns that fall, White was particularly critical of the Democrats' use of alcohol. Although as a novice reporter he had handed around his share of beer to Bent Murdock's political friends, in November 1904 he wrote to Sallie of his outrage at seeing the streets filled with "tough looking" men working for Democratic candidates: "There were crowds of young men and considerable drinking. They were [mostly] Eagles" (a predominantly working-class fraternal organization). In response, he went to the Current Club "and poked it to them good and strong about the whisky business which is running this town."[34]

White was not the only concerned Emporian. The Congregational minister, Frank Ward, announced from his pulpit that the had investigated the town's morals and found them worse than he had ever seen them. The City Federation of Women's Clubs was also alarmed by what they perceived as the lack of enforcement of laws against liquor, gambling, and prostitution. In March its Committee on Suppression of Vice wrote the city council to express its concern; the communication was read and duly placed on file. Early in November a deputation of women called upon Mayor Martin to present resolutions protesting an infestation of "strangers, both men and women," and calling upon the city officers "to use their authority to purify the moral atmosphere."[35]

According to a letter written by Jennie Kellogg and published in the *Gazette,* Martin had insulted the women, neglecting to rise when they entered and treating them with contempt. Kellogg, herself an attorney, reported: "One of the members asked if it is not the duty of the police to arrest anyone found breaking the law along these lines. For answer he sneeringly said: 'That shows how much you know (pause) about law.' " When another woman asked whose duty it was, then, to locate offenders, he responded, " 'Your husbands are business men on the street, and if there are any such places, they probably know where they are.' " Kellogg continued: "After the committee had recovered from this insult, the question was asked: 'Why do we have policemen at all? What are they supposed to do?' He answered, 'To keep the peace.' " She concluded, "When man has so far strayed from his creator's intention concerning him that he can call protecting vice 'peace,' it is time for those who do know the difference to lend a hand."[36]

As the April 1905 municipal elections drew near, it became clear that vice would be the dominant issue. The Law and Order League, which White described as "an informal effort to put down vice," began to seek a candidate in early January. Representatives from the churches met to select as their candidate "a business man . . . who is in favor of prohibiting joints." They chose Orange B. Hardcastle, a partner in a prosperous local furniture and undertaking firm. Before the primary election to select delegates to the Republican city convention, the *Gazette* urged the election of the Hardcastle ticket, which it described as the "business ticket": "the people of Emporia had been saying for years that they wanted a conservative, successful business man to run. And that in Mr. Hardcastle they had found just such a man. He has held aloof from factional quarrels and has been his own master."[37]

Hardcastle won the Republican nomination because of the reformers' zeal in getting their people to the polls. After his nomination by acclamation at the convention, he vowed to "be for the people, and for a clean administration." The convention proceeded to nominate a slate that carefully balanced factions and pro- and anti-Meffert forces.[38]

This reconciliation of longtime factional enemies had been several years in developing. It reflected the death or retirement of local factional leaders such as C. V. Eskridge and Calvin Hood, and was motivated by a common

desire to regain local political dominance. Early in 1904 White had proposed a compromise in order to "clean" the Populists out of the courthouse.
A subsequent county convention nominated Martindale ally George Plumb
and Hood ally C. A. Stannard for the county's two state representatives. In
their acceptances, both men called themselves "businessmen" and avowed
that their campaigns would shun the usual "political" practices. After
White's allies scored major victories in the 1904 county election, several
Martindale allies called for a truce.[39]

Recognizing the political advantage to be gained by appealing to their
interest in reform, the Republicans also welcomed women into their ranks.
Their 1905 city convention elected women to exactly half of the places on
the central committee. In contrast, no women were included on the opposing committee, selected at the "Citizens' Convention" that renominated
Martin for mayor. As both parties hastened to register their own in prepara-
tion for the general election, women came out in large numbers, particularly in the predominantly middle-class northern wards. The result was a
record voter registration, with women constituting nearly half the total.[40]

White opened the campaign with a strong attack upon Martin's administration. While professing the highest respect for him as a person, he insisted
that the Democratic mayor's tolerance of private lawbreaking was undermining the community:

> John Martin does not believe there is any harm in a fellow getting a glass
> of whisky on the quiet in a joint if the joint is not too public. He does not
> believe that the presence of a drinking club where young men and boys and
> old men, too, for that matter, may get liquor by pretending to evade and not
> obey the law is a bad thing. He does not believe that the presence of a few
> tinhorn gamblers in a town, hurts the town, if they run their games quietly
> and keep the limit down. Nor does he believe that if these tin horns bring
> their women with them, and the boys around town have a good time, there is
> any harm if these things are not flaunted in the people's faces. As a result of
> this attitude toward whisky and gambling and women—the town has not been
> wide open but the lid has been tipped up enough to let out a nasty smell. . . .

White's denunciation of these "quiet" evils insisted that there could be no
distinction between public and private morality; rather, values of home
and family must permeate the community. White blamed Democratic hypocrisy for the fact that the town had not increased in business or population in the previous two years, and for the moral peril of its young men.
"Four young business men in this town are now going to hell on the whisky
route from a booze parlor, who two years ago were straight." He concluded,
"Which do you want—a continuation of the good fellow policy or a return
to the principles of civic decency and administration of law, for which Emporia has stood for many years."[41]

The *Times* retorted that, on the contrary, the town had never been so
free of "evil doers." The Democratic paper characterized Martin as an efficient mayor whose "attentive business methods" had reduced expenses and
increased revenues. It was confident that "only those who are spooks, the

diseased of liver, the bearers of deranged stomachs, the mentally rippled, can or do find fault with John Martin's administrative policy."[42]

After its opening salvo, the *Gazette* rarely mentioned the election on the editorial page, but elsewhere provided "news" to prove White's points. On March 31 a front-page article entitled "Sickening Testimony: Emporia Boys Debauched with Joint Whiskey in Sight of the Mayor's Business Office" detailed the testimony of several sixteen- to nineteen-year-olds who had bought liquor at a joint that, though open several years, "has never been disturbed by city authorities." A story highlighted in a box at the top of the page asked Emporia parents whether they wanted their sons exposed to such joints and houses of ill repute, which, it charged, were tolerated even within five hundred feet of the high school. Nevertheless, at the close of the campaign White tried to mitigate the resentment of those whom he had attacked by characterizing it "A Good Natured Contest." Disclaiming any desire to tell Emporians how to vote, he nonetheless promised that Hardcastle would clean up the town. "And finally brethren let us live in Emporia in good fellowship toward one another, and remember that a clean town is the best kind of a town from a business standpoint."[43]

Hardcastle won with 55 percent of the vote in an election that drew 83 percent of registered voters to the polls. His victory was widely credited to the women, for, according to Martin's own figures, men gave him a majority of 157 while women gave Hardcastle a margin of 429. The geographical distribution of the vote suggested that there was another major point of division: the northern wards voted for Hardcastle, the southern for Martin. A *Gazette* reporter quipped, "A few people in the south end of town thought that the town ought to be divided into North and South Emporia. . . ." Though he did not make explicit the meaning of this split, Emporians would have known that it reflected class differences. Although their mayoral candidate lost, voters in the Second and Third wards elected two "Citizens'" candidates to the city council: carpenter Martin Grosz, a leader of the Second Avenue opponents of the Orient Railroad, and Henry Hedgecock, proprietor of a small restaurant near Second Avenue and the Santa Fe yards.[44]

The Republican victory was only the beginning of a long campaign to enforce prohibition in Emporia. Illegal joints were repeatedly raided and closed, although most soon reopened elsewhere. The Law and Order League helped hold down the town's legal expenses by retaining its own attorney, former Populist W. A. Randolph, who prosecuted many of the cases. It also tried to halt the trade in alcohol conducted legally by many Emporia druggists through the loophole that allowed them to dispense alcohol for medicinal purposes. The league attempted to revoke the licenses of druggists who flouted the law most flagrantly, and fought each application for a renewal of such liquor licenses.[45]

Constant vigilance was necessary because not all Emporians were as committed to temperance as the Law and Order League. When city police raided the local Eagles lodge in the summer of 1907, they found many lockers containing beer. A few were marked with the names of prosperous Emporia businessmen, but the majority were used by artisans or blue-collar workers. Stiff penalties were meted out to seven men, but dropped when they withdrew their appeal to the district court and promised to behave themselves thenceforth. Charges were not dismissed, however, against one man, who left town before the trial, whom the mayor and city attorney considered the ringleader. He was, conveniently, an outsider: the *Gazette* reported with some satisfaction that "he came here from Missouri to conduct the beer end for profit."[46]

As in the attempt to run William Meffert out of town, the prohibitionists' efforts to purify Emporia engendered more conflict than enduring reform. Yet White insisted that such vigilance was worthwhile: "Emporia is the largest town in Kansas that has no open joints. . . . Conditions here are kept this way by an everlasting fight but the fight is worth the while." At the very least, it enabled him and other Emporians to publicly demonstrate their dedication to civic virtue.[47]

In these same years, public debate in Emporia was also much taken up with questions of civic improvement, as the booster agenda shifted from railroads to local services. Although Emporians were less sharply divided over these questions than over moral issues, they did have differing priorities in urban development. Many businessmen were most concerned about improving the business district to promote retail trade, while other citizens thought that the emphasis should be placed on services that would improve the standard of living in the neighborhoods. Demands for expanded public services also repeatedly raised the question of how to gather the necessary capital, which in turn prompted debates over municipal versus private ownership and the difference between local and outside investors. All of these debates would be carried out within the terms of the booster ethos. Although White continued to advocate economic growth, he began to argue that Emporia would not benefit if improvements came at the cost of local self-determination. As he did so, he drew upon the potential within boosterism for distinguishing between local and "foreign" interests.[48]

Early in 1902 the Business Men's Association launched a campaign for a bond issue to build a new electric light plant. The existing plant could produce only a night current for street lights, and it was already inadequate to fulfill residents' demands. Unlike the Orient project, this bond issue would not be handed over to a private enterprise but would create a municipally owned plant. The turn toward public ownership reflected not an ideological change of heart but the difficulty of interesting private capitalists in the project. Local boosters pragmatically accepted the involvement of local government as a way of raising the necessary money, even as some were using laissez-faire arguments to oppose railroad regulation.

Although White was away in California, the *Gazette* threw all its energies behind the bond issue. The newspaper always backed bond issues for local improvements, but in this case it had an added incentive, for daytime electricity would power its new linotype. Reporters surveyed local businesses and organizations to show that the additional users of a day current would raise revenues and enable the city to install more street lamps. "It would mean more light in your part of town," the paper promised. It published letters from Mit Wilhite and Jerry Evans promoting the bond issue. H. C. Whitley, perhaps representing an older generation of Emporians, argued that it would be sufficient, and cheaper, simply to upgrade the existing plant. Another dissenter was blacksmith Dudley Smith, who would soon also appear in print as a defender of Dr. Meffert.[49]

Advocates of the plant focused on the economic benefits of a modern facility, but occasionally they raised more theoretical issues. J. J. Wright, a local physician and a Populist, responded to Whitley's objections by lauding the principle of municipal ownership itself: "Indeed the private citizen who has a thought of his environments, walks with a firmer tread and has a respect, who knows that he is a stockholder in the public utilities of his place and that his suggestion counts in the manner of conducting them." It is significant that this comparison of local government to a stockholder's corporation, which is often cited to demonstrate the capitalist bias of Progressivism, was here used by a Populist to indicate the democracy of public ownership of utilities. The *Gazette* itself depicted municipal ownership as a way to both preserve local autonomy and hold down costs to consumers. One item asked ominously, "How would you like to sell the present plant to a corporation and the privilege of building an electric street car line and thereby increase the cost of domestic street lights for an occasional street car ride?" It reported the rumor around town that "eastern capitalists" had made such an offer. The bond issue passed in all wards, and the new plant began operation in the summer of 1903.[50]

Demands for improvements in other public services engendered tensions between local entrepreneurs and outside corporations. In 1900 the city council, responding to criticism of the high rates charged by the Bell-owned telephone company, granted a franchise to a new Independent Telephone Company. It quickly attracted many of Bell's subscribers, setting off fierce price competition. Conflicts heightened in 1905, when the Independent was purchased by Warren W. Finney, an ambitious young newcomer to Emporia.[51]

In these years, local government was much occupied with issues of physical improvements that created conflicts because they involved distributing limited resources among the various areas of town. The city council was inundated with petitions for new street lights, sidewalks, gutters, and sewers, and the needs of the business district seemed generally to win out over those of the neighborhoods, particularly in south Emporia. Demands for some improvements also pitted boosters who wanted to make Emporia as modern as possible against property owners who were reluctant to pay the costs of progress. When Emporia faced a smallpox epidemic in 1900, White argued that the town's reputation required that such outbreaks be prevented by improving its sanitation facilities. Noting that fewer than one-fifth of Emporia homes had sewer connections, he advocated that these be made compulsory: "Let the city make the connection and charge it to the taxes. This is a business proposition which must be met in a business way." In 1904 the city began to pave Emporia streets, stirring controversy because residents on the affected streets were charged a proportion of the costs.[52]

All of these efforts to expand public services were consistent with nineteenth-century boosterism. Simultaneously, however, boosters also began to demand new kinds of government involvement in economic affairs in order to aid local development. They couched their arguments in booster terms, and as the intensity of their appeals mounted they increasingly emphasized the moral dimension of the booster ethos. Thus would boosterism become progressivism.

As discriminatory rates and inadequate service continued to handicap their businesses, Emporians in ever larger numbers demanded effective railroad regulation. Jerry Evans was a case in point. Active in the state and national Lumbermen's Associations, he appeared frequently before the Interstate Commerce Commission to protest railroad rates for lumber. In 1902 he decided to take his cause to state government, and ran for the legislature in hopes of promoting stiffer regulation. When the *Gazette* praised him during the campaign as "one of the town's most energetic and progressive business men," the word "progressive" was clearly synonymous with "booster." He was elected, but the 1903 Kansas legislative session failed to produce any significant changes because state Republicans were embroiled in a power struggle between the new reform faction and the establishment. By the end of 1904, however, the challengers had won their first major victory with the election of Edward Hoch as governor—and William Allen White finally made his move to the reform alliance.[53]

During the legislative session that followed in early 1905, this spark of resentment against big business was fanned to a blaze of insurgency by independent Kansas oilmen's protests against Standard Oil. Oil fields in southeastern Kansas had boomed since 1900 but were now facing a disastrous drop in oil prices, which they blamed on Standard. Governor Hoch took up their cause, proposing that the state build its own refinery to compete with Standard. The issue quickly caught on among Kansans, who accepted Hoch's and the oilmen's arguments that Standard was a threat to everyone, consumer or small businessman. According to a letter from Mayor John Martin published in the *Topeka Daily Capital*, Emporians were united in favor of the plan to build a state refinery, and the county's new "business" legislators, George Plumb and C. A. Stannard, both voted for the bill.[54]

The debate over the state refinery catalyzed a statewide reform movement by setting the stage for an alliance between state government and local business against the domination of "foreign" corporations. In political terms, it drew many Kansas businessmen into the new insurgent Republican coalition. Foremost among the arguments made in favor of a state refinery was that it was not Populist "socialism," but the only way for respectable businessmen to protect their livelihoods from what Hoch termed the depredations of "great aggregations of capital, all of them socialistic in character."[55]

Ida M. Tarbell's *History of the Standard Oil Company,* which after appearing in installments in *McClure's Magazine* had been published as a book in 1904, gave credence to the independents' claims. It also aided the development of Kansas insurgency by pointing the way to a reform rhetoric with which to oppose the power of large corporations without questioning capitalism itself. Small businessmen could hardly attack the basis of the economic system, as many Populists had done. But they could condemn the "trusts" if they were somehow in defiance of the moral injunctions of the booster ethos. Tarbell's *History* documented Standard's contempt for norms of fair economic competition. She also repeatedly emphasized that it had been the independent oilmen, not Standard, who had been true boosters, risking all to settle the frontier and nurture their new communities.[56]

Tarbell visited Kansas to report on the conflict between the independents and Standard for *McClure's,* and while visiting the Whites in Emporia gave a "stirring" address at the Normal School. The *Gazette* used the occasion to counter conservative Republican charges that the present unrest was no different from Populist "demagoguery." This movement, it argued, was due to a rise in the "moral sense of the people" based on new "public information given by writers like Miss Tarbell." Her *History* was "fair, unbiased, carefully thought out, verified by sworn testimony and composed without hysterics." In contrast to Populist propaganda, it implied, her story "did not inflame the people," but "informed them." At the same time, it had irrefutably documented the "story of the life of a powerful financial creature without soul, endowed only with brains, bereft of conscience." White further emphasized the moral dimension of the conflict by reprinting an editorial from the Iola *Register* that argued that the question was "as much a moral issue as it is a financial one." Tarbell, it said, had shown that Standard's history was "covered all over with crime against the moral law."[57]

Insurgency gathered further momentum in 1906, when business and political leaders from throughout the state launched the Kansas Civic Voters League to take on the railroads. Its president was J. S. George, a Hutchinson wholesaler and head of the Kansas Federation of Commercial Interests, which had long advocated rate regulation. Prominent among the league's founders was J. E. Evans of Emporia. Its members included Kansas businessmen and shippers who were united by common resentment of the preference given to Kansas City enterprises in rates and services. They planned to push for railroad reform planks in the Republican platform at the state convention in May.[58]

Evans pressed White to join the movement, but it also appealed to the latter as a businessman paying high railroad rates for newsprint. After the league's creation, White wrote George about his idea to "enlist the newspapers of Kansas" in the struggle: "It seems to me that there are a dozen papers in Kansas of somewhat more than local influence who would be willing to publicly support the League." Like White, publishers of these new progressive newspapers had been freed from Republican party control by increased circulation and advertising revenues. They were now in a position to use their powers of publicity to circumvent the conservative party leadership by reaching out to "the people" directly.[59]

In March the *Gazette* proclaimed it the duty of "every well informed man or woman" in Emporia to attend an organizational meeting for a local branch of the league. He reiterated the difference between this movement and Populism: *this* was the response of the "thinking," "conservative element of the American people" to increased information about "the encroachments of organized corporate capital."

> . . . the best brains of the honest cautious sane, American citizenship must be enlisted in this struggle or it will be lost to the people. The men leading this movement in Kansas are men of that sort. They are not fanatics. They are not cranks. They are business men whose sincerity of purpose may not be questioned.

A few days later he continued, "Don't you think a thing that interests the greatest shippers in Kansas, the wholesale grocers, the cattle shippers, the wholesale implement man and miller, would interest you? Don't you know we are all in the same boat?"[60]

At the Republican convention, the league lost the battle to place antirailroad measures in the party platform, and the reformers turned to extraparty channels. They reorganized as the Kansas Republican League, popularly known as the Square Deal Republican Club. Its executive committee included both of Lyon County's state legislators, C. A. Stannard and George Plumb. Both men were stockmen, and Plumb was also president of the Kansas Live Stock Growers Association. As White had suggested, sympathetic newspapers promoted the league and compiled a pamphlet stating the positions of Republican candidates on issues of railroad regulation. Called *The Square Deal Handbook*, it was printed on the high-speed presses of the Topeka *Mail*, a mass-circulation weekly newspaper published by Arthur Capper. Finally, the league organized a rally in Topeka, for which White arranged an appearance by Robert M. La Follette, the Wisconsin senator who was publicly bucking the Republican party establishment.[61]

Characteristically, White threw all his energies into the league. Just as he had done for the street fair and the Orient Railroad, he simultaneously organized events and validated them by orchestrating the press coverage. He wrote a friend at the *Kansas City Star* to criticize its lack of coverage of "this Kansas situation": "Unless I am fooled . . . there is the blamedest explosion fizzing in the fuse out here that the state has seen since 1890. . . . It seems to me that the Star is missing some good stuff by not sending a man out to report this thing."[62]

Once he had broken with the Republican leadership, White unleashed antipartisan rhetoric that he had previously reserved for Populists. He celebrated the league in *Gazette* editorials as an uprising of "the people" against "the politicians" who were in cahoots with corporations seeking unfair advantages. Again he insisted that there was an essential difference between this movement and Populism: "The curious thing about this movement is that it does not interest what may be called the ne'er-do-wells of any community. It appeals to the middle classes. . . . It is a queer manifestation of the growth of the spirit of kindness and decency in American politics."[63]

Meanwhile, this spirit did not prevent the emergence in Emporia of a heated controversy over the future of the municipally owned electric plant. This conflict for the first time pitted White against his erstwhile booster allies over differing ideas about the best way to promote the town's welfare. Many business leaders were convinced that the thing Emporia most needed was a trolley system, and they were willing to give up municipal ownership of the electric plant to get it. But White had become just as firmly convinced that municipal ownership of public utilities was the key to both equity and local self-determination.

After several years of fruitless efforts to interest investors in building a streetcar line in Emporia, leaders of the Business Men's Association concluded that they could secure one only by offering ownership of the town's electric plant into the bargain. When the idea was first proposed in 1906, White warned his readers, "Don't Be Fooled." Only through municipal ownership could the people "say what the price of light shall be."[64]

When the city council seemed amenable to selling, White raised the same principle of participatory democracy that was being upheld by the Kansas Civic Voters League to circumvent the power of the Republican organization. He argued that the matter should be submitted to a citizens' referendum, because "the plant belongs to the people and not to the council. . . . To sell it without consulting the people at a special election would be morally a crime that would follow a man as long as he lived in this town—even though he had the law for it in a stack of law books a mile high."[65]

To support his point, White surveyed businessmen on Commercial Street. A slim majority sided with him, but, significantly, Mit Wilhite and Jerry Evans opposed him and strongly advocated selling. Most who favored sale did so because they believed that getting a street railway was essential to the town's growth, although a few also advocated the principle of private ownership. W. W. Finney argued, "I believe I can run this telephone system better and more economically than a municipality can, and it is the same way with the electric plant." Opponents of selling the plant expressed fears of losing control to "outsiders": grain dealer G. I. Bontecou said, "Unless we [own the plant], it gives those outsiders too much of a chance to hold up the city." And lumberman Carl Ballweg stated, "I don't see any reason for giving it to outsiders to hold us up." The vast majority favored having a referendum on the question.[66]

The matter rested there for the time being, but for several years it remained very much in the air. The demand for electricity continued to increase and to require further investment to expand capacity. In late 1907 White launched a one-man editorial campaign to head off the demand to sell the plant by making the municipal government more innovative. In several successive *Gazette* issues he published front-page articles highlighted in large boxes, scolding the city government for its lack of action on important energy problems. He lamented the council's failure to bring natural gas to Emporia: "Why do people leave Emporia every month to live in natural gas towns? Because living is cheaper and more comfortable than it is here. . . . It is all right to keep Emporia a clean town. But in keeping Emporia a clean town, let us see to it that we are not merely washing a corpse." He also chided the city's "unspeakably stupid and extravagant" management of public utilities for failing to institute innovations like selling steam from the pumping station for heat.

> This is no dream. What we are doing now is merely backwoods business. The electric light and water works plants of other towns sell heat, and there is no reason why Emporia should stay in the tall timber of old fogyism. The thing to do is to pinch the sleep out of ourselves—to keep abreast of the times—to build a city here, and not jog along in a rut.[67]

When the issue of selling the plant came up again in 1908, White argued that to sell the plant would be both unjust and backward. It was unfair "to make the people pay for the street car losses by increases in lights and power." And "the municipal ownership of electric lights is along the line of progress. . . . To turn this town over to another company . . . would be to put the clock back in this town a dozen years." Behind the scenes, he was also trying, without success, to head off the issue by attracting an interurban streetcar line.[68]

White's criticism of the town's administration as "backwoods" and his advocacy of municipal ownership as "progressive" underline his continuing adherence to the booster belief that a community must keep abreast of the latest social developments to keep up with its competitors. He differed with his opponents over means, not ends. At the same time that he broke with his colleagues on the issue of the electric plant, he joined with them in promoting yet another civic improvement that has also been identified as progressive: the commission form of city government.

By 1907, business leaders and journalists in many American cities and towns were vying to demonstrate their "progressive" spirit by reorganizing their municipal governments along "business lines." Although the idea of the city commission originated in Galveston, Texas, as an efficiency measure in the wake of its disastrous 1901 flood, the idea did not spread beyond the South until Des Moines, Iowa, added the initiative, referendum, and recall to the package. Like the period as a whole, the "Des Moines Idea" was a mixed bag of elitist, corporatist, and democratic elements that boosters touted as the latest essential civic improvement.[69]

The Emporia Business Men's Association began to push for the reform early in 1907, when it dispatched a delegation to Topeka to urge that enabling legislation include cities of Emporia's size. Jerry Evans headed a committee to draft the appropriate legislation. The Current Club hosted a public debate on the commission; a vote taken afterward favored adopting the system "overwhelmingly."[70]

White was at first cool to the idea, commenting in the *Gazette* only that it "is being considered generally by advanced thinkers in municipal government." He came out in favor of the idea a few days later, saying that it would do away with ward politics and "make it possible to get high grade progressive men to devote their time to the town." He grew increasingly enthusiastic about the idea, and by October was calling it "a business proposition in which every citizen is vitally interested." He employed the analogy between a corporation and municipal government that was frequently invoked in discussion of the system: "Every taxpaying citizen of Emporia is a shareholder in an important enterprise—an enterprise involving a waterworks system, sewerage system, electric light plant, and a dozen other varieties of property which may be ranked as valuable assets of incumbrances, according to the management thereof." The city's increasing responsibility for public services made the commission system's promise of streamlining management of local government more desirable. A major reason for White's support, however, was its inclusion of measures providing for direct democracy. These had grown dear to his heart—and he hoped they would help block the sale of the electric plant.[71]

When the plan came before the voters early in 1910 the *Gazette* mounted a promotional campaign on its behalf, printing a standing editorial endorsing and explaining the measure and running daily front-page boxes featuring a wide range of arguments for it. The Current Club organized a public meeting to promote the measure. Although in some cities reorganization was opposed by labor groups and established politicians, there seems to have been little resistance to it in Emporia. The new system was approved in all wards by a vote of 1,047 to 213. If, as was the case in other cities, proponents of the change had hoped to ensure business domination in local government, they were disappointed. The three men elected to the first commission had previously been employed as a plasterer, a stonecutter, and a real estate agent; at least two were Democrats. Of the three defeated candidates, at least two were Republicans.[72]

The electric light plant issue soon began to heat up again, and once more White mounted a full *Gazette* publicity campaign, this time against selling the plant to private developers. Gathering evidence to prove that streetcar companies paid little in taxes, he wrote his former reporter Charles Vernon, now editing a paper in Manhattan, Kansas, that this conflict "has taken four times as much grit" as his reform battles in state politics. "No body cared particularly about that. But the Newmans, and Wilhite and George Jones and Cutler and Mr. Dunlap and all of the big financial influences in town are against me and against me pretty hard."[73]

This time, his energetic campaigning failed. His opponents mounted a lively campaign of their own, holding public meetings at the Whitley

Opera House to counter White's publicity machine. Mit Wilhite gave a rousing speech at the election-eve meeting, in which, according to the *Times*, "he mounted to the very heights of oratory and proceeded to 'skin' the opposition," particularly one "W.A." While claiming to favor municipal ownership of public utilities in principle, the Democratic *Times* argued that Emporia's need for streetcars "is a fact, not a cherished theory." Because "local capitalists" had failed to take up the matter, this was the only way to get a streetcar system. Turning White's populist rhetoric on its head, it argued, "The street car is everybody's. Those who have carriages or automobiles do not need it." Moreover, "the construction of a car line will furnish employment for a lot of laboring men who want work. . . ." Emporians approved the sale by a three-to-two margin, and a year later the new streetcar company began service on Commercial Street and Twelfth Avenue. The enterprise was a financial failure, however, and never extended service to residential areas.[74]

By the close of the first decade of the twentieth century, both White and Emporia had set themselves on a path that some were beginning to call "progressive." Taken together, the campaigns that were waged and the changes that were accomplished suggest a progressive spirit abroad in Emporia. But the pattern blurs upon closer inspection. Few Emporians backed every reform, and many who assumed "progressive" positions on some issues abandoned them on others. Nonetheless, as they promoted these changes, Emporians adapted booster arguments to contemporary purposes, fashioning a common language with which to explain and justify civic reform. It was by no means a coherent or internally consistent philosophy, but it had strong resonance for many Americans seeking to reconcile change with inherited values.

As a local booster and the publisher of the *Gazette*, White used this common language to promote specific goals in Emporia and in Kansas. As a nationally known author, he also applied the rhetoric of booster progressivism to a wide range of social and political developments across America. In so doing he would encourage a belief that these changes were part of a unified national movement. He accomplished this by abstracting from his experiences in reforming Emporia, obscuring the conflicts and contradictions in the reality. For White and his national readers, Emporia would become a model progressive community.

6

Spokesman for Community

In 1910 William Allen White responded to a colleague's request for a photograph by sending two pictures. He explained,

> I don't seem to be able to get all my various split-up characters under one canvas. Of the two pictures that I am sending you one is Bill White of the Emporia Gazette who is rather handy in the fourth ward and sometimes does business on the county central committee, a good advertising solicitor and sometimes takes a hand at reporting and is not highly regarded in our best circles. The other picture is the statesman who has terminal facilities at Topeka and traffic agreements in New York.
>
> Now about the author; I have never been able to get him before a camera. He is no friend of mine and I have never seen him. . . . His work, when it is good, surprises me as much as anybody. I should like to have his photograph as well as you, but I have never got it.[1]

William Allen White the author may have been an enigma to himself, but it was this persona that was most widely known outside Kansas and that speaks most directly to us today through his novels, essays, and innumerable magazine articles. His career as a nationally recognized author emerged simultaneously with, and drew upon, his roles as a prosperous businessman, defender of local righteousness, and insurgent politician. At first his authorial ambitions were primarily literary, as he emulated the local-color short stories and dialect poetry that were popular in the 1880s. After "What's the Matter with Kansas?" he became known as a spokesman for the Midwest and a knowledgeable observer of political affairs. The middle-class readers of the new popular magazines like *McClure's* and *Collier's* appreciated White's skill in translating recent events into familiar and generally reassuring terms. As he became identified with reform causes during the first decade of the new century, these interpretations reflected his conviction that the many campaigns then under way were part of a unified movement, a movement that would later be labeled progressivism.

Just as White adapted booster rhetoric to advocate his local reform causes, his writing for a national audience underwent a parallel transfiguration. In his political reporting, essays, and novels, White's interpretation of turn-of-the-century America can best be understood as a projection upon the national scene of an idealized vision of the small town that had its roots in the booster ethos.

After "What's the Matter with Kansas?" brought White to their attention in 1896, editors of many national magazines looked to him as a spokesman for the Midwest. For the rest of his life he would be called upon to represent "public opinion" in the nation's heartland, just as small-town editors have typically been the first persons consulted by outsiders seeking to size up local sentiments. *Collier's,* for example, in 1903 solicited five hundred words from White on "What the West Thinks of the Trusts Now."[2]

At the same time, White became known in literary circles as a new western exponent of realism. In reviewing White's first book of stories, *The Real Issue,* in the lierary/humor magazine *Life,* Robert Bridges wrote that many of the stories contained "real Kansas" in both its despair and "the aggressive hopefulness and good sense that will ultimately be its salvation." The book's second edition added the subtitle "A Book of Kansas Stories."[3]

As the demand for his writing grew, so did White's network of literary and journalistic acquaintances. Through his first publisher, Chauncey Williams, he met many luminaries of Chicago's flourishing literary scene. Ever the energetic self-promoter, he invited himself to visit his poetic model James Whitcomb Riley. When the two hit it off, White asked Riley to put in a good word for him with William Dean Howells.[4]

His literary world expanded yet further in June 1897, when he visited New York and was taken under the collective editorial wing of *McClure's Magazine.* Since its appearance in 1893, the magazine had become one of the most popular and prosperous of a new generation of mass-circulation magazines. Its editors, S. S. McClure and John Phillips, and many of its staff were transplanted midwesterners who thought of their magazine as reaching beyond the Appalachians for its readers, unlike its eastern-oriented "genteel" predecessors. White's vivid, vernacular style was just what they wanted to address this audience. As Phillips and senior staff writer Ida M. Tarbell guided the awestruck small-town editor around the metropolis, the group became fast friends. White explained, "They thought as we thought in Emporia about men and things." Tarbell recalled White:

> He was a little city-shy then, or wanted us to think so. As I was one of the official entertainers of the group, it occasionally fell to me to "take him by the hand," as he put it, and show him the town. I could have hardly had a more delightful experience. He judged New York by Kansas standards, and New York usually suffered.[5]

As Tarbell's comment suggests, White may have found it to his advantage to play something of a country-mouse role when visiting his urban colleagues. Certainly he learned early on that many of them envied him his small-town life, with its more relaxed pace and lack of urban vexations. Soon after his first visit to Chicago, he wrote rather self-consciously to Chauncey Williams of their contrasting longings:

> There you are up in the city . . . surrounded by the machines and the contrivance man has made, and the hollowness and emptiness of it all throbbing like a drumbeat in your ears, and here I am sitting at my little old desk, the

door of my office opening on the street and the spring ebbing and flowing on the soft breath that flutters in, bearing the purring noises of the quiet rural street. . . . And I want to come up to be with you and you want to come down and be with me. It is strange the unrest that sometimes—always I guess—possesses us.[6]

Many of these new friends had grown up in rural or small-town America, and though their careers had brought them to the cities, many of them were not comfortable with the crowded, impersonal conditions of their new homes. For example, both Tarbell and Phillips of *McClure's* bought country houses, to which they retreated as often as possible, and staffer Ray Stannard Baker quickly moved to the suburbs to avoid urban congestion. White seemed a welcome tie to a life they had lost, and they urged him never to leave Emporia. For Tarbell, White's "crowning achievement" would be "remaining first, last, and always the editor of the Emporia *Gazette*."[7]

City-bred friends like Theodore Roosevelt were similarly attracted to White's connection with a way of life that seemed more authentic than their own. When Richard Watson Gilder proposed that Owen Wister write Roosevelt's biography for *Century*, Roosevelt replied that White would do it better because he "has lived near the rough side of things." Roosevelt enjoyed presenting White to his provincial eastern friends as a typical specimen of the Middle American. He once invited White and John Singer Sargent to lunch and pressed White to talk about Emporia. "I gave a picture of western town culture," White recalled, "that I am sure John Sargent never imagined and could scarcely believe."[8]

Ever sensitive to the expectations of others, White was doubtless aware of the benefits of playing upon his small-town roots and his preference for town life when he visited his urban friends. Yet he was not merely posing. His increasingly frequent trips to Chicago, New York, and Washington convinced him that the city could not be his permanent home. In 1904 he praised stories by the young writer Dorothy Canfield: "I particularly like the one about the fellow who got home sick for the country. I never go to the city but what I have that feeling come over me. I am a born Country Jake." He also asserted that "a man in my business" could not grow in the city. Even his exposure to urban "culture," such as a performance of Shaw's *Man and Superman* that he saw in 1905, deepened his distaste for sophisticated city ways. He found it "so obviously clever that it tired me," he wrote Sallie. "Also it was basically nasty though few will see it so."[9]

Sallie White encouraged her husband in these views. In 1903, when McClure made one of his frequent attempts to lure White to New York, offering him the editorship of a political weekly, Sallie made it clear that "we are *not* going to New York to live for Sam McClure's Weekly—that goes even without saying."[10]

White's varied roles in Emporia gave him special knowledge that contributed to his literary career. He proved adept at translating this knowledge into terms a national audience could appreciate. In 1899 McClure's newspaper syndicate published White's portrait of Fred Funston, hero of the Philippine conflict, billing it as "the first really accurate and striking story" on Funston, because the writer was "an old school-mate and comrade." Between 1899 and 1901 he published in *Scribner's* a series of short stories based upon his experiences in the back rooms of "practical politics." These were collected in *Stratagems and Spoils,* published by Scribner's in 1901. In the summer of 1900 he began to write for *McClure's* a series of portraits of prominent political figures that drew generously upon his knowledge of the characters of political men. These pieces were ideally suited to the *McClure's* human-interest formula, for although they reported the facts of each man's life, their predominant motive was to reveal the innermost personalities of their subjects.[11]

After Roosevelt's accession to the presidency, White was increasingly asked by national magazine editors to report on national politics. These requests resulted not only from his presumed access to the new president, but also from his ability to blend realistic political reporting—often from an "insider's" perspective—with sage yet optimistic interpretations that appealed to his middle-class audiences. The *Saturday Evening Post* put it well in late 1902 in promoting White's upcoming series of reports on Washington politics:

> There are perhaps three or four men in the length and breadth of the country who can write on political topics as sanely, shrewdly and clearly as Mr. White; but not one of them possesses in like degree his fine native humor or his ability to wring the last drop of human interest out of his subject and into his writing. Mr. White has also the rare gift for stripping a complex theme of its non-essentials and showing it forth in its simplest terms.[12]

A gifted political commentator, White also became known in these years as a spokesman for a particular way of life: that of the midwestern small town. Eastern publishers who subscribed to the *Gazette* to read White's political editorials began to note his comment on local life as well. Frank Doubleday clipped such pieces and sent them to his colleagues Edward Bok of *Ladies' Home Journal* and George H. Lorimer of the *Saturday Evening Post,* who agreed that these "sketches of *Folks*" would appeal to their audiences. In late 1902 Doubleday offered to publish a volume of White's editorial sketches on local people and "things as they look in Emporia." White apparently doubted the value of such work, but Doubleday persisted: "I am surprised to see you take such a provincial view. If it's good stuff, it's good stuff, no matter where printed or how printed."[13]

White's own travels out of Emporia and his growing awareness of his urban colleagues' fascination with the small town gave him a new perspective on his accustomed way of life. He began to abstract from their immediate contexts aspects of community life that he had heretofore taken for granted. Subsequently he would offer to his national audience an idealized image of the small town as the embodiment of essential virtues, from neighborliness and equality to unity, service, and morality. Increasingly he would present these small-town virtues as characteristic of the animating spirit of the various reform causes of the time. Though they would sometimes be couched in the fashionable language of evolutionary social thought, his ideas remained rooted in the maxims of the booster ethos.

To make this continuity clear, boosterism's central tenets must be more precisely defined. The booster ethos was a set of closely interrelated assumptions about the nature of community and economic growth that were so embedded in the small-town, middle-class culture of White's day that he treated them as self-evident truths. These assumptions were rarely, if ever, expressed in the abstract, but they permeated booster rhetoric.

Although it clearly served the interests of local business by positing economic growth as the primary good and businessmen as the town's natural leaders, boosterism insisted that prosperity and growth involved the community as a whole rather than the actions of isolated individuals. Ignoring the radical individualism of classical liberalism, boosterism assumed, as had its Puritan antecedents, that prosperity depended upon the nonmaterial, even spiritual condition of the community as a whole. In this sense, boosterism was fundamentally idealist. Deviance from moral norms, whether by a philandering Dr. Meffert or a beer-drinking Eagle, could be tolerated only at peril to the community's moral health and *therefore* its economic well-being.[14]

In a society that still lacked powerful institutions of government, there was some justification for these concerns. Much of the day-to-day functioning of the small town depended upon citizens' voluntary actions. As in the polis of the classical republican vision, the well-ordered community required a loyal, unified populace willing to sacrifice self-interest to the common good.

The booster's primary means to cultivate these necessary virtues was exhortation. In the nineteenth century the local newspaper had taken on the role of defining the common good and preaching these virtues. From his earliest days in Emporia, White had proclaimed that the mental and moral condition of the people was the precondition for all success. In June 1895 he described a flourishing Emporia as "the best town in Kansas" and reported that "the reason for all this prosperity is very simple. The people of this town are honest hard-working people. They are a church building school protecting people. . . . That kind of people always prospers."[15]

A second basic assumption of the booster ethos was that the local community was a self-contained, interdependent whole. Boosters depicted their towns as networks of households, each exchanging its particular good or service for those of every other household. Because of this reciprocity, all economic interests were identical: what benefited one would eventually add to the prosperity of all. Within this system, money merely facilitated exchange, like the body's circulatory system.[16]

This interdependent system would break down if money was allowed to flow out of it. Lacking formal means to prevent residents from trading outside the community, boosters relied instead upon each citizen's loyalty,

a virtue that they preached unceasingly. Throughout his career White proclaimed the virtue and necessity of demonstrating one's loyalty by "buying
at home." In late 1899 he predicted that Emporia would soon gain new
industries if its townspeople would "patronize home industries."

> Enough money is sent out of town every year for flour, cigars, toilet prepara-
> tions, cough syrups, blood medicines, iron work, upholstery, etc., to bring the
> new buildings and fill them with prosperous people. Help yourself by helping
> the town and remember that every cent counts and will help make the grand
> total.[17]

Because of the importance of loyalty within this interdependent community, nowhere was it preached more ardently than in that classic of
small-town journalism, the jeremiad against the mail-order business. Long
before and long after his conversion to progressivism, White returned to
this subject. In 1901 he pronounced that the woman who bought a mail-
order house "hurts this town more than a saloon. She sends money out of
town that should keep Emporia people at work: she breeds idleness, the
mother of crime."[18] One of the most vivid examples of his mastery of the
genre was a campaign he mounted in June 1905. His rhetoric here demon-
strates the close connection within the booster ethos between economic
growth and the virtues of reciprocity, loyalty, and unity.

His first sermon on the subject stated the problem: "Emporia has fewer
people in it than it had two years ago." Then he revealed the cause: "Emporia is suffering from the mail order disease."

> Emporia sends enough money away to mail order houses to support two more
> drygoods houses, another grocery store and a big clothing store. These stores
> would support twenty-five families, and they would support five or six others.
> The man who sends a dollar to a mail order house is a bad citizen no matter
> how he wiggles out of it.[19]

In subsequent issues White elaborated upon this opening statement in
ever more vivid terms. The mail-order trade was a sign of moral decay, of
the "dry rot" of disunity in the civic edifice. "The first sign of the dry rot
in a town is that it runs to mail order business." That things were reaching
an acute stage in Emporia was indicated by the fact that even the merchants and, worst of all, the town councilmen were doing it.

> Sears, Roebuck and the mail order people are running this town. The people
> who pay the taxes and run the stores are getting the worst of it, and the
> merchants who have to build the churches and school houses and pay preach-
> ers are complaining about hard times that they and their wives are many of
> them making.
> . . . The only way we can build up Emporia is to pull together. A dollar
> saved in Chicago is lost to Emporia. The dollar that goes to the Emporia
> grocery store or dry goods store, stays in town, and helps to pay Emporia debts,
> and make Emporia business. But the mail order dollar bids good-bye to the
> town and its prosperity at the city limits, and never comes back.[20]

This free course in booster economics was capped two days later in the strongest terms in an editorial, "Mail Order Leeches":

> The man who buys his goods of a mail order house, and expects his neighbors in Emporia to buy goods of him, or to buy labor of him or to buy professional service of him is economically a leech. He is sucking industrial blood out of the town and gives none back. He sends his profits out of town like a Chinaman, and has no more right to a standing in the community than a foreigner. We are all neighbors industrially in this town and the man who sends away for his goods is not one of us. He is of another industrial system, and deserves no man's support in Emporia. . . .[21]

White's denunciation of the mail-order patron as "not one of us" and deserving of "no man's support in Emporia" reveals a second means, after exhortation, of promoting proper booster virtues: the threat of rejection by "public opinion." Boosters relied upon the fusion of personal identity and public reputation common to small towns, assuming that the fear of public shaming would inspire observance of the proper virtues even among the unconverted. As will be illustrated more fully in the next chapter, White often used his newspaper to shame errant citizens, or threaten to do so. In his "dry rot" editorial he condemned city policeman Al Randolph for having the effrontery to wear a "mail order policeman's uniform": "If the editor of this paper were mayor—which Heaven forbid—Al Randolph would be fired on the spot."[22]

The booster connection between unity and prosperity was manifested in the insistence that the community present a common face to the outside world, especially during movements to promote economic development. During the drive to bring the Orient Railroad to Emporia, White had demanded, "There should be neither cliques, factions nor rings" in the town's pursuit of the railroad, and he attempted to suppress opposition from the Second Avenue residents.[23]

Given its emphasis on demonstrated loyalty to the community, the civic virtues of boosterism could not exist in private. The citizen's participation in public celebrations or service in civic organizations not only promoted specific practical ends but, ultimately was an end in itself. Universal public activism was the best way that a community could demonstrate to the outside world—and to itself—the predominance of booster virtues. For these reasons, White reveled in promoting public occasions like the street fair, when "every one did his part" and "no one shirked," and when the component virtues of the booster ethos were momentarily made vividly manifest. Service was the immanence of the booster spirit.[24]

This booster ethos formed the core of White's social thought. He had espoused his booster belief in community interdependence and the moral basis of prosperity and had advocated the cardinal booster virtues of loyalty, unity, and service well before his national writing career took off in the first decade of the twentieth century. Although his broadening experiences and widening range of personal contacts in this period may have changed his attitudes toward specific reform issues, his emerging progressive reform philosophy remained well within the booster ethos. He simply integrated the fashionable ideas and language of progressive social thought into this structure.

White could graft these ideas onto the booster ethos because a vision remarkably similar to the booster belief in the interdependent local community dominated social thought in the early twentieth century. A conception of society as an organism, which like other organisms was subject to evolution, had challenged the individualism of nineteenth-century philosophy. A number of American intellectuals such as John Dewey and Jane Addams had grown up in small towns or rural communities and fashioned philosophies that promised to extend the remembered communal cohesion of their childhood to a national plane. Influenced by Herbert Spencer's ideas of social evolution, these intellectuals argued that people and institutions alike were part of a unified society, their very existence dependent upon their connection to the whole. Choosing an optimistic reading of Darwin's theory of evolution, they also equated evolutionary change with progress, and exulted in its inevitability.[25]

White does not seem to have read the most sophisticated statements of these organicist evolutionary ideas, but he was aware of currents of thought as they appeared in the magazines and more popular sociological works. He later recalled having read the "better known works of Herbert Spencer" around the turn of the century. Spencer's ideas about social evolution and his organicism seem to have merged easily with White's booster beliefs in local growth and interdependence.[26]

He might also have been inspired to translate his booster rhetoric into the language of evolutionary organicism by reading Charlotte Perkins Gilman's *Human Work*, which McClure, Phillips & Co. published in 1904. White considered it "a great book" and told Phillips he would like to review it if he could "find a place to put it." *Human Work* was Gilman's attempt to summarize her philosophy, which she had been developing for years in numerous books, magazine articles, and public lectures. She argued that society was literally an evolving organism and that human consciousness itself was a social creation. Human beings shared in the widening social consciousness brought by evolution only through their participation in the life of the whole—through their work.[27]

Although Gilman considered progress inevitable in the long run, social problems existed because people persisted in perceiving reality in terms of autonomous individuals. Poverty and injustice would thus be eliminated through a kind of cognitive conversion, in which one finally perceived the organic nature of society and acted accordingly. Individual unhappiness, too, was caused by the inability to understand one's true place as a participant "in that huge, thrilling, organic life in which the individual thrives unconscious—of which the world is lodged in each of us." Ultimately Gilman's vision was a spiritual, even religious one, in which true happiness was achieved when an individual felt as one with the forces of progress:

"in the ceaseless development of that measureless vitality, this vast, ever-increasing Social Life, to feel, now and again—always oftener,—the distant music of the universe grow clearer. . . ."[28]

White, Gilman, and the other progressive thinkers departed from Spencerian social thought in rejecting Spencer's materialistic assumption that social cohesion resulted automatically from functional interdependence. Instead, they fashioned an idealistic variant of evolution in which true community was achieved through shared values and sentiments. In making this adaptation, progressive philosophers drew upon European social science, but for White the sources seem closer to hand. He later counted Emerson, Whitman, and Dickens, along with Spencer, as his "spiritual inspirations" at the turn of the century. But underlying these sources was the booster assumption that civic health rested primarily upon the "spirit" of the community.[29]

White's progressive ideas, like his booster assumptions, were generally embedded, as interpretations, in his reporting on particular events. As a free-lance writer, White was well aware that his work must respond to the interests of readers, as these were determined by magazine editors. His style of lively, "realistic" reporting framed by interpretations that fit with his readers' assumptions was just what the new popular magazines like *McClure's, Saturday Evening Post,* and *Collier's* wanted. It was this ability to tease out a theme immanent in day-to-day reality to which the editors of *Saturday Evening Post* referred when they spoke of White's "gift for stripping a complex theme of its non-essentials and showing it forth in its simplest terms." These terms, more often than not, expressed values that were familiar to his middle-class audiences, perhaps because many were themselves current or former residents of small towns.[30]

He felt less comfortable with the more abstract and restrained style of the older genteel magazines. He complained that the *Atlantic* editors had removed "all the best things" from his 1897 article, "apparently with an oyster-fork." And he admitted to Theodore Roosevelt that "a certain self-consciousness" made it hard for him to write for the *Century.*[31]

White wrote a series of articles for the *Post* about the 1902–1903 session of Congress, which constituted a common man's primer on the actual, "inside" workings of government. Yet his characterizations of men and institutions consistently assessed their moral qualities. No muckraker, he assured his readers that the works of the House were "wholesome and fair" and that senators were "representative American citizens." About Congress as a whole, he concluded that somehow "in the process of political crystallization Nature rejects the impurities and draws together by almost divine prescience those things that are clean and of good report, and makes them the ultimate legal expression of the American spirit." As for the president, White characterized Roosevelt as "an attorney for the people" who acted according to "the law of conscience and common sense" rather than "written law." He lauded the new Department of Commerce and Labor as the "Fair-Play Department," whose guarantee of publicity for corporate actions would ensure their honesty and fairness. Although the new Commissioner of Corporations was not given the power to compel arbitration in strikes, White argued that "he can give the public the real facts," and that "public sentiment is a compulsory arbitration board from which there is no appeal. . . ."[32]

Similarly, an article written one year later in a more muckraking style for *McClure's Magazine* framed its detailed recounting of facts about fraud in the post office with an introduction and conclusion that established the real meaning of the episode. Roosevelt's handling of the case, according to White, was "the most important manifestation" of the "moral uplift" the president was providing the nation. Conversely, his actions were embodiments of "the visible growth of moral perception" that was "springing from the people."[33]

By 1905—when he had emerged fully as a crusader for state and local righteousness—White also sought to express in more explicit terms his understanding of the underlying meaning of the events he was observing. He asserted a new faith, not only in reform, but also that there was a spiritual force guiding the changes, providing an underlying unity to the disparate outward forms. To express these ideas he chose as his forum the genteel *Atlantic,* for which he had not written since 1897. "The Golden Rule," which appeared in October 1905, was his first attempt "to set down what seems to be the current economic morals of the country at this time." In keeping with its social-evolutionary basis, it began with a pseudoanthropological description of the moral development of humankind since it had begun to live in groups. White traced this as the slow, painful growth of a "spirit of obligation" as manifested in "the smaller matters of their daily lives, in their simple relations with their fellows." Encoded in the golden rule, this growing recognition of one's "duty to others" was to White the motive force of all human progress. This duty represented the boosters' virtues of loyalty and service raised to a higher plane.

Further growth would be necessary if the current age's problems of the maldistribution of wealth were to be solved. White asserted the organicist view that "wealth is the natural accretion of all the people" and that for any great fortune it could be shown "that the people were to a great extent partners in its accumulation." But the solution of these problems would not be achieved "until there is developed among the masses a kindness and an honesty in dealing with one another, in the minutiae of daily life, broader than the standard of humanity and integrity of American life today. . . ." Nonetheless, in the loosening of the party system in politics and the new prominence in public life of "the man of ideals, the man of culture, the man who appeals to the spiritual side of the people," he saw evidence that "the American people during recent years have been growing in mental and moral vision, and in spiritual force." Ultimately, like Charlotte Perkins Gilman, he considered such progress inevitable, for "all we know of life is that Christ's teaching tallies with some great force that is moving the current, and that he who follows that teaching moves with the current, and not against it."[34]

Through the essay's evolutionary drapings one can see distinctly the structure of the booster ethos: the belief in community interdependence; the call for reciprocity, loyalty, unity, and service; and the emphasis upon the spiritual basis of all progress. As a good booster, White was attempting in his essay to make his vision a reality through exhortation of his fellow citizens. As he had done with his street fair in Emporia, he also hoped to foster a new civic spirit by proclaiming it already a reality. He did not use the word "progressive," but he was striving to convince his readers that there was a new spirit abroad in America. Later many people would come to equate this "spirit" with the progressive movement.

In 1906 White joined John Phillips, Ida Tarbell, and a number of other former *McClure's* staff members in purchasing the *American Magazine*. The group hoped to, as White put it later, "carry the torch of an evolutionary revolution to the world." White developed the ideas of his *Atlantic* piece further in an essay in the *American Magazine* entitled "The Partnership of Society." He originally wrote it as a commencement address, and the *American* editors rightly introduced it as more "a modern lay sermon" than an essay.[35]

This sermon elaborated upon the organicist principles he had introduced in "The Golden Rule." An isolated, "unorganized" human soul, he asserted, was "unthinkable." As important as the role of the individual "instinct of self-preservation" had been in evolution, there was another instinct, "the centripetal force of society, the instinct of race preservation," which had found its fulfillment in humankind. Since then, all civilizations have been experiments "in establishing justice between men," and even today the most modern issues are struggles for justice. But now, he insisted, though man has progressed far in the material realm, he must rediscover the instinct for "passionate service" that the primitive man once felt for his tribe. The "comforts of our complex life have deadened our hearts to what we should continually feel is the mainspring of that life—our debt to humanity." That debt could not be repaid with money. "Only by service to one's fellows can one call up from his soul the latent sense of duty to humanity which moves through this life of ours, and works among us for the promotion of eternal righteousness."[36]

The culmination of these attempts to express his progressive faith came in a book that combined concrete reporting with the abstractions of his essays. *The Old Order Changeth: A View of American Democracy* appeared first in 1909 as a series of articles in the *American Magazine*. There he surveyed the progress of reform efforts throughout the United States to demonstrate his thesis that they were all manifestations of the same "spiritual growth in the hearts of the American people." Unlike earlier articles in which he had discovered an underlying progressive trend within current events, White collected evidence to support his predefined theme. He chose the work's title before he began, and wrote to reformers and reform organizations requesting information about their activities. One form letter asking for information explained his intention of giving a "comprehensive view of the progress made in the various states in the last six or eight years. . . ."[37]

The opening chapter framed the rest of the book by presenting the steam engine as the symbolic source of present conflict because it had established a dialectic between democracy and capitalism. The advent of steam had lightened labor, thus providing time for reflection that gave rise to demands for democracy. On the other hand, it gave heightened power to capital, which became ever more greedy as it served only selfish ends. He emphasized here and throughout the book that the virtues and vices of capitalism did not reside in any one economic class, but were "a part of the public character." The present conflict between democracy and capital was "a struggle in every man's heart between the unselfish and the selfish instincts of his nature," a "contest in the heart of the common people."[38]

The second chapter traced the rise in the last half of the nineteenth century of an "extra-constitutional" government based on greed: the boss system. Perhaps in mitigation for his own participation in it, White emphasized that, whatever its wrongs, the system epitomized the state of morals of the day. In his solicitude for the needs of business, the boss "merely reflected his environment," and in favoring the rights of capital over human needs, the courts "merely saw as we all saw in those times."[39]

The first signs of change in public opinion came with the Spanish-American War, when "the spirit of sacrifice overcame the spirit of commercialism." Since then there had been, for the American people as for White himself, a "movement which indicates that in the soul of the people there is a conviction of their past unrighteousness." However it be labeled or in whatever form revealed, this movement "is one current in the thought of the people." The subsequent chapters documented this assertion by describing the achievements of various reform movements: institution of the secret ballot, direct primary, initiative, recall, and referendum; regulation of corporations; enforcement of prohibition; cleanup of urban corruption; improvement of education. He described the activities of myriad organizations from labor unions to conservation groups as illustrations "of what organized good will can do." He predicted that even the courts, which theretofore had been the greatest brake to the fulfillment of the public will, would eventually change to reflect "the moral impulse that is stirring in the nation." Steam, metaphorically understood, had wrought all these changes by expanding the people's consciousness. Mankind would conquer the dialectical dangers of steam "by no new set of morals, but by awakening to the widening life that steam has brought, and applying to that greater life his divinely given kindness."[40]

White's sermons on the spiritual meaning of the practical measures of his age contributed to the conviction that Americans were witnessing a unified, coherent groundswell of "public opinion." White himself became

identified nationally as a spokesman for that groundswell, or "movement."
In this way, he replicated his triumph of the street fair, when he had both
created an event and interpreted it.

The most beloved and influential of his writings for a national audience
were not his interpretive political reporting or his inspirational sermons,
however, but continued to be his descriptions of small-town life. These
portraits of Emporia—or thinly fictionalized versions thereof—served as
allegories for his progressive vision.

Early in 1905 White took up the idea that Frank Doubleday had proposed several years before of compiling a book of sketches of small-town
characters. He chose, not surprisingly, to write a fictional account of life as
seen through the window of a small-town newspaper office. The sketches
appeared serially that fall and winter in the *Saturday Evening Post* and
early in 1906 were published as a book, *In Our Town*.[41]

To people his stories, White drew liberally upon his colleagues at the
Gazette and his fellow citizens in Emporia, adding touches of fantasy and
whimsey and heavier doses of pathos. Many of his characters represent
familiar types—the unscrupulous speculators of bygone days, the vitriolic
partisan editor, the ambitious society hostesses, the all-knowing young reporter—to produce a composite portrait of small-town society. Because it
attempted to depict accurately the texure of daily life, *In Our Town* must
be classified as a work of realism. Like its successors by Sherwood Anderson
and Sinclair Lewis, it portrayed thwarted passions, social pretensions, and
everyday human hypocrisies. But, more akin to its near-namesake by Thornton Wilder, the author's attitude toward his subjects was one of compassion
and affection. White's keynote in the book was "kindness": it was the quality that enabled the members of his fictional community to live together in
relative peace despite their many failings, and it was the quality that he
hoped to instill in his readers. He concluded with a call for a broader consciousness of our commonality:

> Passing the office window every moment is someone with a story that should
> be told. . . . If each man or woman could understand that every other hu-
> man life is as full of sorrows, of joys, of base temptations, of heartaches and of
> remorse as his own, which he thinks so peculiarly isolated from the web of
> life, how much kinder, how much gentler he would be! And how much richer
> life would be for all of us![42]

Although the book paid little attention to politics and none to reform,
it did contain echoes of the ideas that White expressed nearly simultaneously in his essay on "The Golden Rule." Indeed, the book showed the
identity between his local boosterism and his broader "progressive" ideals.
He was at pains to emphasize that, though it might be divided into scores
of "crowds" for social purposes, there were no class divisions in his town,
where a young Welsh printer could acquire more general respect that a
foppish gentleman of leisure.

Though he underlined the townspeople's charity in their dealings with each other, White also vividly illustrated the power of public opinion, once righteously aroused, to punish unrepentant wrongdoers. "By the Rod of His Wrath" chronicled the ostracism of John Markley, a wealthy banker and once its most "prominent citizen," who cast aside his devoted but colorless wife for a lusty young divorcée. The community quietly but efficiently and implacably cut Markley out of its recognition, and, angry and unrepentant, he disintegrated psychologically and physically. The editor, speculating on the meaning of Markley's downfall, wondered

> whether or not the God that is the spirit of things at the base of this material world might not be indeed the spirit that moves men to execute His laws. . . . Was it God, moving in us, that punished Markley "by the rod of His wrath," that used our hearts as wireless stations for His displeasure to travel through, or was it the chance prejudice of a simple people?[43]

White clearly believed it was the former. This "spirit" he would elsewhere call public opinion.

The magazine- and book-reading public responded enthusiastically to *In Our Town*'s blend of realism and sentiment. It sold better than any of his previous works, and many ordinary Americans wrote to tell him how much they liked his stories. Newspaper editors and reporters commended the authenticity of his portrayal of their jobs. One reported that "you sketched our police and society reporters so accurately they were rather angry." Local-color writer Alice French praised him: "You do know the Middle West! . . . It is the real thing." Fellow writer-reformer Brand Whitlock commented, "You have put in it not only the life of your town, but the life of my town, and of all American towns. . . ." From the White House, Roosevelt lauded White's vision of the American small town: "The people you describe are the people that I know and the people that give me whatever of strength I have. . . . you write in a [spirit] as far removed as possible from the spirit of the muckraker, and you portray a community in which it is evident that there is a spirit that can be appealed to when the need arises. . . ."[44]

Roosevelt and White agreed that such a spirit was typically American, but both tended to view it as more native to the small town than to the metropolis. Even as, in his more abstract statements of his progressive faith, White expressed his belief that a spirit of righteousness was arising throughout the nation, he revealed an ambivalence about the promise of urban America in his discussions of small-town life. He increasingly portrayed the small town—where everyone knew each other, the essential "comforts" of life were available to all, and a rough social equality prevailed—as the natural home of progressive virtues.

White's emergence as a progressive subtly altered his thinking about the small town. Increasingly his *Gazette* editorials celebrated the simple things of the town's life as often as they advocated reform or growth. When it suited his rhetorical purposes, White had long celebrated the homely graces of life in Emporia in the *Gazette*. But his involvement in progressive causes heightened his awareness of questions of quality of life rather than growth for the sake of growth alone. In 1905, about the same time he was writing the sketches for *In Our Town,* he related in the *Gazette* the sad plight of an Emporian who had moved to Kansas City.

> How would you like to live in a town where they didn't hesitate to tell you you couldn't renew your notes, where your next door neighbor didn't know your name, where no one ever brings any lettuce over in the spring, or any peas over in the summer, . . . where . . . babies are born and weddings celebrated in your block and you know nothing about it? . . . Money is all right— but there is no good reason why one should sacrifice all his happiness for it.[45]

This new emphasis on the quality of life did not mean that White had ceased to be a booster. Indeed, he discovered that extolling small-town virtues could itself be a form of boosterism, for quality of life could be used to attract residents. This was particularly true in a college town like Emporia, where boarding out-of-town students contributed to the local economy. Students' parents needed to be assured that their children were safe from moral contamination. Similarly, when the Santa Fe Railroad announced plans in 1906 to assign thirty to forty workers and their families to Emporia, White attributed the decision to the fact that it was "A Good Family Town."

> As a cold-blooded operating proposition, the railroad company can get more out of a day's work from a man living in a town like Emporia than in a city like Topeka. . . .
> Other towns have bragged of their material advantages and have won. Emporia believes there is something in setting forth her spiritual advantages. Let us see what it will bring?[46]

White often celebrated the quality of life in Emporia in the context of arguing for particular local reform causes such as prohibition or municipal ownership of utilities. When he expressed a vision of the ideal community for a national audience, however, he omitted such mundane—and divisive— details. In an essay, "Emporia and New York," also written in 1906, the prosperous small town was not the product of progressive virtues, but their very incarnation. John Phillips thought it "one of the loveliest pieces that you have written" and published it in the January 1907 *American Magazine.*[47]

Like *In Our Town,* "Emporia and New York" expressed White's ideals in concrete, personal terms rather than abstract principles. The essay went much further, however, because there White offered an actual town, his Emporia, as the embodiment of communal virtues. He used the names of real Emporians—Charley Vernon the reporter, W. T. Soden the proprietor of the flour mill, George Newman the dry-goods merchant, Frank McCain the plasterer—as illustrations of his points, even as he argued that Emporia was merely typical of "nearly every country town of the east and north and west." The essential quality of these towns was their intense democratic spirit, which he contrasted with New York, "typical of urban America," where "class lines are set." Although he noted the various gradations of Emporia "society," he emphasized that "our cut-glass circle is not a wide circle, nor is its circumference wall impassable." That women prominent in Emporia society had risen from the ranks of the "hired girls" he considered as much as its "self-made men" to be "proof of our real democratic spirit."[48]

White argued that Emporians and New Yorkers were essentially the same kind of people, separated only by "differences of provincialism": "What New York can't see is how we can live in Emporia with so little going on at the opera house; and what we can't see is how a man who can have one hundred feet of lawn and a kitchen garden to sprinkle with the hose every evening after work, can permit himself to be locked up in a long row of five and six story cell-houses. . . ." Nonetheless, the underlying theme of the essay is that these material conditions of life in Emporia were the very factors that fostered its democratic spirit.[49]

Foremost among these conditions was equality of opportunity, beginning with the public schools, where any child could become a leader, and aided by equality "of financial backing, of social standing," that "guarantees a democratic community." Citing the case of plasterer Frank McCain, White argued that Emporia had no class divisions. Not only was McCain somewhat better off materially than his counterpart in the Bronx, McCain's children were rising in the world. "His son is a lawyer, graduated from the high school and the law department of the state university, and the only thing that will keep him from being governor of his state is his politics." (Presumably, he was a Democrat like his father.) What was more, in Emporia, according to White, McCain was not a social stereotype, "not a plasterer at all, but a man among men." His opinion was "more valued than is the opinion of many a store keeper or professional man." In fact, McCain was elected Emporia's mayor only a few months after this article appeared, though, of course, the *Gazette* backed the Republican nominee as the "people's" candidate.[50]

White argued that the well-to-do Emporian also benefited from such general equality: "For there is something in touching elbows with men at work—men who are your equals and make you acknowledge it a thousand times a day—that gives a man a philosophy worth more than millions."[51]

Too, in Emporia, people were not too busy to honor the truly important things in life. White described the amazement of his reporter Charley Vernon on a trip to New York, where he witnessed a millionaire's funeral procession, numbering fewer than twenty carriages, ignominiously "clattering down the street at a fast trot." In contrast, "we have had only one funeral in our town of a man worth a million, and that was three miles long." In fact, when a prominent or well-beloved man died, all local businesses closed their doors for the funeral. "But unless one contends that the death of a friend is a mere incident of the day, like the loss of an old hat, we here in Emporia see some things more sanely and more humanly than they do in New York, where death in a house only interests the servants next door."[52]

White maintained that these distinctions were caused by material conditions such as overcrowding. In small towns, people knew their neighbors and had less need to preserve their privacy than when they lived closely together. "[W]hen they live as we live here in Emporia, every family on its fifty-foot lot . . . they feel the need of drawing one another together." Consequently, he asserted, no one suffered from want in Emporia, "even though we have no more food to give than New Yorkers; but we have what is more essential than food in the human partnership—we have a strong social sympathy."[53]

This social sympathy was "the basis of whatever real difference there is between New York and Emporia, between the city and the country." Cities needed formal institutions to express society's charitable spirit, but in Emporia people just naturally shared a common life. Relief was spontaneous, through "the social sympathy, the touch of nature always found among neighbors of every class and clique that 'makes us wondrous kind.' " For White, such neighborly sympathy was the root from which sprang the more complex sense of community spirit that was fundamental to both boosterism and progressivism as he saw it.[54]

This "spirit" was also a major theme of his first novel, *A Certain Rich Man,* in which progressivism served as a driving force in the plot. He described progressivism as the upswelling among "the people" of an idea that questioned "the divine right of wealth to rule." This idea would triumph, he believed, because public opinion was the fundamental force in human society:

> What you and he think is more powerful than all the material forces of this universe. For what you and he think is public opinion. It is not substantial; it is not palpable. It may not readily be translated into terms of money, or power, or vital force. But it crushes all these things before it. When this public opinion rises sure and firm and strong, no material force on this earth can stop it.

As in *In Our Town,* this public sentiment was "God moving among men."[55]

White had attempted to write a great American novel after the success of *The Real Issue* in 1896. It was the story of the rise of a country town in the last quarter of the nineteenth century, and as he first sketched it, it had "a fight and a foot race on every page." He had abandoned the work by the turn of the century, but the reception of *In Our Town* encouraged him to try again, and he and Sallie vowed to write "a full-length, man-sized novel." This time White had an organizing principle for his novel, based on his own "conversion" to progressivism. The novel's structure was the parable of the prodigal son, and he acknowledged in his *Autobiography* that it was probably "the story of my own inner life."[56]

White set his story against the backdrop of the evolution of the town of Sycamore Ridge, Kansas, from a rough frontier community to a modern city. In the manner of Dickens or Harriet Beecher Stowe, White peopled his story with a large, boisterous cast of vividly realized small-town characters, many of whom had actual counterparts in Emporia or his childhood El Dorado. He recorded daily life in the Midwest in rich detail and at times exhibited the skill in realistic psychological portraiture that had earlier prompted William Dean Howells to consider him part of a contemporary trend toward "psychologism."[57]

The story followed the rise of John Barclay from poor but honorable origins to one of America's most wealthy, powerful, and corrupt men, a quintessential robber baron. Yet even as Barclay succeeded, White grimly traced his moral degeneration as the fulfillment of his unbridled selfish greed. Eventually, with the dawning of the progressive movement, Barclay's crimes were uncovered and denounced. Unlike *In Our Town*'s John Markley, however, who was in many ways a prototype, Barclay redeemed himself. Unlike naturalist writers like Theodore Dreiser, White believed that the human psyche was shaped by the individual's conscious relationship to society, not determined by physical or economic circumstances. An individual could therefore be transformed, as in an earlier age he might have undergone a religious conversion, by reestablishing his connection with true social values. Much as Dickens's Scrooge was redeemed by the three ghosts of Christmas, John Barclay was first humbled and then restored to his true self by progressive public opinion. Barclay was capable of redemption in part because he had retained his mother's love and in part because, despite his wealth, he had maintained his ties with folks in Sycamore Ridge. Abandoning the part of his wealth acquired through financial manipulations and unfair business practices, he returned to his first, legitimate occupation as a miller of grain and, in the ultimate act of selflessness, died trying to rescue a woman from drowning in the millpond.[58]

This sprawling novel may seem to late-twentieth-century tastes an unpalatable mixture of Frank Norris and Charles Dickens, yet contemporary readers and critics welcomed its fusion of realism and idealism. Yale English professor William Lyon Phelps praised it as "a true work of realistic art: it tells the truth and at the same time, shows a strong moral grasp of life." One reader exulted that it was not only "a true story" proven by "daily experience and observation" but also a story with a moral: "How refreshing! like an oasis in the desert of the purposeless stories of to-day." Many responded to his characters as though they were real people. One character in particular, a kindly local harness maker–poet named Watts McHurdie, was said to have written a famous Civil War song, and numerous readers wrote asking how they could obtain a copy of it. Reformers such as James R. Garfield applauded the book's accurate portrayal of social problems, while clergymen were attracted to its "religious view of life." Social Gospel minister Walter Rauschenbusch commented, "There is more faith in the spiritual life in your book than in many a sermon." The novel ultimately sold a quarter of a million copies.[59]

White and his readers considered progressivism as a whole a matter of uniting the spiritual and the material, not simply of achieving structural reforms or efficiency. He shared this view with Theodore Roosevelt, who wrote White in 1908 to praise an editorial that expressed "just what I have been trying to do when you say that my effort is to teach men that 'this is not essentially a material world, but that it is a practical world of spiritual things. . . .'" As in boosterism, this coupling of the practical and the ideal seems paradoxical, if not downright hypocritical, to later observers. It was, however, fundamental to the perspective of small-town boosters and to many participants in progressive reform causes.[60]

This union of practical and ideal was central to the distinctions progressives often made between themselves and their Gilded Age predecessors. Again, Roosevelt applauded White for understanding the difference: "I want to avoid being a fool of the goo-goo or mugwump kind and be perfectly practical, and face men and events as they are. At the same time I want to make things better and not worse." Similarly, White protested to a political opponent that he was no "long hair dreamer." "By the time you get back of a $200 pay roll every Saturday night in a country town and keep the city and county printing cinched up against all comers . . . you will have done a fairly practical job of work in this practical world."[61]

For White, true reform could be achieved only through spiritual growth, and consequently he was uneasy with those progressive colleagues who pursued progress through specific structural reforms rather than moral exhortation. He responded to a Socialist critic by arguing that "spiritual evolution" must precede "economic evolution." "I do not believe that it should be possible to very greatly improve present day conditions by any law or system of laws. . . ." When a reader of his essay on "The Golden Rule" proposed the founding of an educational assembly to promote the ideal, he responded that "generally speaking, I do not believe that much can be accomplished by Assemblys and Associations. . . ." Nonetheless, in keeping with the booster ethos, he valued public activism almost regardless of its concrete results. He told another Socialist correspondent, "It is all right to keep kicking, but I think the best good that comes from kicking is in the awakened moral sense and enthusiasms of the men who kick."[62]

For similar reasons, he attacked a bill in the 1908 Kansas legislature to guarantee bank deposits because it would discourage rather than encourage sound business ethics. "It is an unfortunate phase of the rising tide of civic reform that too many of its devotees and advocates, rely too much on law, and not enough on the spiritual growth of the people to remedy obvious evils." Instead, he advocated self-regulation under state supervision: an organization of bankers "could throw out crooked bankers and by throwing them out advertise their weakness and incompetency, so that depositors could govern themselves accordingly."[63]

In hindsight, it is clear that this kind of government-sponsored self-regulation, one of the structural legacies of the period, could easily be exploited by big business in its own interest, but it is misleading to argue that those who advocated it were necessarily apologists for a new corporate order. For

White, the booster, such regulation simply represented an extension to the national economic order of the kind of community discipline that had governed local behavior. To his way of thinking, such organizations would employ the same means of ensuring conformity to local norms: exhortation and threats of public shaming. He, like many progressives, relied upon publicity to enforce group norms, because this was how he was accustomed to enforcing them at the local level.

White's repeated pronouncements in national magazines and books that the many reform efforts of his day were all manifestations of the same "spiritual growth in the hearts of the American people" encouraged the belief among many Americans that there was such a thing as a unified progressive movement. This emphasis upon spirit and process rather than the content of each cause might well have made a broad-based national progressive coalition possible by obscuring the real social and ideological differences between its members. Similarly, White's projection of his vision of an idealized local community upon the nation as a whole overlooked the fundamental tensions between the demands of localist and nationalist progressives. As increasing numbers of men and women began to call themselves progressives, the interests of a nationally centralized movement would overshadow the aims of localists. In transfiguring his booster progressivism into terms suited for his national audience, White would unwittingly contribute to the decline of the local community autonomy that he had struggled to defend.

7

Community Journalism

In 1916 William Allen White celebrated the small-town newspaper in *Harper's Monthly Magazine* as "the incarnation of the town spirit": "Our papers, our little country papers, seem drab and miserably provincial to strangers; yet we who read them read in their lines the sweet, intimate story of life. And all these touches of nature make us wondrous kind. . . ."[1]

This article, "The Country Newspaper," expressed a vision of the small-town newspaper that is still central to the way in which community journalists see their responsibilities today. To reach this point, White's ideas about community journalism had evolved in the first decades of the twentieth century even as its economic foundation shifted from party patronage to advertising. Like many progressives, White insisted that the growth of true community depended upon communication. But where others applied this idea to the task of fostering a sense of community in large cities or the nation as a whole, White applied them to his role as editor of the *Emporia Gazette*. He envisioned the small-town newspaper as an agent of community, in which seemingly unimportant local news unified the town's residents. "It is the country newspaper," he explained in *Harper's*, "bringing together daily the threads of the town's life . . . that reveals us to ourselves. . . ." He concluded:

> Therefore, men and brethren, when you are riding through this vale of tears upon the California Limited, and by chance pick up the little country newspaper . . . when you see its array of countryside items; its interminable local stories; its tiresome editorials . . . don't throw down the contemptible little rag with the verdict that there is nothing in it. But know this, and know it well: if you could take the clay from your eyes and read the little paper as it is written, you would find all of God's beautiful sorrowing, struggling, aspiring world in it, and what you saw would make you touch the little paper with reverent hands.[2]

Seen through White's perspective, the small-town newspaper embodies some attractive qualities—appreciation for the simple pleasures of life, celebration of the common man and woman, and understanding of the deep human needs for belonging and recognition. More than any other journalistic genre, the small-town newspaper's locals illustrate these qualities by redefining "news" in terms of equality, familiarity, and continuity. White's growing appreciation of locals was consistent with his deepening recognition of the value of community in American life.

Nonetheless, we will also see that, as practiced in the *Gazette,* this vision of community journalism reinforced the authority of economic elites in Emporia. It discouraged open discussion of controversies. It countenanced the public shaming of individuals in the interest of enforcing moral norms. And despite White's denial of the existence of classes in Emporia, the *Gazette* did not treat all Emporians equally.

This was so because, like his vision of the small town as progressive ideal, White's understanding of the responsibility of the local newspaper remained rooted in the booster role he had assumed when he first became editor of the *Gazette.* As booster of his town's economy, he had used his newspaper's publicity to encourage community loyalty, whip up enthusiasm for local improvements, and discourage the expression of dissent. During this period White broadened his paper's definition of the relevant community to include a larger number of Emporians. He was motivated by the need for ever-larger circulation to gain a share of the increasing advertising revenues, as well the desire to act according to his new progressive identity. But his booster progressivism also led him to continue to use his paper to promote his vision of morality, unity, harmony, and progress.

White's ideas about community journalism emerged gradually from their booster roots. From his earliest days as editor of the *Gazette,* he argued that the newspaper's news and advertising fostered booster values. A good businessman, he insisted that vigorous advertising sustained an interdependent local economy. Soon after his arrival in Emporia, for example, he criticized local merchants who patronized a traveling salesman's "fake advertising scheme": "The proper way to advertise is in the home newspaper. . . . The home papers go into the homes; the money put into the home papers stays at home and helps to build up Emporia." Like any local business, the newspaper deserved its citizens' loyalty, but it was unique in that it could also help other merchants bridge the gap between public and private worlds.[3]

After rural free delivery began, White developed further the idea that the newspaper encouraged local loyalty. In 1901 White again addressed local merchants, in an editorial entitled "The Gazette and Emporia." Local merchants, he asserted, were "up against a serious proposition." RFD was hurting their trade, and since farmers no longer came to town to collect their mail, "the only way the merchants of Emporia can get at the farmers is through the local newspapers." Not all advertising media were alike, however. A good booster newspaper, working for the town in its news as well as its advertising, provided the best setting.

For 365 days in the year the Gazette stands up for Emporia. It stands for the town, for a decent town, for a wideawake town, for a live town. If you have a town scheme to work—what do you do? You bring it to the Gazette—

whether it is a street fair, a new court house, a new railroad, a wholesale house or a temperance movement. . . .

Now it follows that the Gazette must have made friends. It has made lots of them. . . .

Mr. Emporia business man you want trade. Go after it. You can reach the people of this town and county only in one way to compete with mail order houses: That way is through the Emporia Gazette. . . . The Gazette reaches all the people. It is the home paper of Emporia and of Lyon county.[4]

In promising to combat the mail-order menace, White referred to more than the power of information. To overcome the handicap that small businesses faced in price competition with large-scale retailers, the local newspaper proposed to instill a sense of community loyalty that could transcend mere economic interests. Although White treated this new approach to marketing in characteristically "businesslike" terms, his plan was to appeal to consumers' feelings and civic spirit. He drove this point home a few days later in an editorial on "Business Principles."

The methods of twenty, fifteen, ten or even two years ago will not meet the conditions of business life of today in Emporia. An old citizen of Lyon county, whom all business men know, said one day this week: "I am friendly to Emporia and like to come here to trade." He voiced the feelings of many others. Mr. Business Man, it is your work to increase and perpetuate this friendly feeling. "He that would have friends must show himself friendly." Outsiders are working hard to cultivate these friendly business relations with your legitimate customers. Advertise, gentlemen, advertise your goods. . . .[5]

In other words, the newspaper could create an affective community to replace the merely geographic community being undermined by improved transportation and communication. Beyond creating an appropriate context for advertising, the newspaper's content itself fostered a sense of community. Over the next decade, as White idealized community cohesion into the "sympathy" of which democracy was made, he remained aware that it was also good for business.

Similarly, White realized that it was good for business to expand the *Gazette*'s coverage beyond narrow partisan interests, to pay attention to the lives of ordinary Emporians and farmers within the town's trading territory. Even before he received newspaper canvasser Rose Edington's advice to "put people's names in your paper," White had known that local news was one of the most important features of his newspaper, at least from the point of view of many of his readers. But he was embarrassed at its provinciality. In 1899 he discouraged a newspaper colleague who wanted to subscribe to the *Gazette,* explaining,

I fear that you have over-estimated the Emporia *Gazette.* It is simply a little country daily and weekly, devoted entirely to chronicling the important fact that Bill Jones brought in a load of hay to-day. And Thomas Hughes is recovering from a sprained hip, and that John Smith is putting a new porch on his property on Sylvan street.

Sometimes I write a little editorial, and sometimes I do not; but when I do, I hang it on the hook, and if the local crowds it out, it simply has to go over until the local news gets scarce. . . . This may sound a queer programme to people used to a metropolitan paper; but it makes money for the *Gazette,* and that is one of the things the *Gazette* is running for. . . .

Shortly before his nervous breakdown in 1902, White apologetically turned down the proposal of a Washington correspondent to provide special coverage of the Kansas congressional delegation. The *Gazette* was "a load of hay paper," he said, wherein "it is vastly more important to the 'Gazette's' financial success to know that William Jones of Pike township is in town with a load of hay, than it is to learn of the details of the pending revolution in Washington."[6]

Nonetheless, his emerging progressive vision of community prompted White to reevaluate the significance of local "load of hay news." He found virtue in economic necessity. In "The Country Newspaper," he admitted, "Of course our country papers are provincial. We know that as well as any one." But "so far as that goes . . . all papers are provincial." And the small-town newspaper's "daily chronicle of the doings of our friends" fostered an essential feeling of community. He continued:

When the girl at the glove-counter marries the boy in the wholesale house, the news of their wedding is good for a forty-line wedding-notice, and the forty lines in the country paper give them self-respect. When in due course we know that their baby is a twelve-pounder, named Grover or Theodore or Woodrow, we have that neighborly feeling that breeds the real democracy.[7]

For both practical and philosophical reasons, then, White insisted that the *Gazette* contain abundant local news. This emphasis continued through the first two decades of the twentieth century, even as he shifted much of the newspaper's day-to-day editorial responsibilities to his staff. Such continuity was possible because of his employees' complete agreement with his conception of community journalism.

As White's free-lance writing career expanded after 1900, he grew increasingly frustrated by the daily demands of running the *Gazette.* Though he had begun to delegate responsibility for routine mechanical and business decisions as the newspaper prospered, he was still closely tied to its editorial management. He found this irksome; he had hoped that financial security would bring a measure of freedom to write. As he described this dilemma to a friend in 1904, "I often feel like cutting loose from the *Gazette,* and yet, there is nothing like a base of supplies." Moreover, whenever he left the newspaper for any length of time, Sallie White had to remain behind to run it, which was hardly a satisfactory arrangement.[8]

White made his first major efforts at reorganizing the *Gazette's* editorial management in the summer of 1907, when he took off with his family for several months in the Colorado Rockies to work full time on his novel. He explained to his readers in an editorial, "Good-by, Vain World," that "the editor" had "some work to do which seems to him more important, if not so profitable and pleasurable as running the *Gazette,* and he feels that he must take to the woods to do it." He named Laura French, his proofreader and telegraph editor, city editor. During his absence he formally named Walter Hughes manager of the *Gazette,* with "final authority" in all policy matters that might arise. Henceforth, the paper's masthead and stationery carried both White's name and that of "Walter E. Hughes, manager."[9]

The burden of day-to-day editorial direction fell upon the shoulders of Laura French, who became in effect White's managing editor. He was fortunate to have in her a woman of experience, intelligence, and absolute dedication. Thirty-eight years old in 1907, she had risen from compositor to proofreader and editor at the *Gazette.* She knew thoroughly the fundamentals of journalism and the English language, but she was more committed to the principles of community journalism as it was practiced at the *Gazette* than she was to an abstract profession. She compiled a stylebook for the newspaper that codified White's policies, and then enforced these rules with a vehemence that most cub reporters thought autocratic, but reflected her sense of responsibility to her employer. In a talk on the "Business Girl" to women students at the Normal School, she advised any woman seeking to advance in her career to "study your employer. . . . Know what his policy would be in every situation and endeavor to carry it out." White once praised her for this ability to reflect "the absolute color and shade" of his opinion. A single woman of strong opinions, she was not exactly popular with her male colleagues at the *Gazette.*[10]

One of French's most important roles at the *Gazette* was to educate the successive generations of young men whom White hired as cub reporters. At the turn of the century, a journalist would have been more likely to start out, as did White and French, as printer's devil or compositor. But after the *Gazette* acquired linotypes, few if any reporters emerged from the back room. Typically, an aspiring reporter started as a stringer while in high school or college. If he looked promising, White hired him full time, at a starting salary of around six dollars a week. The cub covered the "street," gathering locals, the railroad news, and short items. Eventually, if he stayed around for several years, he could rise to "star" reporter, who handled the bigger news of city hall and county courthouse. Generally, after a reporter had worked for the *Gazette* for a number of years and had begun to receive higher wages, White called him in to announce, "You have learned as much as we can teach you," and shove him out of the nest, helping him find a place on a larger newspaper.[11]

Over the years, so many of the region's best journalists had started at the *Gazette* that it began to be known as the "White School of Journalism." It may have been White's school, but it was Laura French who taught the classes. In a sense, she was cast in the role of heavy, for it fell to her to initiate the newcomers, and, as craft tradition has it, cubs must be properly humbled by fierce exercise of the blue pencil before they can become good reporters. Reporters' reminiscences of these years invariably include memories of French, none of them with much affection. One described her as "the boss of the newsroom who with one word could cut a cub reporter to size." Freed from this unappealing task, White could play the role of benign if somewhat distant father to his young reporters. While French drilled them in fundamentals, he could urge upon them the virtues of kindness. Her ability repeatedly to reproduce the editorial work force also benefited White economically, because it enabled him to keep wages low.[12]

Laura French ensured that the *Gazette* reflected White's desires, even as she relieved him of the daily details of editing his newspaper. White continued to keep careful watch over the final product to ensure that it met his standards. Whenever he was away from Emporia, he scrutinized the newspaper every day and paid particular attention to the locals. He wrote French from his retreat in Colorado to complain, "It seems to me that there is not enough local in the paper, considering everything." On another occasion, he praised the staff: "You never made so good a paper—lots of little short stuff and lots of good stories."[13]

As White implied in his *Harper's* essay, the characteristic contents of the *Gazette,* as of any small-town newspaper, was news about local people, whether in their normal, day-to-day activities or the special moments of their lives—their births, weddings, and deaths. At the most mundane level were the locals that reported Emporians' daily activities: visits, shopping trips, improvements to the house, family reunions, illnesses and recoveries. These were of interest to Emporia readers precisely because of their familiarity, because they knew the people being written about. Locals were often as brief as "Mrs. Bert Hyle is sick" or "Mr. and Mrs. Ted Jones of Arvonia are here visiting." They noted changes in the features of the town: "S. M. Loveless is putting a new foundation under and a new roof over his house at 821 Cottonwood street." They celebrated simple personal achievements: "One of the handsomest bouquets that has come to the *Gazette* office this season was a bunch of roses from Mrs. W. C. Harris's garden." They reported progress in a neighbor's health: "Miss Anna Davis, who has been sick in St. Mary's hospital for the past two weeks, was able to be taken to her home yesterday." They recorded the movements of the town's more prominent citizens: "Mr. and Mrs. A. H. Plumb have gone to Cape May, N.J., for the summer." They lampooned the leisure activities of local shopkeepers: "J. W. Lostutter and Dick Turner went fishing last night. They were gone three hours and got 0 bites. However, they have one consolation, they got wet and caught cold, and that's something." In short, locals possessed none of the drama or uniqueness generally associated with "news" value.[14]

The *Gazette* also devoted ample space to stories about the major life passages of its citizens. Weddings, of course, were a staple and frequently appeared on the front page. Most stories about local weddings paid loving attention to all the details of the celebration, including the decoration of the church or home and the participants' costumes. The length of the articles tended to be proportionate to the parties' social standing, but every ceremony that was more than a few words before the justice of the peace received at least several paragraphs. The 1899 wedding of Esther Griffith and Charles Jones garnered nearly a full column of the *Gazette*'s front page and dwelled on every detail of the preparations ("it was a violet wedding"). The story concluded, "The *Gazette* is happy to join these friends in wishing this couple the happiness that their many wholesome qualities of mind and heart deserve. The union of these two young people brings together two of the best families in town, old settlers, and substantial citizens. The wedding was most happy in every way." Such statements acknowledged that weddings were not merely personal events, but milestones in the life of the community as a whole.[15]

Even the much humbler Truit-Sallee wedding in 1903 received its "fortyline wedding-notice," again with attention to dresses and decorations ("Ferns, palms and smilax were used effectively") and closing commendation: "The bride is a popular young woman who deservedly holds a high place in the estimation of a large circle of acquaintances and friends and the groom is a genial young man who has earned by his enterprise a high position in G. W. Newman's store." Similarly, a story on the wedding of a local black couple concluded: "Mr. Terry has an ice cream parlor at 911 Commercial street, and is one of Emporia's most highly esteemed young colored men. Mrs. Terry lived for years at the home of Mrs. Robert L. Jones, and has the respect of everyone with whom she is acquainted."[16]

Such extended coverage of local weddings often included descriptions of attendant customs that have since passed from our culture. The *Gazette* report of the Jones-Dickson wedding concluded, "Accompanied by the guests, the bride and groom were escorted to their newly furnished and cozy cottage at No. 602 Exchange street. The College crowd had here made itself evident and mottoed paper hearts were displayed in every conceivable place. It was a happy beginning of a prosperous future." Frequent references to the noisy receptions accorded the newlyweds show that the ancient custom of charivari had not yet died out in small-town America. After one wedding, the *Gazette* noted that "the small boys used their inherent right to make the night hideous with a charivari."[17]

Deaths of Emporians received even more attention, usually with a frontpage notice at the time of death, a longer story about the funeral, and, for many residents, an editorial eulogy. White was a master of the last genre, employing the occasion to preach a small sermon upon the text of a particular virtue that the departed had embodied. These virtues were generally those he considered essential to the well-being of the community as a whole. An early example was written upon the death of John Jones, a Welsh-born minister who had been a pioneer settler of Emporia. White began by noting that essential feature of the small-town funeral, the procession: "The other day in Emporia, the longest funeral procession that has formed in ten years followed the Rev. John Jones three long miles in the hot July sun out to Dry Creek Cemetery." What did such a turnout mean?

The reason so many people lined up behind the hearse that held the kind old man's mortality was simple: they loved him. He devoted his life to help-ing people. In a very simple way, without money or worldly power, he gave of the gentleness of his heart to all around him. We are apt to say that money talks, but it speaks a broken, poverty-stricken language. Hearts talk better, clearer, and with a wider intelligence. . . .

When others gave money—which was of their store—he gave prayers and hard work and an inspiring courage. He helped. In his sphere he was a power. And so when he lay down to sleep hundreds of friends trudged out to bid him good-by with moist eyes and with cramped throats to wish him sweet slumber.

And then they turned back to the world to make money—to make money—what a hollow impotent thing! What is a man profited if he gain the whole world and lose his own soul?[18]

White believed it important to commemorate the deaths of those who had contributed something to the community, regardless of their wealth or social standing. When one of the leaders of Emporia's black community died, he published a eulogy, noting to a colleague, "We make it a point in the office to write some obituary notice about every worthy citizen whether rich or poor and it is generally my job to do it." Even in later years, when he had turned over to others much of the day-to-day writing of the *Gazette,* White prided himself on writing the last words over his friends and neigh-bors, just as he had promised in his salutatory editorial.[19]

Taken together, these staples of small-town journalism, the locals and the formulaic reporting of weddings and funerals, seem well suited to White's goal of fostering a feeling of community. Such human-interest news emphasizes the universality of human experience rather than social dis-tinctions, its continuities rather than its disruptions. In their sheer every-dayness and repetitiveness, locals replicate and reinforce the persistent face-to-face contact that is generally considered a basic condition of community. Similarly, as cultural historians have become aware, significant life-cycle events such as weddings and funerals serve communal as well as personal functions. Public participation in such events in some ritualized fashion has been a crucial means of creating and reinforcing communal ties, as well as of dramatizing the social status of the host.[20]

Beyond these most formulaic of news stories, the rest of the *Gazette's* contents embodied the booster and progressive ideal of the town as a uni-fied and interdependent whole. First, it ceaselessly exhorted Emporians to participate in community life. From the 1899 street fair on, White orga-nized and then energetically promoted every imaginable sort of public celebration to draw together residents of Emporia and Lyon County and thereby encourage a sense of belonging to the community. Afterward, he interpreted these events as evidence of the town's civic spirit. For example, a 1907 editorial praised a meeting of local businessmen to plan Emporia's fiftieth-anniversary celebration as proof of "A New Spirit Abroad."

Emporia needs more such meetings—full of the spirit of enthusiastic cooperation, full of belief in the town, full of the spirit of mutual help to make Emporia a bigger better town.

This spirit has been growing in Emporia for the past five years. . . . And
it has brought real fruit. There is more building, more growth, in every way
in this town than ever before. . . . Every one does his part. The town pulls
together. There is no longer any "crowd"—except the big Emporia crowd. . . .

There is a new spirit abroad in the town, and it is the spirit of intelligent
progress.

As in this editorial, the *Gazette* consistently portrayed the level of participation in public activities as an index of the community's moral and economic health.[21]

Year in and year out, the *Gazette* recorded in detail local observances of
every holiday of the American civil religion and included the names of
those who participated and comments on the meaning of the day for Emporians. American historians have begun to recognize the role of such events
in building American communities. If participating in the actual event created a sense of belonging to a community, the newspaper's recording that
event in print enabled those who could not be there to participate vicari-
ously, and reminded later inhabitants of its significance.[22]

Less overtly, but more continuously, everyday news and editorial comment also sought to reinforce communal ties. Here White's progressivism
merged neatly with his drive to expand the *Gazette*'s readership, for paying
attention to a broader segment of the population attracted new readers as
well as expanded the definition of the relevant community. When White
first bought the *Gazette,* it typically reported on the regular meetings of the
organizations, such as the G.A.R. and the Masons, that contained the
town's most prominent citizens. Over time, the paper increased the number of organizations on which it reported, thus widening its definition of
the visible community. In 1904, for example, the *Gazette* instituted a union
directory and promised to "print all the news and announcements of union
labor in Emporia."[23]

In the days of the factional press it had been common policy to celebrate
service to the community by the gentlemen who backed the newspaper
while ignoring the contributions of factional opponents. W. Y. Morgan,
and White himself in his early years as editor, had been particularly zealous
in praising the beneficences to Emporia of Calvin Hood. But increasingly
White highlighted the actions of humbler citizens, including those who differed from him politically. In 1905 he published a "Roll of Honor" of the
names of thirteen farmers who had done the spring plowing and planting
for a sick neighbor. "You hear a great deal in the papers about the politicians of this community and what able men they are. The newspapers aren't
to blame, because the people insist on having stories about the smartness
and worth of the politicians printed, but no story about any Lyon county
statesman is as good as this story."[24]

Such commendatory editorials became a hallmark of White's practice of journalism, and he lavished considerable care upon them. The occasion might be as simple as Charles Knittel's achieving the first crop of home-grown potatoes. Or it could be the thirtieth anniversary of Maggie Ballweg's millinery shop, which prompted a long editorial entitled "Thirty Years of Maggie."

> Maggie is as much a part of Commercial street today as Newman's or Mr. Dunlap the banker or Rorabaugh's store, or the Mit-Way Hotel or the Normal School or Soden's Mill. . . . She is found taking her place as a business woman beside her business colleagues in every good movement in the town; yet no woman in all the town, peeping from behind the curtains of her own parlor windows, has preserved more of the eternal feminine about her than Maggie Ballweg. She has been a business woman, but first of all a wife and mother. She has succeeded in all her enterprises.[25]

Editorials and locals also sought to create a sense of cohesion by emphasizing the community's continuity over time, for a sense of community requires a vision of the town as a seamless progression from glorious past to promising future. Continuity with the past can be established through civic celebrations, but a community's future is represented, symbolically and literally, by its women and children. The survival over time of every culture depends upon the willingness of women to bear and rear children and of children to follow in their parents' footsteps. Much of White's recurring concern about "gadding" young women and dissolute young men reflected the need to protect Emporia's future mothers and business leaders.[26]

Nonetheless, the *Gazette* celebrated continuity across the generations more often than it expressed foreboding. As much as White fretted about the wild ways of Emporia's girls, he was also optimistic that the "natural" cycles of women's lives would persist. In an editorial entitled "About Your Ma," he advised today's young woman that if she thought her ma was stodgy, "you have another guess about ma, young woman."

> About forty-odd years ago, if all the old settlers don't lie, and probably they don't, your ma was the swiftest proposition that ever came down the Burlingame Road. . . . When your pa got your ma, he had to keep her on ice, she was so torrid, until she was thirty-five. . . .
> Well, as we were saying, when your ma married your pa, and you and the other children came one after another, your ma had to be up a good deal nights, when she could hear the fiddle and piano going in the other end of town, where it didn't interest her as much as it once did. She had a chance those nights . . . to do a good deal of serious thinking. And she acquired a lot of sense. She knows things that you won't know for a long, long time. A woman sitting up at night tending babies has time to form conclusions that are the resolvents of many years of undigested youthful impressions.[27]

Similarly, stories about children in the *Gazette* confidently portrayed them as Emporia's future. In one of his special Saturday editions in 1900 White ran a photograph of the town's "Boy Choir." The caption concluded:

"They are the boys who will make Emporia thirty years from now. It will pay you to be considerate and respectful to them now if you desire a large funeral and a kind word said for you after you die." In another issue a photograph of a group of adolescent girls, whom White jokingly labeled "Trundle Bed Trash," bore a similar inscription: "They are just getting into long skirts this year and are beginning to harbor secret ambitions for tailor made gowns, Knox sailors and diamond rings. . . . Heaven knows, it will be a short enough time before they will be cutting out of the *Gazette* a description of themselves 'gowned in white satin'. . . ." The caption noted that "most of this crowd are native-born Emporians and some of their fathers and mothers belonged to the Emporia trundle bed trash twenty years ago." Significantly, White not only emphasized Emporia's continuity but claimed a central role for the newspaper in the rite of passage of marriage itself.[28]

Communal ties are maintained by group discipline as well as approbation and reassurance, and White asserted the newspaper's responsibility to embody the "spirit" of the town by calling down shame upon the heads of wrongdoers as well as by praising benefactors. Like the Puritan minister publicly singling out errant members of his congregation, he was capable of naming names in his editorial sermons, as he had done to Al Randolph for wearing a mail-order uniform. In 1906 he castigated Dave Jones for demanding a high price for a lot on Commercial Street that the Emporia Artificial Ice Company needed to build a cold storage plant. "According to current business standards" it might be acceptable for Jones to gouge the corporation, but in this case "the corporation is not the only sufferer." The whole community would benefit from the new enterprise. White urged his readers to consider

> Now what would Christ have done? Would he have held his property at the figure which he thought the corporation might pay—or would he have taken what the judgment of the neighbors seemed to think it worth? We call ourselves a Christian community—yet how many real Christians are there who in a single business transaction would not find an excuse to deceive themselves into doing the thing that Christ would not have done. There is really no use trying to reform the world until we reform the people in the world.[29]

On the other hand, White reserved the right to withhold the publication of news if it served his purpose of promoting community. Although he shared with today's journalists a belief in the power of the press, he realized that what did not appear in a newspaper was often as powerful as what did. He understood the importance in a small town of a person's reputation and knew that sometimes the threat of public exposure would be enough to bring about repentance and reformation. In one case at least, he gave editorial "First Notice."

> Mr. Boy take notice: The fact that you were mean drunk last night and tried to whip your father is kept out of today's paper on account of your

mother and sister; but the next time you don't get any more consideration than any other plain drunk. . . .

But the next time you get full of drug store booze and go up home and bawl around like a jackass, and flourish your club—the Gazette is going to dump you right where you belong—in with the loafers and drunks and black-guards who are the contempt of all honest men, and what is more you needn't send your father and mother around to beg you off. The time to think of them and their disgrace is before you get drunk.[30]

Occasionally the *Gazette* acknowledged its power to publish or suppress damaging news, but generally it did so in a humorous way. In 1900 it commented,

The other day the *Gazette* published an item about a young man who filled up on bad whisky, kicked a door in at the house of a questionable character and for his trouble was shot twice in the legs by the "lady" of the house. The boy's name was kept out of the paper because he has got a pretty fair punish-ment and learned a valuable lesson. Since then fifty people—twenty-five being young girls—have pestered the reporters of this paper for the name of the young man.

In 1902 an item on the notorious third page quipped, "You hear lots of people kicking about what the *Gazette* says about them, whereas they ought to be rejoicing to think that it doesn't say lots worse things it knows about them and doesn't print."[31]

At the same time, much of what a small-town newspaper printed was not "news," in that many people already knew about it. In such cases the news-paper served other functions through its reporting. In the case of celebra-tions or life-cycle events it provided public recognition and a record for posterity. In the case of scandals it defined what might be considered "pub-lic knowledge." When a distraught local woman protested that a *Gazette* story about her ex-husband's remarriage had shamed her, White tried to re-assure her.

The whole town . . . knew about Mr. Benedict's marriage to Henda Cleav-enger. The matter could not have received one bit more publicity than it had by appearing in the paper. By printing it fairly and squarely, you make it a matter of public record and it at once stops all venomous gossip and puts forever at rest all insinuations that would float in the air and puts yourself in your true light, which is certainly not a light in which you have anything to be ashamed of. Your course in this community has been honorable and is above any reproach. . . .[32]

Nonetheless, White assured her that he would have withheld the story if she had asked him to.

Such a selective policy concerning publicity left the *Gazette* open to charges of favoritism, and in the early 1910s White established a formal policy of printing news of scandals only when it became a matter of court record, as in the case of divorces. In 1913 he announced:

A few months ago the town buzzed with a sad story. It did not appear in the *Gazette*. It will not appear in the *Gazette*. The sad stories of life, unless they are forced into publicity by court record, or by some crisis of a public event, are not, as a rule, good reading. . . . The important things of life are its kindnesses, its nobility, its self-denials, its great renunciations.[33]

White maintained that there was no such thing as inherent "news" value in a story. He justified suppressing sensational news on the ground that the newspaper's fundamental purpose was to serve the welfare of the community, not some abstract "right to know." He made this purpose explicit in 1921 in responding to a reader's complaint that the *Gazette* had ignored two recent divorce scandals among the "big bugs" while it published the names of poor drunks. White said that "the community has a right" to the basic facts about divorce decrees, "but the harrowing details that mark the wreck of any home are not news. . . ." On the other hand, "The man who fills up with whisky and goes about making a fool of himself becomes a public nuisance. . . . Publicity is one of the things that keep him straight." He concluded, "The bum and the divorce are treated always from the standpoint of the community interest."[34]

He evaluated each event according to its probable effect—upon the subject, the reader, and particularly the community as a whole. He attempted to instill into his reporters a sensitivity to the human side of the news. Calvin Lambert, who became the *Gazette*'s city editor in 1919, said at White's death,

It seemed to me that the foremost thought in Mr. White's newspaper work was kindness. He always insisted that his reporters write the news as kindly as possible. Sordid stories offended him. A suicide, a murder, a sensational divorce, an errant son—all these were tragedies to Mr. White, and he insisted that the reporters omit details which added grief to the relatives.[35]

Similarly, White was aware that the reported news was rarely all there was to the story. In a small town, he believed, most readers would bring to each news account knowledge of its context and would therefore read it more sympathetically. In "The Country Newspaper" he explained that "the beauty and the joy of our papers and their little worlds is that we who live in the country towns know our own heroes." He attempted to instruct his readers that the same was true for "foreign" news. A 1907 editorial, "A Telegraph Story," preached forbearance.

The dispatches from day to day contain the outlines of all there is of the passion and humor and tragedy of human life; but only outlines, for the narratives are of necessity boiled down to the smallest compass. . . .

The supreme court affirms the lower court's sentence of five years upon an ex-county judge who got away with certain money that was intrusted to him while he was in office. Not knowing the judge, we breathe some nice moral platitude to the effect that one's sin is sure to find one out; but, knowing the judge—

It is a pitiful thing. An old man, badly crippled: a sensitive man, an honorable man, a scholar and recluse, a gentleman of refined tastes, goes to the penitentiary because he has a fool family. He will never emerge from the penitentiary alive. The disgrace will kill him soon.

For years this old man was an ornament to his community, and people were proud of him. . . . But he had a wife and daughters who burned money. They wore a path to the local milliner's and the only thing they ever read was the fashion magazines. They toiled not, neither did they spin but Solomon in all his glory was not arrayed like them.

The judge's humble salary wasn't a taste for them. . . . what can a man do with a lot of vociferous women after him? He can go to the penitentiary. . . .

The dispatch relating the story of his doom was in yesterday's Gazette.[36]

Although it was most likely not planned that way, everything about the *Gazette*'s content and design in the first decades of the century also reflected and reinforced White's insistence upon the primacy of the local community. Even the front page, which White described in *In Our Town* as "the parlour of our paper," sustained an impression that Emporia stood at the center of the universe. Typographically, the *Gazette*'s appearance was unsophisticated in comparison with urban dailies. Its seven ruled columns were extremely gray, and the size of headlines rarely varied. The layout itself was routine: two major stories of the day were carried in two columns in each upper corner, with two-column headlines. The next two inner columns carried "star boxes": short, sometimes humorous items, one local and one national, surrounded by stars. The center column typically contained the major local news story, and a mixture of national and local news filled out the half of the front page below the fold. This unvarying layout, as well as an absence of variation in the headlines according to estimates of "newsworthiness," blurred distinctions between "big" national and "little" local news. The result was a sense of homogeneity in which all stories appeared of equal importance.[37]

After 1903, when White acquired his first linotype, the *Gazette* received the world's news fresh from the Associated Press. Nevertheless, at least a third of the front page was typically devoted to local events. Stories of weddings, city council and school board meetings, and church conventions jostled promiscuously with world and national news of more "historic" import. In addition, the Associated Press tended to report national news in a matter-of-fact, even bland style that minimized its dramatic impact. This style meant that each local newspaper could interpret the news according to its own lights and thus shape its picture of the outside world to a local perspective.[38]

The Associated Press did, however, report the major scandals, such as the dramatic trials of Henry Thaw for the murder of Sanford White. Editor White was ambivalent about whether the *Gazette* should publish such stories. When Kansas newspapers were full of the "sickening details" of the trial of a small-town minister under the "white slave" law for the abduction of a sixteen-year-old parishioner, White defended the extensive coverage. "The Stuckey trial," he argued, "comes as an object lesson and sermon just when it should do the most good. It expounds emphatically the great truth that the way of the transgressor is hard." If a single girl was saved from ruining herself by reading the stories, the newspapers' wisdom "will be fully vindicated." On the other hand, insisting that "the news is what the newspapers play up," he argued the following year that such sensationalism was "bad for public morals, and a newspaper that prints such things inveterately should be declared a nuisance."[39]

The difference between good sensationalism and bad seems to have rested with whether an appropriate moral could be drawn from the story. White often used his editorials to instruct his readers in the proper interpretation of the wire service news. When the Gazette's front page contained dramatic stories about the execution of three youths for murder, an editorial on page two, entitled "Obedience," drew the moral: "It is a miserable story, and it has a terrible end. The story is printed here that boys may see how in the end meanness is unprofitable. The boys belonged to a gang of youngsters who believed they were smarter than organized society. There is nothing to that theory." Even the sordid Thaw case had a moral: "The Gazette's verdict of the Thaw case is all made up. Thaw isn't crazy: he was just easy. White got his; little Evelyn will get hers, and some way ought to be devised for a special dispensation to reach out and hand her mother what is clearly coming to her."[40]

The Gazette also made national news more meaningful, and yet more familiar, to its readers by emphasizing its connections with their own experiences. A reporter who came to the Gazette in the 1920s recalled White's insistence that "much of the national and world news is really local news" and his instructions to "probe deeply to find out and report what the effect will be on the homes and the people in them." This sense of the continuity between Emporia and the world "out there" was reinforced by the Gazette's practice of reporting national and international news through the eyes of Emporians who were involved. Whenever the nation was at war, the newspaper published letters from local boys at the front. For example, in 1900 the paper printed the full text of a letter from Ralph Avery, with this introduction: "It gives an account of three Emporia boys who are now in the volunteer army in the Philippines, where they went through their first real battles, and how it felt. The description of the fighting is good and it will pay everyone to read it, not alone because it is entirely Emporian, but because it is interesting."[41]

News of natural disasters, with their concomitant suffering and loss of life, has been a staple of journalism from the first printed broadsides. In the days before institutionalized relief, Emporians responded spontaneously to such news by organizing as a community to help the victims. These efforts were encouraged and recognized by the Gazette. As soon as reports of the 1900 Galveston flood reached town, City Marshal Dan Dryer and policeman John Burns began carrying subscription papers for a relief fund up and down Commercial Street; the Gazette reported that a mass meeting would be held that night. And in 1903 the paper announced: "Every public spirited and charitably disposed woman in town is requested to come to the Whitley hotel parlor tomorrow to help make bed ticks for the Topeka flood sufferers. . . . There are 100 ticks to be made and that means work." Such efforts were no doubt less effective than those mounted later by professional relief agencies, but they made it possible for Emporians to unite and act upon their sympathies rather than remaining isolated and passive bystanders.[42]

During the Progressive Era, politics and government dealt increasingly with questions that affected the daily lives of Americans, and the *Gazette* emphasized this connection by focusing on how national and state legislation translated into local experience. For example, an item on the new pure-food law dealt primarily with how it had changed the taste of Coca-Cola. Even before the publication of *The Jungle,* concerns about the quality of "foreign" processed food, not to mention child labor practices, were satirized in an editorial, "Watch Your Lard."

> Users of lard made in Wichita will confer a favor on a bereaved family in that town, by following the instructions printed below from the El Dorado Republican.
> "A 13-year-old boy by the name of Drake Watson, who was working in a Wichita packing house, disappeared at three o'clock Friday and it is suggested that he fell into the leaf-lard vat. He was not exactly holocausted or incinerated, but he was probably exhaled, evaporated, or to speak professionally, 'rendered.' The deceased, demised, exhaled, or 'rendered' young man leaves a father who 'drew' his wages, and a step-mother who often failed to patch his pants. However, if any of the housekeepers who use Wichita packing house leaf-lard should find any stray buttons, buckles or the like, pertaining to the paraphernalia of a 13-year-old boy with a step-mother, in their pie dough, it is hoped they will send word to the bereaved parents. . . ."[43]

Emporians also participated in the general interest in reform ideas during the period by attending the frequent public lectures by prominent reformers. Large audiences heard Eugene V. Debs, sociologist E. A. Ross, single-tax advocate John Z. White, and muckrakers Ida Tarbell and Lincoln Steffens. Afterward, their talks were reported in full in the *Gazette.* The 1906 news story on Debs commented, "Debs is a pleasing and forceful speaker—not given to oratory, and a man of rather conservative cast for a Socialist, and he pleased his audience immensely."[44]

In his editorials, just as in his magazine articles, White sought to interpret the news of the period's varied political, economic, and social reform movements as all facets of the same historical tendency. After prohibitionist O. B. Hardcastle's election as mayor in 1905, White concluded, "What has happened in Emporia recently has been repeated all over the country. The law-breakers, the tin-horn element, the good fellows and those who think they control politics, and tie up with them, have been defeated by the law-abiding people. . . . The conscience of the people is quickening." In 1906 he pointed to the battles being waged between "the people and the politicians" in states from New Hampshire to Georgia to Nebraska and found them all a "manifestation of the growth of the spirit of kindness and decency in American politics." Emporia was right there at the forefront of history.[45]

For many of us who live in impersonal urban and suburban America, White's celebration of community in the *Gazette* bears a nostalgic attraction. Yet one must keep in mind that the *Gazette*'s portrayal of life in Emporia also had aspects that are less appealing. Rooted as it was in boosterism, the *Gazette* defined community in ways that served the interests of local business and consistently placed businessmen in the center of community life. It did not treat all Emporians equally. And, as illustrated by White's readiness to attack publicly those who resisted the "community's" interests and to suppress dissenting opinions, his vision of community had little room for values of personal freedom and self-expression. His insistence upon communal morality and unity severely limited his tolerance of diversity.

When White said in "The Country Newspaper" that "we who live in the country towns know our own heroes," he drew examples from a variety of occupations in Emporia. But it was George Newman whom he termed our merchant "prince" and Al Ludorph, a hack driver, who filled the role of "villain": "Boston people pick up their morning papers and read with shuddering horror of the crimes of their daily villain, yet read without that fine thrill that we have when we hear that Al Ludorph is in jail again in Emporia. For we all know Al; we've ridden in his hack a score of times."[46]

Shakespearean theater has its "high" characters, kings and princes who speak in blank verse and carry out the burden of the dramatic action, and its "low" characters, peasants and artisans who speak in prose and provide comic relief. Such differential treatment reinforces social hierarchies, and there was often a similar division of function among the classes in the *Gazette*. Although this tendency was mitigated to a degree by the need to attract a large readership, most often "prominent" Emporians played the major roles, with the poor forming the dramatis personae for low humor.

Because of the centrality of business in White's vision of community, the activities of Emporia's commercial elite were automatically defined as newsworthy. Conversely, the *Gazette* was particularly reluctant to publicize controversies when prominent citizens were involved. Occasionally the newspaper even admitted this, as in a humorous item in 1905: "Another good story has been spoiled because of the prominence of the families involved. The Gazette would like to have a law passed, making it a crime punishable by hanging, for the members of prominent families to commit any wrong." Scandalous or humorous stories reinforced the "otherness" of outsiders or marginal members of the community. Since respectability was identified with middle-class norms, those who either could not or would not conform were fair game for public ridicule. Black Emporians in particular bore the brunt of this distinction in the *Gazette*.[47]

Much of the unequal treatment of black Emporians was caused by the difficulty that even well-meaning white Americans like White had in envisioning racial minorities as full-fledged members of the community. To the extent that blacks conformed to middle-class values, White acknowledged them. But they had no rights to any form of alternative culture apart from the booster standards of propriety. White's vision of community demanded complete homogeneity.

White's attitudes toward and treatment of blacks were far more tolerant than those of many Americans of his day. Several times when he attended formal dinners during his travels, he made sure to sit beside Booker T. Washington when others refused. In the *Gazette*, blacks were accorded the titles of Mr., Mrs., and Miss, often denied them in other newspapers. Black voluntary societies were covered in much the same way as white. Booker T. Washington's visit to Topeka in 1905 merited a large front-page article complete with a photograph of the educator. Susan Tipton, matriarch of a prominent black family, was honored with a front-page top-of-column story upon her death: "She was one of the kindest souls in town and her going will bring sadness to a great many people in Emporia besides her relatives." The *Gazette* saluted the homecoming of local black soldier Lloyd Stafford, who had seen "hard and dangerous service" in China during the Boxer Rebellion.[48]

But blacks were not treated equally. Black Emporians were nearly always differentiated from their fellow townspeople by the appellation "colored" after their name or elsewhere in the news item. The *Gazette*'s reporters often used a condescending tone in news items about black Emporians. For example, one began, "The swellest wedding in colored circles occurred last night. . . ." Another related the story of "Henry Davis, the aged negro hod carrier on the new court house," who had lost his balance while carrying a hod full of mortar up a flight of stairs. In trying not to spill it, he had fallen off, landed squarely on his head, and been knocked unconscious. But, according to the story, "Mr. Davis came to, jumped up and started to work and said he was not hurt, one bit." Which "substantiates the old theory that a negro's skull is unbreakable."[49]

While White and the *Gazette* praised local blacks who fulfilled booster norms of respectability, they had no tolerance for those who did not. In answer to an inquiry about the situation of blacks in Emporia, White asserted that although the older generation did all right, "the younger generation is often lazy and trifling" because they clustered in too large numbers in towns. Moreover, black Emporians who stepped beyond the bounds of propriety received less consideration than whites in similar situations. In 1902 the *Gazette* reported "a little altercation" that had escalated into a "free for all scrap" between two black men, whose names were given; but an anecdote in the same issue about a white man who pulled a gun on another did not mention any names. The difference was that the black men had been arrested and fined, while the white man had not, although he had been restrained by a policeman. Similarly, much of the *Gazette*'s differential treatment of the races reflected that of the rest of society. It could be said to be merely reporting matters of public record in noting that "Ann Henderson and John Duncan, both colored, who have been congregating too much together, have been given until Wednesday to leave town." Or that police had "arrested Lewis Hunt and Jack Reana, two of the drunkest negroes that ever hit the town."[50]

Many of the *Gazette*'s inconsistencies in treating different social groups arose from White's refusal to recognize their different economic situations. Quarrels among middle-class families generally took place within the shelter of those large, comfortable houses on their fifty-foot lots that White was so fond of describing, whereas poorer blacks or whites could not afford such privacy. According to the *Gazette*'s policy, if a quarrel remained private—within the house—it was not news that the community should know; if it took place on the streets, it inevitably became a public matter. When a black woman threatened her husband's lover with a pistol on an Emporia street, the *Gazette* reporter took full advantage of the dramatic material by writing up the story as though it were a theater review. The front-page story was entitled "A Great Show" and concluded:

> The acting was superb throughout. The little Washington woman as the villain, who was breaking home ties, was done with concentrated scorn. . . . Fanny Powell in the emotional role displayed much power and her crying and screaming brought prolonged applause. It was the best black face show that has been in town for a long time.

Similarly, the arrest of nine young black men for crapshooting was written up as a mock society event, complete with dialect dialogue, and entitled "Emporia's Four Hundred." The names of the blacks were printed; that of a white hack driver who was also arrested was not.[51]

The most blatant discrimination against blacks in the *Gazette* decreased with time, but a new minority group that was just beginning to emerge in Emporia was also treated unequally. In 1907, the Santa Fe began importing Mexican laborers to work on its roadbeds. Soon whole families lived in railroad cars and shacks along the railroad south of town. But, as far as the *Gazette* was concerned, these new residents were invisible. Only occasionally, when they were arrested for fighting or made some other unmistakably "public" action, did they enter the *Gazette*'s definition of community: "Today is railroad pay day, and crowds of the Mexican laborers, who are working on the track, were on the streets and in the stores today, spending their money."[52]

There was also little room in White's conception of community journalism for genuine diversity of opinion. In "The Country Newspaper" he interpreted the declining numbers of competing newspapers in each town as a positive sign "that the spirit of these communities is unifying." The days of the partisan press, when "many newspapers babble[d] the many voices arising from the disorganized spirits of the place," he likened to "those curious phases of abnormal psychology . . . wherein a dual or multiple personality speaks."[53]

Boosterism's demand for unity denied the legitimacy of personal rights wherever these conflicted with the public interest. Like many progressives, White believed that rights inhered in society, not in autonomous individuals. His primary concern was for the effects of the news upon the community as a whole. He argued in a 1913 editorial that a Socialist who had been prevented from making a speech on a Hutchinson, Kansas, street had no inalienable right to speak. "Free speech and free press are not rights of an individual. An individual has no rights either of property or of conscience or of speech, which violently conflict with society as it is established about him." He said this not because he disagreed with the man's views, for he admitted that Socialists had proposed ideas twenty years ago that were now "highly respectable." Their error, he said, was that they were too far ahead of the rest of society, although social progress would eventually catch up with them. This rejection of individual rights inherent in boosterism would find its fullest expression during World War I.[54]

Given the more and less appealing aspects of this philosophy of community journalism, one must still ask, how much influence did the *Gazette* really have in Emporia? Did the newspaper have the unifying effect on its readers that White envisioned in "The Country Newspaper"? How did readers respond to what they read in the *Gazette*? Such questions are hard enough to answer today, with the tools of survey research at our disposal. We cannot, unfortunately, administer to shades of Emporians past a questionnaire designed to quantify whether reading the *Gazette* made them "wondrous kind." But there are some bits of evidence that enable us to make at least a few tentative statements.

Emporians then and later delivered mixed verdicts upon White's and the *Gazette*'s influence in Emporia. As early as 1902, a former Emporian commended White for his "influence for good in the town." David Hinshaw, a local boy who began as a country correspondent for the *Gazette*, later credited White with healing the "generation-old town row." He admitted that "a few fortunate funerals clearly helped, but the benign influence of a great and kindly spirit was largely responsible for the vastly finer Emporia of today." On the other hand, the son of the longtime president of the Normal School commented, "There was a saying, and it was partly true, that if you wanted something defeated in Emporia, get the *Gazette* to support it." White's defeat on the electric plant issue demonstrated that, even when he threw the full weight of his newspaper behind a cause, he could not count on imposing his way of thinking on specific issues upon Emporians.[55]

This inconclusiveness is not surprising. The longstanding debate over whether the press has the power to force its will upon the people, or is merely a passive reflection of public opinion, has proven impossible to resolve in those terms. It is more profitable to view the question of influence as a matter not of simple linear cause and effect but of mutual interaction between newspaper and audience.

As a "practical" businessman and free-lance writer, White was well aware that he had to please his audience if he wanted to succeed financially. Consequently, even before he began to appreciate local news as the foundation of community, he published such "load of hay" news because his readers wanted it. James Whitcomb Riley had once advised him that "the real success of [writing] depends upon *not* how it pleases *the author,* but how it pleases his *audience.*" White not only accepted this dictum but passed it on when the opportunity arose. When he and his *McClure's* colleagues bought the *American* in 1906, White warned John Phillips that "the great danger before you is that of being too Purposeful." He advised instead a strong dose of humor: "You should have the sharp claque of the slap stick and the rattle of broken glass down the sky-light to indicate the course of the Dutchman's journey."[56]

It was easier to be receptive to one's audience when, as a small-town editor, one was literally surrounded by it. Long after he stopped soliciting for advertising, White continued to perambulate Commercial Street to test the waters of public opinion. He evaluated responses to political developments, as he described to a colleague, by getting out "on the street" and talking "to the merchants and farmers and people generally." He sought out the opinions of those of different political persuasions, like his pressman Jim Yearout, who was the son of a local Democratic leader: "he kinda took interest in what makes that little guy click like that." In many local issues, White delayed taking a stand until he had a sense of where opinion lay. He often employed a technique much like that which Theodore Roosevelt has been credited with inventing at the national level—the trial balloon. White would make a noncommittal comment about an emerging issue and wait for the response from his readers before taking a definite stand. At times this gave an impression of inconsistency, but except for instances in which he felt important principles were at stake, it kept him from taking on losing causes like the electric plant issue.[57]

Nonetheless, the *Gazette* did achieve significant influence over the public expression of ideas in Emporia, by virtue of its success in dominating the town's newspaper field. By 1907 the *Gazette* had a circulation in Emporia of nearly eighteen hundred, reaching at least three-quarters of the families in town. The *Republican,* dealt a serious blow by the failure of the First National Bank in 1898, had changed hands several times after C. V. Eskridge's death in 1900. Early in 1903 it had been sold again, to an editor backed by a group of White's factional enemies, but the paper finally ceased publication in 1905. White claimed that it failed because Emporians knew it was a kept "organ": "Subscribers will go where they can get the news with the least bias. . . ." But readers might have been attracted just as much by the improvements in the *Gazette* made possible by White's ability to mobilize the capital to acquire advanced machinery and, above all, his instituting the Associated Press wire service news. During the controversy over the electric plant, White's opponents tried to found yet another daily, the *Journal,* edited by William Martindale's son Edgar, but it was short-lived. After 1905 the principal alternative to the *Gazette* was a weekly Democratic paper, the *Times,* supplemented by a handful of tiny weeklies in outlying Lyon County villages.[58]

In the days before radio and television, the *Gazette* was an integral part of daily life for many Emporians. An afternoon paper, it figured prominently in the evening ritual in many households. Margaret Soden, the daughter of a prominent local businessman, recalled that her father read the *Gazette* every evening after supper: "He sat in a certain chair—I can see him as plain as anything—sitting there, smoking a cigar and reading the *Gazette.* And, 'Do not talk to Daddy! Don't talk to your father, your father's reading the paper.'" In the Soden family at least, the prevailing attitude was "If the *Gazette* said it, it was right." But even if one didn't always agree with it, she insisted, "the *Gazette* was just part of living here in Emporia." During Janet Cleveland's childhood in rural Lyon County, her mother entertained the whole family in the evenings by reading aloud from the *Gazette.* "She always looked through it first to see what was in it, who died, who was married and all that." The *Gazette* also served her and her brothers and sister as a primer. She still has a tattered 1902 copy with circles drawn around the words that she could read at five years old.[59]

Each reader approached the newspaper differently, according to his interests. One might read primarily the national and political news, while another, like the young Margaret Soden, might look through it "to see if it had anything about anybody I knew." Scrapbooks kept by Emporians during this period demonstrate a lively interest in news of the births, deaths, and weddings among a surprisingly wide network of family and neighbors, as well as a fascination for human-interest items of all kinds. Although few Emporians would have read everything in the *Gazette,* it is likely that, with fewer distractions to fill their evening leisure hours, most read more of the paper than is common today.[60]

With such a large proportion of Emporians reading the *Gazette,* White did have the power—within the limits established by his readers' interests— to decide which events and issues received extensive coverage and thus were brought to general attention. As we have seen, he used this power to promote values of community harmony, morality, and business leadership. At times, such as in the campaigns against Dr. Meffert and for enforcement of prohibition, these values contradicted each other. On those occasions, he accepted controversy in the interests of morality, but he sought to dampen conflict in many other moments of potential tension. When a local woman accused a man from a prominent county family of attempted rape, the *Gazette* reported the sensational trial in only the most neutral terms. White even sent proof sheets of the stories to the attorneys for both sides, for their approval. At the conclusion of the case, the news story closed with an admonition to all parties to put bad feelings aside: "It is a disgrace to this community that such bad blood exists."[61]

In White's earliest days at the *Gazette,* he attempted, with only limited success, to use this power to define important issues against local Populists and his factional opponents. After 1900, in order to enlarge his readership, he toned down his partisan rhetoric in the newspaper and emphasized local human-interest reporting. By downplaying the many local feuds that had been engendered by Emporia's longstanding factional divisions, White may well have helped to foster feelings of goodwill in his community. Nonetheless, even such "unbiased" stories contained a larger bias toward his booster beliefs. As the *Gazette* prospered and the investment required to start even a small-town newspaper increased, Emporians found fewer opportunities to express controversial points of view.[62]

A second form of influence, more subtle but perhaps even greater, lay in the newspaperman's power to describe events. Through his choice of language, White affected Emporians' means of thinking about them. Again, this ability was shaped by the interplay between his purposes and the limits of the language he employed. In order to be effective, his characterizations of events had to fit within established rhetorical structures and patterns of belief. White excelled in this regard, for according to his need he was able to draw upon a dazzling repertoire of rhetorical traditions ranging from the Old Testament to a salty midwestern vernacular. His exuberant facility for language pleased Emporians even when they disagreed with his ideas. The son of a Populist farmer said, "My father didn't always like William Allen White too well but he liked his writing—he was a wonderful writer." Despite the fact that he was a Democrat, James Yearout read White's editorials regularly: "There was a little extra something there that would just fascinate you and you get the feeling within. . . . It seemed it was home like, just like you and I sitting here talking."[63]

Although White's political editorials were reprinted throughout Kansas and the nation, Emporians remembered and treasured most his editorials on local subjects. A former Emporian recalled on White's death, "Mr. White's best editorials to me were not those on national affairs which impressed the country, but the local ones, particularly his incisive characterizations of his friends who died and his always human comment on life in a prairie town." Margaret Soden can still quote from the obituary he wrote when her grandmother died: "One of the most beautiful things that I think he ever wrote was after she died. . . . It's a lovely thing."[64]

For at least a few, White's ability to name events in the *Gazette* altered ways of thinking. David Hinshaw testified to the editor's influence in his life:

> Forty years ago as a farm boy, I once filled a bad chuck-hole in the road near my home, solely because travelers were severely jolted as they drove over it. Only my father's hired men had seen me do it, and they ridiculed the act. Sometime thereafter a *Gazette* editorial, in discussing good citizenship, said that the man was a good citizen who on his own initiative took a shovel and filled holes in the road. Within ten minutes after reading that editorial I had grown six inches in mental and moral stature. In filling that hole I was only being neighborly. But when Editor White, who did not know of my action, called such deeds evidences of good citizenship, he opened a new world for me.

White had only taught the boy a word, but along with it came a new identity and in time careers as a progressive organizer and pioneer public relations counselor.[65]

It was in this opportunity to articulate—to give effective expression to—the experiences of Emporians that White's greatest influence lay. He referred to this interrelationship between newspaper and community in "The Country Newspaper": "The newspaper is more than the voice of the country-town spirit; the newspaper is in a measure the will of the town. . . . [A newspaper becomes] dominant and authoritative because it interprets and directs the community."[66]

But perhaps nothing better illustrates the complex and intimate relationship between writer and audience, editor White and Emporia, than two public gatherings that occurred in 1909 and 1910. In the summer of 1909, just as *A Certain Rich Man* was due to be released, all the Whites, including children Billy and Mary and mother Mary Hatten White, sailed for Europe. It was the fulfillment of a long-awaited dream, for which the Whites had been saving for ten years, and the family romped happily through a Grand Tour of the Continent and England. They did not learn until their return voyage that *A Certain Rich Man* was a substantial success, selling out four editions almost immediately.[67]

In Emporia, proud residents bought more than twenty-five hundred copies, nearly one for every fourth person in town. A few citizens began to plot a suprise homecoming for their now-most-famous citizen. The ringleader seems to have been the *Gazette*'s star reporter, Brock Pemberton, but members of the organizing committee also included prominent Emporians and White's allies in many reform campaigns. Days before the family's scheduled arrival, a poster appeared around town, asking "every man, woman and child on the townsite" to welcome them at the Santa Fe station: "William Allen White is Emporia's most prominent man, and the First citizen of Kansas. Honor him and Our Town and yourself by coming out."[68]

When the train bearing the Whites pulled into the station, it was met by the town's Silver Cornet Band, playing "Hail the Conquering Hero"—just as it had done when he returned from his convalescence in 1902. This time the air was filled with banners, proclaiming "The Homecoming of Colonel Hucks," (referring to White's early short story by that name), "In Our Town Once Again," and "What's the Matter with Kansas, Hey Bill?" The family was escorted to open hacks, paraded to the bandstand in Humboldt Park, and regaled with a program in which townspeople assumed the roles of the residents of *A Certain Rich Man*'s Sycamore Ridge—in many cases, characters that seemed to have been patterned after themselves. For example, Sheriff Tom O'Connor performed the duties of fictional sheriff Jake Dolan, as marshal of the parade, and the venerable Civil War veteran Colonel J. M. Steele gave an address in the costume of the novel's Colonel Martin Culpepper. The town's quartet sang sentimental ballads of which "John Barclay's mother" had been particularly fond, and at the end the family was escorted home to the strains of "Home, Sweet Home." Literature and

Homecoming celebration gathered at the Santa Fe station, 1909
(William Allen White Memorial Library, Emporia State University)

life seemed perfectly fused in a moment of goodwill and celebration. Emporians seemed happy to identify themselves with the images that White had created. Learning of the homecoming, Ida Tarbell wrote, "I never have read anything lovelier in my life than the account of your home-coming. We all wept over it. Aren't you glad you staid by Emporia?"[69]

The following year, White found himself at odds with many of the same men who had organized his homecoming, over the issue of selling the municipal electric light plant to private developers. Despite the *Gazette*'s strenuous opposition, voters approved the sale in a referendum made possible by progressive legislation that White had promoted. When the results became clear, the victors hired the same town band for a celebratory parade that ended in a serenade on the Whites' front lawn. It was an amiable charivari, and White appeared on the front porch to make a few friendly remarks. But the meaning of the moment was clear: White was being compelled to accept gracefully the will of the majority, to acknowledge that in this case "the people" had spoken in contradiction to the *Gazette*. To remain in a relationship with his local audience, White knew that at times he had to accede to its power over him.[70]

Prompted by his emerging progressive ideas and by the changing economic nature of journalism, White had developed a new understanding of the purpose of the small-town newspaper, one that remains at the heart of community journalism today. In the *Gazette* he simultaneously celebrated and fostered a feeling of community that was based on the assumption that all its members shared his booster beliefs. In pursuing this vision he honored Emporians and their daily lives; he placed them at the center of a universe of concentric circles emanating outward from "Emporia, U.S.A." If this vision was provincial and often unequally applied, it nonetheless affirmed for many of its readers that their lives were significant and meaningful.[71]

Still, this vision also contained fundamental contradictions based on the newspaper's functions as embodiment of community on the one hand and mediator with the outside world and promoter of economic growth on the other. This contradiction became increasingly visible after 1910, as the focus of progressive reform efforts shifted toward the national sphere and as the national mass-production economy affected more and more of daily life. Furthermore, with the imperative of the greatest progressive reform of them all, the "war to end all wars," White's insistence upon unity and service sanctioned the serious repression of individual liberties.

PART III

Nationalizing the Community

8

Booster Nationalism

In his *Autobiography* William Allen White recalled that during the First World War he and the *Gazette* had energetically supported every measure on its behalf:

> I was on all of the money-raising campaigns, chairman of a "Special Gifts" committee—which means I helped to look after the larger givers. Every country editor's job is to conduct, directly or indirectly, his town's drive for progress and benevolence; and it was no new experience for me to pound the streets of Emporia with a subscription paper in my hand.[1]

White recognized that his role in promoting Emporia's full participation in the war effort was a continuation of his local booster activities. Indeed, the war years in Emporia, with their unremitting citizen activism, their patriotic unity, and their self-sacrificing enthusiasm for the common good, were a booster's dream. In many ways the war merely intensified the essential characteristics of boosterism. When President Woodrow Wilson decided to rely principally upon an aroused public opinion, rather than a greatly expanded state, to prosecute the war, he tapped boosterism's tremendous rhetorical and organizational power. He also unwittingly unleashed boosterism's capacity to foster oppression as well as loyalty.[2]

Even before the beginning of World War I, however, the booster ethos had increasingly come to serve national rather than local ends. Although it was obscured by White's and other progressives' tendency to equate the local and national communities, the momentum of reform in the second decade of the twentieth century moved to the national level. As the focus of political action shifted from the cities and states to Washington, progressives who advocated reform by centralizing power in the national government assumed leadership of the movement. These nationalist progressives, gaining prominence through sheer energy and effectiveness as institutional innovators, adopted new methods of shaping public opinion and promoting reform. These methods included special-interest lobbying groups, the new "profession" of public relations, and techniques of community mobilization that united central planning with local execution.

Though he was largely unaware of the long-term implications of his actions, White aided this nationalizing and centralizing shift. By supporting new nationalist organs of progressive publicity, he gave legitimacy to their centralizing programs and obscured the real differences between those who called themselves progressives. Similarly, at the local level he and the *Gazette* helped to introduce agents of centralization to Emporia. As a community leader, White spearheaded local drives, such as a campaign to build a YMCA center, that were directed by national organizations. The *Gazette* incorporated increasing amounts of nationally oriented news, publicity, and advertising. This decade of White's editorship of the *Gazette,* then, showed that the small-town newspaper could be an instrument of centralization just as effectively as a protector of the local community.

William Allen White's political activities in the 1910s reflected the shift within progressivism from local to national spheres of action. When several insurgent Republican legislators from Kansas became embroiled in controversies with party leaders in Washington, they drew White more deeply into national politics. In the hot, emotional summer of 1912, he found himself leading, albeit reluctantly, a new political party. From then until the Progressive party's dismal defeat at the polls in 1914, White devoted much of his time to party matters: planning state and national strategy, raising funds and organizing, campaigning, and, in his spare time, boosting the new party through his newspaper and magazine articles.[3]

The progressive movement encompassed a wide diversity of organizational approaches, as White's activities illustrated. He relied heavily upon time-honored practices in his work as a state politician. Here, the *Gazette* was his primary organizing tool. During the early struggles between pro- and antireform factions in Kansas, it had been his most effective means of distributing publicity. When Robert La Follette spoke on behalf of Kansas insurgents in 1908, White made sure that sympathetic publishers received full and immediate reports via wire and stereotyped plate. Progressive-minded journalists communicated frequently through meetings, correspondence, and the exchange of newspapers, and they were major sources of information about local politics. For example, in 1910 the insurgent Republican state chairman, Jonathan N. Dolley, sent White a list of "friends" in Burlingame, Kansas, that had been supplied by a local editor.[4]

The customary newspaper exchange network, in particular, continued to be an important form of progressive communication. As political conflict mounted in Kansas, newspapers from other areas sought to exchange papers with the *Gazette,* in order, as one put it, "to keep in touch with public sentiment in Kansas." The applicant added, "You might find The [Milwaukee] Journal of some use in regard to the trend of politics in this section of the country." During the 1914 campaign, White expanded upon this traditional practice by offering cut-rate subscriptions to the weekly *Gazette,* which served in effect as a Progressive newsletter. He even offered a special combination deal: "the Gazette and a dozen Murdock and Allen buttons for $1.00 for one year, with 50 cents of the dollar going into the state campaign fund."[5]

The many *Gazette* alumni who published small-town newspapers in the area amplified White's voice within this network. He had given these editors their start and helped them find places as editors in their own right. His motives had been benevolent, but he had also built a cadre of like-minded journalists indebted to him. During White's campaign to establish a Progressive party, he used this referral process more self-consciously to ensure a network of sympathetic journalists. Progressives hoping to establish a beachhead in their communities often wrote White asking for the names of young men who could launch Progressive newspapers.[6]

These alliances proved invaluable whenever White orchestrated news to create the impression of a spontaneous movement in public opinion. For example, alumnus Rolla Clymer became editor of the El Dorado *Republican,* Bent Murdock's old paper, in 1918. He recalled that White maintained their friendship long afterward through correspondence, "messages of friendliness and wisdom and faith." Clymer explained how White worked:

> Occasionally he would drop an offhand line to say that Joe Dobbins might be good material for attorney-general or lieutenant-governor, and that I might profitably look into his qualifications. Then, after I had done so and had timidly written a few words to the effect that Joe might shed glamor on the state service, Mr. White would pick up my remarks in his column.
>
> Observing, in the manner of one making a great discovery, that "the papers around the state" were beginning to mention Joe Dobbins, he would forge ahead in slashing, 12-cylinder fashion to boost the candidate he had already hand-picked and launched upon his trail to the stars.[7]

Other midwestern progressives promoted the movement through long-familiar forms. The editor of the Optima, Oklahoma, *Optimist* even proposed embodying it in a fraternal organization: "Call it the society of the Square Deal and each member a Knight of the Square Deal, and let each Knight wear upon his breast a bronze button with the words 'Knight of the Square Deal' upon one side with the picture of Roosevelt and some other words and suitable emblem on the other." He envisioned lodges in each town, but with few officers and "no secret work." He believed that this would not only take the movement out of party control, but attract to it people of all parties, religions, and classes.[8]

Without abandoning his traditional methods, White also used the new national media to further local political ends. He knew that progressive-minded national magazines could often counteract adverse coverage in partisan local newspapers. For example, when progressive U.S. Senator William Borah was acquitted of charges of fraud in 1907, White urged him to let *McClure's* do an article on the case, pointing out that many Americans "look to the magazines for their final judgments" and that newspapers had ignored or mishandled the story of his vindication. Similarly, in 1908 he urged Norman Hapgood and Brand Whitlock to help Joseph Folk's campaign for the U.S. Senate in Missouri by providing publicity in *Collier's* and *Everybody's.*[9]

While it contributed to the achievement of local ends, using these mass-circulation magazines also increased the power of the national media. Magazine editors such as John Phillips of the *American Magazine* were aware that their coverage of what was often local political infighting had helped to create the impression of a national movement. When White attacked Kansas senator Chester Long in the Kansas City *Star,* Phillips urged him to write a similar piece for his magazine. He told White about Lincoln Steffens's idea of getting "all the magazines" to focus upon different members of Congress simultaneously. "The idea is to affect legislation and the reorganization of the House." A few days later White forwarded an article, asking, "How would this do for my September contribution to the Government by Magazines. . . ."[10]

In much the same way, some Americans who called themselves progressives were fashioning new national organizations to rationalize and centralize the process of "reform." Among them, enterprising young publicists, single-issue reform groups, professional associations, and corporations developed systematic, large-scale techniques to mobilize public opinion. Although throughout the nineteenth century American reformers had sought to arouse public opinion on behalf of their causes, such efforts became more systematic and effective in the Progressive Era. These would in time overshadow the more informal and locally based journalistic practices.[11]

In this period, too, reformers created their own publicity departments instead of relying upon personal ties to journalists like White. The Progressive party speedily established a publicity bureau soon after its birth. David Hinshaw, the young Emporian whom White had taught about citizenship and who had helped White organize the Kansas Progressive campaign in 1912, was a staff member in 1914.[12]

At the same time, enterprising publicists founded independent organizations expressly to disseminate progressive publicity throughout the nation. Their projects served simultaneously to advance progressive causes and to create jobs for themselves in the growing communication industry. As a nationally recognized figure, White was frequently solicited to lend his support by contributing articles or merely allowing his name to be listed as an advisor. Announcing, "We have it in for the Associated Press," the president of the Twentieth Century Company informed White in 1910 of his plans to syndicate news about progressive causes, which he claimed the AP was mishandling. He asked White to let them use his name as an associate director and to recommend correspondents to cover a gamut of progressive issues from public ownership of utilities to "Any Victory of Genuine Democracy." Other young progressives launched magazines, such as *The Progressive News,* dedicated to publicizing the movement. The most long-lived project of this younger generation of progressive journalists was, of course, *The New Republic.*[13]

Although the centralizing goals of these organizations contradicted White's localist perspective, he did offer at least nominal support to many of them. As a consequence, his network of progressive acquaintances and his national reputation as an activist continued to widen. Early in 1910, Raymond W. Pullman, who had formerly handled publicity for Gifford Pinchot's U.S.

Forest Service, wrote White about his plan for a "Publishers' Conservation League, to promote the Roosevelt-Pinchot conservation policies." He was backed by a friend of Pinchot's, E. A. Van Valkenberg of the *Philadelphia North American,* and had already rounded up six other prominent reform-minded publishers. White was one of another thirty-six whom Pullman hoped to enlist in an "educational campaign."[14]

Shared language bridged—and obscured—many differences between progressives. Like most successful rhetoric, the wonderfully elastic concepts of "efficiency" and "conservation" could mean different things to different people and thereby seem to unite groups with differing goals. In this case, the Conservation League's invocation of conservation gave it license to take on a wide range of projects.

> Newspapers which collectively wield the power of publicity can have no higher duty than to stand against all waste and to stand for public economy as embodied in improved agricultural methods, development of waterways and fisheries, forest preservation, extension of transportation facilities, prevention of mine accidents, pure food, economical distribution of products, and those two things most important of all—the proper care and protection of the child and the maintenance of public health. Conservation in the broadest sense does not mean any one, but all of these things.[15]

Pinchot's promotion of conservation through the rule of scientific experts ran contrary to White's booster definition of progressivism. Nonetheless, faced with such a formidable list of undeniably worthy causes, White allowed his name to be placed on the association's new letterhead as a member of the Advisory Board. His friendship for Theodore Roosevelt probably also played a role, for it often blinded him to the significant differences between his outlook and Roosevelt's.

White rarely used the word "efficient," but when he did he meant it simply as a synonym for the booster term "businesslike." Certainly, he had always opposed "waste" when it was produced by corrupt or shiftless Populist or Democratic "politicians," but the concept operated more in a moral than a scientific dimension. On the other hand, for the more urban progressives, "efficiency" connoted technical expertise or the dominance of professional or corporate elites. Men like industrialist George W. Perkins who joined the progressive bandwagon in this period used the word to promote a nationally centralized, rationalized society led by enlightened corporate managers. The National Civic Federation embodied their vision. Again, despite the many differences between his philosophy and that of this wing of the movement, White allowed his name to be listed as one of four hundred sponsors of the Federation's "National Industrial Survey."[16]

The emergence of public relations as a specialized occupation epitomized the rise of systematic, centralized organizational forms in this period. Previously, although a few businessmen and politicians had employed "press agents," most relied upon informal, reciprocal relationships with newspapermen like White to foster favorable public opinion. In response to the increased independence of newsmen like White, many large national corporations hired public relations "counselors." Arguing that antibusiness attitudes were caused by misinformation spread by "demagogues," they sought to give the public their employers' side of the story. For example, in 1915 a new "special representative" for the Katy railroad wrote White to correct some statements he had made in an editorial: "In my judgment many similar stories . . . are published, not because editors desire to do railroads an injustice, but because railroads are sometimes shortsighted in not giving the editors fair opportunity to get at the real facts."[17]

Just as these new centralized, systematic ways of organizing communication were developing in coexistence with decentralized, informal styles, the pages of the *Emporia Gazette* conveyed messages from both local and national sources. Foreign and brand-name advertising, in particular, continued to increase during the 1910s. Although the contents of national and local advertising were often similar, they conveyed strikingly different visual impressions. National agencies could produce far more sophisticated and effective graphics than could the *Gazette*. This contrast, widening over the years, eroded the *Gazette*'s ability to portray the local community as the center of its citizens' cosmos.[18]

Foreign and brand advertisements provided the most visually striking aspect of the newspaper in these years. Messages for Ivory Soap, National Biscuit Company products, Armour's Glendale Oleomargarine, Calumet Baking Powder, and Sunkist Seedless Oranges invariably stood out on the newspaper page by virtue of their superior design and vivid illustrations. Their messages, however, remained familiar appeals to product quality, wholesomeness, and dependability. Armour, for example, appealed to maternal instincts by employing adorable round-faced cherubs to speak for Glendale Oleomargarine.[19]

At the other extreme in terms of design sophistication stood local advertising, which still consisted of simple type-filled boxes announcing the availability of certain goods or asserting the dependability and economy of their wares. A few businesses added generic illustrations, such as a cartoon of "Ben the Booster" in the Emporia Lumber & Coal Company ads. The *Gazette* purchased the cuts or plate for these illustrations from commercial type foundries or received them in exchange for advertising space. Retailers of women's clothing such as Newman's and Rorabaugh's used more fashion illustrations in their ads, but the typographical descriptions of the products continued to overshadow the pictures. Although they added visual interest to the advertising, rarely were these illustrations more than a decorative touch; words and images did not produce a unified message.[20]

Many local merchants who sold national brand products included pictures of them in their own advertisements. Brand manufacturers now provided such promotional materials as part of their sales programs. Illustrations appeared most frequently for technologically new products: stoves, electric fans and sweepers, the new "victrolas," and, above all, automobiles. Like the illustrations in local advertising, they simply enlivened the text rather than forming part of its message. Men's brand-name clothing advertisements were an exception, being entirely produced by the manufacturer, with only a space at the bottom for the local store's name. Some of these were the most advanced advertisements in the newspaper, combining words, images, and decorative detail to create an impression of dignity and sophistication. Ironically, they imparted to their mass-produced men's wear the aura of the hand-tailored suit that the products were making a thing of the past.

During this decade, too, motion picture advertising began to appear in the *Gazette*. Local theaters bought ever-larger amounts of space through the decade, but their advertisements continued to be plain type-filled boxes announcing the theater and the name of the coming attraction. The producer, director, or actors might receive mention if they were well known. As the decade progressed, a line of small, light type came to describe the film itself: for example, *The Case of Becky*, with Blanche Sweet, was "A thrilling and dramatic story of a young woman possessed of two personalities." Adjectives alone could not adequately convey the excitement promised by the new medium.[21]

Advertising by movie producers themselves was a harbinger of things to come, as the volatile film industry began to pursue a new market strategy of product differentiation through the star system. In 1916 Metro Pictures launched a series of stylish ads in the *Gazette* to promote its products. One presented an array of photographs of their stars and said, "These are some of the Big Stars appearing in Metro Pictures. Is your theatre showing them?" In time, Emporia theaters advertised with brand names, just like other merchants. The Electric Theater announced that it was showing films by Paramount and Artcraft Pictures Corporation, billed as "identically the same pictures that are shown at the Strand, Rialto, New York, and Circle Theaters on Broadway."[22]

Soon publicity releases accompanied the advertising. The *Gazette* had always published as news promotional stories about the theatrical troupe playing at the Whitley Opera House, often favorable reviews copied from other newspapers. After the turn of the century, photographs of one of the company's illustrious members occasionally appeared. These "puffs" were simply reciprocal favors in exchange for paid advertising and free passes to the productions. When motion pictures came to Emporia, the practice was easily transferred to their features. As the motion picture industry matured, however, its public relations departments learned to exploit such customs of reciprocity more systematically. Emporians were thereby first introduced to such glamorous actresses as Theda Bara, "considered by many the greatest of emotional actresses."[23]

Such advertisements barely suggested future trends; overall, they did not change the appearance of the *Gazette* enough to distract readers from its focus upon the local community. Yet behind the scenes the advertising industry made advances in organizational techniques analogous to those of the public relations profession. Going beyond designing advertisements, agencies and manufacturers planned complex, coordinated campaigns employing several media. For example, Armour & Company's campaign kit for Glendale Oleomargarine included large advertising cards, announcing "As advertised in the Emporia Gazette." It asked the paper to distribute these to retail stores in Emporia, explaining, "We believe that by directly linking the retail stores with the advertising the campaign will be more productive." It also provided the stores with "Sales Helps," instructing them how to connect the advertising with "the window displays and novelties" it provided. The *Gazette* reported that the merchants welcomed all the attention.[24]

Other promotional campaigns required the local merchant to pay for the advertising, again placing the newspaper in the role of mediator. The Peninsular Chemical Company wrote the *Gazette* about its plan for a three-month campaign and said that it had sent a copy of its new ad book to its local agent. "If he has not already taken up this advertising, it would be a good idea to call on him and discuss the matter."[25]

Increasingly, such campaigns provided promotional material intended for the newspaper's news columns themselves. Food companies seeking to increase the consumption of their products supplied recipes that featured them. These appeared either in the advertising itself, as in a campaign for Sunkist oranges in 1917, or in supplemental materials distributed to the newspapers. For example, the Lord & Thomas agency enclosed recipes for "Jiffy Jell" along with its advertising order and asked that they be forwarded to the household editor. "Be sure and send a copy of the issue containing the ad and recipes in the enclosed wrapper to the advertiser, also a copy to us," they instructed.[26]

Advertisers appropriated progressive rhetoric for their own purposes, demanding "cooperation" in return for their increased expenditures. Some merely asked the *Gazette* to provide them with information about likely distributors for their products. The Pilot Motor Car Company asked for help in recruiting dealers, justifying its request by pointing to the returns it would reap: "You create another customer for your advertising space. . . . At least 80 per cent of our advertising appropriation is spent in local papers in cities where we have dealers." Others, however, asked the *Gazette* to persuade merchants to order products for which it received advertising. At first, Walter Hughes balked at such requests and asked a colleague for his opinion. "We feel that this is an imposition on the newspapers, but do not wish to be unfair to advertising agencies. If other newspapers are doing this soliciting and canvassing, we want to do it too."[27]

Requests for "cooperation" often formed part of a carrot-and-stick approach that promised the newspaper more advertising in the future. In 1916, Lord & Thomas placed a small order for California Fruit Growers Exchange advertising, but promised that "by co-operating on the special Christmas and Orange day large advertisements" the *Gazette* could nearly double its business with the Exchange. The agency warned, "It is needless for us to say that the papers getting the largest amount of co-operation

will of course be the first considered on future advertising on this account."
Such cooperation required the *Gazette* to round up advertising for Sunkist
from at least five local fruit dealers, all to run on "Orange Day." The agency
also suggested that it might want to give retailers proof sheets of the advertising to display in their windows. It added, "Some publishers have
also expressed a willingness to make occasional mention of our client's
brands in their local news columns; in fact, there are several effective methods of co-operation, and while we do not insist upon any specific assistance,
we certainly expect your hearty cooperation. . . ." Similarly, the International Silver Company noted with its contract that this was a trial campaign, "and co-operative effort on the part of the publisher [is] absolutely
necessary." It commented ominously that some papers did not seem to be
cooperating: "And some of these publishers complain that national advertisers do not use newspapers instead of magazines."[28]

The Association of National Advertisers went beyond these demands,
asking newspapers to publish editorial material—one might say propaganda—on behalf of advertising itself. The president of the Remington
Typewriter Company, which advertised in the *Gazette,* wrote:

> You are sellers and we are buyers of space. The more this space is worth to
> us—the greater is bound to be your return. We believe that nothing will do more
> to enhance this value than a campaign of education such as we now plan—de-
> signed to instruct the public on the true function of advertising and the rea-
> sons why advertised products have a legitimate claim on their patronage. Pub-
> lishers of newspapers and other periodicals all over the country have already
> done so much in this line of their own volition that we feel that your co-
> operation is assured from the outset.

He enclosed an article entitled "To Investigate the Influence of Advertising on Prices," which he called "the first gun in this campaign." He also
suggested that the paper might want to adapt some of the materials in
its own editorials. "Needless to say," he concluded, "the members of the
Association of National Advertisers are intensely interested in this campaign." They would consequently be given the names of all publications
that used their publicity. A month later, after the *Gazette* sent the issue
in which the first article appeared, the secretary of the association replied,
"We assure you that your co-operation with this Association is very much
appreciated."[29]

Cooperation had its rewards. At the end of 1917, the *Gazette* commented
that it had had more "foreign" advertising that year than ever before. This
increase took place in spite of America's entry into the European war and
the fact that the paper had raised advertising rates in response to substantial increases in the cost of newsprint.[30]

As a small business, then, the *Gazette* was thriving. But it was also gradually becoming as much an agent of national corporations as of local interests. It was also surrendering to these advertisers a certain degree of
the independence it had only recently gained when freed from dependence

upon party patronage. In much the same way, as a community leader White encouraged an alliance between local booster means and national organizational ends. Before this, boosters had emulated other cities' improvements, but now the desired reform was coordinated from the top down by a nationally centralized organization. Emporia's 1914 drive to build a home for the YMCA illustrates the extent to which national organizations harnessed booster rhetoric and energies. White was the driving force behind the campaign, exactly as he had been of the street fair fifteen years before. Although both drew heavily upon booster rhetoric, the YMCA drive united local participation with national direction. Such campaigns set the stage for the mobilization of booster energies on behalf of the war to end all wars.

Despite his many state and national activities in this decade, White continued to be closely involved in local affairs. Even as he directed the Kansas campaign for the Bull Moose party in 1914, for example, he masterminded the mayoral candidacy of Robert M. Hamer, an attorney and fellow Current Club member who happened to be a conservative Republican. Similarly, he continued to keep an eye on the local liquor situation, warning District Court Judge William C. Harris about the "rising activity of bootleggers in Emporia. . . ." He had not published anything about it, he said, "because it would hurt the town as a student town and . . . it would probably be said that I was calling attention to the shortcomings of political opponents." He urged Harris to warn the county sheriff and attorney "that it doesn't need newspaper publicity to disseminate the news."[31]

White's biggest local project during the first half of the decade was to raise seventy-five thousand dollars to build an impressive home for Emporia's YMCA. He was deeply committed to the idea of the YMCA not because of religious feeling but out of concern that boys were growing up in an increasingly restrictive and corrupt society. His turn-of-the-century "Boyville" stories revealed a powerful nostalgia for the vanished world of his childhood, when growing boys had been free to roam the fields and woods unhindered. He often expressed concern that, without such experiences, boys would grow up too staid and "soft." When his own son was ten, White confided to a friend that he thought young Bill was too well-behaved for his own good. The YMCA represented a hope of preserving youth's morals and masculinity in an overcivilized environment. He told a prospective donor that the YMCA was a "place where the boys could go to feel perfectly at home . . . under the decent environment of manly directors." No doubt the booster imperative that a community have all the amenities that other towns had also played a role in his thinking. When the local ministerial association organized a group in 1907, the *Gazette* commented that "in towns where these organizations exist, it is said that fewer boys loaf in the pool halls and on the streets."[32]

White had agitated for a YMCA since the middle of the 1900s, but could stir little interest among his townsmen until the advent of moving pictures in 1907 and a vaudeville house in 1913, which aroused the concern of many Emporians about the effects on their children. The town's progressive mayor, John Glotfelter, tried to prevent the establishment of the first nick-elodeon theater, reasoning, according to the *Gazette,* that it would "tend to give children the habit of going to such places." The *Gazette* did not echo his reservations, perhaps because the new manager advertised regu-larly and promised to show such edifying features as a filmed Passion play. More substantial movie houses soon appeared and also advertised gener-ously in the newspaper. As was typically the case with progressive regula-tion, Emporians attempted to reconcile the benefits of economic growth with its tendency to undermine community values: they ensured the health-fulness of movies shown in town by instituting a municipal censor.[33]

In late 1913, the county attorney requested an injunction restraining the new movie house, the Star Theater, from presenting vaudeville perfor-mances. He was responding to a petition from members of the City Federa-tion of Women's Clubs, the city superintendent of schools, the high-school principal, and the Congregationalist and Presbyterian ministers. The educa-tors and the municipal movie censor had investigated a performance and found the vaudeville sections "vulgar, full of improper suggestion and in-nuendo." The superintendent asserted that it was "tending to corrupt the morals of young people, who composed 90 per cent of the audience." "The whole performance was abnormal for the life in Emporia," he concluded. "It might pass in Chicago, but not in Emporia."[34]

Henceforth, Emporians found themselves more responsive to reformers' efforts to protect the town's youth. In March 1914, citizens voted 1,923 to 1,312 to close the town's pool halls, where boys congregated to play pool and smoke cigarettes. In May, a large, well-organized group of volunteers launched an intensive ten-day drive to raise funds for a YMCA building.[35]

White had been trying to get such a drive off the ground for nearly three years. Even now, many "knockers" resisted the idea, for the community was just beginning to recover from the economic effects of a bad crop failure the preceding summer. In March, White had refused to publish a letter from Episcopal minister Carl Nau criticizing the drive, on the ground that the decision to launch it had already been made. "Your letter could not affect that decision," White explained. "It could only make it a small Y.M.C.A., and I do not believe that your object would be to cripple the movement." Once such a civic activity was under way, boosterism decreed, no good citizen should do anything that might interfere with its success.[36]

White chaired the drive, and his exhaustive efforts followed the general pattern of his earlier booster projects—organizing projects to involve the people, ceaselessly exhorting their participation in the newspaper, and pri-vately appealing to the loyalty of his friends. For ten days, beginning on May 19, Emporia and its hinterlands were the object of the most intense and carefully organized fund-raising campaign they had ever experienced. Significant differences, however, separated this drive from its predecessors. In this instance, participation was counted primarily in terms of donating money. And although Emporians carried out the drive, the national YMCA organization had planned and directed it.

The *Gazette* called it the "famous scientific whirlwind ten-day campaign." The YMCA's plan systematized and intensified the traditional process of fund raising through personal contact, or, one might say, peer pressure. Before the drive began, volunteers compiled card files with the names of people likely to subscribe money. The *Gazette* announced, "There are four thousand names on the information cards of the YMCA committee in this town, and every one of that number will be expected to give something." One hundred canvassers, all men, received these cards and contacted every person named at least once within the ten days of the drive to "invite" contributions to the building fund.[37]

To reduce the diffidence that volunteers might have about asking money of their neighbors, the drive employed sophisticated motivational techniques. Volunteers were divided into ten teams, which competed for the largest amount of pledges. They met for lunch each day at the drive headquarters in the Commercial Club rooms, where their results were calculated and the leading team announced. A member of that team then had the honor of moving the hands of a big clock mounted on the Citizens National Bank building, on the corner of Commercial and Sixth, to record progress toward the fund-raising goal. In addition to spurring their efforts by stimulating competitiveness, this practice created smaller, more cohesive subgroups to encourage a sense of team loyalty. At each day's luncheon the volunteers heard an inspirational talk from one of the prominent Kansans whom White had recruited.[38]

To complement the fund raiser's personal appeals, the *Gazette*'s relentless publicity whipped up public enthusiasm for the project. Each day the paper carried a large box on the front page exhorting Emporians to open their hearts and pockets, a long article in the center column on drive activities, and, on inside pages, editorials, cartoons, and more news stories promoting the drive. The appeals rang every conceivable rhetorical change. Invidious comparisons showed what other Kansas towns had already accomplished. The interdependent local economy was invoked: "Ninety-five per cent of the money spent for this $75,000 building will flow right back to Emporia for labor, and lumber, and stone, and dry goods, and furniture, and fittings, and plumbing, and painting and hardware. We are really only swapping dollars among ourselves." Business sense and morality were again united: "The men in [the campaign] are hard-headed business men, who know that the town as a town is worth more to them as a market if the boys and young men are strong and clean and wholesome." The *Gazette* emphasized the unity of all local interests by pointing out that YMCA boards always included a "union labor man" and a farmer. The building would be located "within reach of every railroad man in town." Efficiency-minded progressives received assurances that "Every dollar spent for a YMCA building takes ten dollars from the community's cost of jails and courts." And "A Y.M.C.A. building in a town bears the same relation to the town's morals that sanitation and hygienic living bear to the town's health."[39]

Nor did the paper ignore religious considerations: "The Y.M.C.A. will do many things for Emporia. . . . But chiefly it will promote the spirit of Christ in this community—the spirit of service, of brotherhood, of spiritual regeneration. . . . It will bring new members into the church trained for effective work." These statements appeared on Saturday; pledge cards would be distributed in all the churches the next day. "Go to Sunday School determined and prepared to give sacrificially for a cause that will make Emporia a cleaner, better town for all the years to come; for your children, and their children, through all the years." There was indeed something for everyone.[40]

Mit Wilhite's appeal, published in the *Gazette*, combined many of these arguments and demonstrated their close ties to the booster ethos:

> [YMCA] means better boys and that means better business for my hotel; better credits, and a better class of patrons. I'm willing to admit that, like every other business man, I'm looking after my own interests, just as the Gazette is, and every other business man. But also, my interests are like the other business man, and what's good for me is good for all. And more than that, I'm no knocker. I've been in every good thing in town and I'll not miss this.[41]

Moreover, Wilhite's appeal indicates the passion with which "true boosters" regard their cause. Admitting that at first he had thought it the wrong time for a drive, he insisted: "But the time to talk of that is past. If the campaign fails now it will hurt the town. . . . It's got to win. It would be a black eye if we lost, and I'm right here to tell you that the bunch meeting up there in the Commercial Club rooms never fails." Once the project had been publicly launched, there could be no looking back. Wilhite's sense of civic—and masculine—honor was touched. "We may be wrong about starting; but we've started, and we can't stop till we win, without hurting the town. No man who claims to be a booster has any business on the outskirts of this fight. He must get in, and get in where it is thick and hot, and where his licks count."

For the first time in this campaign, a new visual form of persuasion reinforced this familiar booster rhetoric in the *Gazette*. Many cartoons and drawings, provided by the national YMCA organization, promoted the drive. They were printed with standardized electrotypes, to which each local newspaper added typographical touches to localize the illustrations. These additions were generally so awkwardly done, however, that the effect emphasized the disjunction between the universal and the particular. Early in the campaign, the paper sported an attractive promotional banner across the entire front page, just below the masthead, composed of a series of illustrations explaining "What the New Building Will Mean to" entities ranging from "The Young Man," shown in coat and tie reading a book, to "The City and State" and "The Future Home." Nowhere in the illustration itself was there anything specific to Emporia. But along the sides, in a different typeface from that used in the drawing itself, were the words "$75,000 by May 29 for a Y.M.C.A." and "Emporia's Investment in Her

Young Manhood." The plain sans-serif typeface supplied by the *Gazette* looked out of place beside the more stylish lettering used in the illustration. Another drawing depicted a valley between sheer cliffs on right and left. At the right, over the cliff's unfenced edge, tumbled long lines of boys, one after another. At the bottom of the cliff a broken boy on a stretcher was being lifted into an ambulance. But the cliff on the left hand had a fence, labeled "Association Work," which held masses of boys safely away from its edge. In the center, in a cursive type, were the words "Fence or Ambulance"; at the top, in the *Gazette*'s type, it said, "The New Y.M.C.A. will Save the Boys of Emporia."[42]

As the campaign came down to the wire, the drive appealed to civic pride and simple excitement. The sheer size of the goal created a sense of drama, as citizens wondered whether the volunteers could reach it. Emporians were urged to come out and wait "for the returns" as though it were an election night. They would be entertained by a band concert in the street outside the rooms where the results were being tabulated. Whistles would blow every thousand dollars added to the total. All eyes would turn toward the clock in the final moments. The *Gazette* vowed, "The fight will last until midnight."[43]

The paper described the interest in outlying towns and villages. The drive, it claimed, was the focus of all eyes:

> These things are set down so that this town may realize how much it means to win—not merely here in Emporia, but all over the country. Tens of thousands—literally—are watching the outcome of this campaign. From all over the world eager eyes of our friends and former residents are watching the clock. To fail—but that is an impossible contingency. We MUST win. As it was ten days ago in the beginning, so it is now, and ever shall be world without end.

Far more was at stake, it seemed, than the mere size of the new YMCA building.[44]

Meanwhile, White worked feverishly, personally soliciting political allies and family friends alike. When all other arguments failed, he appealed to personal loyalty. He wrote to Thomas O'Connor, who as a Catholic was alienated from the evangelical Protestant organization:

> This Y.M.C.A. campaign is a very personal matter with me. I know the limitations that the association puts on Catholics and it is not right and it is not fair but I am not to blame for it. . . . I shall be responsible for the failure or success of this thing. I have never made a personal laydown on you before, but I want you to fill out this card and return it to me.

He wrote a former Emporia resident, "I am sending a letter like this to all my good friends and I hope that we can make a good showing." And he cajoled his old booster colleague Robert L. Jones:

> I do not care what you think about the Y.M.C.A. I do not care what you think about the high-jinks of the boys on the street turning the clock, but I do care what you think of your old side pard, and your old side pard will be

blamed if this campaign fails. . . . I can tell you in confidence that I have given $2,000.00 and intend to give more, and I want you to help protect my ante.[45]

As the deadline loomed, White did indeed give more, adding another thousand dollars to his pledge. He was also forced to call in some personal reserves. A few days after the campaign had ended, he wrote to A. O. Rorabaugh, his old advertising ally, whose dry goods business had prospered so well that he had moved on to bigger things in Wichita. White reminded him that the last time he was in town "I hit you for a subscription and you said if right at the last we needed something to make up the fund, I could put you down. Well, that time came as, of course it had to come." White himself had signed a pledge card for Rorabaugh in order put the drive over the top. "It was absolutely necessary in order to get this thing across. . . . I had worked all the morning on it before I decided that I would be justified in using your promise in this way. I hope for old sake's sake and for the sake of the town where we both got our start that this will not make you unhappy."[46]

The appeals to booster values and personal loyalties that put the YMCA drive over the top resembled those that had achieved many other causes in Emporia. The day after, White wrote the customary editorial pointing out the "true" meaning of the drive. "It was a great victory for the town because it united everyone. If the building should burn down the day after it was built, it would have been worth all of that for the fine spirit of fellowship and mutual help that it developed in the town." Yet he unconsciously gave an ironic twist to his interpretation by noting that the spirit of community had been achieved through an imported system. The men had followed "a tried and perfected system, and they accomplished what seemed rather wonderful to those who did not know how it was being done." It was the combination of the national organization's "splendid system" and the "tireless, hopeful, intelligent work" of the Emporia men that had won the day.[47]

White moved on from his YMCA fund-raising drive to organize the 1914 campaign for the Bull Moose party in Kansas. But when that ill-fated party lost miserably at the polls, he had to admit that his hopes of founding a progressive third party had failed. He told Theodore Roosevelt that he and all the Progressive leaders were "dead tired." He recognized that the party had not unified the people. "Our vote was a town vote, an upper middle-class vote. . . ." Many of his reform comrades experienced the same weariness. Sighing, "I have had my fill," John Phillips told White in 1915 that he was leaving the *American Magazine*. "Besides, between you and me, I don't believe I can edit the competitive, popular magazine in these days, as the game is now done and run."[48]

Yet White had not given up altogether on the crusading spirit, for he had no sooner written off the Progressive party than he launched a local campaign to raise money for the Belgian Relief Committee. During the relief drive, the *Gazette* tried to shock its readers out of their complacency by painting a grim picture of children and old people in Belgium starving "while we live in our accustomed luxury." Exhortation was no longer enough, however. White had learned that it must be reinforced by the new organizational techniques. He warned a colleague in another town not to let leadership of the relief drive get "into the hands of any preacher. It is a business man's job." To White this now meant the new method of systematic face-to-face convassing. Public meetings alone were useless, and "turning the job over to a preacher, means there will be a lot of tears shed, but not much money." By the end of the month, Lyon County residents had donated five thousand dollars, enough to buy a thousand barrels of flour.[49]

By now, it seemed, White regarded a cause as little more than a pretext for launching the public drives that created community spirit and, perhaps, sustained his local leadership. Ever since his street fair, White had promoted civic virtue by organizing events that demanded group participation and cooperation. At first he had advocated such spirit as a means to economic prosperity, but with his progressivism came a desire for civic spirit in itself.

Experience showed, however, that genuine community cohesion was difficult to achieve and even harder to sustain. It was helpful if public drives somehow created a sense of urgency that heightened the need for unity. In the case of the YMCA drive, fear of the town's "losing the fight" and being shamed in the eyes of the watching world became a powerful force for "cooperation," if not cohesion. Recent experience had also shown that exhortation should be backed by "systematic" methods that reinforced traditional personal pressures.

By the time America entered the war, then, many of the qualities that would become associated with wartime "hysteria" had already been foreshadowed in Emporia and in the *Gazette*. The booster ethos had long advocated self-sacrifice to the common good and demanded unified participation in every community project. Community life, and the *Gazette,* had already become "nationalized" by 1917 to a far greater extent than at the turn of the century—whether in matters of reform, entertainment, consumption, or communication. Life in Emporia was by no means a completely standardized product of nationally centralized agencies, but such organizations had achieved far greater influence over the community's day-to-day experience. The First World War merely accelerated this process.

America's entry into the Great War provided a genuine cause for urgency. White, like many other reformers, seized upon the war as a powerful tool with which to forge a higher community. During the war years, spurred by White and the *Gazette,* Emporians supplied the emotion and energy, but planning and approval came from Washington.[50]

As the carnage in Europe mounted after 1914, the war came home to Emporians every day in the *Gazette*. The Associated Press dispatched ever more extensive accounts of the war to America, and the newspaper received war news from other sources as well. The first and most striking change that the war brought to the *Gazette* was the appearance, in early 1915, of front-page photographs; most of them were war-related, although some were about human-interest stories in America. Since White had made it a policy never to pay for such material, and since they invariably portrayed the Allies favorably, these photographs probably resulted from Allied propaganda efforts.[51]

Instead of depicting the ravages of war directly, these photographs focused upon the less threatening human dimension of the conflict by showing individual Englishmen, Frenchmen, or Belgians: nice, normal people caught in the midst of war. One photograph featured a little girl who alone of all her family had survived the sinking of the *Lusitania*. Another showed British soldiers obviously relishing being shaved by French women barbers. Perhaps one of the most effective—if these were indeed intended as propaganda—was a photograph of swarthy, sinister "Franz von Rintelen, German Agent," said to have "spent huge sums of money in an attempt to embroil the United States and Mexico."[52]

From 1914 to 1917, White's feelings about the European war underwent an evolution typical of many of his countrymen's: from aversion to aquiescence to enthusiasm. In 1914 he announced that there was no difference between the belligerents. After the sinking of the *Lusitania,* he took the part of the Allies but feared the effects of war on American society. He wired President Wilson, "Running amuck with the rest of the world will accomplish nothing for humanity." In 1915 he joined the League to Enforce Peace, which he saw as a middle ground between pacifism and outright war. As the war dragged on and the American economy fattened on its war industries, White grew uneasy. As 1917 dawned, he wrote a stinging jeremiad in a New Year's Day editorial: "As a nation we are rich with blood money. . . . Our prosperity is cursed and tainted. Some day we shall have own own fiddler to remunerate. 'Vengeance is mine, saith the Lord, I will repay!' And he has a little bill against this United States." When America finally entered the war, White vowed, like a good booster, "Having gone into the fight we must wage it so that the world will know that our entrance has counted. We must hit and hit hard and hit as quickly as we can."[53]

Once war became inevitable, White, like many progressives, found silver linings. Perhaps it *could* serve positive ends. "A great moral victory and a great advance in civilization must come of the war as compensation for the devastation," he concluded. He began to hope that war could purify and strengthen community spirit.[54]

By the end of the war White would argue that the war had indeed done for America what progressive politics had been unable to do—reawaken and cleanse its spiritual consciousness. He wrote in the *Gazette,*

Seriously and frankly, the United States before the war had in many respects been losing some of the vigor which has been the heritage of the nation. And with the days of our industrial and agricultural pioneering gone, a period of prosperity had been making us soft with luxury. The virility and the clearness of American thinking and action had been slipping. . . .

Then came the war. . . . It has aroused our intellects to an appreciation of our shortcomings and it is hardening us again, as individuals, and as a nation, in ways of physical and mental existence. . . . [The war's] suffering and grief will reawaken the national consciousness, clarify our mental powers and restore our national vision.

Throughout the war, White predicted that the enlarged wartime role of government foreshadowed the realization of many progressive goals. He hoped that by wholeheartedly supporting the war he would also help to channel its energies into permanent progress.[55]

In promoting this greatest of all civic campaigns the *Gazette* played the role it had always played—calling attention to a cause vital to the community's well-being, exhorting the people to action on its behalf, rewarding those who did more than their share, and shaming those who did less. For the duration of the war and through the Versailles Conference, the war dominated the *Gazette*'s news, editorials, features, and advertising. It carried several columns a day of Associated Press dispatches from Europe and additional columns of news of the war effort in America from wire service reports or the press releases that flooded in from the countless new war-related bureaucracies. It carried unremitting publicity for drives for Liberty Loans, Baby Bonds, the Red Cross, the YMCA—there seemed never to be a moment when there was not some drive going.[56]

Government press releases were reinforced by the artistic creations of the Division of Pictorial Publicity of the Committee of Public Information, which pioneered the use of emotion-laden images to inflame readers' patriotism. Either as illustrations alone or as part of advertisements, these drawings added unaccustomed visual style to the *Gazette*. Local merchants sponsored many of these advertisements, and their names appeared at the bottom, just as they did in standardized ads for national brands. Occasionally the merchant added a message of his own, such as the War Saving Stamp advertisement "patriotically donated by Poehler Mercantile Company." It listed the names of brands that the store carried and promised, "By buying these brands you will be able to save money with which to buy War Saving Stamps."[57]

The *Gazette* went far beyond these imported manifestations of patriotism, however. It heightened the intensity of wartime enthusiasm by treating participation in the war effort as yet another, but far more compelling, booster cause. The newspaper argued that Emporia's contribution revealed as much about its spirit as did its support of a YMCA.

Indeed, when it came to mobilizing the nation for war, the government used much the same system as the YMCA. In preparing for entry into the war, Wilson's Council on National Defense had proposed creating a network of "community councils of defense" on the local level so that all citizens could be "reached through personal contact." Once the task of industrial mobilization began, however, this local structure was superseded by one based on what one historian has called "the new communities of production, distribution, and consumption—communities vertically organized and far-flung." Nonetheless, even here the administration often depended upon public opinion to enforce its regulations. Bernard Baruch used threats of public shaming to enforce the pricing policies of his War Industries Board, reportedly promising one industrialist that if he refused to comply with WIB's directives, "you will be such an object of contempt and scorn in your home town that you will not dare to show your face there."[58]

Meanwhile, the local community remained the fundamental unit when it came to raising manpower and funds, and organizers combined time-honored booster appeals with the new face-to-face fund-raising system. Looking back on the war effort a decade later, White was struck by the "nearly automatic way" in which Emporians organized themselves. That is, they went about war mobilization just as they had the many previous local campaigns.

> Within a month [of the declaration of war] our Chamber of Commerce had lent its files and our Y.M.C.A. building was crowded with workers. The County was card indexed. Every family in the county was on the card index with his financial rating and when the call came for work these cards were given to team captains who again gave them to team workers and in four or five days Emporia filled her quota. . . .

The *Gazette* assured Emporians that fund raisers would be neither spiteful nor "smart alecky," but because they believed in a righteous cause, "they will insist that Lyon County give its dollars as freely as it has given its men."[59]

When it came to enlisting young men to serve their country, the federal government chose to work through local draft boards made up, in the words of Selective Service administrator Enoch H. Crowder, "of friends and neighbors of the men to be affected." On the day appointed for registration for the draft, the *Gazette* in a front-page box instructed Emporians to "Hang Our Your Flag," and in another box on the same page suggested that the day should be one of "serious meditation upon the solemn duty that lies before us." It published the names of all registrants.[60]

The *Gazette* backed the official power of the boards with communal praise and pressure. It gave extensive publicity to Lyon County soldiers, from their enlistment and training to frequent reports in a "Camp and Field" column on the front page. A number of the *Gazette* work force enlisted, including three who served in France, and White promised that their jobs would be waiting for them when they returned. Their places were filled temporarily by young women. The newspaper had nothing but contempt for those men who shirked their duty. The *Gazette* published the names of all those who requested draft exemptions and criticized a young Emporia man for taking an exemption as a minister, predicting that the war itself would do much to promote religion. White joined a group of nationally known writers and artists called the "Vigilantes," whose aim was to "arouse the youth of the nation to their duties in peace and war." The *Gazette* also published the group's writings.[61]

Beyond the government's official demands, however, "booster patriotism" expected every member of the community to contribute according to his station and ability. The *Gazette* honored women's traditional wartime contributions—nursing, making clothing, and preparing bandages—but in this war it became evident that housewives were more important as consumers than as producers of goods. The *Gazette* published reams of materials from the Food Administration instructing women on how to comply with the changes in patterns of food consumption mandated by war needs. They provided numerous recipes and hints about what to serve on wheatless days or how to use a new product such as corn oil. Food manufacturers also sought the imprimatur of patriotism for their products. Calumet Baking Powder united progressive home economics, the war effort, and advertising interests in a campaign featuring a series of articles by "eminent Domestic Scientist" Maude Marie Costello. Calumet's advertising agency billed the articles as "an educational campaign that shows how to bring down living expenses. Housewives who read and follow this series of articles, certainly will be doing a bigger 'bit' towards the conservation of foods." An Armour ad proclaimed, "The war will be won in the kitchens of America."[62]

Men and women alike were expected to contribute financially to the limit of their abilities—and beyond. The *Gazette* lauded Mrs. Mary Rishel, who had given her last fifty cents to one fund drive because "She wanted to feel that in this town, she rowed her own weight in the boat." The newspaper reasserted the booster ethic of reciprocity: "A man in a newly established business in Emporia, a stranger to the town, gave $50 without so much as asking 'how much is expected.' See that you patronize him." And an editorial contrasted a "rich" Emporia woman who had a son in France, and donated liberally to the Red Cross, with a "rich" man who, it was said, had hidden his assets from the assessor and who bought few war bonds. A French woman who was fund raising asked both for a donation; the woman gave fifty cents, the man five cents. "God bless one of Emporia's richest women, and God forgive one of Emporia's richest men," the paper commented. Emporians had little trouble figuring out to whom it referred.[63]

Typically, White poured his own energies and money into the cause. He put much of his savings into war bonds, and toward the end of the war Walter Hughes had to borrow money to cover a huge bond purchase that White had made on the spur of the moment. Above all, he considered his greatest responsibility to be educating local-minded people about America's new responsibilities as a world leader. At the invitation of the Red Cross, but at his own expense, he traveled to Europe in the fall of 1917 to write about its work there. From this trip came a number of articles on behalf of the Red Cross and a book, *The Martial Adventures of Henry and Me,* that attempted to make the war intelligible to small-town Americans.

He also wrote publicity materials for the Red Cross, for the Treasury Department's bond drives, and for the Committee on Public Information. Back at home, he spoke to audiences in rural schoolhouses and churches throughout Lyon County. As he told Walter Lippmann, "Incidentally, I have been soliciting for the Y.M.C.A. and using that as a reason for the meetings, but what I have been trying to do is to get this war to the farmer."[64]

In proper booster fashion, White also hoped to turn mobilization to the town's benefit. He promoted Emporia as a site for a training camp, telling his congressman, "These soldiers will be country town boys for the [most] part, who are clean, wholesome, vigorous young chaps, and who should not have the temptation of the saloon, the gambler and the prostitute anywhere near them." Their safety would be "absolutely guaranteed" in Emporia, for "Our community wouldn't stand for it for a minute."[65]

Most significantly, he considered censorship of wartime news to be perfectly consistent with his vision of community journalism. His editorial "Local Censoring" drew an explicit and revealing connection between the typical booster role of the newspaper and its wartime functions.

> Considered in the light of the rules in existence on the average conscientious newspaper, the four great principles of the new censorship might have been laid down by a newspaper editor.
>
> "They must be accurate in statement and implication," says the first regulation regarding dispatches. The same requirement for news will be found on page 1, paragraph A of any cub's primer in the country.
>
> "They must not supply military information to the enemy," says the second. Every day a good editor is meeting in his own field the same requirement. He is withholding information which would bring harm and no possible good to his town.
>
> "They must not injure the morale of our forces here, or at home or among our Allies," says the third. Every day in the week, the conscientious editor is insisting that the news he prints does not injure the morale of his community.
>
> "They must not embarrass the United States, or her Allies in neutral countries," says the fourth. The editor is withholding news which embarrasses and which cannot help his town, or the agencies which are of benefit to the town.
>
> The government started the war by regarding the press as a nuisance, except when it might be of use in appeals for funds for carrying on the war. There was more or less of a sentiment that newspapers were not essential to the winning of the war. Slowly this sentiment has been breaking down. At the outset of the war, 95 per cent of the newspapers of the United States were insisting that as a war measure, all foreign language papers should be suppressed for the duration of the war. The war has entered its second year, and Congress is beginning to talk about what the newspapers have advocated.[66]

During the war, White and many other newspaper publishers showed little concern for questions of free speech or free press, but then, they had rarely done so before. Nor was White sensitive to the rights or feelings of townsmen who failed to demonstrate proper enthusiasm for the cause. Even after the fighting had ended, the *Gazette* reported that the "Emporia slacker committee" had exacted donations from two working-class men who had been reported "for failure to subscribe and for showing an improper attitude toward solicitors." The committee visited one at the behest of his boss, the proprietor of the Lenox Restaurant, who wanted to be able to put up a "100 per cent" sign in his window.[67]

In wartime, just as during a booster campaign, those who refused wholehearted support endured denunciation as "kickers." White blistered his old progressive friend Joseph Bristow, whose criticism of conscription, White insisted, gave "aid and comfort to every disloyal Socialist, every noodleheaded pacifist, every treacherous German citizen, and every white-livered coward slinking from his American duty." When a mutual friend objected, he replied privately: "I wish America might have been able honorably to keep out of the war, but America was not. . . . There is only one way to get out of the war, and that is to fight out, and we will flunk out a lot quicker if men like Bristow . . . justify all the mollycoddles and sapheads in their weak and wobbly attitude toward the war." Though he professed sympathy with many of the goals of the agrarian Non-Partisan League, he insisted that its "pacifism and pro-Germanism" made it "an enemy to the country."[68]

He was still less concerned about the rights of the area's German-American population. As quoted above, he advocated the suppression of German-language newspapers, and he publicly recommended the deportation of Lyon County resident Gottlieb Sattler, who, he said, had lived in this country for thirty-seven years but "had kept his soul in Germany." He applauded the rejection of "hyphen" identities as reflections of "Americanization," one of the "solidifying effects of the war." "One of the things the American freedom cannot tolerate is the clannishness of the old blood ties. To be an American a man must be an American and nothing less." At the same time, he lauded those who publicly professed their loyalty, such as German-born businessman Carl Ballweg, who in 1917 sent out Christmas cards avowing his devotion to his adopted land. In good booster terms, Ballweg admitted his interdependence with his community, saying that he and his fellow immigrants had "sponged on all America had, her free lands, her free schools and above all, her spirit of open-hearted comradeship. . . . We would be recreants, ingrates, perjurers and curs if, in the hour of her need, we counseled with her enemies and were disloyal to her cause."[69]

In these various ways, boosterism became nationalism. The mobilization of Emporians on behalf of the war influenced everyone's behavior and language. The war's organizational practices even affected the ways that Emporians went about familiar community affairs. In 1918, local women's organizations launched an intensive drive to "enlist [each] home in the national movement for greater conservation of child life. . . ." They planned to visit every home in the county to investigate children's conditions and instruct mothers in proper child care. Even the Gazette's traditional spring sermonette on the homeowner's lawn-care responsibilities took on a more ominous tone:

> Too many lawns are frowsy in Emporia. Too many yards need care. We have Red-Crossed and YMCAed and Baby-bonded around so enthusiastically that we seem to forget that, after all, Emporia must go on for centuries as a home town.
>
> Now that the Red Cross drive is almost over in the town, it is up to Emporia to clean up. The civic committee of the Chamber of Commerce is beginning to have feelings. It will call on the negligent home and lot owners soon, if they don't perform.[70]

It was during the war that the language of "efficiency" most clearly predominated. In the interests of winning the war, efficiency was a means that threatened to become an end. For example, the *Gazette* praised both the spirit *and* effectiveness of the local Red Cross, particularly "its efficient chairman Carl W. Nau." It editorialized against "mental slackers" who wasted valuable time in woolgathering. "Success in these strenuous times and in the equally exacting period which will follow the war will come only to the man who is able to be on the job mentally as well as physically. . . ." Even the churches adopted the rhetoric; the local Presbyterian church advertised a lecture on "Church Efficiency."[71]

Nonetheless, Germany's reputation for efficiency caused some reservations about the concept. White defined German *Kultur* as "a certain efficiency of government obtained by keeping the majority of the people out of all voice of governmental affairs, a certain low cost of manufactured products . . . made possible by enslaving the workmen." In contrast, he exulted that his friend Henry Allen had gotten the Republican nomination for governor in Kansas while remaining in Europe working for the Red Cross and YMCA. "That, after all, was the core of his campaign: Faith in the folks. If the folks are not to be trusted, democracy is a farce and the Germans are right."[72]

Under pressure of the war, time-honored habits of communal discipline through exhortation and personal pressure had become more systematic, more efficient. In the process, their coercive powers and potential for intolerance were considerably heightened. Although there were few instances of violence against German-Americans or others suspected of disloyalty in Lyon County during the war, the rights of many were roughly handled. Ironically, this intolerance was the result of American disinclination to entrust the central government with sweeping formal powers. The Wilson administration counted upon aroused public opinion, rather than national bureaucracies, to enforce its policies. Although it deplored vigilante violence against those suspected of disloyalty, it must be counted as having encouraged it.[73]

The war represented an unparalleled intrusion of national forces into the community's life. The fact that they operated through familiar community processes only made the intrusion all the greater, for they were thereby transformed into instruments of national goals, and became only secondarily expressions of community cohesion.

The First World War brought to a climax the progressive alliance of localist and nationalist reformers. With the war's end, the alliance would collapse, leaving behind little of its initial spirit, but much of its organizational skeleton, for historians to examine. Nevertheless, it is not wholly accurate to say only that the Progressive Era was a transition from one method of organization to another, for in the small towns of America much of the booster ethos remained alive, if attenuated. But that world was increasingly dominated by the growing national corporate economy and its allied federal administrative structure. Henceforth, community activities would most often be planned and directed by parent national organizations.

The 1920s would see the fuller realization of this process. Once again, the *Gazette* was in the forefront of this change, as the newspaper was transformed from a defender of localism into an agent of the national media.

9

Mass Media Come to
the Small Town

While visiting Washington, D.C., in 1923, William Allen White received an invitation to the White House. He had been there many times before, but not since Warren Harding had become president. He had grown accustomed, during visits to previous presidents, to being questioned about the political "situation" out west, but Harding did not want to talk politics. He wanted to talk about the newspaper business. Like White, he had begun his career as a newspaperman, and he still owned the Marion, Ohio, *Star*. The two men sat in the Oval Office and swapped notes about newsprint prices, advertising rates, and printers' wages back in Emporia and Marion. According to White, Harding mused,

> You know every day at three-thirty, here in the midst of the affairs of state,
> I go to press on the Marion Star. I wonder how much advertising there is. . . .
> I would like to walk out in the composing room and look over the forms before they go to the stereotyper. There never was a day in all the years that I ran the paper that I didn't get some thrill out of it.[1]

By 1923, clearly, neither White nor Harding could by any stretch of the imagination be considered mere small-town newspapermen. Although White continued formally as editor of the Emporia *Gazette*, he increasingly left editorial decisions to a younger generation of newsmen that included his son William Lindsay White. From the twenties on, White devoted a much larger share of his attention to national affairs. His shrewd observation of politics and life in general earned him the affectionate title "Sage of Emporia."

Yet, as their Oval Office conversation illustrates, neither man could sever his ties to the occupation that had shaped his life and identity, even as their careers moved beyond their original roles. White, in particular, always prided himself on being a community leader in Emporia, and during the twenties he eagerly directed another period of economic expansion at the *Gazette*. Nonetheless, his national stature and changing local conditions placed a certain distance between him and his neighbors. He became more a respected figurehead, and at times an irritating gadfly, than a native leader. Just as he was established in the nation's imagination as *the* Small-Town Newspaperman, White ceased to play that role in Emporia.

After the war, White continued in his accustomed role as spokesman for the Midwest. Increasingly, however, this role entailed not simply representing his region but defending his small-town world view against aggressive urban critics. Cultural differences between city and country in America had been growing for some time but had been obscured for many during the prewar years by a common commitment to reform. Wartime regimentation and postwar repression made these cultural differences all too clear, and a younger generation of intellectuals turned from promoting reform to asserting individual freedoms. "Progressivism" lost favor to "liberalism."

With a foot in each world, White struggled to mediate between these increasingly antagonistic mentalities, which he characterized as the "Emporia" and the "New York" points of view. He steered an erratic public course, tacking wildly between localism and cosmopolitanism, between values of community and individualism. However sophisticated he appeared to his liberal urban friends, White's heart remained with the small town. Even as he acknowledged criticisms of its intolerance and complacency, he continued to argue that the small town provided the best conditions for a humane way of life. Yet, ever the booster, he also attempted to refute imputations of provinciality by helping to keep Emporia "up-to-date" intellectually and materially. His boosterism prevented him from fully understanding how such efforts to keep abreast of urban trends undermined one's sense of the importance of local life.

For the *Gazette,* these postwar years brought economic expansion and further technological improvements. Yet, whereas the boom in advertising patronage twenty years before had momentarily strengthened the newspaper as an independent, community-building institution, this further economic growth undermined that role. The paper's expansion in size and circulation led to its segmentation, the extensive use of standardized materials, and a diminished emphasis upon local news. By the middle of the 1920s, the *Gazette* was less a home town newspaper than before, for it reflected the fads and foibles of urban America as much as the life of Emporia.

As wartime mobilization slowly wound down and Americans sought to resume their normal lives, the Emporia *Gazette* passed into the hands of a new, younger generation of journalists. Laura French, exhausted from doing double service during the labor-short war years, left the *Gazette* in 1919 for what she thought of as a long vacation. Young Calvin Hood Lambert took her place. When she announced her intention to return, White explained that there was no opening for her. But White paid for his lack of loyalty to his devoted employee, for with French's departure he lost the staunchest defender of his vision of community journalism. Lambert, the son of White's former factional ally and just home from service in France, had his own ideas about how to run a newspaper. Unlike French, Lambert and succeeding editors were interested less in mirroring White's mind in all that went into the paper and more in publishing a paper according to prevailing practices in the larger journalistic profession. They struggled to make the *Gazette* more cosmopolitan.[2]

Earlier in the century, the expanding advertising industry had changed the *Gazette*'s appearance and content. In the twenties, it did so even more forcefully. Demand for advertising, which had remained relatively constant during the war years, increased dramatically immediately after the Armistice and continued to mount thereafter. In his *Autobiography* White recalled this increase and attributed it largely to foreign advertising: "From the East came thousands of dollars in advertising, calling attention to national products—automobiles, radios, phonographs, tobacco, oil, transportation—a long list of things which once were luxuries and were becoming the common comforts of the people." Nonetheless, demand for advertising rose almost equally among foreign, brand, and local purchasers.[3]

Emporia's merchants, competing for consumers whose range of choice had been widened by ownership of automobiles and the advent of parcel post, turned to the *Gazette* for aid as they had twenty years before. They showed themselves ever more eager to "cooperate" in the sophisticated, multifaceted advertising campaigns planned and distributed by advertising agencies. Combined advertising programs, in which ads by different local merchants featuring the same product shared a page with a larger ad paid for by the manufacturer, became commonplace. For example, the maker of Mazola, Karo, and Argo Corn Starch declared June 17, 1927, "Corn Products Day" and filled an entire page with local and foreign advertisements promoting its products.[4]

To keep an acceptable balance between news and advertisements, the *Gazette* expanded in size as advertising increased. The paper grew from an average of 6.8 pages in 1916 to 12.7 pages in 1926. This immediately strained the printing capacity of the old Duplex press. By mid-1919 Walter Hughes was already thinking about adding a deck in order to print a twelve-page newspaper. He did not pursue this idea, but it had become clear that increased advertising and a circulation nearing four thousand required a new press.[5]

Just as in the purchase of the Duplex eighteen years before, moving up to a more powerful press meant a significant investment of capital at a time of rising printing costs. Furthermore, the postwar economic recession hit particularly hard in Kansas. Not until early 1924 did White buy a new press, a Duplex tubular plate press that printed from curved stereotyped plates mounted upon a cylinder. Making these plates from page type forms added another step in the production process and required purchasing stereotyping equipment and hiring another employee. But it printed thirty thousand pages an hour in up to sixteen-page editions. Press, stereotyping equipment, and a thirty-horsepower motor cost White thirty thousand dollars.[6]

Similarly, as in the period of the *Gazette*'s first major expansion, 1903 to 1906, the purchase of the press formed part of a larger program to expand the newspaper's circulation. At the end of the war, the daily *Gazette* remained primarily a local paper, with 56 percent of its 3,904 subscribers in Emporia and fully 94 percent within a twenty-mile radius. Its circulation had stayed nearly constant for a decade, reflecting the limited capacity of the old flatbed press to print the paper and of the railroads to deliver it. Now, however, the purchase of a powerful new press not only made it possible to expand the paper's circulation: it made growth imperative in order to pay for the increased capital investment.[7]

Consequently, as soon as the new press was in place White launched an all-out campaign to expand the *Gazette*'s circulation to a fifty-mile radius of Emporia. The paving of many roads in the area now made it feasible to use automobiles to deliver newspapers to outlying towns. To attract new subscribers in these towns, White published an early edition of the *Gazette* that reached the most distant homes by suppertime. He hired reporters to cover the news of these communities. He visited the chambers of commerce of each little town within the targeted area to promote his expanded *Gazette*. He sent his son, Bill, just back from college, to drum up circulation and train new carriers in these towns. By the end of the twenties, the *Gazette*'s circulation had risen to well over six thousand.[8]

The new press also made it possible to use dry mats, or papier-mâché molds, for the first time. Using the stereotyping equipment, a worker poured lead into these molds to produce the equivalent of a column of type, an engraved image, or a half-tone photographic cut, but at far less cost than any of these. Mats had been in use for several decades, but the *Gazette* had lacked the facilities to use them.[9]

The new ability to use mats significantly altered the way the *Gazette* looked in the twenties, for now it was as easy to print visual images as words. Advertisers had long preferred mats because they offered cheaper and more convenient distribution, but by the twenties they had also supplanted boiler plate as the means of distributing syndicated news, features, and photographs. Mats would help make the *Gazette* a more stylish, "cosmopolitan" newspaper.

The widespread use of mats for both brand and nonbrand advertising speeded the dissemination of urban trends in fashion and decoration in the twenties. Impressed by the quality and effectiveness of the government's wartime propaganda, agencies produced increasingly sophisticated advertisements. They abandoned the cluttered composition typical of previous years and combined words and images to achieve a unified aesthetic effect rather than trying to present a great deal of information. Designers also used white space to draw attention to their messages, and effectively balanced areas of type and illustration. This increased stylishness only made locally produced advertising seem more drab and old-fashioned. Consequently, even local merchants who did not feature national brands used all-purpose advertisements produced by commercial designers and sold in dry mat form.[10]

With a few significant exceptions, however, advertisements in the *Gazette* in the twenties did not depart from the prewar emphasis upon familiarity and quality in its appeals to consumers. Conspicuous in its rarity was the manipulation of emotions that so concerned media critics then and now. Rather, the cumulative effect of increased advertising was more subtle, and perhaps in the end more insidious, as it heightened urban influence over many aspects of everyday life.[11]

By far the most striking change from the prewar *Gazette* occurred in advertisements for motion pictures. Employing energetic and arresting designs in place of the modest all-type prewar announcements, they made the most innovative use of typography and illustration in the newspaper. Visual liveliness was accompanied by "peppier" copy, epitomized in this advertisement: "the flapper was 1923—the MODERN is 1925, you're years behind the time till you see—We Moderns, chic and charming Colleen Moore makes a lame sister out of the flapper. She starts something new—AND HOW!!" Where previously movie ads had, if anything, understated their products, these ads were often more titillating than the movies themselves. An ad for *His Secretary* with Norma Shearer, for example, promised shocking revelations of "the temptations, the romance, the adventure" found by "the millions of young girls who seek to get ahead in the world of business. . . . Here is the drama of our sisters and daughters who offer themselves on the altar of business." Moreover, movie advertisers no longer depended upon words to convey an impression: an illustration of Gloria Swanson doing a fan dance had infinitely more effect than mere words such as "exciting" and "sensational."[12]

Whatever the cultural effects of the more sophisticated designs, the increased volume of advertising undeniably changed the newspaper. It demanded a larger newspaper, prompting the purchase of a more powerful and complicated press. Doubling the number of pages entailed far more than simply multiplying the prewar *Gazette* by two, however. It drastically changed the paper's organization and contents. More pages required more text, and to fill the additional space the staff turned to standardized news and features distributed by the Associated Press, syndicates, and public agencies more often than local news.

Enlargement also made it possible for the first time to segment the *Gazette* into departments devoted solely to certain subjects. The prewar newspaper had sometimes reserved particular positions on a page for one type of news or advertising, but it had been too small to allow for completely separate sections, such as had emerged in urban newspapers by the late nineteenth century. Consequently, editorials, society news, items on local entertainment offerings, and country locals had been jumbled together on the same page. By the middle of the twenties, however, the *Gazette* was divided into separate sections—editorials, sports, homemaking, entertainment, society, and even automotive and real estate.

This segmentation, clearly, resulted from advertising needs rather than some sudden division of Emporians into special-interest groups. Each section contained advertisements directed at a particular consumer audience:

barbershops, tobacco, and sporting goods on the sports pages; women's clothing in society; groceries in homemaking; and movies and vaudeville in entertainment.

With segmentation, the *Gazette* lost a certain sense of cohesiveness, of addressing and reflecting a unified, homogeneous community. No longer could it be assumed that everyone would go through the newspaper from cover to cover, as had been implicit in the composition of the newspaper in early days, with its closely packed columns, often without headlines to set stories apart. In the interests of advertisers, the *Gazette* now addressed its readers as individual consumers rather than as members of a single community. No doubt some Emporians appreciated the ease with which they could read only those stories in which they were interested. Nonetheless, this fragmentation diminished the extent to which Emporians shared a common experience through reading the *Gazette*.[13]

Those who lived far from Emporia and subscribed to the weekly *Gazette* in the postwar years retained more sense of a unified community than those who read the daily paper. As improved transportation lowered rural demand for the weekly, White began to send it to people around the country who subscribed primarily to read his editorials. This practice prevented inflating the daily circulation figures with subscribers outside the Emporia trade area, thus satisfying local merchants who were unwilling to pay higher advertising rates for readers who were not prospective customers. The four-page weekly contained no advertising but included his editorials and some local news. White charged just enough to cover the cost of the newsprint.[14]

Much of the material in the new sections of the daily edition was now either general consumer-oriented news, often produced by industrywide public relations firms, or specific promotional "news" about the very products advertised. Such stories attested to the growing sophistication of American advertising and public relations practices. Publicity agents had begun to appreciate the benefits of making life more convenient for small publishers, and they flooded newspapers with material suitable for these special pages. Much of it, both news and photographs, came in mat form. A contemporary publicity manual recommended offering a mat service, as it "is especially welcome to the editors of the country press, for it obviates the necessity of setting up the type, and has the added advantage of carrying its own illustrations."[15]

Publicity releases now routinely accompanied advertising contracts. For example, on the day the new car models were introduced in 1927, three of the *Gazette*'s eight pages carried heavily illustrated mat advertisements from Emporia agencies for Hudsons, Chryslers, Oldsmobiles, Chevrolets, Fords, Studebakers, Nashes, Oaklands, and Willys-Knights. Feature articles with such headlines as "Manufacturer Says Two Cars Save Family Money," "Give New Oakland 100,000 Mile Test," and "Chevrolet Trucks Lead Their Field" surrounded these ads. Similarly, corporate publicity departments often provided the homemaking tips and recipes on the Friday-evening "Market Basket Page." On "Corn Products Day," the only non-advertising copy on the page was a recipe column, "Modern Method of Preparing Delightful Foods," in which all the recipes called for the advertised brands.[16]

Nowhere was this alliance between news and advertising more apparent than on the amusement page. At a time when photographs of Emporians remained rare, the *Gazette*'s pages glittered with the faces of Hollywood's latest starlets, and promotional "news" stories featured movies playing in Emporia. News and advertising mirrored each other so much that it was sometimes hard to tell them apart. On one occasion, the entertainment page contained large advertisements for *Stage Struck* with Gloria Swanson and *We Moderns* with Colleen Moore. The news consisted of stories and publicity photographs of Moore and Swanson in the same costumes and poses as in the ads.[17]

The rest of the news in the *Gazette* reflected the same movement toward standardization according to urban models and away from detailed coverage of local events. In addition to publicity releases, most of the *Gazette*'s extra pages were filled with material from the Associated Press and one or another of the flourishing news and feature syndicates. When the *Gazette* acquired its new press, it switched to the full Associated Press news report in place of the pony edition it had received since 1903. This required installing a direct leased telegraph wire from Kansas City and hiring a telegraph operator to transcribe the news.[18]

The Associated Press underwent a transformation of its own in the twenties, replacing the sober but reliable reporting that had been its hallmark with a more lively and human-interest approach. To a great extent, it was forced to this change by competition from other syndicates such as Hearst's International News Service, Central Press Agency, and the United Press Agency, which had discovered that such liveliness—what detractors called sensationalism—sold better than more factual reporting. By the mid-1920s even many AP members, including White, supplemented their AP news with materials from these agencies. The United Press, in particular, grew rapidly in the twenties, and in 1928 it had almost as many clients as the AP. AP's chief of traffic, Kent Cooper, had long urged the cooperative to enliven its coverage and offer features and photographs, but he had been consistently overruled by more conservative leadership. When he became general manager in 1925 he quickly moved to change editorial policy and introduce a new feature service. Soon thereafter AP added a mat photograph service.[19]

Dismayed though he was by the tendencies of journalism in the twenties, White felt he had to follow the trends. In early 1927, he wrote Cooper to commend his new feature mat service:

> I have been buying Central Press stuff and United Press stuff for a year or two, and if the Associated Press service continues I shall be glad to drop them both. As it is I've dropped the red letter mail service which I have been buying from the United [Press]. Personally as between two newspaper men, I

loathe the whole business. . . . But I run a paper in a town without competition and I have to give the morons and nitwits something for their money.

Loathe them or not, White's *Gazette* used a considerable amount of Central Press and UP material even after the AP feature service began.[20]

One reason for the divergence between White's tastes and the *Gazette*'s
contents was the fact that his new, younger staff now made most editorial
decisions. They considered many of their boss's ideas old-fashioned, particularly his aversion to comic strips and his fondness for locals. Eventually
their journalistic visions prevailed.

For a long time White adamantly refused to have comics in his newspaper, but in 1920 he finally acceded to his staff's arguments. He proclaimed his continuing opposition even as he acknowledged defeat: "The
boss is whipped . . . the force has beat him. He thinks that [comics] make
a low appeal; that their humor is broad, and their level of intelligence
negligible. But the force maintains that they sell papers." By mid-decade
the *Gazette* carried daily "The Gumps," "Bringing Up Father," and "The
Figgers Family," and it had a full-page version of "The Gumps" on Saturday evenings, since it did not publish a Sunday edition. In fact, the paper
put aside its former prejudice to the extent of running a mat ad in January
1927 calling attention to "National Laugh Month" and advising its readers
to "Laugh and Grow Fit every day by following the fun elements in The
Emporia Gazette."[21]

The divergence between White's vision of journalism and his staff's reflected different conceptions of the *Gazette*'s proper role. This divergence
appeared most clearly in a continuing conflict over the paper's locals. According to Frank Clough, Lambert's successor as city editor, both William
Allen and Sallie White constantly complained that there weren't enough
locals in the paper. But the editors argued that the *Gazette* was no longer
a local paper and should emphasize "its district news, its Associated Press
reports, and its features rather than its strictly Emporia news." Clough told
Mrs. White on one occasion, "the *Gazette* is just like a boy who is too big
for short pants and his parents don't think he is big enough for long ones."
" 'Go along with you,' she retorted. 'Tell your reporters we need some more
local items and don't let your pants get too big for you.' " The two generations finally compromised on a policy of publishing the locals that were
brought to the *Gazette* but seeking out only items concerning "the town's
more prominent citizens." From the point of view of White's earlier broader
vision of community, such a compromise amounted to defeat.[22]

Through the magic of the telegraph and the convenience of dry mats, the
Gazette received from the syndicates the "hottest" news of the twenties,
much of it human-interest features and photographs prominently featuring
urban socialites and the latest Hollywood celebrities. It published political
cartoons and syndicated political columns on its editorial page, syndicated
photographs of sports heroes on the sports page, and photographs of the

latest New York or Paris fashions on the society page. Frequently there were also full-page montages of "The Day's News in Pictures," purchased from the Central Press Agency, containing photographs of political figures, aviators, explorers, socialites, and bathing beauties.[23]

It was also through these services that the *Gazette* registered the journalistic shock waves that had originated from the new big-city tabloids. Brash, irreverent, and risqué, tabloids like the *New York Daily News* altered all journalism in America by testing the boundaries of legitimate news. However much newsmen like White might lament the misuse of screamer headlines and full-page photographs, the exploitation of sex and murder stories, they felt compelled to offer at least a mild form of competition. Consequently, the case of "statuesque blonde" Ruth Snyder and "her corset salesman paramour" Henry Judd Gray for the murder of her husband received extensive attention in the *Gazette* via AP and Central Press. Running accounts in 1927 of the New York City trial, verdict, sentencing, and execution accompanied large, grim photographs and drawings of the condemned couple.[24]

This case had barely ended when another sensational trial opened in Los Angeles, in which film actor Paul Kelly was tried for the murder of musical comedy star Ray Raymond over the love of actress Dorothy MacKaye. While giving the trial ample space, the *Gazette* felt called upon to comment editorially upon this rash of murders:

> Today the American press is getting its new murder from the Pacific coast in a nice juicy tale of slaughter that comes buzzing over the wires, just as the last click of the grisly horror from the Snyder case is slowly ticking into the long silence. Every week the press of the land is soaked with blood. . . . Murder will not only out but it will soak its blood into the consciousness of the American people.

The editorial did not consider whether this impression of slaughter might not be the result of the press's scramble to exploit such "juicy" tales rather than a sign of changing mores. Instead, in a parody of those calling for repeal of prohibition, it advocated that laws against murder be abolished because they clearly only tempted people to break them.[25]

During the heyday of urban "ballyhoo" in the mid-twenties, the *Gazette* reported all the sensations: the "Peaches" and "Daddy" Browning marriage and separation, the Rhinelander annulment suit, the Scopes "monkey trial," and, of course, the Lindbergh flight and its aftermath all received day-by-day detailed attention through AP dispatches and Central Press photographs. The generally gray front page sported an uncommon banner headline the day Lindy landed in Paris, along with a large photograph of the "Flying Fool." In succeeding days, an illustrated Central Press series traced the life of Lindbergh as told "exclusively" by his mother. The paper cheered his triumphal return to America with an oversized decorative banner, "Welcome Lindbergh!"—probably from a Central Press mat—complete with stars and bunting, soaring airplanes, and photos of Lindbergh and Coolidge. In the center of the page, a large sketch of Lindbergh hovered over a spread American eagle.[26]

In comparison to such excitement, the stories that had been the staples of the *Gazette*—the daily comings and goings of Emporians, their marriages and childbirths and deaths, their cycles of civil celebrations—retreated. They were still recorded in the newspaper, but they received less space proportionately and absolutely, were relegated to stock columns, and were overshadowed by the sheer amounts of other news. Nor were they illustrated like the wire service and syndicated stories. Half-tone engravings remained expensive, and the *Gazette* did not have its own photoengraving equipment. According to Frank Clough, Sallie White resisted acquiring such equipment because she opposed photographs in the paper. She insisted that newspapers should concentrate instead on "word pictures." "Perhaps I'm old-fashioned," he quoted her as saying many times, "but I still believe that a story well written—briefly, entertainingly, and to the point—means a lot more to the reader than a photograph." However admirable her sentiments may have been in the abstract, in practice her aversion to technological change helped relegate her beloved local news to obscurity.[27]

Although the *Gazette* continued to report weddings and other social events, they were segregated in the society pages. No longer the "forty-line" stories that White had praised in "The Country Newspaper," the short notices paid little attention to the details of the events. At one time, those interested in fashion trends could have gathered intelligence from descriptions of dresses worn at local parties; now they could turn only to Central Press photographs and reports by "Mme. Lisbeth" about what was current in world capitals. Although no photographs appeared of newlywed Emporia couples, readers were regularly treated to stories and pictures of the weddings of the rich, well born, or simply notorious. Thanks to Central Press, Emporians were treated to "one of the first photos" of the daughter of the American ambassador in Berlin and her groom.[28]

This disparity in treatment may have reflected some readers' desire for news of the glamorous and sensational, as White seemed to believe, but its immediate causes were improvements in the technologies of communication and printing. Because mat services had many subscribers, they could provide stories and photographs at prices far below the cost of filling a comparable amount of space with unique local news. The AP feature mat service cost the *Gazette* only $1.50 a week, and the photo mat service $3.50.[29]

Such economies of scale can be realized only with a mass-produced product. When that product was news, mass production did not merely standardize but qualitatively changed news contents. While some of the increased news appearing in the enlarged *Gazette* concerned significant national and international events, at least an equal amount can only be described as "human interest."[30]

In some ways, the wire service human-interest news was similar to the *Gazette*'s locals, for both treated many of the universal themes of human experience: childhood and youth, love, marriage, death, and the pursuit of achievement. Nevertheless, the two conveyed fundamentally different messages about these themes. As White had acknowledged in "The Country Newspaper," its "sweet, intimate stories" could interest only people who knew one another. To appeal to a large, dispersed audience, mass-produced human-interest stories treat the extraordinary, the aberrant, the disruptive. Stories about weddings and divorces, for example, might appeal to the same human fascination with love, but the latter is more emotionally charged because it is, or at least was, more unusual, more threatening to social order. Consequently, human-interest news reverses the messages about social order and continuity conveyed by local news.[31]

For example, human-interest stories about young women in the twenties had parallels with locals in previous years. At the beginning of White's editorship, the *Gazette* contained lively pieces like this:

> The west side girls are working a partnership game that is making half of the boys in town go wild. They each get a fellow in a sisterly sort of anxious way that completely disarms suspicion and tells him how much the other girl likes him. One dose is usually enough and the way the boys are biting is scandalous. The boys pay the livery and candy bills. These girls ought to go into politics.

Such items brought White criticism for "sensationalism." Yet even after the *Gazette* had become somewhat less spicy, it often commented on the various foibles of Emporia girls, such as their weakness for anything in a uniform:

> Last Sunday, a body of Pennsylvania troops came through Emporia, and Emporia girls by the dozens flocked to the train, and scraped up acquaintance with men whom they never had seen before, and who, in all probability, they never will see again. It has been the same in Emporia on other days, and it has been the same in other towns. Women fall for brass buttons.[32]

In the twenties, however, this formula reached a perverse kind of apotheosis in the "flapper." The *Gazette* followed the trend, as in this AP story:

CHARLESTON IS TOO TAME
ADDICTS TRY PARACHUTE JUMPING

> Charleston enthusiasts here are turning to parachute jumping to obtain an added kick. Matching her life against the luck she believed attached to her, Teresa M. Kirshe, 18-year-old stenographer, yesterday crawled onto the wing of a plane bucking a strong wind at 2,160 feet and leaped clear. Her luck held. Now her sister Mary wants to borrow the parachute.[33]

With increased journalistic attention to crime in the twenties, the flapper also assumed a more dangerous demeanor. When she was not jumping from airplanes in a compulsive search for thrills, the flapper as she appeared through wire service stories was running completely amok. Thus we find Central Press photos of seventeen-year-old Dorothy Perkins of New York, who was on trial for the murder of the man her father had chosen to be her

husband. She was said to have killed him because "she preferred the atten-
tions of a 35-year-old man." Hard-faced Maxine Spangler was pictured,
cigarette in hand, in a wire release, following sentencing for check forgery.
The headline read "Must Have Her 'Smokes.'" Describing her as a "16-
year-old flapper," the caption quoted her as saying "I'd as soon be in the
pen as any place if they'll just give me plenty to smoke." It concluded, "her
aged father spent his all trying to make good the checks."[34]

Compared to such behavior, the transgressions of Emporia girls had been
trifling adolescent flings. As portrayed in the newspapers of the twenties,
flappers challenged traditional values in much more fundamental ways, by
smoking and drinking, refusing to be ruled by patriarchal authority, and
committing adultery and even murder. They seemed to threaten the very
continuity of society. A revealing photograph in this regard appeared in the
Gazette above the caption "The More Dolls the Fewer Flappers—Acting on
this theory the Professional Women's League is encouraging interest in
dolls for very young ladies. Miss Martha Hogan appears both interested
and interesting." In the photograph the aforementioned young woman,
fetching in a short skirt, sits surrounded by baby dolls. This visual juxtaposition of flapper and baby doll reflected the perceived threat that young
women would refuse to marry and bear children, thus undermining the
very continuation of society.[35]

These symbols of disruption and discontinuity jarred markedly with the
local aspects of the *Gazette,* which, although in attenuated and segmented
form, still recorded the cyclic continuities of its community. There was
little evidence that Emporia was experiencing a "jazz age" among its own
youth. In fact, one of the rare local photographs to be found in the *Gazette*
during this period showed College of Emporia students studying their
catechism lessons, hardly the behavior of "flaming youth."[36]

The contrast between local news and syndicated human-interest stories
in the *Gazette* conveyed a sense of marked divergence between Emporia
and an outside, increasingly cosmopolitan world. Small-town and urban
cultures did indeed grow farther apart in the twenties, but the changing
means of producing news heightened the perception of difference. This
divergence may have made Emporians all the more determined to preserve
their way of life against growing immorality, but it also emphasized that
their community's values no longer dominated the nation.

Emporians could no longer gain the impression from reading their local
newspaper that Emporia—or their own lives—mattered much in the scheme
of things. While some may have welcomed the *Gazette*'s "peppier" copy
and more stylish appearance in the twenties, they may also have felt a concomitant waning in their sense of the importance of their everyday lives.
For, rather than focusing on homely local events, the paper increasingly
dramatized faraway people and places. Instead of celebrating the life
passages of their friends and neighbors, it reported the abnormalities of
strangers. In "The Country Newspaper," White had concluded, "it is this
country newspaper that reveals us to ourselves." By the end of the twenties

the *Gazette,* with its more attractive advertising, celebrity photographs, and livelier news, no longer could be said to reveal Emporia to Emporians. Without intending it, the *Gazette*'s expansion in the twenties brought a sense of the marginality of small-town life.[37]

For William Allen White, the postwar years were a paradoxical time of ever-widening horizons and rising reputation on the one hand and loss of direction and dismay at the drift of American society on the other. A turning point of sorts came when White turned fifty, early in 1918; he was so distressed by the onset of "maturity" that he burst into tears while dressing for his birthday party. Nonetheless, as soon as the Armistice was announced, he scrambled to make sure that he would be present as a reporter at the Peace Conference. His months in Paris during the winter of 1918–19 marked the beginning of a new international phase of his life. His experiences, which included appointment as an American representative to the abortive Prinkipo Conference, constituted a heady, intensive education in European politics and culture. He later confessed, however, that he understood little of what was actually occurring at the Peace Conference. "After all, I was just Republican precinct committeeman in the Fourth Ward of Emporia, Kansas, who had been on the state committee and had been on the National Committee. . . ."[38]

It was also in Paris that White received the shocking news of Theodore Roosevelt's sudden death. "Not since my father's death," he recalled, "had grief stabbed me so poignantly as those headlines cut into my heart. . . ." As 1919 wore on back in America, he watched appalled as the demands for "100 per cent Americanism" that he had himself made during wartime were turned against all forms of domestic dissent. And a year later he found himself, to his self-disgust, joining the Kansas delegation to the Republican National Convention in supporting Harding for president. He was torn, as often in his life, "between the desire to jump in the fiery furnace as a martyr, and the instinct to save my hide and go along on the broad way that leadeth to destruction." In his *Autobiography,* looking back on that moment, he believed that Roosevelt's death and the collapse of the League of Nations had "created in my heart a climax of defeat," an enervation of purpose.[39]

Struggling to regain his sense of purpose in the twenties, White attempted to serve as he had in the past, as a spokesman and mediator. But he encountered the formidable challenge of bridging a widening cleavage between between small-town and metropolitan America, between Emporia and New York. Even as he tried to keep in step with changing postwar currents of thought, he sought to remain loyal to small-town booster values. The effort led him to actions that often appeared erratic and contradictory to both his local and his metropolitan audiences.

The biggest intellectual change of the twenties was White's emergence as a defender of the liberal value of free expression, which as a booster he had formerly subordinated to the need for unity. It is not clear precisely when this change occurred, for nowhere does he acknowledge having made one. During the war, as we have seen, he denied the precedence of rights of free press or speech. Although he later claimed to have been troubled by the harassment of pacifist progressive colleagues like Jane Addams, he felt that he could say or do nothing while the war continued. His European travels also enabled him to observe the Allied nations' prosecution of the war, and he was surprised to learn that the United States had been the most restrictive of freedom of press and speech. Consequently, in 1919 he supported clemency for Eugene V. Debs, arguing that "Other nations were much more liberal than we were." As the end of the war brought only an intensification of repression, he found himself assuming a new role as advocate of tolerance.[40]

Meanwhile, White also took the side of tolerance in a messy local controversy surrounding College of Emporia president and fellow Current Club member Henry Coe Culbertson. Culbertson had antagonized many of his Presbyterian constituents, partly by his inefficient handling of the college's finances, but mainly by his habit of appearing in public with pretty female parishioners. He maintained they were "family friends," but less sophisticated Emporians interpreted his behavior in another way. In mid-1917, Culbertson left Emporia in the midst of controversy. With White's help he got a job in the wartime Food Administration; later he spoke on behalf of food conservation for the Speakers' Bureau. Nonetheless, he left implacable enemies in the Presbyterian Synod, which in late 1918 brought him to ecclesiastical trial on charges of financial and sexual misconduct.[41]

The situation resembled the Meffert affair a decade and a half before, but this time White used his influence to discourage conflict rather than to arouse the forces of righteousness. He insisted that Culbertson was innocent of actual wrongdoing. He tried to shield him from negative publicity by asking newspaper colleagues to keep the story out of the papers. Even as he criticized Culbertson's persecutors as narrow-minded, however, he faulted him for his poor "social sense." His explanation of Culbertson's behavior revealed his continuing appreciation of the significance of public behavior in a small town.

> I've jawed him by the hour about that. He never could see why when he and Mrs. Culbertson received Miss Hurst in their home as a social companion, he should not make her a social companion outside of their home when occasion arose. So he did it. I have women working for me whom I have employed for ten and twenty years. I am very fond of them as friends. But I know that I cannot make any public recognition of any relation between them and me but a business relation. This Culbertson could not get into his head. He grew up in a city; he didn't understand the country town viewpoint.[42]

White's travels had enabled him to understand both the "city viewpoint" and that of the "country town," which assumed the community's right to regulate its members' public behavior. Personally he continued to accept communitarian norms, for they went to the core of the small-town way of life. Hence, when Culbertson's successor at the College of Emporia revealed an interest in investment, White warned, "You can't afford to do it, as the head of a College. . . . If a community knows that a College man is dabbling in speculative ventures, he will lose his influence. . . . and your influence is worth more to you than any money you might make."[43]

As the gap between these "city" and "country" perspectives widened in the 1920s, White scrambled to somehow accommodate both individualism and community. He was in a sense trying to preserve the balancing of opposites that had formed a dynamic tension within both boosterism and progressivism: materialism with idealism, progress with community. But the poles had grown increasingly difficult to reconcile.

His response to modernist trends in American culture reflected a parallel ambivalence. He wanted to remain alive to change, but he also longed for the comfort of the familiar. His contradictory desires were illustrated in his 1915 request of Frank Lloyd Wright to "do over" his nineteenth-century house. He told Wright that it "is one of those old fashioned houses, warted all over with bow windows, and towers and gables and fibroid tumors, acute angles, meaning nothing and merely serrating the sky line . . . it is about as discouraging a proposition as you could imagine." Yet he and Sallie preferred to renovate rather than build anew, because "it is our home and the children were born here, and there is a certain sentiment in having lived in a place 16 years." Wright promised to try but warned that "the house might pass away under the aesthetics of the necessary surgical operation." In fact, the Whites did find his plans "too devastating on the old house and destructive," and when the house was finally renovated after a fire in 1920, they used the designs of a Kansas City architectural firm.[44]

Similarly, although he had been inspired to become a writer by the then avant-garde works of Howells and Howe, he was repelled by the direction that literature had taken by the 1920s. His own stories and novels attempted to infuse realism with moral meaning, an approach that postwar disillusionment had made unfashionable among intellectuals. *A Certain Rich Man* had been a great success in 1909, but when his second novel, *In the Heart of a Fool,* finally appeared in 1918, it encountered a greatly changed critical climate. Francis Hackett attacked it in the *New Republic* as "written by the romantic Puritan [in White], with propaganda behind it." White protested that "a story is a good story only if it does have a purpose—some sort of moral purpose." Nonetheless, after attempting a few light short stories in the early twenties, he ceased writing fiction altogether.[45]

White's ambivalence toward postwar trends in urban culture was also evident in his attitude toward his son's education at Harvard in the early twenties. After attending his father's alma mater, the University of Kansas, for a year and a half, "Young Bill," as he was called, decided that it was not intellectually demanding enough. He wanted to attend Harvard, and his father was proud to send him there. In his *Autobiography* White credited his son's Harvard experience with providing a "liberal education for his parents too"—liberal in the twentieth-century as well as the classical definition of the term.[46]

But his letters to Bill at the time revealed misgivings, for he hoped that his son would return one day to take over the *Gazette*. He knew that at Cambridge Bill would be immersed in an alien culture, one that might easily unfit him for life in Emporia. Although the Whites were tremendously proud of their son's activities at Harvard, they were alarmed when he returned home to visit sporting sophisticated evening dress, a coonskin coat, and a cane. The father's letters consequently reflected his conflicting desires to allow his son to make his own decisions but still prevent him from straying too far from the appointed path. He pressed Bill to cultivate the friendship of people who would be good influences. These included former *Gazette* reporter Brock Pemberton, now a successful Broadway producer. Pemberton, White believed, had "the Emporia point of view."[47]

White also feared that, in the new age of prohibition, his son's actions at college might harm his own reputation as a reformer. During Bill's first semester, he warned him to be careful of

> that incidental drinking that college people do. In your case it is rather different from others, because I am widely known as a prohibitionist. Whenever I go away in America . . . I always turn my glass down and I earnestly hope you will do the same thing with the college boys. It would be a reflection on me which I don't think you would wish to make. . . .

Even "away in America," White was quite concerned about maintaining appearances.[48]

When, in his senior year, Bill began to talk about getting a Rhodes scholarship to Oxford, the moment of decision seemed at hand. He had to decide to which world he would ultimately belong. The elder White replied,

> You ought to decide rather definitely that if you accept the Rhodes Scholarship, you will give up all thought of coming back to run the Gazette. . . . You will come back in your middle-twenties out of touch with the young people of the town, out of touch with the ideals of the community, and in the years when you should be drilling yourself in the practice of your profession, you will be acquiring a lot of utterly useless academic atmosphere, erudition and ideals which will have to be pounded out of you at great expense by the Gazette, if ever you come back to it.[49]

A few days later, he returned to the question when Bill asked if he should send a night telegram with the score of the Harvard-Princeton football game. White explained that a night telegram would arrive too late for publication on Saturday and that the news would be cold by Monday. Bill's ignorance of this obvious journalistic fact only proved how essential it was that he begin his "practical" education immediately.

> It is to know these things and know them so casually that the temptation to spend three dollars for a night letter would not remotely tempt you, that you should get to Emporia as soon as you can if you are going into the newspaper

business on The Gazette. . . . You are getting too old now to let another year slip by without getting the fundamentals of the business in which you need to earn your living. You don't need culture; you don't need erudition; you don't need the broadening influence of travel so much as you need a time table of the trains going in and out of Emporia, to know where they are going, where they originate, what their equipment is and how many train men they carry.

When it came to matters of newspaper business, White was decidedly unambivalent.[50]

Bill White did return to Emporia and did take up his father's business. In fact, many of the Gazette's editorials from the mid-twenties to the mid-thirties that were believed to be the work of William Allen White were actually written by his son. Eventually, in 1934, feeling that he needed to get out from under his father's shadow, Bill left Emporia to write for national magazines in Washington and New York. In time he achieved recognition in his own right as a novelist and war correspondent.[51]

White's political activities in the twenties followed the same pattern of ambivalence. After the Progressive party's collapse, he had returned to the Republican fold. Always an astute "practical politician," he managed to regain significant power in Kansas politics as one of the leaders of the progressive faction in the party. Nonetheless, twice in the twenties he shunned politics as usual to take on unpopular liberal causes. By singlehandedly opposing the restriction of free speech and denouncing the Ku Klux Klan, White gained the respect of urban liberals but outraged his Kansas colleagues.

In 1922, White clashed publicly with his friend Henry Allen, whom he had helped elect governor of Kansas, over the principle of freedom of speech. In Kansas as elsewhere, conflicts over labor had increased after the war, as conservatives appropriated the authority of patriotism and anti-communism to suppress union activity. When railroad shopmen went on strike, Allen, swayed by what White called a "silly terror of Bolshevism," invoked the state's new compulsory arbitration legislation to put down the strike. White defended the local shopmen as peaceful and patriotic citizens and at one point dissuaded Allen from sending in troops in response to "purely faked up" reports of violence.[52]

Then the local union asked Emporia merchants to display signs stating "We are for the striking railroad men 100 per cent." Under the authority of the arbitration law, Allen banned the signs as likely to encourage violence. White, newly sensitive to First Amendment issues, refused to obey the ban. Instead, he displayed the sign, amended to read "forty-nine per cent," and he announced that he would increase the figure each day that the strike remained peaceful. He challenged Allen in an editorial: "Either we have free speech and a free press in this country, or we have not."[53]

Allen threatened to arrest White. Merchants on Commercial Street shook their heads, commenting, "Well, White's gone crazy again." But White was playing to a wider audience than Emporia. When word came that his arrest was imminent, he asked Calvin Lambert to drive him into the country (he had never learned to drive a car). They wandered aimlessly until four in the afternoon, when White announced, "We can go back now, so I can get arrested." Lambert realized that White had wanted to delay his arrest so that the story would receive full coverage in the next morning's newspapers.[54]

The charges against White were dismissed before they came to trial, but in the aftermath of the controversy he defended his actions in an editorial, "To an Anxious Friend." A concise but powerful statement of the necessity for free speech as "the wisdom of the people," it was immediately reprinted throughout the country and received a Pulitzer prize the following year.

> You tell me that law is above freedom of utterance. And I reply that you can have no wise laws nor free enforcement of wise laws unless there is free expression of the wisdom of the people—and, alas, their folly with it. But if there is freedom, folly will die of its own poison, and the wisdom will survive. That is the history of the race. It is proof of man's kinship with God. You say that freedom of utterance is not for time of stress, and I reply with the sad truth that only in time of stress is freedom of utterance in danger. No one questions it in calm days, because it is not needed. And the reverse is true also; only when free utterance is suppressed is it needed, and when it is needed, it is most vital to justice.
>
> Peace is good. But if you are interested in peace through force and without free discussion—that is to say, free utterance decently and in order—your interest in justice is slight. And peace without justice is tyranny, no matter how you may sugar-coat it with expedience. This state today is in more danger from suppression than from violence, because, in the end, suppression leads to violence. Violence, indeed, is the child of suppression. Whoever pleads for justice helps to keep the peace; and whoever tramples on the plea for justice temperately made in the name of peace only outrages peace and kills something fine in the heart of man which God put there when we got our manhood. When that is killed, brute meets brute on each side of the line.
>
> So, dear friend, put fear out of your heart. This nation will survive, this state will prosper, the orderly business of life will go forward if only men can speak in whatever way given them to utter what their hearts hold—by voice, by posted card, by letter, or by press. Reason has never failed men. Only force and repression have made the wrecks in the world.[55]

The nation applauded White's libertarian sentiments. They marked a significant departure from the booster ethos demands for unity and loyalty, but he did draw upon his accustomed rhetorical opposition between the "law" and the "spirit" of the "people." Nonetheless, his son recalled, very few Emporians understood why he was making such a big fuss over a sign. He was supported by the striking shopmen, a number of college professors and ministers "who could think about abstract things such as civil liberties," and "a few of those thick-and-thin friends most men always have." But, Bill White remembered, "respectable Emporia thought he was out of his mind."[56]

Two years later, White again courted national publicity and local criticism in his nationally publicized campaign against the Ku Klux Klan. In the early years of the decade the Klan had quickly gathered strength in Kansas. Despite—or perhaps because of—White's repeated ridicule of the Klan in the *Gazette,* its membership rose in Emporia. Klan members gained control of the police department and in the spring of 1924 succeeded in electing one of their own as mayor. When a conservative Republican who was reputed to have Klan support defeated two progressive Republicans in the Kansas gubernatorial primary, White announced that he was running for governor as an Independent to protest both parties' failure to denounce the Klan.[57]

Just as a younger White had resented the image of Kansas created by the "wild-eyed" Populists, he again battled to redeem his state's reputation. He was troubled by the increasing popularity of the liberal view of small-town America as the bastion of ignorance and repression. This attitude was epitomized by sociologist John Mecklin's assertion that year that "The Klan makes a powerful appeal to the petty impotence of the small-town mind." In announcing his candidacy, White explained, "I want to be governor to free Kansas from the disgrace of the Ku Klux Klan. And I want to offer Kansans afraid of the Klan and ashamed of that disgrace, a candidate who shares their fear and shame."[58]

Because he was in the race to publicize a cause rather than to get elected, White made no effort to create a genuine political organization. His staff consisted of Calvin Lambert as his press agent and Bill White as chauffeur. The national press nonetheless followed every step of his six-week campaign, and the *New York Times* and the London *Daily News* even sent reporters. White gave them colorful copy as he protested the Klan's denial of civil rights: "The gag rule first came into the Republican Party last May when a flock of dragons, kleagles, cyclopses and fieries came up to Wichita from Oklahoma and held a meeting with some Kansas terrors, genii and whangdoodles. . . . A few weeks later the cyclopses, pterodactyls, kleagles, wizards and willopus-wallopuses began parading in the Kansas cow pastures, passing the word down to the shirt-tail rangers that they were to go into the Kansas primaries and nominate Ben Paulen." As he had once labeled Populists an unrepresentative "rag-tag" element, White characterized the Klan as a "small minority" of Kansans. He implied that they were importations from Oklahoma, which seems to have replaced Missouri as a source of social infection. He even compared the Klan to "the Soviet of Russia."[59]

And just as in the publication of "What's the Matter with Kansas?", White's crusade received mixed reviews from his many different audiences. The national press hailed his courage and independence. Around Kansas, his campaign was criticized as the tactics of a spoiler. He was said to be merely promoting himself and his liberal faction in the Republican party. Boosters deplored the fact that he was drawing negative national attention to Kansas, for many argued that the Klan's power was already on the wane.

On the other hand, urban liberals such as Walter Lippmann criticized White for not also attacking President Coolidge and Kansas Senator Arthur Capper for their evasive stands on the KKK.[60]

White's crusade, like his first famous editorial, garnered national prestige but threatened his local influence. His son recalled the campaign's aftermath: "The morning after the election, the Eastern Seaboard press was hailing William Allen White for having swept the Klan from Kansas. Back home we had another view." White had failed to carry his own county, "the deepest humiliation a politician can have. . . ." His family knew that despite "the glowing editorials written by Liberals across the land . . . it had been a bone-crunching defeat." As "practical politicians" they knew that "it would take us several years of hard work to pick up the pieces of this Noble Victory and stick them together again."[61]

Such widely publicized stands, combined with his continuing support of progressive reform issues in the face of postwar conservatism, won White the respect of growing numbers of those Americans who were beginning to call themselves "liberals." To them he represented an island of sanity in a sea of ignorant, small-minded Americans, who were being increasingly manipulated by the media in the interests of big business. In his 1923 critique of American journalism, *Some Newspapers and Newspaper-Men,* Oswald Garrison Villard called White the only "interesting and vital" newspaperman between the Mississippi and the West Coast. Rather than seeing White as part of his region, Villard could attribute his staying in Emporia only to his desire to be a "big frog in a small puddle." In the *Century,* Ernest Gruening called White the one "shining example" of an editor who was a conspicuous leader in his community.[62]

These writers viewed the typical small-town newspaper as a tool of both corporate propaganda and provincial ignorance. Kansas sociologist Carroll D. Clark reported on the sorry plight of such papers in a 1926 article in the *New Republic,* "The Small Town Press Sells Out." Basing his argument on an idealized picture of the turn-of-the-century newspaper, Clark deplored the large amounts of syndicate and publicity material being carried in small-town papers, but had even harsher words for such a paper's local news. He regretted that it did little to educate its readers out of their "gullibility, timorousness, suspiciousness, intolerance" and "distorted" notions of the important social problems of the day. He sneered, "Undoubtedly to their readers there is a real and brightening interest in the news of marriages, births, funerals, conversions, family reunions, school exercises, and holiday celebrations. But there is nothing in the recitation of this endless life cycle to lift the populace out of its narrowing confines." There could hardly be a more vivid illustration of the divergence between prewar progressivism and postwar liberalism than a comparison between White's celebration of the country newspaper in 1916 and Clark's condemnation in 1926.[63]

However they might laud White as an exception to the current state of middle-class American civilization, these liberals were frequently exasperated by what they perceived as his inconsistencies and his inability to carry his beliefs to their logical conclusions. They would be particularly mystified by his attacks on Al Smith in 1928 and his refusal to endorse Franklin Delano Roosevelt's candidacies in the 1930s. Similarly, his biographers have characterized his refusal to shift to the Democratic party in the thirties as evidence of his fundamental inconsistency. Walter Johnson concludes that he was simply "a strange mixture of broad, kindly tolerance and small, narrow provincialism—a composite American."[64]

What they did not understand was that, despite his widening horizons and the increasingly varied activities that took him away from the *Gazette* and from Emporia, White continued to think of himself as a small-town newspaperman. His identity was inseparable from that of the editor of the *Emporia Gazette,* and that role, or bundle of roles, represented for him the ideal balance of ideals and action. Several times he had thought of freeing himself from its distractions and devoting himself to writing, but always something happened to draw him back into the political fray or the next community fund drive. When in the thirties a friend commented that White might have been a great writer if he had left politics and journalism alone, he responded, "I don't regret that I came out of the cloister and have lived my life in my own way."[65]

Throughout his life, White prided himself on staying involved in local affairs. As late as 1942 he bragged to his friend Edna Ferber, "I get up as much copy as anyone arund the shop and, of course, have my finger in a lot of local pies." Despite his new acceptance of ideals of free speech, he remained loyal to booster economic ideas. In 1929 he helped gather subscriptions to bring a cheese factory to Emporia. He bragged that he had never in his life voted against a local bond issue. He made a point of dropping in to shop in local stores that advertised in the *Gazette,* even when he didn't need the products. He was troubled by new marketing practices, such as the loss leader, that encouraged price competition between local merchants. And in the dark days of the Depression, he warned shoppers and merchants alike against "the tendency to go 'cheap'" in terms straight out of the booster handbook:

> Now a word to the advertisers. You can't make any money selling goods at a loss. . . . Carry quality goods, advertise quality goods—goods that you can stand back of as represented. . . .
> And now for the community. Remember this: Cheap merchandising makes a cheap community. . . . When everybody prices a different leader, the whole merchandising structure of a town is on a minus cost basis and sooner or later the bats fly in at the windows of that town, the coyotes run in the streets, and the sheriff's auctioneer is the town's merchant.[66]

The contradictions in White's thought continued to be those inherent in the booster ethos. As a businessman he advocated economic growth, and as a newspaper publisher he defended advertising as an engine of that growth. Even when his liberal friends attacked advertising as an instrument of corporate power, White held to an essentially Hamiltonian view. He described advertising in 1939 as "the marketing agent that creates the necessary new economic wants which in turn keep the mill wheels whirling and men at work in what was once upon a time—at least well before October 1929—a comparatively well ordered national industrial economy." Yet he was aware that economic growth could be harmful to community. He resisted the argument that mail-order houses would run the small merchants out of business, even as he acknowledged, "I suppose a man cannot put his hands against the tide, when it has an economic reason for its current."[67]

Despite the region's declining agricultural population, White continued to emphasize Emporia's identity as a commercial and educational center. His opposition to attempts to attract large industries made him unpopular with both entrepreneurial and working-class Emporians. As one of his former pressmen commented, many workers felt that White hurt their chances to get better jobs: "He called this the Athens of Kansas and they disliked him for it."[68]

Nonetheless, changes in the local economy made the booster ethos less relevant. Chain stores entered Emporia in force in the twenties, requiring independent merchants to adopt their competitive pricing strategies. The chains were managed by men who sought to rise by moving up within their corporations rather than boosting their local community. White mused in 1927:

> Every morning I swing into Commercial Street and pass a thoroughfare of commerce as different from that which I came into thirty years ago as if it were a new city. Our drygoods stores are all owned, so far as the majority of stock is concerned, by big buying associations in larger cities. The same is true of our lumber yards, our notion stores, many of our drug stores, and a few of our meat markets. The country merchant, deacon in the church, member of the school board, a leading citizen, pillar of society, local philanthropist, and sometimes petty tyrant of the small urban community, has passed. Instead, we have the snappy young manager who may appear any morning in any store from any place, join the Chamber of Commerce and the Rotary Club, help in the annual drives of the Red Cross, the Y.M.C.A. . . . let the auditor of the chain stores run his business morals, and so, climbing upward in the business scale one day, disappear in a cloud of glory to Kansas City, Omaha, or St. Louis. . . .[69]

As indicated by the organizations that this "snappy young manager" joined, the practice of boosterism had become bureaucratized by the twenties. Many of the roles once played by the local newspaperman—organizer of community activities, fund raiser, promoter of harmony, mediator between groups—had been assumed by local agents of national organizations. Learning from the efficiency of wartime, the Community Chest systematized and centralized local fund raising. The Lyon County Retailers' Association, with the services of a full-time staff and an extensive national information exchange network, took over the problem of assessing credit-worthiness. The Farm Bureau, which had come to Emporia in 1914, mediated town-country relations. National service organizations such as the Rotary Club, organized in Emporia in 1917, worked against the factionalism that had dominated the turn-of-the-century community. In 1924, White praised service clubs for having "wiped out these old feuds in American towns . . . even if the big city highbrows do laugh at the 'Rotes' and the Lions and the Kiwanis."[70]

The Business Men's Association that White and a few other ambitious young men had organized in 1897 had given way to a more formal Commercial Club in 1910. It in turn was superseded in 1917 by an even more systematically directed chamber of commerce, with ties to the National Chamber of Commerce. When in 1919 White received a proposal for a trucking service, he referred them to the chamber of commerce: "It is a live crowd and could do more good than anyone else to get your proposition before our people."[71]

Although White's vision of community had less and less to do with the realities of postwar Emporia and America, it nonetheless appealed to a great many Americans who did not share the modernist intellectuals' contempt for the small town. Many who had moved to the cities in search of economic opportunities looked back with nostalgia, and often loneliness. Subscription files for the weekly *Gazette* for 1918–21 showed that many out-of-town readers were former Emporians who wanted the paper's "home news," as many called it. C. R. Rice wrote from Spokane, Washington, "we get very lonely so far from our Kansas home, and we both enjoy the Gazette very much because there are names in it every week that we know." Mrs. J. P. Ramseyer of Streator, Illinois, protested, "I can't get along with out the news of the home town, and home folks." In Hollywood, California, Josephine Watson appended a note to her renewal that her copy was read by "*four* old Emporia families—and all *enjoy it.*"[72]

Many of White's magazine readers were attracted to White as much for his personal image as for his political commentary. For such people, often themselves recently removed from small-town origins, White came to embody the world that they had lost. Ever since he had written *In Our Town* White had cultivated a voice that was mellower, kindlier than the one he raised in righteousness. John Phillips was referring to this voice when he wrote in 1910 concerning some political articles he wanted:

> I should like to have in the magazine the simple wholesome familiar spirit that you get into your Gazette editorials. . . . I have been wondering if there was anything in taking a character in whose mouth you put observations. But, after all, I think it is best to have them very simple things—you, William Allen White, talking plainly to the readers of the American Magazine.[73]

In the intervening decades, William Allen White *became* this character—the wise, kindly Small-Town Editor, an idealized composite of the roles he had played in Emporia. He played his part exceedingly well. He recognized his ability to reach ordinary Americans through this persona, and employed it consciously, though not cynically. When he wanted to educate Americans to the meaning of the war in Europe, he wrote *The Martial Adventures of*

Henry and Me as a first-person travelogue, recounting the adventures of two middle-aged midwestern small-town newspapermen "going out to a ruthless war without our wives." By showing the war through these admittedly provincial eyes, White hoped make it more intelligible to ordinary Americans. To a fellow Emporian he explained his frequent use of comparisons between his war experiences and things in Emporia:

> I was trying to put the background of America back of the spectacle of the war so that our own people who know our own background might visualize and realize the war. . . . Now of course Emporia was only put in as a symbol—a symbol of America—all middle class. . . . So I kept working in details of the Emporia background to make these Americans see that their very life was woven into the vast fabric of destiny that is passing over the loom of the fates in this war.[74]

Unlike writers of the realistic school, or later practitioners of documentary, White did not intend these "details" to be unmediated material facts. Rather, they were appeals to shared beliefs and ideals as reflected in his protagonists' responses to their experiences. *Martial Adventures* was an allegory, in which his main characters enacted facets of the American character. Similarly, White's last novel, *In the Heart of a Fool,* also published in 1918, attempted to make an allegorical statement about the struggle between idealism and materialism, against the background of industrial warfare. Intellectuals praised his treatment of the war but lambasted the novel for its moralizing. Thereafter, White expressed his moral vision through nonfiction writing and his public crusades.[75]

In the twenties, Emporia emerged again and again as a symbol of what was good about small-town America. In 1920 a *New Republic* article discussing possible presidential candidates dismissed Henry Allen with the flip remark "He is from Emporia. Have you ever been in Emporia?" White rose to the challenge. It was the booster reflex—to defend one's home town against all comers—but White defended Emporia "not as a particular village, but as a typical midwestern town." "For it seems to me that these midwestern towns have developed a type of civilization just as commendable as the civilization developed in the larger centers." He took up Emporia's equitable distribution of material things: waterworks, electric lighting, telephones, spacious homes, good schools and other public institutions. He catalogued its many cultural offerings. Then he turned to "life":

> There one is puzzled. It is hard to say whether a community in which there is a fairly equitable distribution of wealth, a fairly high grade of literacy, a fairly low degree of poverty, and practically no crime, is worth while. Perhaps Athens with none of these things gave more to the world than more righteous and circumspect cities. Doubtless Babylon gave less. About our own larger cities with their inequities of living conditions, who can surely tell the truth? . . . Only if there is any merit in establishing a nearer approach to the approximate justice of God in the relations of life, than is found in larger cities, these small towns have some merit. . . .

He concluded, "So perhaps it may not be the last word of wisdom to dismiss all the considerable amount of aspiration and struggle, all the 'long days of labor and nights devoid of ease,' which scores of their citizens year after year, have put upon their local problems, with the snippy snort,—'ever been in Emporia?' " Here, clearly, were drawn the battle lines of the twenties: art versus democracy, individual expression versus public service, New York versus Emporia.[76]

Through the twenties White found himself in the thick of the "revolt against the town," and although he praised Sinclair Lewis's writings for the quickening effects of his criticisms, he repeatedly argued that Lewis was one-sided. In "The Other Side of Main Street" he praised the work of Dorothy Canfield as more balanced in seeing the "truth" as well as the "facts" of small-town life. He argued that "it is a question whether one sees externals or internals." Much of his writing in succeeding years attempted to show Americans the "internals" of their lives.[77]

The single piece of writing that most effectively defended White's small-town ideals and made him personally known to millions of Americans was, however, completely unpremeditated. In May of 1921, White's sixteen-year-old daughter, Mary, was killed in an accident. She had been an exuberant and popular girl, and all Emporia was shocked by her death. Both the Whites were devastated with grief, and for many years neither could speak of their daughter without tears. Nevertheless, they went to the *Gazette* office the day after Mary's funeral and together wrote her obituary. For more than two and a half decades White had commemorated the deaths of his fellow Emporians; he felt that his townsmen would expect something even on this occasion. "Mary White," the obituary that he wrote in her honor, immediately became a minor literary classic. This moment of greatest tragedy in White's life also marked the triumph of his vision of community. His editorial celebrated not only a girl, but a way of life.[78]

MARY WHITE

The Associated Press reports carrying the news of Mary White's death declared that it came as the result of a fall from a horse. How she would have hooted at that! She never fell from a horse in her life. Horses have fallen on her and with her—"I'm always trying to hold 'em in my lap," she used to say. But she was proud of few things, and one of them was that she could ride anything that had four legs and hair. Her death resulted not from a fall but from a blow on the head which fractured her skull, and the blow came from the limb of an overhanging tree on the parking.

The last hour of her life was typical of its happiness. She came home from a day's work at school, topped off by a hard grind with the copy of the High School Annual, and felt that a ride would refresh her. She climbed into her khakis, chattering to her mother about the work she was doing, and hurried to get her horse and be out on the dirt roads for the country air and the radiant green fields of the spring. As she rode through the town on an easy gallop, she kept waving at passers-by. She knew everyone in town. For a decade the little figure in the long pigtail and the red hair ribbon has been familiar on the streets of Emporia, and she got in the way of speaking to those who nodded at her. She passed the Kerrs, walking the horse in front of the Normal Library, and waved at them; passed another friend a few hundred feet farther on, and waved at her.

The horse was walking, and as she turned into North Merchant Street she took off her cowboy hat, and the horse swung into a lope. She passed the Tripletts and waved her cowboy hat at them, still moving gaily north on Merchant Street. A Gazette carrier passed—a High School boy friend—and she waved at him, but with her bridle hand; the horse veered quickly, plunged into the parking where the low-hanging limb faced her and, while she still looked back waving, the blow came. But she did not fall from the horse; she slipped off, dazed a bit, staggered, and fell in a faint. She never quite recovered consciousness.

But she did not fall from the horse, neither was she riding fast. A year or so ago she used to go like the wind. But that habit was broken, and she used the horse to get into the open, to get fresh, hard exercise, and to work off a certain surplus energy that welled up in her and needed a physical outlet. The need has been in her heart for years. It was back of the impulse that kept the dauntless little brown-clad figure on the streets and country roads of the community and built into a strong, muscular body what had been a frail and sickly frame during the first years of her life. But the riding gave her more than a body. It released a gay and hardy soul. She was the happiest thing in the world. And she was happy because she was enlarging her horizon. She came to know all sorts and conditions of men; Charley O'Brien, the traffic cop, was one of her best friends. W. L. Holtz, the Latin teacher, was another. Tom O'Connor, farmer-politician, and the Rev. J. H. Rice, preacher and police judge, and Frank Beach, music master, were her special friends; and all the girls, black and white, above the track and below the track, in Pepville and Stringtown, were among her acquaintances. And she brought home riotous stories of her adventures. She loved to rollick; persiflage was her natural expression at home. Her humor was a continual bubble of joy. She seemed to think in hyperbole and metaphor. She was mischievous without malice, as full of faults as an old shoe. No angel was Mary White, but an easy girl to live with for she never nursed a grouch five minutes in her life.

With all her eagerness for the out-of-doors, she loved books. On her table when she left her room were a book by Conrad, one by Galsworthy, "Creative Chemistry," by E. E. Slosson, and a Kipling book. She read Mark Twain, Dickens and Kipling before she was ten—all of their writings. Wells and Arnold Bennett particularly amused and diverted her. She was entered as a student in Wellesley for 1922; was assistant editor of the High School Annual this year, and in line for election to the editorship next year. She was a member of the executive committee of the High School Y.W.C.A.

Within the last two years she had begun to be moved by an ambition to draw. She began as most children do by scribbling in her school books, funny pictures. She bought cartoon magazines and took a course—rather casually, naturally, for she was, after all, a child with no strong purposes—and this year she tasted the first fruits of success by having her pictures accepted by the High School Annual. But the thrill of delight she got when Mr. Ecord, of the Normal Annual, asked her to do the cartooning for that book this spring, was too beautiful for words. She fell to her work with all her enthusiastic heart.

Her drawings were accepted, and her pride—always repressed by a lively sense of the ridiculous figure she was cutting—was a really gorgeous thing to see. No successful artist ever drank a deeper draft of satisfaction than she took from the little fame her work was getting among her schoolfellows. In her glory, she almost forgot her horse—but never her car.

For she used the car as a jitney bus. It was her social life. She never had a "party" in all her nearly seventeen years—wouldn't have one; but she never drove a block in her life that she didn't begin to fill the car with pick-ups! Everybody rode with Mary White—white and black, old and young, rich and poor, men and women. She liked nothing better than to fill the car with long-legged High School boys and an occasional girl, and parade the town. She never had a "date," nor went to a dance, except once with her brother Bill, and the "boy proposition" didn't interest her—yet. But young people—great spring-breaking, varnish-cracking, fender-bending, door-sagging carloads of "kids"—gave her great pleasure. Her zests were keen. But the most fun she ever had in her life was acting as chairman of the committee that got up the big turkey dinner for the poor folks at the county home; scores of pies, gallons of slaw, jam, cakes, preserves, oranges, and a wilderness of turkey were loaded into the car and taken to the county home. And, being of a practical turn of mind, she risked her own Christmas dinner to see that the poor folks actually got it all. Not that she was a cynic; she just disliked to tempt folks. While there, she found a blind colored uncle, very old, who could do nothing but make rag rugs, and she rustled up from her school friends rags enough to keep him busy for a season. The last engagement she tried to make was to take the guests at the county home out for a car ride. And the last endeavor of her life was to try to get a rest room for colored girls in the High School. She found one girl reading in the toilet, because there was no better place for a colored girl to loaf, and it inflamed her sense of injustice and she became a nagging harpy to those who she thought could remedy the evil. The poor she always had with her and was glad of it. She hungered and thirsted for righteousness; and was the most impious creature in the world. She joined the church without consulting her parents, not particularly for her soul's good. She never had a thrill of piety in her life, and would have hooted at a "testimony." But even as a little child, she felt the church was an agency for helping people to more of life's abundance, and she wanted to help. She never wanted help for herself. Clothes meant little to her. It was a fight to get a new rig on her; but eventually a harder fight to get it off. She never wore a jewel and had no ring but her High School class ring though she was nearly seventeen. "Mother," she protested, "you don't know how much I get by with, in my braided pigtails, that I could not with my hair up." Above every other passion of her life was her passion not to grow up, to be a child. The tomboy in her, which was big, seemed loath to be put away forever in skirts. She was a Peter Pan who refused to grow up.

Her funeral yesterday at the Congregational Church was as she would have wished it; no singing, no flowers except the big bunch of red roses from her brother Bill's Harvard classmen—heavens, how proud that would have made her!—and the red roses from the Gazette forces, in vases, at her head and feet. A short prayer: Paul's beautiful essay on "Love" from the Thirteenth Chapter of First Corinthians; some remarks about her democratic spirit by her friend, John H. J. Rice, pastor and police judge, which she would have deprecated if she could; a prayer sent down for her by her friend, Carl Nau; and, opening the service, the slow, poignant movement from Beethoven's Moonlight Sonata, which she loved; and closing the service a cutting from the joyously melancholy first movement of Tchaikovsky's Pathetic Symphony, which she liked to hear, in certain moods, on the phonograph, then the Lord's Prayer by her friends in High School.

That was all.

For her pallbearers only her friends were chosen: her Latin teacher, W. L. Holtz; her High School principal, Rice Brown; her doctor, Frank Foncannon; her friend, W. W. Finney; her pal at the Gazette office, Walter Hughes; and her brother Bill. It would have made her smile to know that her friend, Charley O'Brien, the traffic cop, had been transferred from Sixth and Commercial to the corner near the church to direct her friends who came to bid her good-by.

A rift in the clouds in a gray day threw a shaft of sunlight upon her coffin as her nervous, energetic little body sank to its last sleep. But the soul of her, the glowing, gorgeous, fervent soul of her, surely was flaming in eager joy upon some other dawn.[79]

As he had done on countless previous occasions, White here distilled into a few clear, simply described images the essence of a life. It was appreciated by his local audience, who had known Mary; he recalled, "The town was deeply moved by it." But the tragedy of this death and the sincere but contained grief of its expression made of the obituary a piece of literature that transcended local interest. A few days after it appeared in the Gazette, Franklin P. Adams reprinted it in the New York Tribune, and thence it moved quickly throughout the country. It was reprinted in countless newspapers and magazines. Alexander Woollcott read it in his very first Reader radio program, and other radio programs followed suit. White wrote his son, "It was really better than I thought. And to tell the truth, Bill, it seems really better than it is. It was such a simple, inevitable thing to do that I see no grace and little merit in it."[80]

The editorial touched the hearts of a broad range of Americans. Christopher Morley of the New York Evening Post asked to include it in an anthology, saying, "what you wrote is not only honorable to yourself as a father and a writer; it adds honor to all who follow the calling of decent self-respecting journalism." An Indiana banker requested a copy of the editorial, explaining "The writer lost an only daughter of about this age. . . ." For decades thereafter, "Mary White" was reprinted in hundreds of collections of essays, particularly schoolbooks. One editor said, "I think it appropriate to perpetuate in a high-school book the memory of what seems to me an ideal American high-school girl." Consequently, subsequent generations of Americans know William Allen White principally through his commemoration of his daughter.[81]

The tragic death of an innocent child possesses a universal appeal that makes it a frequent subject for human-interest stories. In White's hands, skilled but at this moment utterly without design, the obituary fulfilled yet transcended the human-interest formula. It would stand as a shining rebuke to the sordid and superficial journalism of the twenties. The Mary White who was immortalized in her obituary was indeed an ideal of American girlhood, and an embodiment of the progressive values that her father cherished. She was therefore a perfect antithesis to the mass media's reigning female figure, the flapper. For all her nearly seventeen years, Mary was completely innocent of sexuality or feminine wiles. Uninterested in the "boy proposition," she had never had a date. She cared nothing for clothing or jewelry and continued to wear her hair in pigtails. Yet despite her purity, Mary was by no means the fragile, passive girl of the Victorian feminine ideal. She was, instead, exuberant, vital, and full of actively expressed love for humanity.

She was, in other words, the epitome of progressive girlhood, uniting physical vigor and unpretentious social consciousness. Like her hero and family friend Theodore Roosevelt, Mary had been frail as a child, but through exercise had shaped "a strong, muscular body." She loved the out-of-doors and was a thoroughgoing "tomboy." She was a "hardy soul" and "mischievous without malice."

Mary had been as one with her community and alive with concern for everyone in it. What made her happy was "enlarging her horizon" and sharing with others. She knew and was friendly to "everyone in town," including the police judge, the traffic cop, and "all the girls," regardless of race or class. She was active in school and civic organizations. Lacking formal piety, she nonetheless joined the Congregational Church because she believed it could help people. The "most fun she ever had in her life" was organizing a Christmas turkey dinner for the poor. And her last project before her death was agitating for a rest room for black high-school girls. Though White insisted, "no angel was Mary White," her father's image of his daughter embodied his ideals every bit as much as angelic Little Eva had represented sentimental Victorian values.

Although White's vision of community would lose its dominance over the *Gazette* and life in Emporia in the twenties, Americans' wholehearted response to "Mary White" demonstrated its continuing imaginative power. In his *Autobiography* White predicted, "Probably if anything I have written in these long, happy years . . . survives more than a decade beyond my life's span, it will be the thousand words or so that I hammered out on my typewriter that bright May morning under the shadow and in the agony of Mary's death."[82]

Epilogue

By the close of the twenties, William Allen White was no typical small-town newspaper editor, but he had become America's archetypical Small-Town Editor. Shrewd yet kindly, courageously individualistic yet deeply rooted in his community, White's national image symbolized a humane native American tradition that, by the Depression, even urban intellectuals had begun to search for. Fittingly, it was the national media, which had undermined the small-town newspaper's real influence, that disseminated and shaped this image of White. Urban newspapers and mass-circulation magazines told and retold the story of his career. Teachers of journalism compiled anthologies of his editorials. Fellow Emporians wrote biographies of their most famous citizen. This clebration of White climaxed in 1938, when his seventieth birthday prompted an outpouring of attention in media ranging from the venerable *Atlantic* and *Christian Century* to journalistic upstarts *Life* and *Look*.[1]

Announcing "An American Institution is 70," *Life*'s commemoration of the event was also a nostalgic salute to small-town America. Its five-page spread opened with a large photograph of a kindly, white-haired old man, who was, simply, "The Country Editor." A short text framed the succeeding photographs by establishing White as a multifaceted archetype: "He is the small-town boy who made good at home. To the small-town man who envies the glamour of the city, he is living assurance that small-town life may be preferable. To the city man who looks back with nostalgia on a small-town youth, he is a living symbol of small-town simplicity and kindliness and common sense."

The following photographs celebrated the community as well as the man. One showed White being serenaded outside the *Gazette* building by "a thousand Emporians led by Mayor Lostutter and the 161st Field Artillery band." In another, White greeted the massed membership of the Rotary Club outside his home, to which they had "marched in a body" to give him a basket of roses. Others depicted White alighting from his car on his way to work, greeting "almost everybody" on his way down busy Commercial Street "on his daily round," and self-consciously sipping a Coke at Warren Morris's drugstore. One page was devoted to photographs of the *Gazette* newsroom and four of his most dedicated employees. The final page was filled with a single large photograph. It showed White, his ample back to the camera, working at his battered rolltop desk, oblivious to the mountains of papers, newspapers, and books threatening to cascade about him. On top of the desk and on the wall behind are photographs and mementos of national leaders past and present, evidence of a long and distinguished career. But the text below the photograph has only the heading "The Country Editor at his desk: here 'Mary White' was written."[2]

Ironically, these loving images of small-town America were recorded and disseminated by the photo-magazine, the latest development in mass journalism. With its large photographs and minimal text, *Life* was far removed from the unillustrated, type-filled pages of the *Gazette* in 1895. Yet, as the story of William Allen White's career illustrates, even then economic and technological changes were under way, transforming not only the appearance but the roles of the small-town newspaper. By the time *Life* celebrated the Country Editor and his Small Town, both had become popular stereotypes and objects of nostalgia. Gone was the young William Allen White: a brash, feisty young editor, eager to show his stuff; a shrewd businessman; a relentless crusader for righteousness. White's image in *Life* was as a kindly old man, the symbol of a vanished age.

Life had begun by reiterating the well-known story of White's rise, so like that of a Horatio Alger hero:

> Every small-town boy who ever dreamed of becoming a newspaperman knows the story of how William Allen White, with 27 years behind him and $1.25 in his pocket, rode the Santa Fe into Emporia, Kan., one day in 1895, borrowed $3,000 and bought the Emporia *Gazette,* and next year wrote an editorial called "What's the Matter with Kansas?" which made him nationally famous overnight.

Like Horatio Alger's stories, this version bore stronger resemblances to fairy tales than to the reality of White's success. Nonetheless, small-town boys who dreamed of becoming newspapermen would have learned soon enough that there was even less chance in 1938 that the story would be repeated.

At the beginning of the twentieth century, William Allen White became a national figure by admirably playing the many roles of the small-town journalist at a unique historical moment. As booster and progressive, White attempted to unify and defend his community. As newspaper publisher and magazine writer, he took advantage of opportunities created by improved communication technologies and a consumption-based economy. Ultimately, the power of communication to transcend geographic boundaries and shape national networks overwhelmed its potential to foster local community. William Allen White the publisher undermined the work of William Allen White the community-builder.

Notes

Abbreviations

EG   *Emporia Gazette* (daily edition)
ER   *Emporia Republican*
ESU   William Allen White Collection, William Allen White Memorial Library, Emporia State University, Emporia
ET   *Emporia Times*
KU   William Allen White Papers, Kansas Collection, Kenneth Spencer Research Library, University of Kansas, Lawrence
LB   Letter books included in LC
LC   William Allen White Papers, Manuscript Division, Library of Congress, Washington, D.C.
LCHM   Lyon County Historical Museum, Emporia

Introduction

1. William Allen White, *The Autobiography of William Allen White* (New York: Macmillan Company, 1946), pp. 257–58.

2. For Franklin's account of his arrival, see *The Autobiography of Benjamin Franklin,* Leonard W. Labaree et al., eds. (New Haven: Yale University Press, 1964), pp. 75–77. The many biographies of White that focus upon his national career include Walter Johnson, *William Allen White's America* (New York: Henry Holt and Company, 1947); Everett Rich, *William Allen White: The Man From Emporia* (New York: Farrar & Rinehart, Inc., 1941); Frank C. Clough, *William Allen White of Emporia* (New York: McGraw-Hill Book Company, 1941; Greenwood Press reprint, 1970); David Hinshaw, *A Man From Kansas: The Story of William Allen White* (New York: G. P. Putnam's Sons, 1945); John DeWitt MeKee, *William Allen White: Maverick on Main Street* (Westport, Conn.: Greenwood Press, 1975); and E. Jay Jernigan, *William Allen White* (New York: Twayne Publishers, Inc., 1983).

3. My understanding of face-to-face communication has been greatly influenced by the work of Fr. Walter J. Ong, most recently *Orality and Literacy: The Technologizing of the Word* (New York: Methuen & Co., 1982). As will become clear, however, I do not follow Fr. Ong's polarization of cultures into oral or literate. Rather, I have come to believe that there is a continuum among and within societies between purely oral and purely literate and that small towns in the nineteenth century had strong oral components. Certainly, journalism as a highly conventional genre has many of the same characteristics that Fr. Ong ascribes to oral expression.

4. Recent studies of nineteenth-century communities have shown that, far from being self-sufficient individualists, businessmen were tightly bound into local networks of personal relationships that controlled the distribution of credit. See, particularly, Anthony F. C. Wallace, *Rockdale: The Growth of an American Village in the Early Industrial Revolution* (New York: W. W. Norton & Company, 1978), and Paul Johnson, *A Shopkeeper's Millennium: Society and Revivals in Rochester, New York, 1815–1837* (New York: Hill and Wang, 1978).

5. Communication scholars have begun to recognize that communication is best understood as an interactive rather than a linear process and to call for studies examining the concrete context in which meanings are created and communicated. These developments are summarized by Robert A. White in "Mass Communication and Culture: Transition to a New Paradigm," *Journal of Communication* (Summer 1983): 279–301; and Michael R. Real, "Media Theory: Contributions to an Understanding of American Mass Communications," *American Quarterly* 32 (Bibliography Issue, 1980): 238–258.

6. Similarly, Elizabeth L. Eisenstein argues that understanding of the effects of the introduction of printing has lagged because printing falls outside standard fields in historical scholarship. Eisenstein, *The Printing Press as an Agent of Change: Communications and Cultural Transformations in Early Modern Europe* (New York: Cambridge University Press, 1979), pp. 3–24. David D. Hall has noted that the study of printing and journalism, the "history of the book," requires a synthesis of intellectual and social history. Hall, *On Native Ground: From the History of Printing to the History of the Book* (Worcester, Mass.: American Antiquarian Society, 1984). Similar interdisciplinary approaches have particularly benefited the study of early America. See Rhys Isaac, *The Transformation of Virginia, 1740–1790* (Chapel Hill: University of North Carolina Press, 1982), and John Putnam Demos, *Entertaining Satan: Witchcraft and the Culture of Early New England* (New York: Oxford University Press, 1982). I have also benefited from Laurel Thatcher Ulrich's use of the sociological concept of "role analysis" to study colonial women's lives in *Good Wives: Image and Reality in the Lives of Women in Northern New England, 1650–1750* (New York: Alfred A. Knopf, 1982; Oxford University Press paperback, 1983).

7. The William Allen White Papers in the Manuscript Division of the Library of Congress contain nearly two hundred shelf feet of materials, including 80 bound letter books and over 450 containers of correspondence. Other papers are contained at the William Allen White Memorial Library, Emporia State University, Emporia, Kansas; at the Kansas Collection, University of Kansas Libraries, Lawrence, Kansas; and in smaller numbers in other collections.

8. The booster ethos bears striking parallels with the classical republican tradition as explicated in recent years by J. G. A. Pocock and others. Intellectual historians have only recently begun to assess the continuities with political or economic ideas in the later nineteenth century. Pocock, *The Machiavellian Moment: Florentine Political Thought and the Atlantic Republican Tradition* (Princeton, N.J.: Princeton University Press, 1975); Gordon S. Wood, *The Creation of the American Republic, 1776–1787* (Chapel Hill: University of North Carolina Press, 1969); Drew R. McCoy, *The Elusive Republic: Political Economy in Jeffersonian America* (Chapel Hill: University of North Carolina Press, 1980); Dorothy Ross, "The Liberal Tradition Revisited and the Republican Tradition Addressed," in John Higham and Paul K. Conkin, eds., *New Directions in American Intellectual History* (Baltimore: Johns Hopkins University Press, 1979), pp. 116–31.

9. Boorstin's rich description of the peculiar emphasis upon growth and community spirit among the builders of American "upstart" cities is the starting point for any study of boosterism. Boorstin, *The Americans: The National Experience* (New York: Vintage Books, 1965), Part Three. Atherton describes the country town's combination of "idealism, optimism, materialism and faith in progress" in *Main Street on the Middle Border* (Bloomington: Indiana University Press, 1954), p. xvi and passim. Robert R. Dykstra describes the ambitions of town-building businessmen in five frontier Kansas towns in *The Cattle Towns* (New York: Atheneum, 1976). Carl Abbott describes the growth strategies of four cities in *Boosters and Businessmen: Popular Economic Thought and Urban Growth in the Antebellum Middle West* (Westport, Conn.: Greenwood Press, 1981). And studies of various American communities in the nineteenth century have noted the intense concern with growth of many members of local elites. See, for example, Michael Frisch, *Town Into City* (Cambridge, Mass.: Harvard University Press, 1972), and Don Harrison Doyle, *The Social Order of a Frontier Community: Jacksonville, Illinois, 1825–70* (Urbana: University of Illinois Press, 1978).

10. Boorstin, *National Experience,* pp. 115–16.

11. Most prominent among the studies of this political reorientation is Richard L. McCormick's *From Realignment to Reform: Political Change in New York State, 1893–1910* (Ithaca: Cornell University Press, 1981). See also his essays "The Party Period and Public Policy: An Exploratory Hypothesis," *Journal of American History* 66 (1979): 279–98; and "The Discovery that Business Corrupts Politics: A Reappraisal of the Origins of Progressivism," *American Historical Review* 86 (1981): 247–74.

12. Daniel T. Rogers offers a provocative interpretation of progressivism as a "constellation" of three "languages of discontent" that gave "those who called themselves progressives . . . a set of tools" with which to effect change. Rogers, "In Search of Progressivism," *The Promise of American History: Progress and Prospects* (Baltimore: Johns Hopkins University Press, 1982), pp. 113–32.

13. Local-history sources for Emporia include the *Gazette* and other local newspapers, city directories, censuses, scrapbooks, and records of local government and civic organizations. Much of this material is located in the Lyon County Historical Museum in Emporia. Biographical data from these sources were gathered on hundreds of Emporia residents in order to identify lines of economic and factional cleavage. Community studies that provided important models include Paul Boyer and Stephen Nissenbaum, *Salem Possessed: The Social Origins of Witchcraft* (Cambridge, Mass.: Harvard University Press, 1974); Robert A. Gross, *The Minutemen and Their World* (New York: Hill and Wang, 1976); and Mary P. Ryan, *Cradle of the Middle Class: The Family in Oneida County, New York, 1790–1865* (New York: Cambridge University Press, 1981). A recent anthropological study of an American town, which argues that individualism must be understood within the context of community, is by Hervé Varenne, *Americans Together: Structured Diversity in a Midwestern Town* (New York: Teachers College Press, 1977). On the need to examine the forum of "public culture," see Thomas Bender, "Wholes and Parts; The Need for Synthesis in American History," *Journal of American History* 73 (June 1986): 120–36.

14. George M. Fredrickson made this point persuasively in a review article, "Down on the Farm," in the *New York Review of Books,* Apr. 23, 1987, pp. 37–39. Although my thinking about the *Gazette*'s role in Emporia and the transformation of boosterism into an instrument of nationalism has benefited from discussions of

the theory of "hegemony," for example, in the end that theory fails to provide an explanation of how hegemonic consensus is produced. Lacking that, its theoretical terms such as "historical block" offer little understanding not also provided by more commonly understood language such as "coalition." Where possible, I have chosen to use language familiar to nonprofessional historians. On hegemony, see T. J. Jackson Lears, "The Concept of Cultural Hegemony: Problems and Possibilities," *American Historical Review* 90 (June 1985): 567–93; and Thomas Bender's "Comment" on the panel "Defining Our Terms: Cultural Hegemony," at the 1985 Meeting of the Organization of American Historians.

1. The Education of a "Somebody"

1. *Emporia News*, quoted in William Allen White, *The Autobiography of William Allen White* (New York: Macmillan Company, 1946), p. 3.

2. David Riesman, Christopher Lasch, and, most recently, Jackson Lears have assumed the dominance in the nineteenth century of a personality type described by Riesman as "inner-directed," characterized by a strong, autonomously defined sense of self. While such a type was the goal of Victorian reformers and may or may not have been characteristic of the educated urban upper-middle classes to whom Lears specifically refers, it remains to be seen whether it ever achieved dominance among rural or small-town Americans. Riesman, with Nathan Glazer and Reuel Denney, *The Lonely Crowd: A Study of the Changing American Character*, 3rd ed., rev. (New Haven, 1969); Lasch, *The Culture of Narcissism: American Life in an Age of Diminishing Expectations* (New York, 1978); T. J. Jackson Lears, *No Place of Grace: Antimodernism and the Transformation of American Culture, 1880–1920* (New York: Pantheon Books, 1981), pp. 12–15, 34–37.

3. White, *Autobiography*, pp. 22, 39. See also Jean H. Baker, *Affairs of Party: The Political Culture of Northern Democrats in the Mid-Nineteenth Century* (Ithaca, N.Y.: Cornell University Press, 1983).

4. The classic discussion of the role of newspapers in promoting new towns is Daniel J. Boorstin's *The Americans: The National Experience* (New York: Vintage Books, 1965), Chapter 17. On the founding of Emporia see Laura M. French, *History of Emporia and Lyon County* (Emporia: Emporia Gazette Print, 1929), pp. 1–7; EG, July 4, 1907.

5. French, *History of Emporia*, pp. 12, 27, 37, 52.

6. William E. Connelley, *The Life of Preston B. Plumb* (Chicago: Browne & Howell Company, 1913), pp. 60–65, 216. Daniel Boorstin depicts several such town-building "leading citizens" in *The National Experience*, pp. 115–23. The role of reputation and civic spirit in achieving standing is described by Patrick Palermo in "Rules of the Game: Local Republican Political Culture in the Gilded Age," *The Historian* 47 (Aug. 1985): 483–85.

7. White, *Autobiography*, pp. 9, 42–43, 84–85.

8. Ibid., pp. 9, 10; Vol. P. Mooney, *History of Butler County Kansas* (Lawrence, Kansas: Standard Publishing Company, 1916), p. 140.

9. White, *Autobiography*, p. 9. Quotation from Mooney, *Butler County*, p. 132.

10. H. H. Gardner, quoted in Mooney, *Butler County*, p. 140; J. M. Sotterthwaite, "Dr. Allen White, As I Remember Him," unpublished manuscript, n.d., KU.

11. Mooney, *Butler County*, p. 140; Sotterthwaite, "Dr. Allen White"; White, *Autobiography*, p. 21–22, 51, 85.

12. White, *Autobiography*, pp. 22, 61, 81, 84. See also Palermo, "Rules of the Game," pp. 491–92.

13. White, *Autobiography*, pp. 61, 62, 77.

14. Ibid., p. 83.

15. Ibid., pp. 7–8, 43, 61.

16. Ibid., pp. 44, 58, 60, 84.

17. Ibid., pp. 7, 35, 61.

18. Ibid., pp. 25, 30, 36.

19. Ibid., pp. 91–92.

20. Rolla A. Clymer, "Thomas Benton Murdock and William Allen White," *The Kansas Historical Quarterly* 23 (Autumn 1957): 249; White, *Autobiography*, p. 92.

21. White, *Autobiography*, pp. 74, 101, 122, 139, 137 (quote).

22. French, *History of Emporia*, pp. 50–55; White, *Autobiography*, p. 100.

23. White, *Autobiography*, pp. 101–102.

24. Ibid., pp. 103–106, 147; diary is on microfilm made by Walter Johnson, Reel 4, Kansas State Historical Society, Topeka.

25. White, *Autobiography*, pp. 109, 118.

26. Ibid., pp. 69–71, 109, 111; William E. Connelley, *History of Kansas Newspapers* (Topeka: Kansas State Printing Plant, 1916), p. 152. White recalled his age as ten or eleven, but the *Democrat* was not founded until March 24, 1881, when he was thirteen.

27. White, *Autobiography*, pp. 110, 112.

28. Ibid., pp. 112–13, 118.

29. Ibid., p. 118. Carolyn Dyer's research into the business history of antebellum Wisconsin newspapers has effectively dispelled the myth of the frontier journalist as an independent and individualistic artisan, setting up shop with only the proverbial "shirt-tail full of type." Rather, newspapers have required more capital investment than most men could provide on their own, and from the earliest days were supported by political patronage. Carolyn Stewart Dyer, "The Business History of the Antebellum Wisconsin Newspaper, 1833–1860: A Study of Concentration of Ownership and Diversity of Views" (Ph.D. dissertation, University of Wisconsin–Madison, 1978), and "Political Patronage of the Wisconsin Press, 1849–1860: New Perspectives on the Economics of Patronage," in *Journalism Monographs* (forthcoming).

30. Elizabeth F. Baker, *Printers and Technology* (New York: Columbia University Press, 1957), pp. 3–5; James Moran, *Printing Presses, History and Development from the Fifteenth Century to Modern Times* (Berkeley: University of California Press, 1973), pp. 148, 157.

31. White, *Autobiography*, pp. 114–19 (quote on p. 115); Leonard W. Labaree et al., eds., *The Autobiography of Benjamin Franklin* (New Haven: Yale University Press, 1964), p. 100. On the work culture of printers in the nineteenth century, see William S. Pretzer, " 'Love of Grog and Desperate Passion for Clean Shirts': The Tramp Printer in Nineteenth Century America," paper presented at the Annual Meeting of the Organization of American Historians, Apr. 3, 1981.

32. White, *Autobiography*, pp. 118, 123–24.

33. Ibid., pp. 130, 135, 141, 153.

34. Ibid., p. 131.

35. Ibid., pp. 134, 155–57.

36. Ibid., pp. 131–32.

37. Ibid., pp. 132–33. On the prominent role of personal ties and reciprocity in

political culture, see Paula Baker, "The Culture of Politics in the Late Nineteenth Century: Community and Political Behavior in Rural New York," *Journal of Social History* 18 (Winter 1984): 167–93; Richard L. McCormick, "The Party Period and Public Policy: An Exploratory Hypothesis," *Journal of American History* 66 (Sept. 1979): 279–98; and Palermo, "Rules of the Game," pp. 491–94.

38. White, *Autobiography*, pp. 131, 149–50.

39. Ibid., pp. 140, 143, 144, 177, 198–99, 256.

40. Ibid., pp. 154–55, 158–59.

41. Ibid., p. 163.

42. Ibid., pp. 145, 153–54.

43. Ibid., p. 90.

44. Ibid., p. 182.

45. Ibid., p. 182; printed postcard, dated Nov. 10, 1890, ESU; White to I. D. Marshall, stamped as received July 7, 1890, KU.

46. White, *Autobiography*, pp. 186–87.

47. Ibid., pp. 189, 183, 186, 198, 197.

48. Ibid., pp. 93, 199.

49. Ibid., pp. 201, 205–206 passim.

50. Ibid., pp. 207–208; Icie F. Johnson, *William Rockhill Nelson and the Kansas City Star* (Kansas City: Burton Publishing Company, 1935).

51. Mooney, *Butler County*, pp. 149, 437; Jean Folkerts, "William Allen White: Editor and Businessman during the Reform Years, 1895–1916," *Kansas History* 7 (Summer 1984): 130; White, *Autobiography*, pp. 222–23.

52. White, *Autobiography*, pp. 190, 222; Walter Johnson, *William Allen White's America* (New York: Henry Holt & Company, 1947), p. 60; Frank Luther Mott, *A History of American Magazines*, 4 vols. (Cambridge, Mass.: The Belknap Press of Harvard University Press, 1957), IV: 97; Garland to White, June 21, 1894, ESU.

53. White to Paine, n.d. (ca. Jan. 22, 1893), ESU.

54. William Lindsay White, "Life With William Allen White Was Lively," *Kansas City Star*, Sept. 22, 1968, pp. 8–9F; Marion Ellet, "Sallie White," EG, June 24, 1968. Bertram Wyatt-Brown defines southern honor as "the cluster of ethical rules, most readily found in societies of small communities, by which judgments of behavior are ratified by community consensus." *Southern Honor: Ethics and Behavior in the Old South* (New York: Oxford University Press, 1982), p. xv.

55. White, *Autobiography*, pp. 227–30, 237–38. On Nelson's reform orientation, see David Paul Nord, *Newspapers and New Politics: Midwestern Municipal Reform, 1890–1900* (Ann Arbor: UMI Research Press, 1981), pp. 122–23.

56. White, *Autobiography*, pp. 255–56; William Allen White, "Early Draft of Autobiography," unpublished manuscript (ca. 1927–28), Ch. 5, p. 2, ESU.

57. White to Albert Bigelow Paine, two letters, n.d. (early 1893), ESU; White, *Autobiography*, pp. 245, 256.

58. Morgan quoted in *Kansas: The First Century*, 4 vols. (New York: Lewis Historical Publishing Company, 1956), II: 426; Mooney, *Butler County*, p. 482; White, *Autobiography*, pp. 256–57, 260.

2. The New Editor

1. William Allen White, *The Autobiography of William Allen White* (New York: Macmillan Company, 1946), p. 259; [Laura French], "History of the Emporia Gazette," unpublished typescript, n.d. (ca. 1945), in possession of Mrs. William Allen White, p. 21.

2. EG, June 3, 1895.

3. White to Charles M. Vernon, Apr. 3, 1908, LB 11, LC.

4. Laura M. French, *History of Emporia and Lyon County* (Emporia: Emporia Gazette Print, 1929), pp. 42, 233; Jacob Stotler, *Annals of Emporia and Lyon County, 1857-'82* (Emporia: n.d., n.p.), p. 20; William Allen White, "Early Draft of Autobiography," unpublished manuscript (ca. 1927-28), Ch. 5, p. 19, ESU.

5. White, *Autobiography*, pp. 314, 315.

6. Alfred Theodore Andreas, *History of the State of Kansas*, 2 vols. (Chicago: A. T. Andreas, 1883), II: 848-49, 851, 853-54; James D. Kemmerling, "A History of the Whitley Opera House in Emporia, Kansas: 1881-1913," *Emporia State Research Studies* 18 (March 1970): 5-7; EG, July 16, 1900; French, *History of Emporia*, p. 27.

7. French, *History of Emporia*, pp. 222-35. See Dun & Co. reports on Stotler in Vol. 12, pp. 266, 267, 291, R. G. Dun & Co. Collection, Baker Library, Harvard University Graduate School of Business Administration.

8. William E. Connelley, *The Life of Preston B. Plumb* (Chicago: Browne & Howell Company, 1913), p. 221; Andreas, *History of Kansas*, II: 850; White, *Autobiography*, p. 441.

9. White, *Autobiography*, p. 267.

10. White to Charles M. Vernon, April 3, 1908, LB 11, LC.

11. Walter Johnson, *William Allen White's America* (New York: Henry Holt and Company, 1947), pp. 78-79.

12. White, *Autobiography*, p. 197.

13. Such claims have been made about similar editorial statements made by the first penny papers in the 1830s in Michael Schudson, *Discovering the News: A Social History of American Newspapers* (New York: Basic Books, 1978), and Dan Schiller, *Objectivity and the News: The Public and the Rise of Commercial Journalism* (Philadelphia: University of Pennsylvania Press, 1981).

14. EG, June 4, 1895.

15. Ibid., June 3, 1895.

16. Ibid., June 4 and 7, 1895. On White's disdain for sports, see William Lindsay White, "Life With William Allen White Was Lively," *Kansas City Star*, Sept. 22, 1968, pp. 8-9F.

17. EG, June 6 and 7, 1895.

18. Ibid., June 5 and 11, 1895. Patrick F. Palermo discusses the role of boosterism in integrating newcomers in "Boosterism, Politics and the Community: Using Interactionism in Historical Research," in the possession of the author.

19. EG, June 7, 1895.

20. Ibid., June 3, 5, 6, and 8, 1895.

21. Ibid., Oct. 5, 1895; White, *Autobiography*, pp. 264-65. White recalled that the story had been about a wedding, but it was in fact about the engagement.

22. EG, June 12, 1895.

23. White, *Autobiography*, pp. 268-69.

24. He got the billboard space in trade for newspaper advertising. Since the Opera House was a large user of advertising, *Gazette* ads in its programs and on its scene curtain may also have been exchange propositions. Ibid., p. 271; Kemmerling, "History of the Whitley Opera House," p. 14.

25. ER, May 21 and June 4, 1895; EG, June 4, 1895.

26. ER, June 18, 1895; EG, July 6 and 15, 1895.

27. ER, July 16 and 18, 1895; EG, July 2, 16, and 20, 1895.

28. ER, July 19, 1895; EG, Aug. 6, 1895.

29. This agreement, dated April 1896, on the stationery of the Hotel Whitley, is in a hand other than White's, and is unsigned. Although this might indicate that it was not finally ratified, it is doubtful that White would have kept it in his papers if the deal had not been completed. The document is in the William Allen White Collection, ESU; Emporia City Council Proceedings, Vol. II, July 5, 1886, and Vol. III, City Clerk's Office, Emporia.

30. EG, June 11, 1895. On the Gazette's use of "plate," see White, "Early Draft of Autobiography," Ch. 7, p. 8, ESU.

31. EG, June 3, 1896; April 12, 1901, LB 2, LC.

32. "Forty Years: New Man, Old Issues," New York Times Magazine (Aug. 9, 1936): 2.

33. White, Autobiography, p. 266.

34. Ibid., p. 266; White to Way and Williams, [Aug. 15?] and Aug. 29, 1896, typescript copies in manuscript division, Newberry Library, Chicago. See Joe W. Kraus, "The Publication of William Allen White's The Real Issue," Kansas Historical Quarterly 43 (Summer 1977): 193–202. On Way and Williams, see Robert M. Crunden, Ministers of Reform: The Progressives' Achievement in American Civilization, 1889–1920 (New York: Basic Books, 1982), p. 155.

35. White, Autobiography, p. 278. For selections from his editorials in this period, see Everett Rich, William Allen White: The Man from Emporia (New York: Farrar & Rinehart, 1941), pp. 85–87, 92; Johnson, White's America, pp. 90–92.

36. Quotes contained in Philip Mangelsdorf, "When William Allen White and Ed Howe Covered the Republicans," Journalism Quarterly 44 (Autumn 1967): 454–60.

37. EG, August 15, 1896.

38. Rich, William Allen White, p. 92.

39. Morton to White, Aug. 26, 1896, ESU.

40. Rich, William Allen White, p. 92; Johnson, White's America, p. 95, refers to a letter from the chairman of the Republican Congressional Committee asking White for the price of reprints; F. H. Peavey to the Gazette, n.d., ESU; "Personal Notes," Harper's Weekly 46 (Feb. 1, 1902): 155.

41. Walter Johnson, White's America, p. 95; Rich, William Allen White, pp. 91–95; John DeWitt McKee, William Allen White: Maverick on Main Street (Westport, Conn.: Greenwood Press, 1975), pp. 40, 47.

42. Rich, William Allen White, p. 93. Arthur Guy Empey was a writer whose book about World War I, Over the Top, brought him short-lived celebrity. White to Chauncey Williams, n.d. [January 1897], ESU.

43. EG, Feb. 1, 1944.

44. ET, Aug. 21, 1896, and Dec. 1, 1897. The envelope and clipping are now in the possession of LCHM.

45. EG, Dec. 9, 1896, and Feb. 12, 1897; White to Warren R. Anderson, Oct. 13, 1899, and White to Doubleday & McClure, Sept. 22, 1899, both LB 1, LC.

46. Acting commissioner to John M. Reynolds, Jan. 19, 1897, and Frank Gaiennie to D. R. Francis, Nov. 19, 1896, Misc. Correspondence, RG 48, National Archives, Washington, D.C.; Annual Report of the Auditor for the Interior Department to the Secretary of the Treasury (Washington: GPO, 1898); White to W. R. Greason, Nov. 20, 1912, LC.

47. Page to White, Dec. 19, 1896; "A Typical Kansas Community," Atlantic 80 (1897): 171–77; Scribner's Magazine 22 (Nov. 1897): 531–48; The Forum 23 (Mar.

1897): 75–83; "Kansas Stories," *McClure's Magazine* 8 (Feb. 1897): 321–30; and "An Appreciation of the West," ibid., 11 (Oct. 1898): 575–80. White was by no means the only Kansan who was enlisted to report on his native state for national magazines. For a listing of such articles, see William H. Seiler, "Magazine Writers Look at Kansas, 1854–1904," *Kansas Historical Quarterly* 38 (Spring 1972): 1–42.

48. *The Forum* 23 (Mar. 1897): 82. His argument echoed Frederick Jackson Turner's assessment of Populism. See "The Problem of the West," *Atlantic Monthly* 78 (Sept. 1896): 289–97.

49. EG, Dec. 14 and 29, 1896.

50. Ibid., Feb. 5 and 25, 1897; 1896 Emporia city directory; EG, July 5, 1902; White, *Autobiography*, p. 100; ET, Aug. 25, 1899. By 1899 the group had changed its name to the Young Men's Business Association, but in 1900 it resumed the name Business Men's Association.

51. EG, Apr. 8, 1897.

52. Aug. 26, 1899, LB 1, LC.

53. White to F. C. Meagley, July 18, 1902, LB 3; White to F. B. Ripley, July 24, 1900, LB 2, both LC.

54. White, *Autobiography*, p. 285. White borrowed the photographic engravings from his former publisher, Chauncey L. Williams, who edited a Chicago magazine called *Show Window*. White to Chauncey L. Williams, June 29, (1899), LB 1, LC. On Keokuk's fair, which is still held annually, see "Keokuk's Street Fair a Wet Fete," Picture Section, *Des Moines Sunday Register*, Aug. 22, 1982, p. 5. White wrote to a promoter who had been recommended by the president of the Salina Street Fair Association, asking his terms. White to George D. Lenson, July 1 (1899), LB 1, LC.

55. EG, Nov. 16, 1898, Nov. 16, 1899.

56. ER, Nov. 16, 17, and 18, 1898. On Jobes's political affiliations, see Robert Sherman La Forte, *Leaders of Reform: Progressive Republicans in Kansas, 1900–1916* (Lawrence: University Press of Kansas, 1974), pp. 20, 100.

57. EG, June 21 and Nov. 16, 1899, July 21, 1900; White, *Autobiography*, p. 314; ET, Jan. 29 and Feb. 2, 1900. On Albaugh's connections, see La Forte, *Leaders of Reform*, pp. 20, 100.

58. EG, June 29, 1899.

59. Ibid., June 27, 1899.

60. See stories headed "Do You Want a Carnival?" (June 30, 1899), "The Everlasting Rust" (July 1, 1899), "Almost Persuaded" (July 3, 1899), "Well Begun's Half Done" (July 5, 1899), "One Hundred a Day" (July 6, 1899), "Still Booming" (July 7, 1899), "Still She Grows" (July 8, 1899), and "The Thousand Raised" (July 10, 1899).

61. William E. Connelley, *The Life of Preston B. Plumb* (Chicago: Browne & Howell Company, 1913); a 1877 Dun & Co. report stated that Newman "does business with Emporia National Bank." R. G. Dun & Co. Collection, Baker Library, Harvard University Graduate School of Business Administration.

62. EG, July 31, 1899.

63. White to Hanford Finney, July 3, 1899, LB 1, LC.

64. White to Leland (July 26, 1899); to H. R. Honnell, Aug. 18 (1899); and to Morrill, July 24 (1899); all LB 1, LC. He also wrote to Republican editors Henry Allen and C. W. Daniels, requesting help in finding tents to house his old soldiers. White to Allen and to Daniels, July 3 (1899), LB 1, LC.

65. See, for example, White to F. P. Cochran, Aug. 12, 1899, and to Frank O.

Bush (post–July 25, 1899); White to Marshall, July 6 (1899); all LB 1, LC. See also J. B. Marshall to White (post–Sept. 22, 1899), ESU.

66. See, for a small sample, White to Linson Bros. (post–July 25, 1899); to Kansas City Zoo, July 24, 1899; to B. Delgarian, Oriental Carnival Co., Aug. 26 (1899); to St. Louis Attraction Co., Aug. 26 (1899); to International Colored Photography Co., Aug. 12 (1899); to Arthur Walker, Sept. 13, 1899; to John S. Phillips, July 3 (1899); to Arthur Winslow and to Fisher Equipment Co. (July 12, 1899); all LB 1, LC.

67. EG, Sept. 2 and 6, 1899.

68. Ibid., Sept. 7, 1899.

69. Ibid., Aug. 29, 1899.

70. Ibid., Sept. 5, 1899.

71. White to S. A. Johnson, Sept. 23, 1899, LB 1, LC.

72. EG, Sept. 22, 1899.

73. Aug. 15 (1899), LB 1, LC. He wrote a similar request to the Missouri, Kansas and Texas agent. White to James Barker, Aug. 15 (1899), LB 1, LC.

74. White to Black, Sept. 11 and 19, 1899; and to Morton, Sept. 15, 1899; all LB 1, LC.

75. White to Mr. Grinnell, Aug. 28, 1899; to *Journal*, Sept. 5, 1899; and to W. D. Smith, Aug. 28, 1899; all LB 1, LC. EG, Sept. 2, 4 ("The Big Doin's"), and 23, 1899.

76. French, *History of Emporia*, p. 71; EG, Sept. 27, 1899.

77. EG, Sept. 29 and 27, 1899.

78. French, *History of Emporia*, p. 71; EG, Sept. 30 and Oct. 2, 1899; White, *Autobiography*, p. 322. The *Gazette* report of the parade neglected to mention White among the automobile's passengers.

79. EG, Oct. 3, 1899.

80. Ibid., Oct. 14, 1899; White, *Autobiography*, pp. 322–23.

81. EG, Oct. 2, 1899.

3. A Practical Printer

1. White to A. E. Stilwell, June 20, 1901, LB 2, LC.

2. See, for example, biographies of two other progressive journalists, Arthur Capper and Joseph Bristow: Homer E. Socolofsky, *Arthur Capper: Publisher, Politician and Philanthropist* (Lawrence: University of Kansas Press, 1962), and A. Bower Sageser, *Joseph L. Bristow: Kansas Progressive* (Lawrence: University Press of Kansas, 1968). Lewis Atherton describes the effects of increased advertising on small-town newspapers in *Main Street on the Middle Border* (Bloomington: Indiana University Press, 1954), pp. 222–29.

3. [Laura M. French], "History of the Emporia Gazette," unpublished typescript, n.d., in the possession of Mrs. William L. White, pp. 21–22; on the water motor, see White to the Fairbanks-Morse Co., Apr. 17, 1900, LB 1, LC.

4. William Allen White, *The Autobiography of William Allen White* (New York: Macmillan Company, 1946), p. 118. White stated (p. 262) that he employed four girl compositors at the *Gazette,* but a photograph of the staff taken shortly before his arrival pictured seven men and one woman. The woman wears a dress, cape, and hat, garb more appropriate to a society editor than a compositor, who would likely have worn a shirtwaist. At least three of the men are attired in the customary

style of compositors: vest and white shirt, with shirtsleeves rolled above the elbows. The photograph appears in "The Emporia Gazette's Album of Memories," a pamphlet published by the *Gazette* for the 1976 Bicentennial. Moreover, shortly after his arrival White mentioned in the *Gazette* that his payroll was around $100 a week, but in the *Autobiography* he recalled it as $45. On the entry of women into printing in the nineteenth century, see Mary Biggs, "Neither Printer's Wife nor Widow: American Women in Typesetting, 1830–1950," *Library Quarterly* 50 (1980): 431–52; and Ava Baron, "Women and the Making of the American Working Class: A Study in the Proletarianization of Printers," *Review of Radical Political Economics* 14 (Fall 1982): 23–42.

5. White to Charles M. Vernon, Apr. 3, 1908, LB 11, LC. White invested $600 in a new job press during his first year at the *Gazette*. Everett Rich, *William Allen White: The Man from Emporia* (New York: Farrar & Rinehart, 1941), p. 75; White to Eugene Ware, Aug. 1, 1902, LB 3, LC; on the press see White to Great Western Type Foundry, July 5 [1899], LB 1, LC.

6. White to Sallie White, Sept. 27, 1904, and Aug. 20, 1905, KU.

7. July 18, 1900, LB 1, LC. Carolyn Dyer documents the wide range of patronage jobs distributed to newspapers in an earlier period in her article "Political Patronage of the Wisconsin Press, 1849–1860: New Perspectives on the Economics of Patronage," in *Journalism Monographs* (forthcoming).

8. White to Theodore Poehler, Jr., Jan. 19, 1900, LB 1, LC.

9. For a sample of correspondence relating to job work, see White to A. R. Raylor, Aug. 29, 1900, LB 1; to Edna Bryan, Apr. 5, 1901, LB 2; to Graham Paper Co., Jan. 7, 1902, LB 2; to J. W. Butler Paper Co., Jan. 15, 1902, LB 3; Mae Austin to the Theo. Poehler Mercantile Co., Jan. 17, 1903, LB 3; to Guy B. Seely, Sept. 8, 1903, LB 4; to Chas. H. Barnes, Apr. 13, 1906, LB 8; to the Reverend William Westwood, July 13, 1906, LB 8; to Crane & Co., Aug. 14, 1906, LB 8; to Teachnor Bartberger, Feb. 25, 1907, LB 9; Fern Forman to Mail & Breeze, June 20, 1907, LB 9; and Walter Hughes to W. N. Tinchor, Aug. 10, 1907, LB 10; all LC.

10. White to Arthur Capper, May 24, 1901, LB 1; White to Great Western Type Foundry, Nov. 29, 1905, and Nov. 8, 1906, LB 9; all LC; French, "Gazette," p. 34.

11. EG, Sept. 18, 1899; Laura M. French, *History of Emporia and Lyon County* (Emporia: Emporia Gazette Print, 1929), p. 78.

12. Richard E. Huss, *The Development of Printers' Mechanical Typesetting Methods, 1822–1925* (Charlottesville: University Press of Virginia, 1974), p. 136; 1897 Mergenthaler Linotype Company circular, quoted in George Everett, "The Linotype and U.S. Daily Newspaper Journalism in the 1890's: Analysis of a Relationship" (Ph.D. dissertation, University of Iowa, 1972), p. 326; Bureau of the Census, *Manufactures 1905, Part II, States and Territories* (Washington: GPO, 1907), p. 317. The average speed of a linotype operator was 5,000 ems (a printers' measure, representing the width of a capital "M") per hour of corrected straight matter. The average hand-setting speed was under 1,000 ems per hour. See Craig Spicher, *The Practice of Presswork* (Pittsburgh: privately printed, 1919), p. 205.

13. White to Mergenthaler Linotype Company, Oct. 9 and 17 and Dec. 3, 1902, LB 3, LC.

14. In 1900 the city directory listed three women as compositors at the *Gazette;* by 1904 no women were employed in this capacity, although one of the compositors, Laura French, had become proofreader. John Schottler had joined the previously all-woman composition force in 1901, continued as a hand compositor for a time, and eventually went to a linotype operators' school. He became foreman of the

composing room in 1924, and was still there around 1945. See French, "Gazette," p. 31; his starting date was found on a list of employees (ca. 1919–20) in the possession of the *Emporia Gazette*.

15. White to Melton, Jan. 24, 1903, LB 3, LC. On wages, see White to Warren Mitchell, May 7, 1901, LB 2; to Julius Melton, Jan. 24, 1903, LB 3; to (?), Sept. 11, 1903, LB 3; and to Charles E. (Kocher), Dec. 21, 1903, LB 5; Mae M. Austin to George N. Moore, Jan. 16, 1903; and to J. A. Reed, Jan. 20, 1903, LB 3; all LC.

16. William Allen White, "Early Draft of Autobiography," unpublished manuscript (ca. 1927–28), Ch. 7, p. 6, ESU; White to Mergenthaler Linotype Co., Oct. 17 and Dec. 29, 1902, and Feb. 2, 1903, LB 3, LC. On Hughes, see French, "Gazette," p. 22; White to W. J. Black, Aug. 26, 1902, LB 3, LC; his starting date was found on a list of employees (ca. 1919–20) in the possession of the *Emporia Gazette*.

17. On the bonus plan in the 1920s see Rich, *William Allen White*, p. 237, and White to W. E. Hughes, Dec. 22, 1920, in possession of the *Emporia Gazette*. On the insurance program see White to Pittsburgh Life and Trust Co., Dec. 15, 1906, and to William Means (and to eight other employees), Dec. 21, 1906, LB 9, LC. If they chose to enroll in the program, employees paid for the premiums through deductions from their pay; the *Gazette* contributed one-twentieth of the premium for each year of employment. On White's holiday parties see interviews with James T. Yearout and Harriet R. Cross, Flint Hills Oral History Project, Lyon County Historical Museum.

18. White to Russell, Sept. 7, 1903, LB 4; Austin to Newton *Republican*, Sept. 11, 1903, LB 4; White to Mergenthaler Linotype Co., April 13, 1904, LB 5; White to Julius Melton, Aug. 15 and 25, 1904, LB 6; to Mergenthaler Linotype Co., Aug. 25, 1904, LB 6; to Melton, Sept. 12, 1904, LB 6; and to Mergenthaler Linotype Co., Oct. 6, 1904, LB 6; all LC.

19. Circulation in 1904 was 2,250; at the end of 1905 it was 2,400. *Gazette* to E. H. Wright Co., Dec. 10, 1904, LB 6; Circulation Statement, Sept. 10, 1906, LB 9; both LC. For a summary of the *Gazette*'s circulation figures, see Sally F. Griffith, "Home Town News: William Allen White and the Emporia *Gazette*, 1895–1930" (Ph.D. dissertation, Johns Hopkins University, 1985), Appendix II.

20. White to E. A. Pierce, Aug. 23, Nov. 8, 14, and 16, and Dec. 8, 1902, LB 3, LC; White to Sallie White, July 12 and 13, 1903, KU; White to Murray Machinery Company, Dec. 5, 1903, LB 5, LC.

21. White to W. C. Markham, July 29, 1904, LB 6, LC. On the Duplex, see James Moran, *Printing Presses, History and Development from the Fifteenth Century to Modern Times* (Berkeley: University of California Press, 1973), p. 205.

22. White to Sallie White, Sept. 8, Oct. 6, and Nov. 14, 1904, KU; White to the editor of the Reading *Telegram*, Sept. 30, 1905, LB 7, LC. In 1907, when the *Gazette*'s bookkeeper recommended the press, she added that "We were told by several different parties that we would regret putting in a Duplex, but such has not been our experience." Fern Forman to A. M. Kennedy, Aug. 9, 1907, LB 10, LC.

23. Sallie White to William Allen White, Aug. 18, 1905, KU. On the Cottrell, see White to G. B. Cottrell & Sons Co., Aug. 31, 1904, LB 6, LC; White to Sallie White, Sept. 13, 1904, KU; Mae Austin to John Moffitt, Mar. 21, 1906, LB 8, LC.

24. White to Sallie White, Feb. 1, 1906, KU; and White to Duplex, Apr. 26, 1906, LB 8, LC. For the date of pressman Sanford Rice's arrival, Apr. 21, 1906, see the listing of employees (ca. 1919–20) in the possession of the *Emporia Gazette*. On paper and ink, see Fern Forman to the Gazette Printing Co. (Phoenix, Ariz.), Aug.

9, 1907, LB 10, LC; Mae Austin to Mrs. M. A. Doud, June 2, 1906, LB 8, LC. The newspaper first appeared in its new seven-column format on June 2.

25. EG, June 15, 1906.

26. Ibid., Oct. 20, 1906.

27. French, *History of Emporia,* p. 73; EG, Jan. 16, 1901. On resistance to RFD, see Wayne E. Fuller, *R. F. D.: The Changing Face of Rural America* (Bloomington: Indiana University Press, 1964), and Atherton, *Main Street on the Middle Border,* pp. 231–33.

28. Rose Edington to White, Mar. 22, 1900 (two letters of same date, one misdated 1899), ESU. See also Rose Edington to White, Jan. 15, 1900, ESU, and White to Edington, Jan. 17, 1900, LB 1, LC.

29. He paid for these subscriptions out of his fees for articles for these magazines. See White to Nellie Bassett, Sept. 3, 1901, LB 2; to George H. Lorimer, Dec. 16, 1901, LB 2; to *McClure's,* May 26, 1904, LB 5; and to Curtis Publishing Co., Mar. 25, 1905, LB 7; all LC. White to John A. Sims, Oct. 24, 1904, LB 6, LC.

30. EG, Aug. 30, 1900.

31. Ibid., Dec. 6, 1900, and Feb. 23, 1901. On the *Gazette's* first use of college students, see White to Bernie Keath, June 4, 1904, LB 5, LC.

32. See White's reference to the *Mail* in his letter to Teachener Bartberger, Apr. 9, 1900, LB 1, LC. The *Mail* was owned by Arthur Capper, who was quickly building a publishing empire in Kansas. See Socolofsky, *Arthur Capper,* especially pp. 45–46.

33. EG, July 28, Sept. 1, 8, and 15, 1900.

34. White to Charles Scott, May 21, 1900, and to American Press Association, Apr. 14, 1900, both LB 1, LC. For a sample of the many requests for cuts, see White to Mattie Eskridge, May 21, 1900; to the *Kansas Issue,* June 14, 1900; and to D. S. Gilmore, July 21, 1900; all LB 1, LC.

35. On "telegraph" news see White to A. N. Kellogg, May 9, 1901, LB 2; on other plate see White to Kellogg, Sept. 15 and Aug. 25, 1899, LB 1; to George Clarke (ca. July 24, 1899); LB 1; to W. L. Witmer & Co., May 15, 1901; LB 2; and to Kellogg, May 27, 1901, LB 2; all LC.

36. White to A. N. Kellogg, May 9, 1901, LB 2, LC.

37. White to C. O. Smith, May 16, 1904, LB 5; to Charles L. Diehl, Jan. 27, 1903, LB 3; to Frank MacLennan, Feb. 2, 1903, LB 3; and to Charles Cleaver, Apr. 6, 1903, LB 3; all LC. George Everett notes a marked increase in the size of urban newspapers after the installation of linotypes. Everett, "The Linotype and U.S. Daily Newspaper Journalism," pp. 270–71.

38. EG, Apr. 9, 1903; Wirt McCarty to Schuyler Searsey (April) 1903, LB 4, LC; White to Sallie White, Apr. 22 and (July ?), 1903, KU; Fern Forman to A. M. Kennedy, Aug. 9, 1907, LB 10, LC.

39. On clubbing, see White to Al Gaylord, May 27, 1901, LB 2; to Kansas City *Star,* Oct. 21, 1901, LB 2; Mae Austin to D. S. Gilmore, Jan. 1, 1903, LB 3; to the Topeka *Capital,* Oct. 22, 1902, LB 3; to John Brisbane Walker, Oct. 27, 1903, LB 4; to *Live Stock Indicator,* Aug. 31, 1902, LB 3; to *American Farmer,* Jan. 17, 1903, LB 3; and to *Inland Poultry Journal,* Aug. 29, 1905, LB 7; all LC. On other promotional efforts, see White to H. U. Mudge, Dec. 18, 1903, LB 5; to J. F. Huckle, Dec. 18, 1903, LB 5; *Gazette* form letter, Aug. 22, 1904, LB 6; and Mae Austin to W. A. Thornton, Sept. 27, 1905, LB 7; all LC.

40. White to Sallie White, July 19, 1905, KU, and to G. B. Cortelyou, Sept. 6, 1905, LB 7, LC.

41. On the advertising industry as a whole during this period, see Daniel Pope, *The Making of Modern Advertising* (New York: Basic Books, 1983).

42. Alfred D. Chandler, Jr., *The Visible Hand: The Managerial Revolution in American Business* (Cambridge, Mass.: Belknap Press of Harvard University Press, 1977), pp. 289–99, and Glenn Porter and Harold C. Livesay, *Merchants and Manufacturers* (Baltimore: Johns Hopkins University Press, 1971), pp. 223–25.

43. For a sampling of White's many exchange deals, see White to F. C. Russell (bicycle), July 10 (1899), LB 1; to David Rolands (an edition of Uncle Remus stories), Aug. 26 (1899), LB 1; to Blixenderfer Typewriter Manufacturing Co., Oct. 7, 1899, LB 1; to Edward S. Martin (subscription to *Harper's*), Dec. 22, 1899, LB 1; to Chauncy L. Williams (office desk), Jan. 12, 1900, LB 1; to Parry Manufacturing Co. (buggy), Apr. 30, 1900, LB 1; to R. P. Remington (printing materials), Sept. 5, 1900, LB 1; to Security Mutual Life Insurance Co., June 18, 1901, LB 2; to N. W. Ayer & Son (Beckwith Round Oak furnace for White's house), July 23, 1901, LB 2; to Nelson Chesman Co. (ink), Mar. 7, 1902, LB 3; to Henry O. Dreer (flower seeds and bulbs), Aug. 26, 1902, LB 3; to Patterson-Sargent Co. (house paint), Oct. 7, 1902, LB 3; Eva Austin to Milton Lindsay (correspondence course), Feb. 15, 1904, LB 5; Mae Austin to Alpine Safe Lock Co. (office safe), Mar. 7, 1904, LB 5; to Dauchy & Co. (type), Dec. (19), 1904, LB 6, Apr. 20, 1906, LB 8, and Feb. 11, 1907, LB 9; to P. M. Haan (hotel accommodations), Mar. 3, 1905, LB 7; and White to H. O. Brown (Victrola phonograph), May 10, 1910, LB 16; all in LC.

44. EG, July 31 and Nov. 22, 1901; Sarah Stage, *Female Complaints: Lydia Pinkham and the Business of Women's Medicine* (New York: W. W. Norton & Company, 1979). Statements about advertising volume are based on measurement of the column inches of advertising contained in 252 randomly selected issues of the *Gazette* from 1895 to 1927. For full details see Griffith, "Home Town News," pp. 547–51.

45. In early 1902, for example, the *Gazette* included advertising for the following nostrums, promising to promote beauty or cure a variety of ills: Beggs' Cherry Cough Syrup, Bellavita Arsenic Beauty Tablets & Pills, Bradfield's Female Regulator, Cascarets, Cramtonic Hair and Scalp Food, Doan's Kidney Pills, Fletcher's Castoria, Hostetter's Stomach Bitters, Kraum's New Red Blood (the product of a local druggist), Krause's Headache Capsules, Lydia E. Pinkham's Vegetable Compound, Mother's Friend, Nervita Medical Co., No-to-bac, Paine's Celery Compound, Parker's Hair Balsam, Ripans Tabules, Rocky Mountain Tea, Scott's Emulsion, S. S. S. (The Swift Specific Co.), and Wine of Cardui. Taken from the advertising sample for Jan.–Apr. 1902.

46. White to Dauchy & Co., May 6, 1901, LB 2, and to [C. H.] Fuller's Advertising Agency, Mar. 29, 1902, LB 2; Austin to Sterling Remedy Co., Oct. 27, 1903, LB 4, and to Martin Rudy, (June 26, 1906), LB 8; all LC. For similar rejections of "objectionable" advertising, see Mae Austin to Nelson Chesman & Co., Oct. 13, 1902, LB 3; to Frank W. Lenhoff, May 22, 1903, LB 4; to Guenther-Bradford Co., Sept. 15, 1903, LB 4; White to J. Walter Thompson Co., Apr. 4, 1904, LB 5, and Mar. 22, 1905, LB 7; Austin to Nelson Chesman & Co. (for Man Medicine), June 16, 1905, LB 7, and to Anderson Chemical Co. (for the Safety Syringe), Feb. 11, 1907, LB 9; all LC.

47. White to Royal Baking Powder Co., June 29 [1899], LB 1, LC.

48. White to Royal Baking Powder Co., Dec. 22, 1899, LB 1, LC.

49. In response to the problem of nonpaying advertisers, White eventually estab-

lished a contract with a collection agency, exchanging advertising for its services. For examples of this sort of problem, see the *Gazette* to Publishers' Commercial Union, March 7, 1902, LB 3, LC.

50. For example, White secured $100 worth of advertising in George P. Rowell's 1900 *American Newspaper Directory* with a like amount of advertising in the *Gazette* for Rowell's patent medicine, Ripans Tabules. White to Peter Dougan, Jan. 17, 1900, LB 1, LC. On Rowell and his *Directory*, see Pope, *Modern Advertising*, pp. 121–23.

51. Apr. 5, 1901, LB 2.

52. White to J. M. Connell, Dec. 24, 1906, LB 9, and to Grandin Advertising Agency, Ltd., Mar. 18, 1904, LB 5, both LC. On the AAA, see Pope, *Modern Advertising*, pp. 158, 170–71. For the *Gazette's* use of post office backing, see figures in *American Newspaper Annual* (Philadelphia: N. W. Ayer & Son, 1916), p. 323; *Advertiser's Directory of Leading Newspapers and Magazines* (Chicago: Charles H. Fuller Company, 1916), p. 110. On the ABC see Pope, *Modern Advertising*, pp. 171–72.

53. White to Willie Sharpe Kilmer, July 3 (1899), LB 1, LC.

54. Sept. 19, 1899, LB 1, LC.

55. This discussion is based on extensive reading in the *Gazette's* business correspondence in the letter books at the Library of Congress. In support of each generalization I will cite merely one or two of the hundred letters possible. See White to R. H. Clarke, Aug. 22 (1899), LB 1; to Scott & (Browne), Oct. 7, 1899, LB 1; to Peruna Drug Manufacturing Co., Nov. 15, 1899, LB 1; to E. Catz Advertising Agency, Apr. 9, 1900, LB 1; to Nelson Chesman & Co., Sept. 3, 1900, LB 1; bookkeeper to Frank P. MacLennan, Mar. 28, 1902, LB 3, and to British Medical Institute, May 26, 1902, LB 3; White to Charles H. Fuller Co., Mar. 15, 1904, LB 5; Mae Austin to Long-Critchfield Corporation, Feb. 6, 1905, LB 7; to Chas. J. Moffett, Apr. 8, 1905, LB 7; to N. W. Ayer & Son, April 24, 1905, LB 7; to Devoe & Raynolds Co., July 29, 1905, LB 7; to Mahin Advertising Co., Sept. 8, 1906, LB 8; to Warren J. Lynch, Dec. 27, 1906, LB 9; and Fern Forman to American Cigar Co., Mar. 9, 1910, LB 44; all LC.

56. George A. Kubler, *A New History of Stereotyping* (New York: privately printed, 1941).

57. Oscar E. Anderson, Jr., *The Health of A Nation: Harvey W. Wiley and the Fight for Pure Food* (Chicago: University of Chicago Press, 1958), pp. 156–57; Ralph M. Hower, *The History of an Advertising Agency: N. W. Ayer & Son at Work, 1869–1939* (Cambridge, Mass.: Harvard University Press, 1939), pp. 112–13, 214, 216; Pope, *Modern Advertising*, p. 195–99.

58. White to C. F. Wyckoff Company, Apr. 4, 1904, LB 5, LC. See White to Nelson Chesman, Mar. 18, 1904; to Liquid Ozone, Mar. 21, 1904; to Willis Sharpe Kilmer, Mar. 18, 1904; to Pettingill & Company, Mar. 22, 1904; and to Munyon & Company, Mar. 22, 1904; all LB 5, LC. For criticisms of these products and their makers, see Samuel Hopkins Adams, *The Great American Fraud* (Chicago: Press of the American Medical Asociation, 1912). James Harvey Young mistakenly describes the *Gazette* in the days before the muckrakers as "anti-nostrum." Young, *The Toadstool Millionaires: A Social History of Patent Medicines in America before Federal Regulation* (Princeton: Princeton University Press, 1961), pp. 210–11.

59. *Collier's,* Oct. 7 and Nov. 4, 1905, reprinted in Adams, *The Great American Fraud,* pp. 6, 148; Mae Austin to Adams, July 26, 1905, LB 7, LC. On the somewhat convoluted origins of these articles, see Mark Sullivan, *The Education of an*

American (New York: Doubleday, Doran & Co., 1938), pp. 183–91, and Young, *Toadstool Millionaires,* pp. 214–19.

60. Stage, *Female Complaints,* p. 161; Adams, *Great American Fraud,* p. 5; Austin to *Collier's Weekly,* Oct. 24, 1906, LB 9, LC. On the *Gazette's* dealings with Cheney, see Mae Austin to Cheney Medicine Co., Feb. 17, Apr. 8, and June 27, 1903, LB 3, and July 10, 1903, LB 4; all LC.

61. EG, Apr. 13, 1906; Austin to Starke Advertising Agency and to S. S. S. Company, Aug. 29, 1905, and to the Pineule Medicine Company, Oct. 3, 1905; all LB 7, LC.

62. Austin to Gundlach Advertising Co., Jan. 14, 1907; Fern Forman to D. D. D., Apr. 8 and 16, 1907; Austin to Chamberlain Medicine Co., Jan. 18, 1907; all LB 9, LC. See Mae Austin to James T. Wetherald Advertising Agency, Nov. 7 and 16, 1905, LB 7, and to Peruna Drug Manufacturing Co., (Feb. 24), Mar. 26, and Aug. 28, 1906, LB 8. Also Austin to Hostetter Co., Mar. 10 and Apr. 20, 1906, LB 8; to Nelson Chesman & Co. (for Wine of Cardui), Feb. 5, 1906, LB 8; to J. L. Stack (for Liquozone), Jan. 18, 1907, LB 9; Fern Forman to E. C. Dewitt & Co., Dec. 20, 1907, LB 10; to E. W. Ross Medicine Co., Jan. 29, 1908, LB 11; to Bogg's Manufacturing Co., Feb. 4, 1908, LB 11; Austin to Morse Advertising Agency, July 9, 1906, LB 8; Fern Forman to Pepsin Syrup Co., Jan. 29, 1908, LB 11; all LC.

63. Forman to Philo Hay Specialties Co., Feb. 15 and 22, Mar. 13 and 21, and Apr. 13, 1908, LB 11; White to the Morse International Agency, Mar. 27, 1908, LB 11; all LC. On mining and stock advertising, see White to Max Yingling, Sept. 15, 1907, LB 10; Fern Forman to Horn-Baker & Co., Oct. 4, 1907, LB 10; and White to W. D. Feng, Mar. 18, 1910, LB 16; all LC.

64. On the shift from curative claims to more subtle emotional appeals, see Pope, *Modern Advertising,* pp. 221–23.

65. *Gazette* to Royal Baking Powder Co., Aug. 15, 1906, LB 8; White to There's a Reason Co., Ltd., July 22, 1910, LB 16; White to Cocoa Cola Co. [*sic*], Sept. 27, 1910, LB 17; all LC.

66. EG, Feb. 18, 1902; *Gazette* to Royal Baking Powder Co., Mar. 6, 1902, LB 3; Austin to Royal Baking Powder Company, Apr. 12, 1904, LB 5; to Calumet Baking Powder Co., Aug. 25, 1904, LB 6; to Royal Baking Powder Co., May 2, 1906, LB 8; Fern Forman to Blaine Thompson Co., Feb. 7, 1908, LB 11; all LC. On the baking powder trade war over alum, and its effects on the passage of the Pure Food and Drug Act, see Anderson, *Health of a Nation,* pp. 133–34, 141–42.

67. EG, Nov. 18 and July 20, 1906.

68. Survey of letter books, LC, and random sample of newspapers, 1900–1907. On the "therapeutic" appeal in turn-of-the-century advertising, see T. J. Jackson Lears, "From Salvation to Self-Realization: Advertising and the Therapeutic Roots of the Consumer Culture, 1880–1930," in Richard Wightman Fox and T. J. Jackson Lears, eds., *The Culture of Consumption: Critical Essays in American History, 1880–1980* (New York: Pantheon Books, 1983), pp. 3–38.

69. White to Willis Sharpe Kilmer, July 3 [1899],, LB 1, LC.

70. Austin to [?] Advertising Agency, June 29, 1903, LB 4, LC. Similar letters were written to Nelson Chesman Co., Mar. 26, 1903; to Dr. Howard Co., Mar. 28, 1903; to Nile E. Lawrence, June 30, 1903; and to Alfred E. Rose, July 14, 1903; all LB 4, LC.

71. White to Daniel J. Sully & Co., Jan. 18, 1904, LB 5. See also Austin to Chicago Telephone Supply Company, May 24 and July 1, 1904, LB 5; White to

P. P. Stone, E. W. Howe, Foley & Co., and Dr. Caldwell's Pepsin Syrup Co., all Mar. 18, 1904; and to Royal Baking Powder, Mar. 21, 1904; all LB 5, LC.

72. White to Procter & Collier, Apr. 23, 1900, LB 1, LC; Cyrus Curtis to White, June 25, 1902, ESU; and Mae Austin to the George E. Van Eleve Co., Apr. 14, 1905, LB 7, LC. See *Gazette* to Frank P. MacLennan, Apr. 8, 1902, LB 3, and White to James T. Wetherold, May 16, 1904, LB 5, both LC.

73. Pope, *Modern Advertising;* Chandler, *Visible Hand;* Kurt Mayer, "Small Business as a Social Institution," *Social Research* 14 (Sept. 1947): 332–49.

74. Atherton, *Main Street on the Middle Border,* p. 55; interview with Lucina Jones, Sept. 26, 1978, Flint Hills Oral History Project, LCHM; Carolyn B. Berneking, "The Welsh Settlers of Emporia: A Cultural History," *Kansas Historical Quarterly* 37 (Autumn 1971): 269–80.

75. EG, Feb. 5, 1900; White to A. O. Rorabaugh, Sept. 3, 1901, LB 2, LC; EG, Oct. 25, 1901.

76. EG, June 18, 1902.

77. Austin to Mahin Advertising Agency, Apr. 7, 1904, LB 5, and to Ryle Advertising Agency, Jan. 27, 1903, LB 3, both LC. See also White to Lord & Thomas, May 31, 1900, LB 1; to Geo. W. Cornwell, May 31, 1901, LB 2; Austin to Frank MacLennan, Mar. 28, 1902, LB 3; to the Liquid Ozone Co., Aug. 12, 1903, LB 4; to Morse Advertising Agency, Dec. 18, 1903, LB 5; to Lyon & Healey, Nov. 16, 1905, LB 7; Fern Forman to Pittsburgh Perfect Fence, Oct. 9, 1907, LB 10, and to Arizona Ostrich Farm, Nov. 8, 1907, LB 10; all LC.

78. Austin to Mahin Advertising Agency, Feb. 3 and 13 and Mar. 23, 1903, LB 3, LC. See also a similar arrangement for the "Loose-Wiles Cracker Company," Austin to Lord & Thomas, Dec. 19, 1906, LB 9, LC.

79. Mayer, "Small Business as a Social Institution."

80. EG, Nov. 22, 1901, and Apr. 10, 1906. See White to Tanner & Brothers, Sept. 30, 1902, and Mar. 26, 1903, LB 3; *Gazette* to Ricker & Son, [May 1] 1903, LB 4; White to Jones & Stone, to N. Guettel, and to Sam Rosenfeld, Apr. 30, 1906, LB 8; to G. W. Newman Dry Goods Co., May 4, 1906, LB 8; and to A. O. Rorabaugh Dry Goods Co., May 5, 1906, LB 8; all LC.

81. White to Advertising Dept., Emery Bird & Thayer, Nov. 4, 1899, LB 1, and to Emery Bird & Thayer, May 2, 1901, LB 2, both LC. See also White to Emery, Bird & Thayer, July 20, 1900, LB 1, LC.

82. See Mae Austin to W. L. Witmer & Co., May 27 and Sept. 9, 1902, Jan. 2 and 27, 1903, LB 3; White to Chauncey L. Williams, March 15, 1910, LB 16; all LC.

83. White to Jones & Stone, Apr. 30, 1906, and to G. W. Newman Dry Goods Co., May 4, 1906, LB 8, LC.

84. White, "Early Draft of Autobiography," Ch. 8, p. 2, ESU.

4. The Making of a Progressive

1. My thinking regarding White's development has been influenced by contemporary developmental psychology, particularly as insightfully synthesized with cognitive psychology by Robert Kegan. See Kegan, *The Evolving Self: Problem and Process in Human Development* (Cambridge, Mass.: Harvard University Press, 1982).

2. EG, Oct. 1, 1901.

3. White to Howe, Jan. 21, 1902; *Gazette* to Frank MacLennan, Mar. 12, 1902, and to John S. Phillips, Apr. 4, 1902; all LB 3, LC.

4. White, in his *Autobiography*, cites both overwork and fear of a lawsuit; Walter Johnson emphasizes the former and John McKee the latter. White, *Autobiography*, pp. 346–47; Johnson, *William Allen White's America* (New York: Henry Holt and Company, 1947), p. 136; McKee, *William Allen White: Maverick on Main Street* (Westport, Conn.: Greenwood Press, 1975), p. 65. On White's reaction to Platt's threat, see his letter to Arthur Scribner, Dec. 20, 1901, in Johnson, *White's America*, p. 48.

5. White to Williams, Mar. 15, 1897, ESU, and Nov. 30, 1897, typescript copy in Manuscript Division, Newberry Library, Chicago; Doubleday to White, Feb. 27, 1900, and Jan. 20, 1901, ESU; White to Doubleday, Aug. 23, 1905, LB 7, LC.

6. Roosevelt to White, Nov. 14, 1901, in *The Letters of Theodore Roosevelt*, Vol. 3 (Cambridge, Mass.: Harvard University Press, 1951), p. 197. For an account of the factional basis of the opposition to Leland, see Robert Sherman La Forte, *Leaders of Reform: Progressive Republicans in Kansas, 1900–1916* (Lawrence: University Press of Kansas, 1974), pp. 14–21. John Morton Blum argues that Roosevelt's dismissal of Leland was part of his general strategy of undermining Hanna's organization. Blum, *The Republican Roosevelt* (Cambridge: Harvard University Press, 1954), pp. 40–42.

7. White, *Autobiography*, p. 297.

8. Ibid., pp. 297–98. John Milton Cooper's comparative biography of Roosevelt and Wilson, *The Warrior and the Priest* (Cambridge, Mass.: Harvard University Press, 1984), vividly recaptures the centrality of the search for honor in Roosevelt's personality and appeal.

9. White to Roosevelt, Oct. 30, 1901, LB 2, LC. See also White to James H. Canfield, Nov. 14, 1901, LB 2, LC.

10. White to Gleed, Nov. 22, 1901, LB 2, LC. Gleed was a director of the Santa Fe, which had turned against Leland.

11. EG, Nov. 22, 1901.

12. Ibid., Dec. 19, 1901, and Jan. 10, 1902. Richard L. McCormick notes a similar emphasis among conservative New York Republicans on loyalty to the GOP as the party of principle. McCormick, *From Realignment to Reform: Political Change in New York State, 1893–1910* (Ithaca, N.Y.: Cornell University Press, 1981), especially pp. 71, 123–24.

13. EG, Jan. 10, 1901.

14. (Ca. Dec. 19) 1901, LB 2, LC. One such refusal, which has been widely quoted, also occurred at this time, when White turned down an offer (tendered through Charles Gleed) from John Brisben Walker to write for *Cosmopolitan*. Apparently, White was not interested in a job in which he would be subject to another editor, but he would consider leaving Emporia. Gleed to White, Nov. 9, 1901, ESU; and White to Gleed, Nov. 16, 1901, in Walter Johnson, *Selected Letters of William Allen White*, pp. 46–47.

15. Jan. 20, 1902, LB 3, LC.

16. Examples of White's letters are in EG, April 1 and 25, 1902. On White's health in the summer of 1902, see White to John S. Phillps, July 23, 1902, Phillips Manuscripts, Lilly Library, Bloomington, Indiana.

17. EG, May 26, 1901; White, *Autobiography*, p. 347; Roosevelt to White, June 4, 1902, C1, LC.

18. EG, March 27 and 28, 1902.

19. Ibid., Oct. 18, 1899; Topeka *Capital* article reprinted ibid., May 19, 1902.

20. For the background of the creation of the board, see Larry Jochims, "Medicine in Kansas, 1850–1900 (Part II)," *Emporia State Research Studies* 30 (Fall 1981). A direct reference to the specification of "gross immorality" is in EG, Apr. 11, 1903.

21. EG, May 29, 1902.

22. Ibid., June 2 and 4, 1902.

23. Ibid., June 9 and 11, 1902.

24. Ibid., July 12, 1902.

25. Ibid., July 14, 1902, Apr. 11, 1903, and Nov. 15, 1904; White, *Autobiography*, pp. 378–79.

26. White, *Autobiography*, p. 379.

27. EG, Nov. 15, 1904. He told the Kansas attorney general that he had "personally stood for the money" for the lawyer. White to C. C. Coleman, Oct. 30, 1904, LB 6, LC.

28. White to Dr. Robey, Dec. 11, 1902, LB 3, LC.

29. White to Bailey, Mar. 30, 1903, LB 3, LC.

30. Apr. 16, 1903, KU.

31. EG, Apr. 11, 1903.

32. White, *Autobiography*, p. 380; EG, Nov. 15, 1904.

33. EG, Nov. 18, 1904.

34. White, *Autobiography*, p. 380; ET, Nov. 25, 1904; White to Bliss Perry, Nov. 25, 1904, in Johnson, *Selected Letters*, pp. 62–63. He wrote essentially the same thing to Theodore Roosevelt, Elihu Root, R. J. Collier, and Norman Hapgood, among others. Correspondence of Nov. 25, 1904, LB 6, LC.

35. Apr. 16, 1903, KU.

36. See White to Sallie White, Apr. 16 and 22, 1903, KU; White, *Autobiography*, p. 353. On White's public political stance in early 1903, see La Forte, *Leaders of Reform*, pp. 33–34.

37. White, *Autobiography*, p. 381.

38. Laura M. French, *History of Emporia and Lyon County* (Emporia: Emporia Gazette Print, 1929), p. 77.

39. White to Roosevelt, Oct. 31, 1903, LB 4, LC; La Forte, *Leaders of Reform*, p. 34.

40. White to J. B. M. Hamilton, Oct. 31, 1903, LB 4, LC.

41. White to C. W. Munn, Aug. 26, 1902, LB 3, LC. On rate protests, see EG, Sept. 27, 1902.

42. White to W. J. Black, Apr. 28, 1904, LB 5; to Wesley Merritt and to Paul Morton, Sept. 8, 1903, LB 4; all LC. For other examples of such mediating advice, see White to F. C. Meagley, July 18, 1902, LB 3; to Paul Morton, Jan. 27, 1903, LB 3; and to Mr. Hamilton, Apr. 20, 1904, LB 4; all LC.

43. White to Lee Gates, Sept. 3, 1903, LB 4, LC; White, *Autobiography*, p. 365.

44. EG, Sept. 3, 1902; White, "A Tenderfoot on Thunder Mountain," *Saturday Evening Post*, Nov. 8, 1902, 1–2, 14–15; Nov. 15, 1902, 3–5; Nov. 22, 1902, 15–16; and Nov. 29, 1902, 3–5, 18–19.

45. White to Sallie White, July 7 and 8, 1903, KU.

46. On his promotional efforts see White to Lee Gates, Sept. 3, 1903, LB 4, LC. On the use of contacts see White to George A. Dorsey (quoted), Nov. 25, 1904, LB 6; to I. B. Perrine, Oct. 5, 1903, and to Mr. McCallius, Oct. 29, 1903, both LB 4; all LC. On efforts as a publicist see "The Boom in the Northwest," *Saturday Evening Post*, May 21, 1904, 1–3, and May 28, 1904, 1–2; White to Perrine, Oct. 5,

1903, LB 4; to Twin Falls Irrigation Co., May 28, 1904, LB 5; and to Van Riper, May 25, 1904, LB 5; all LC. On Perrine's important role in promoting irrigation in Idaho, see F. Ross Peterson, *Idaho: A Bicentennial History* (New York: W. W. Norton & Co., 1976), pp. 130–31.

47. White, *Autobiography*, p. 365.

48. White to Roosevelt, May 1, 1907, LB 9, LC; White to Perrine, Mar. 2, 1905, LB 7, LC. See also White's version of this affair in his *Autobiography*, pp. 365–66.

49. White to Van Riper, May 22, 1905, LB 7, LC; White, *Autobiography*, pp. 367–68. White's treatment of these events in the *Autobiography* is generally true to the evidence contained in his correspondence, execpt that he recalls that the mining journal solicited him for an article, whereas it was the other way around. He also does not mention his longstanding involvement in the mining enterprises.

50. On the important distinction between shame and guilt, see Bertram Wyatt-Brown, *Southern Honor: Ethics and Behavior in the Old South* (New York: Oxford University Press, 1982), p. 155.

51. On the emergence of this group and White's political stance in early 1903, see La Forte, *Leaders of Reform*, pp. 31–34.

52. The emergence of progressive politics in Kansas has been well documented by Robert Sherman La Forte in *Leaders of Reform*, although he is less successful in explaining why a shift from factionalism to issue-oriented politics should have occurred. See, for example, p. 44.

53. Eva Austin to E. W. Blatchford & Co., Mar. 12, 1904, LB 5; Mae Austin to Theo. Hiertz Metal Co., Oct. 5, 1905, LB 7; to Kansas City Paper House, Feb. 25, 1903, LB 3, Aug. 10 and 14, 1903, LB 4, May 23, 1904, LB 5, and Oct. 23, 1905, LB 7; to Kansas City Paper House, June 3, 9, and 14, 1904, LB 5, and Oct. 17, 1904, LB 6; all LC.

54. White to Sallie White, Oct. 6, 1904, KU; *Gazette* to J. W. Butler Paper Company, Mar. 21, 1906, LB 8; to Kansas City Paper House, Mar. 5, 10, 11, and 13, 1903, LB 3; all LC.

55. Mae Austin to KCPH, Aug. 26, 1903, LB 4; White to KCPH, July 17, 1904, LB 6; both LC. See also *Gazette* to Kansas City Paper House, June 24, 1904, LB 5, and July 29, 1904, LB 6; both LC. On turn-of-the-century developments in the newsprint industry, see Naomi R. Lamoreaux, *The Great Merger Movement in American Business, 1895–1904* (New York: Cambridge University Press, 1985), pp. 44, 126–29.

56. Austin to Kansas City Paper House, Jan. 23, 1905, LB 7, LC.

57. EG, June 21, 1905.

58. William Allen White, "Early Draft of Autobiography," unpublished manuscript (ca. 1927–28), Ch. 8, pp. 16–17; White, *Autobiography*, p. 366.

59. Jan. 15, 1907, LB 9, LC; La Forte, *Leaders of Reform*, pp. 80–83. For similar sentiments, see White to F. D. Smith, Feb. 25, 1907, LB 9, LC. Noting that the railroads' actions on behalf of Curtis were no worse than usual, La Forte (pp. 83, 272–73) criticizes White's account of Curtis's nomination as distorted. What he misses is the important change in White's interpretation of acceptable political behavior.

5. Booster Progressivism

1. EG, Nov. 15, 18, and 20, 1899. Plumb's prominent role in lobbying for railroad regulation in the 1890s is detailed in Charles L. Wood, "Cattlemen, Railroads,

and the Origin of the Kansas Livestock Association—the 1890s," *Kansas Historical Quarterly* 43 (Summer 1977): 121–39. Wood notes that the members of the KLA in the nineties were mainly large, well-established stockmen from the Flint Hills area, west of Emporia.

2. EG, Nov. 15 and 29, 1899. For an attack on Populist antimonopoly "demagoguery" as opposed to "business principles," see ibid., Sept. 19, 1900.

3. White to W. C. Edwards, May 4, 1900; to John B. Eaton, May 31 and June 4, 1900; both LB 1, LC.

4. EG, June 5, 1900.

5. White to Francis Brogan, Apr. 11, 1901, LB 2, LC.

6. EG, June 6 and Nov. 22, 1900.

7. Ibid., Dec. 7, 1900.

8. Ibid., Dec. 22, 1900, and Jan. 7, 1901. On the Orient railroad see John Leeds Kerr, *Destination Topolobampo* (San Marion, Calif.: Golden West Books, 1968).

9. White to A. E. Stilwell, Apr. 24, 1901, LB 2, LC; EG, Apr. 26, 1901.

10. EG, Apr. 22, 1901; White to Roosevelt, May 3, 1901, LB 2, LC.

11. EG, Mar. 19 and May 6, 1901; ER, May 28, 1901. An unidentified clipping, dated May 6, 1901, reported that contractors were in town preparing for work. Clipping in "Railroads" file, LCHM. EG, Mar. 6 and 12, 1901. For his social history of Santa Fe workers, James Ducker examined census data on Emporia residential patterns. He states that the Second and Third wards (those south of Sixth Avenue) had higher concentrations of working-class residents than the northern two wards, although he does not present his figures. James H. Ducker, *Men of the Steel Rails: Workers on the Atchison, Topeka & Santa Fe Railroad, 1869–1900* (Lincoln: University of Nebraska Press, 1983), pp. 82–83.

12. White to Agnellus Rom, June 3, 1901, and to L. M. Paret, May 24, 1901, both LB 2, LC.

13. ER, May 3 and June 3 and 12, 1901; Laura M. French, *History of Emporia and Lyon County* (Emporia: Emporia Gazette Printing, 1929), p. 75.

14. White to John A. Eaton, Mar. 18, 1910, LB 16, LC. See petitions to the Emporia city council on Jan. 2 and Feb. 6, 1905, city council minutes.

15. Yearly programs and minutes for the Current Club, which continues to meet regularly in Emporia, are contained in the Current Club Collection, Lyon County Historical Museum, Emporia. David Thelen discusses the rise of such groups in Wisconsin in the 1890s in *The New Citizenship: Origins of Progressivism in Wisconsin, 1885–1900* (Columbia: University of Missouri Press, 1972), Ch. 4. A similar men's discussion group still going strong in Grinnell, Iowa, also dates from this period.

16. Historians of women and the family have recently made significant contributions to an appreciation of the importance of a more explicit differentiation of gender roles in the creation of a new middle-class culture in response to social change in the nineteenth century. Foremost among these are Mary P. Ryan, *Cradle of the Middle Class: The Family in Oneida County, New York, 1790–1865* (New York: Cambridge University Press, 1981), and Kathryn Kish Sklar, *Catharine Beecher: A Study in American Domesticity* (New Haven, Conn.: Yale University Press, 1973).

17. EG, Nov. 24, 1900. See, for example, the local on "Mrs. Bibantucker," who squandered her husband's small wages on hack rides. Ibid., Feb. 20, 1902.

18. Ibid., Dec. 8, 1900.

19. *Saturday Evening Post* 173 (Mar. 30, 1901): 14.

20. Reprinted in EG, May 19, 1902. Additional details from EG, Nov. 15, 1904.

21. Ibid., May 19, 1902.

22. Ibid., July 12, 1902.

23. Names taken from EG, July 11, 1902, and traced to Emporia city directories for 1900 and 1904. One name was not listed in either, and one had no occupation listed.

24. Names taken from EG, July 12, 1902, and traced to Emporia city directories for 1900 and 1904. Another five men and women were listed but had no occupation, and nine, or nearly one-fifth of the total, were not listed in either directory, suggesting the greater geographic mobility of this group.

25. EG, July 12, 1902.

26. French, *History of Emporia*, p. 77; the 1904 directory lists French as living in "rooms" on Constitution Street.

27. White to Sallie White, Apr. 21, 1903, KU; EG, June 10, 1903, and Nov. 15, 1904. William Stahl bought the *Republican* early in 1903, backed by White's factional opponents J. O. Patterson, stockman John Wiggam, Republican congressman J. M. Miller, and William Martindale. White to Sallie White, Apr. 22, 1903, KU.

28. Susan Strasser argues persuasively that the early twentieth century was a turning point in the history of women's domestic labor, as new household appliances and improved public services first began to lighten significantly the physical labor involved in housework. Strasser, *Never Done: A History of American Housework* (New York: Pantheon Books, 1982).

29. EG, May 29, 1900. For an example of Emporians in Colorado, see the *Gazette* column about their activities, "From Manitou," of Aug. 6, 1901.

30. On the emergence of the GFWC and its use of an ideology of "municipal housekeeping," see Karen J. Blair, *The Clubwoman as Feminist: True Womanhood Redefined, 1868–1914* (New York: Holmes & Meier Publishers, 1980).

31. French, *History of Emporia*, p. 74; EG, Aug. 23 and Sept. 18, 1901, and Sept. 3, 1902.

32. White, *Autobiography*, pp. 82, 164, 223–25; EG, Mar. 19, 1901; Robert Smith Bader, *Prohibition in Kansas* (Lawrence: University Press of Kansas, 1986), p. 149. Political patterns in Emporia seem to have followed those described by Richard Jensen and others, with the exception that the Republican factions themselves were often divided over the issue. See Jensen *The Winning of the Midwest: Social and Political Conflict, 1888–1896* (Chicago: University of Chicago Press, 1971); Paul Kleppner, *The Cross of Culture: A Social Analysis of Midwestern Politics, 1850–1900* (New York: Free Press, 1970); and Don Harrison Doyle, *The Social Order of a Frontier Community: Jacksonville, Illinois, 1825–70* (Urbana: University of Illinois Press, 1978).

33. EG, Feb. 11, 1904.

34. White to Sallie White, Nov. 8, 1904, KU.

35. French, *History of Emporia*, p. 81; city council minutes, Mar. 21, 1904; EG, Nov. 5, 1904.

36. EG, Nov. 5, 1904.

37. White to Robert D. Bussey, Jan. 9, 1905, LB 7, LC; EG, Mar. 16, 1905.

38. EG, Mar. 18, 1905. Hugh Holmes, Meffert's new father-in-law, was nominated for the city council, and his lawyer, W. N. Smelser, was nominated for the school board; two signers of the protest against Meffert, W. R. Griffith and J. Frank Kenney, were nominated for police judge and school board member, respectively.

39. White to J. M. Miller, Mar. 5, 1904, LB 5, LC; EG, May 16, 1904; White to Sallie White, Nov. 9, 1904, in possession of Mrs. William L. White. In 1906 White would back the election of former Martindale ally John Wiggam to the Republican central committee, arguing that previous loyalties were now irrelevant because "all factions were dead." EG, Mar. 13 and Apr. 14, 1906.

40. EG, Mar. 20, 21, and 23, 1905. The *Gazette,* while noting that the Citizens' Convention was attended by "men of every brand politically—Democrats, Republicans, Populists, Prohibitionists and Socialists," asserted that "The greatest of these were Democrats." The number of women registered was 1,551, nearly 46 percent of the total of 3,372. This was 62 percent higher than the female registration of 961 two years before.

41. EG, Mar. 20, 1905.

42. ET, Mar. 24, 1905.

43. EG, Mar. 31 and Apr. 3, 1905.

44. Ibid., Apr. 5, 1905, and official returns in city council minutes, Emporia City Office; 1904 city directory. The vote in the northern two wards (One and Four) was Hardcastle 961, Martin 393; in the south (Two and Three), Hardcastle 568, Martin 869. It should be noted that there was stronger support for Hardcastle in the south than there was for Martin in the north.

45. For a sample of the league's activities, see EG, June 23, 1905, June 21, 1906, July 25, Aug. 30, and Dec. 2, 1907, and Nov. 18, 1908.

46. Ibid., Aug. 8, 12, and 30 (quotation), 1907; 1904 city directory.

47. White to Robert D. Bussey, Jan. 9, 1905, LB 7, LC.

48. In *City Building in the New South: The Growth of Public Services in Houston, Texas, 1830–1910* (Philadelphia: Temple University Press, 1983), especially Ch. 5, Harold L. Platt describes a general pattern in urban development, in which as cities grew boosters shifted attention from securing external transportation such as canals and railroads to improving internal services. As this occurred, conflicts arose concerning how to allocate civic resources. Platt describes such conflicts as between the civic elite and "progressive" localists who emphasized neighborhood improvement and feared the loss of local autonomy.

49. EG, Feb. 28 and Mar. 6, 26, 27, and 28 (quotation), 1902.

50. Mar. 22 and 24 and Apr. 2, 1902. On Wright as a Populist, see ibid., July 13, 1895.

51. On the conflict, see ibid., Nov. 17, 1900, July 29, 1901, and May 27, 1905. On Finney, see French, *History of Emporia,* p. 82, and Robert Smith Bader, *The Great Kansas Bond Scandal* (Lawrence: University Press of Kansas, 1982), p. 107.

52. EG, Jan. 29, 1900. See city council minutes for 1903–1906 for numerous examples of such issues. Paving costs were divided among residents of affected streets according to the appraised value of their property.

53. EG, Apr. 19 and Sept. 27, 1902.

54. *Topeka Daily Capital,* Feb. 9 and 16, 1905. See Francis W. Schruben, "The Kansas State Refinery Law of 1905," *Kansas Historical Quarterly* 34 (Autumn 1968): 299–324.

55. Edward Wallace Hoch, "Kansas and the Standard Oil Company," *The Independent* 58 (Mar. 2, 1905): 463.

56. Ida M. Tarbell, *The History of the Standard Oil Company,* 2 vols. (New York: Macmillan Company, 1904).

57. French, *History of Emporia,* p. 81; EG, Mar. 13 and Apr. 10, 1905.

58. On the KCVL and George, see Robert Sherman La Forte, *Leaders of Reform: Progressive Republicans in Kansas, 1900–1916* (Lawrence: University Press of Kansas, 1974), pp. 55–57, 68–70. On Evans, see White to George, Jan. 13, 1906, LB 7, LC.

59. White to George, Jan. 13, 1906, LB 7, LC.

60. EG, Mar. 27 and Apr. 3, 1906.

61. White to La Follette, July 6, 1906, LB 8, LC; La Forte, *Leaders of Reform,* pp. 76–79.

62. White to Ralph Stout, Aug. 9, 1906, LB 8, LC.

63. EG, Aug. 24, 1906.

64. Ibid., Nov. 17, 1904, Mar. 6 and 24 and Nov. 24, 1906.

65. Ibid., Dec. 3, 1906. On KCVL advocacy of direct primaries, see La Forte, *Leaders of Reform,* p. 71.

66. EG, Dec. 3, 1907. Twenty-three businessmen opposed selling, while eighteen favored it.

67. Ibid., Nov. 7 and 9, 1907.

68. Ibid., Apr. 30, 1908; White to O. C. Wales, June 22, 1907, LB 9; to William B. McKinley, Oct. 10, 1910, LB 17; to W. E. Hildebrand, Oct. 17, 1910, LB 17; and Hildebrand to White, Oct. 20, 1910, C5; all LC.

69. Bradley Robert Rice, *Progressive Cities: The Commission Government Movement in America, 1901–1920* (Austin: University of Texas Press, 1977). Rice documents the central role that local newspapers played in promoting the innovation: "The press was both an actor in and a chronicler of the change-of-government struggle" (p. 7).

70. EG, Jan. 23 and 25, 1907; Current Club minutes for Apr. 15, 1907, LCHM.

71. EG, Jan. 25 and 29 and Oct. 15, 1907.

72. Ibid. Jan. 7, 24, and 31, and Feb. 1, 2 ("The Average Man's Weapon"), 3, 5, 7, 8, 9 ("The System—Not the Man"), 10, 11, 12 ("Laboring Men for Commission"), 14, 15 ("A Taxpayers' Government"), 18, and 19 and Mar. 9, 1910. The measure probably took so long to come before the voters because of the extremely stringent qualifying requirements: Kansas law required the signatures of 40 percent of those who had actually voted in the previous municipal election, not simply of the *number* of the vote cast. EG, Jan. 7, 1910.

73. White to Vernon, Oct. 18, 1910, LB 17, LC. See also White to W. F. Ewing, Oct. 18, 1910; to Henry J. Allen, Oct. 18, 1910; to Rodney Elward, Oct. 18, 1910; and to Mayor Bishop, Oct. 21, 1910; all LB 17, LC.

74. ET, Mar. 16 and Apr. 6, 1911; Rolla Clymer, "Reminiscence," *The Emporia Gazette's Album of Memories* (Emporia: Emporia Gazette, [1976]), n.p.; French, *History of Emporia,* pp. 94–95. In the 1920s the streetcar was replaced by bus service.

6. Spokesman for Community

1. White to Jay E. House, Aug. 6, 1910, LB 17, LC.

2. Frederick Palmer to White, Oct. 14, 1903, ESU. For details of his early commissions to report on regional issues, see Ch. 2, note 47. Examples of later articles are "Fifty Years of Kansas," *The World's Work* 8 (June 1904): 4870–72; and "The Glory of the States: Kansas," *American Magazine* 81 (Jan. 1916): 41, 65.

3. "Droch" (Robert Bridges), " 'What's the Matter with Kansas?'," *Life* 29 (Jan. 7, 1897): 6–7.

4. White, *Autobiography*, p. 288; White to Riley, Feb. 11 and 19, 1897, James Whitcomb Riley Manuscripts, Lilly Library, University of Indiana.

5. Ida M. Tarbell, *All in the Day's Work* (New York: Macmillan, 1939; reprint, G. K. Hall, 1985), p. 261; White, *Autobiography*, p. 301. On *McClure's* see Harold S. Wilson, *McClure's Magazine and the Muckrakers* (Princeton, N.J.: Princeton University Press, 1970).

6. Mar. 11, 1897, ESU.

7. Tarbell bought a farm in Connecticut around 1907, and Phillips had a summer home in Duxbury, Mass. Tarbell, *Day's Work*, pp. 260, 262; *New York Times*, Mar. 2, 1949, p. 25; Ray Stannard Baker, *American Chronicle: The Autobiography of Ray Stannard Baker* (New York: Charles Scribner's Sons, 1945), pp. 146–47. On the appeal of country living generally in this period, see David E. Shi, *The Simple Life: Plain Living and High Thinking in American Culture* (New York: Oxford University Press, 1985), pp. 194–95.

8. Roosevelt to Gilder, Sept. 21, 1900, *The Letters of Theodore Roosevelt*, vol. 3 (Cambridge, Mass.: Harvard University Press, 1951), p. 149; White, *Autobiography*, p. 341.

9. White to James H. Canfield, June 4, 1904, LB 5, LC; White to Lewis A. Stebbins, May 19, 1904, LB 5, LC; White to Sallie White, Nov. 3, 1905, KU.

10. S. S. McClure to White, May 6, 1903, ESU; Sallie White to William Allen White, Sept. 1903, KU.

11. List for May 21, 1899, McClure's Syndicate Scrapbook, McClure's Manuscripts, Lilly Library; William Allen White, *Stratagems and Spoils* (New York: Charles Scribner's Sons, 1901). Much of the text of the *McClure's* essays was eventually incorporated into the political portraits in *Masks in a Pageant* (New York: Macmillan Company, 1928).

12. *Saturday Evening Post* 175 (Dec. 27, 1902): 21.

13. Frank N. Doubleday to White, Nov. 28 and Dec. 8, 1902; George H. Lorimer to White, Dec. 3, 1902; and Edward Bok to White, Mar. 4, 1901; all ESU.

14. Robert N. Bellah et al. argue that an ethic of communal responsibility restrained the competitive individualism encouraged by commerce in mid-nineteenth-century America, in *Habits of the Heart: Individualism and Commitment in American Life* (Berkeley: University of California Press, 1985; reprint, Harper & Row, 1986), pp. 38–41. Lewis Atherton notes this fusion of morality and prosperity in *Main Street on the Middle Border* (Bloomington: University of Indiana Press, 1954), pp. 68–70.

15. EG, June 13, 1895.

16. For a similar use of the body to symbolize community interdependence, see Atherton, *Main Street*, p. 63.

17. EG, Nov. 28, 1899.

18. Ibid., Jan. 4, 1901.

19. Ibid., June 17, 1905.

20. Ibid., June 20, 1905.

21. Ibid., June 22, 1905.

22. Ibid., June 20, 1905. The role of public reputation in the formation of individual identity is discussed in Chapter 1.

23. Ibid., June 5, 1900.

24. Ibid., Oct. 2, 1899.

25. Jean Quandt, *From the Small Town to the Great Society: The Social Thought of Progressive Intellectuals* (New Brunswick, N.J.: Rutgers University Press, 1970); R. Jackson Wilson, *In Quest of Community: Social Philosophy in the United States,*

1860–1920 (New York: John Wiley & Sons, 1968). Quandt includes White among her group of "communitarian" intellectuals, with John Dewey, Jane Addams, Josiah Royce, Charles Horton Cooley, and Robert Park. Although White shares with the others the fact that he grew up in small town or rural America—a fact that Quandt sees as fundamental to their emphasis upon community—he seems otherwise inappropriate for the group. He was hardly an intellectual, and the ideas attributed to him were expressed in the course of his commentary about current events. Aside from his acquaintance with Jane Addams, which did not begin until 1908, he had no connection with any of the other writers, and there is no evidence that he read their works. Nonetheless, since these communitarians shared a common background, they, like White, may have been influenced by the assumptions of the booster ethos absorbed during their childhoods.

26. White, *Autobiography*, p. 326.

27. White to John Phillips, June 4, 1904, LB 5, LC; Charlotte Perkins Gilman, *Human Work* (New York: McClure, Phillips & Co., 1904).

28. Gilman, *Human Work*, pp. 388–89.

29. Quandt, *Small Town to the Great Society*, pp. 28–29; Daniel T. Rodgers, "In Search of Progressivism," *Reviews in American History* 10 (Dec. 1982): 124–26.

30. *Saturday Evening Post*, Dec. 27, 1902, 21.

31. White to Maud St. Aubert Johnston, Aug. 3, 1897, ESU; to Theodore Roosevelt, Oct. 14, 1901, LB 2, LC.

32. White, "The Politicians," *Saturday Evening Post*, Mar. 14, 1903, 1–3; White, "The Brain Trust," *Saturday Evening Post*, Mar. 21, 1903, 1–3; White, "The President," *Saturday Evening Post*, Apr. 4, 1903, 4–5, 14; White, "The Fair-Play Department," *Saturday Evening Post*, May 2, 1903, 1–2.

33. White, "Roosevelt and the Postal Frauds," *McClure's Magazine* 23 (Sept. 1904): 506–20.

34. White, "The Golden Rule," *The Atlantic Monthly* 96 (Oct. 1905): 433–41.

35. White, *Autobiography*, p. 387; White to John S. Phillips, July 6, 1906, LB 8, LC; White, "The Partnership of Society," *American Magazine* 62 (Oct. 1906): 576–85.

36. White, "Partnership of Society."

37. White, *The Old Order Changeth: A View of American Democracy* (New York: Macmillan Company, 1910), p. 62. The articles appeared in the *American Magazine* between Jan. 1909 and Feb. 1910. White to John Phillips, Apr. 8, 1908, and White's form letter, Apr. 8, 1908; both LB 11, LC.

38. White, *Old Order Changeth*, pp. 5, 6, 7.

39. Ibid., pp. 20, 23.

40. Ibid., pp. 29, 30, 165, 226, 235–36.

41. White to Maud St. Aubert Johnson, Mar. 1, 1905, ESU; contract between White and McClure, Phillips & Co., Dec. 11, 1905, ESU.

42. White, *In Our Town* (New York: McClure, Phillips & Co., 1906), p. 363.

43. Ibid., pp. 118–19.

44. Mrs. D. L. Andrews, Jan. 3, 1906; Minnie Brown Emerson, Jan. 25, 1906; Virgil V. McNitt to White, Dec. 6, 1905; F. W. Brewster to White, Jan. 6, 1906; Margaret Stantyn Humphreyville to White, Dec. 29, 1905; E. Y. Horn to White, Jan. 20, 1906; Alice French to White, May 23, 1906; Brand Whitlock to White, June 17, 1906; and Theodore Roosevelt to White, June 15, 1906; all ESU.

45. EG, June 14, 1905.

46. Ibid., Apr. 10, 1906.

47. White to Phillips, Oct. 18, 1906, LB 9, LC; Phillips to White, Nov. 10, 1906, ESU.

48. White, "Emporia and New York," *American Magazine* 63 (Jan. 1907): 261, 260.

49. Ibid., p. 261.

50. Ibid., pp. 260, 264; EG, Mar. 15 and Apr. 3, 1907.

51. Ibid., p. 263.

52. Ibid., pp. 258, 259.

53. Ibid., p. 263.

54. Ibid., pp. 263, 264.

55. White, *A Certain Rich Man* (New York: Macmillan Company, 1909), p. 326.

56. White to Chauncey Williams, Nov. 30, 1897, Newberry Library; White, *Autobiography*, p. 373. He recalled that they made this decision in Feb. 1905, after *In Our Town* was published, but that book did not appear until 1906.

57. White to T. B. Murdock, June 10, 1909, ESU; William Dean Howells, "A Psychological Counter-Current in Recent Fiction," *North American Review* 173 (Dec. 1901): 876. He was reviewing *Stratagems and Spoils*.

58. Howells's contrast in the above-cited review between White's and Gorky's "psychologism" also illustrates the differences between progressive realism and naturalism: "The meaning that animates the stories is that our political opportunity is trammelled only so far as we have trammelled it by our greed and falsehood. . . . To come up out of that Bottomless Pit [of Gorky's despair] into the measureless air of Mr. White's plains is like waking from death to life." Ibid., pp. 877–78.

59. William Lyon Phelps to White, Mar. 18, 1910, C4; James M. Stewart to White, June 19, 1910, C6; William H. Foulkes to White, Feb. 12, 1910, C5; White to Jay B. Nash, Jan. 19, 1910, LB 16; to F. B. Scott, Jan. 19, 1910, LB 16; James R. Garfield to White, Nov. 18, 1909, C2; George Brett to White, Dec. 1, 1909, C2; Walter Rauschenbusch to White, July 9, 1910, C4; George Brett to White, Sept. 16, 1909, C2; all LC; White, *Autobiography*, p. 423. For a survey of the critical response, see E. Jay Jernigan, *William Allen White* (New York: G. K. Hall, 1983).

60. Roosevelt to White, June 26, 1908, C2, LC. Historians' confusion over the "true" nature of progressivism is reflected in the debate over whether Roosevelt was a "realist" or an "idealist." John Milton Cooper's fine comparative biography of Roosevelt and Wilson, *The Warrior and the Priest* (Cambridge, Mass.: Harvard University Press, 1984), is an important corrective to the exaggerated emphasis upon Roosevelt's pragmatism.

61. Roosevelt to White, Feb. 15, 1904, C1; White to Mr. Crummer, Sept. 5, 1906, LB 8; both LC.

62. White to Millard A. White, Nov. 7, 1905, LB 7; to Frank Ayer, Oct. 11, 1906, LB 9; to C. J. Lamb, Oct. 11, 1906, LB 9; all LC.

63. EG, Jan. 14, 1908.

7. Community Journalism

1. William Allen White, "The Country Newspaper," *Harper's Monthly Magazine* 132 (May 1916): 887–91.

2. Ibid., p. 891.

3. EG, June 29, 1895.

4. Ibid., Feb. 26, 1901.

5. Ibid., Mar. 2, 1901.

6. White to Warren R. Anderson, Oct. 13, 1899, LB 1; to Isabelle Morrell Ball, Jan. 9, 1902, LB 3; both LC.

7. White, "Country Newspaper," pp. 890–91.

8. White to Eva McK. Wilder, June 8, 1904, LB 5; to Lulu Gardner, Jan. 5, 1903, LB 3; both LC.

9. EG, June 26, 1907; White to Hughes, Aug. 25, 1907, LB 10; both LC.

10. State Normal Bulletin, Mar. 22, 1916, clipping in Gilsom Scrapbook, LCHM; EG, June 11, 1919, and Feb. 29, 1957.

11. Reminiscences of Oscar S. Stauffer, Rolla Clymer, and C. H. Lambert, The Emporia Gazette's Album of Memories (Emporia: Emporia Gazette, [1976]), n.p.; EG, June 4, 1917.

12. Calvin Lambert reminiscences, Flint Hills Oral History Project, LCHM. See also reminiscences of Oscar S. Stauffer, Rolla Clymer, and Murdock Pemberton. Album of Memories; EG, June 11, 1919. According to onetime Gazette correspondent David Hinshaw, White was known among his employees as "Father White." Hinshaw, Father White at Seventy-One (Boston: Atlantic Monthly Company, 1939), p. 9.

13. White to Laura (French), Sept. 15, 1907, LB 10, and to the Gazette (ca. fall 1909), C2, both LC.

14. EG, Dec. 6, 1901, July 5, 1902, July 20, 1906, Feb. 12, 1903, Jan. 14, 1908, Apr. 22, 1904, and May 18, 1905.

15. Ibid., Oct. 19, 1899.

16. Ibid., Apr. 9, 1903, and Sept. 20, 1906.

17. Ibid., Apr. 21, 1903, and July 26, 1900.

18. Ibid., Aug. 1, 1901, also reprinted in Helen Ogden Mahin, ed., The Editor and His People: Editorials by William Allen White (New York: Macmillan Company, 1924), pp. 51–53. This collection contains many examples of this genre.

19. White to Clad Hamilton, Jan. 20, 1910, LB 16, LC.

20. For a description of the social characteristics of community, see Robert Redfield, The Little Community (Chicago: University of Chicago Press, 1956). One of the most notable recent historical analyses of the community-building functions of such life-cycle events is Rhys Isaac, The Transformation of Virginia, 1740–1790 (Chapel Hill: University of North Carolina Press, 1982).

21. EG, May 24, 1907.

22. See, for example, Jean H. Baker, Affairs of Party: The Political Culture of Northern Democrats in the Mid-Nineteenth Century (Ithaca: Cornell University Press, 1983); Don Harrison Doyle, The Social Order of a Frontier Community: Jacksonville, Illinois, 1825–70 (Urbana: University of Illinois Press, 1978); and Lewis Atherton, Main Street on the Middle Border (Bloomington: Indiana University Press, 1954), pp. 190–216. During this period progressive reformers staged civic celebrations consciously designed to promote a feeling of community. David Glassberg, "American Civic Pageantry and the Image of the Community, 1900–30" (Ph.D. dissertation, Johns Hopkins University, 1982).

23. EG, Mar. 16, 1904.

24. Ibid., Apr. 24, 1905.

25. Ibid., Apr. 13, 1906, and Jan. 7, 1915.

26. On the emphasis upon historical continuity in civic celebrations in this period, see David Glassberg, "History and the Public: Legacies of the Progressive Era," Journal of American History 73 (Mar. 1987): 957–80.

27. EG, Jan. 20, 1904; also in Mahin, Editor and His People, pp. 105–106.

28. EG, Apr. 21 and May 12, 1900.

29. Ibid., Mar. 27, 1906.

30. Ibid., Oct. 14, 1904.

31. Ibid., Mar. 8, 1900, and July 19, 1902.

32. White to Mrs. Belle Benedict, Aug. 10, 1901, LB 2, LC. This situation was undoubtedly a source for White's story "By the Rod of His Wrath," in *In Our Town*.

33. EG, June 22, 1913; also in Mahin, *Editor and His People*, pp. 30–31.

34. EG, May 23, 1921; also in Mahin, *Editor and His People*, 39–40.

35. "Calvin Lambert, Former City Editor, Recalls Days on The Gazette," EG, Feb. 1, 1944.

36. EG, Nov. 21, 1907; White, "Country Newspaper," p. 890.

37. White, *In Our Town*, p. 6. On the distinction between "big" and "little" news, see Helen MacGill Hughes, *News and the Human Interest Story* (Chicago: University of Chicago Press, 1940; reprint, Greenwood Press, 1968), pp. 55–70.

38. Average proportions from a random sample of ten issues in 1916, when the European war was big news, were national and international news, 55 percent; state, 10 percent; local (including Lyon County), 35 percent. Journalism historians have argued that the emergence of AP's bland style in the later nineteenth century came from the need to serve a broad range of newspapers regardless of political affiliation. Donald Shaw, "News Bias and the Telegraph," *Journalism Quarterly* 44 (Spring 1967): 3–12, 31.

39. EG, Jan. 8, 1910, and June 2, 1911. The latter is also in Mahin, *Editor and His People*, pp. 29–30.

40. EG, Apr. 22, 1904, and Mar. 1, 1907.

41. T. F. McDaniel, "An Emporian Remembers William Allen White," EG, Nov. 17, 1977; ibid., Feb. 10, 1900.

42. EG, Sept. 11, 1900, and June 10, 1903.

43. Ibid., Jan. 14, 1908, and June 15, 1905.

44. Ibid., Oct. 17, 1906; others: ibid., June 17, 1916, May 18, 1905; French, *History of Emporia*, p. 81. Debs had appeared in Emporia before, when he lectured at the Chautauqua held every year at Soden's Mill. EG, July 1, 1903.

45. EG, May 8, 1905, and Aug. 24, 1906.

46. White, "Country Newspaper," p. 890.

47. EG, Jan. 6, 1905.

48. White, *Autobiography*, p. 292; EG, Sept. 7, 1899 (on a Colored Baptists' Convention), Aug. 29, 1900 (on the formation of a black society "for the general dissemination of knowledge"), June 27, 1902 (on the state meeting of the Colored Eastern Star), Mar. 6, 1903 (on a celebration at the A.M.E. Church), Aug. 29, 1900, Jan. 14 and 21, 1902.

49. EG, Nov. 17, 1899, and Sept. 25, 1903.

50. White to Walter M. Thueing, Dec. 12, 1906, LB 9, LC; EG, Jan. 21, 1902, Dec. 27, 1897, and Dec. 17, 1900.

51. EG, Nov. 17, 1899, and May 11, 1908.

52. Ibid., Aug. 15, 1907. Mexican immigrants became more numerous and permanent in Emporia during World War I. Ted F. McDaniel, ed., *Our Land: A History of Lyon County Kansas* (Emporia: Emporia State Press, 1976), pp. 162–63; Victoria Rindom, "Railroad Attracted Mexicans to Emporia," *Album of Memories*.

53. White, "Country Newspaper," p. 888.

54. EG, Dec. 10, 1913.

55. D. S. Rowland to White, July 20 (1902); KU; Hinshaw, *Father White,* p. 20; interview with Walter W. Butcher, Flint Hills Oral History Project, LCHM.

56. Riley to White, Oct. 8, 1897, ESU (emphases in the original); White to Phillips, July 6, 1906, LB 8, LC.

57. White to J. L. Bristow, Feb. 8, 1911, LB 16, LC; interview with James T. Yearout, Flint Hills Oral History Project, LCHM. One historian labeled "mercurial" such behavior in the case of a conflict between W. W. Finney, owner of the telephone company, and the city government. Robert Smith Bader, *The Great Kansas Bond Scandal* (Lawrence: University Press of Kansas, 1982), pp. 107–10.

58. Statement of Circulation to the Association of American Advertisers (ca. Jan. 1907), LB 9, LC; *Thirteenth Census, Vol. II, Population* (Washington: GPO, 1913) p. 696; French, *History of Emporia,* pp. 223–24, 226; EG, Dec. 13, 1900, and June 3, 5, and 10, 1905; White to Sallie White, Apr. 22, 1903, KU; Edgar Martindale to White, July 9, 1910, C6, LC. The 1910 census counted 2,312 families in Emporia; by that time the *Gazette's* circulation had increased further, but the figure for circulation within Emporia is available only for 1907.

59. Interview with Margaret Soden, May 21, 1982; interview with Janet Cleveland, May 20, 1982.

60. For a fuller discussion of the contents of Emporians' scrapbooks, see Sally F. Griffith, "Audiences and Communities: Readers' Responses to Their Local Newspaper," paper presented to the Strong Museum Symposium, "Reading in America, 1840–1940," Nov. 21–22, 1986.

61. White to Kellogg & Madden and A. L. Redden and M. W. Suddock, May 17, 1904, LB 5, LC; EG, May 19, 1904. Scholars of communication describe the press's "agenda setting" function as its ability to influence the public's perceptions of what issues are important simply by deciding how much space to devote to them. As one put it, the press "may not be successful much of the time in telling people what to think, but it is stunningly successful in telling its readers what to think *about.*" B. C. Cohen, quoted in "Media Theory: Contributions to an Understanding of American Mass Communications," *American Quarterly* 32 (Bibliographic Issue): 241.

62. Jean Folkerts emphasizes White's use of his agenda-setting power against Populism and for business dominance in "William Allen White's Anti-Populist Rhetoric as an Agenda-Setting Technique," *Journalism Quarterly* 60 (Spring 1983): 28–34, and "William Allen White: Editor and Businessman during the Reform Years, 1895–1916," *Kansas History* 7 (Summer 1984): 129–38.

63. Interviews with Charles H. Cowan and James T. Yearout, Flint Hills Oral History Project, LCHM. On limits to expression that are set by social usage see Clifford Geertz, "Ideology as a Cultural System," in his *The Interpretation of Cultures* (New York: Basic Books, 1973), pp. 193–233.

64. Alfred G. Hill, "The Influence of an Editor," *Chester* (Pennsylvania) *Times,* n.d., obituary file, KU; interview with Margaret Soden.

65. Hinshaw, *Father White,* pp. 9–10.

66. White, "Country Newspaper," p. 888.

67. White, *Autobiography,* p. 406.

68. Ibid.; Everett Rich, *William Allen White: The Man from Emporia* (New York: Farrar & Rinehart, 1941), p. 148; homecoming program annotated by Sallie White and poster, ESU.

69. Program, "The Home-Coming of Colonel Hucks," ESU; Rich, *William Allen White*, p. 148; Ida Tarbell to White, Sept. 18, 1909, C2, LC.

70. Rolla Clymer, "Reminiscence," *Album of Memories*, n.p.; French, *History of Emporia*, pp. 94–95; William Lindsay White, "Life With William Allen White Was Lively," *Kansas City Star*, Sept. 22, 1968, pp. 8–9F.

71. Lewis Atherton, *Main Street*, pp. 166–67, similarly argues that the country newspaper "dignified the lives of common people."

8. Booster Nationalism

1. William Allen White, *The Autobiography of William Allen White* (New York: Macmillan Company, 1946), p. 533.

2. For an analysis of the social effects of Wilson's war policies, see David M. Kennedy, *Over Here: The First World War and American Society* (New York: Oxford University Press, 1980).

3. White's Progressive activities are documented in Robert Sherman La Forte, *Leaders of Reform: Progressive Republicans in Kansas, 1900–1916* (Lawrence: University Press of Kansas, 1974), Chs. 11 and 12.

4. See White to editors of Kansas newspapers, July 27, 1908, and letters to White from C. E. Coudery, E. P. Greer, George W. Marble, W. J. Krehbiel, Sheffield Ingalls, A. L. Miller, T. B. Murdock, W. C. Simons, C. E. Wattermire, and H. T. Woods, all July 28, 1908, ESU; Dolley to White, July 14, 1910, C5, LC. White's correspondence files from 1910 through 1914 attest to his work with other newspapers. See, for example, letters to White from Dow Busenbark, June 30, 1910, C4; George N. Marble, July 18, 1910, C6; and Andrew McLaughlin, July 21, 1910, C6; all LC.

5. Milwaukee *Journal* to White, May 25, 1910, C6; Battle Creek *Enquirer* to White, Oct. 9, 1010, C6; Springfield *Republican* to White, Oct. 29, 1910, C6; White to T. C. Wilson, Mar. 4, 1914, LB 24; all LC. Victor Murdock and Henry Allen were Progressive candidates for senator and governor, respectively.

6. White to Charles Vernon, Jan. 13, 1914, LB 23; to H. W. Randolph, June 3, 1914, LB 24; and to Elmer T. Peterson, Nov. 6, 1914, LB 25; all LC.

7. Rolla A. Clymer, "Thomas Benton Murdock and William Allen White," *Kansas Historical Quarterly* 23 (Autumn 1957): 255.

8. E. E. Talboys to White, Sept. 5, 1910, C7, LC.

9. White to W. E. Borah, Oct. 24, 1907, LB 10; to Hapgood, Jan. 22, 1908, and to Whitlock, Feb. 1, 1908, both LB 11; all LC.

10. Phillips to White, May 22, 1908, ESU; White to Phillips, May 25, 1908, LB 12, LC.

11. Historians who have characterized progressivism as primarily a "search for order" have focused upon these organizations. The most influential works in this vein have been Robert H. Wiebe, *The Search for Order, 1877–1920* (New York: Hill and Wang, 1967); Louis Galambos, "The Emerging Organizational Synthesis in Modern American History," *Business History Review* 44 (1970): 279–90; and James Weinstein, *The Corporate Ideal in the Liberal State, 1900–1918* (Boston: Beacon Press, 1968).

12. White to A. W. Wright, Feb. 10, 1914, LB 24, LC; La Forte, *Leaders of Reform*, pp. 217, 247–48. For examples of other organizations see Clara C. Chapin to White, Jan. 25, 1915, C31, and Lilla Day Monroe to White, Nov. 25, 1910, C10, both LC.

13. Ralph Albertson to White, Feb. 26, 1910, C4; Harold W. Sanford to White, C29; both LC. See also George Creel to White, Apr. 20, 1915, C30, LC.

14. Pullman to White, Apr. 4, July 1, and Aug. 29, 1910, C6, LC. On Gifford Pinchot's early publicity efforts at the Forest Service, see Samuel P. Hays, *Conservation and the Gospel of Efficiency* (Cambridge, Mass.: Harvard University Press, 1959), pp. 138–41. On Van Valkenberg's connection with Pinchot, see Weinstein, *Corporate Ideal*, p. 145.

15. Raymond W. Pullman to White, Apr. 4, 1910, C6, LC.

16. Weinstein, *Corporate Ideal*, pp. 3, 124–27.

17. The emergence of public relations in this period is discussed in Richard S. Tedlow, *Keeping the Corporate Image: Public Relations and Business, 1900–1950* (Greenwich, Conn.: JAI Press, 1979), Ch. 1; Z. G. Hopkins to White, Dec. 11, 1915, C32, LC.

18. Statements about advertising volume are based on measurement of the column inches of advertising contained in 252 randomly selected issues of the *Gazette* from 1895 to 1927. For full details see Sally F. Griffith, "Home Town News: William Allen White and the Emporia *Gazette*, 1895–1930" (Ph.D. dissertation, Johns Hopkins University, 1985), pp. 547–51.

19. For samples of Calumet's advertising, see EG, Feb. 17, May 1, and Oct. 12, 1916, and June 4, 1917; for Glendale's, Jan. 11, 1916.

20. *Gazette* to Meyer-Both, Feb. 22, 1918, D9, LC. See also *Gazette* to Meyer-Both Co., Nov. 23, 1916, and Meyer-Both to *Gazette*, Feb. 5, 1917, both D8, LC.

21. EG, May 1 and Mar. 27, 1916.

22. Ibid., May 1, Apr. 24, and Oct. 28, 1916, Oct. 27, 1917. On the role of the star system in the evolution of the industry from competition to oligarchy, see Reese V. Jenkins, *Images and Enterprise: Technology and the American Photographic Industry, 1839 to 1925* (Baltimore: Johns Hopkins University Press, 1975): pp. 292–94.

23. See "New Motion Pictures," EG, May 1, 1916.

24. Ferry-Hanley Advertising Co. to *Gazette*, Oct. 12, 1917, D8, and Jan. 18, 1918, D9; *Gazette* to Ferry-Hanley Advertising Co., Feb. 21, 1918, D9; all LC.

25. Peninsular Chemical Co. to *Gazette*, Mar. 21, 1917, D8, LC.

26. Lord & Thomas to *Gazette*, Dec. 21, 1917, D8, LC. See advertising for Sunkist Oranges, in EG, Jan. 14, 1916.

27. *Gazette* to Dunlap-Ward Advertising Agency, Nov. 6, 1915, LB 50; Mercantile Tailoring Co. to *Gazette*, Oct. 28, 1916, D8; Lord & Thomas to *Gazette*, Feb. 20, 1917, D8; Pilot Motor Car Company to *Gazette*, Mar. 14, 1917, D8; American Tractor Co. to *Gazette*, Jan. 10, 1918, D9; *Gazette* to A. M. Clapp, Oct. 21, 1915, LB 50; all LC. See also *Gazette* to National Drug Co., Nov. 12, 1915, LB 50, LC, declining to call on Emporia druggists.

28. Lord & Thomas to *Gazette*, Nov. 2, 1916, Feb. 5 and [13], 1917; International Silver Co., Nov. 10, 1917; all D8, LC.

29. A. C. Reiley to *Gazette*, Feb. 15, 1917, and Secretary-Treasurer, Association of National Advertisers, to *Gazette*, Mar. 17, 1917, both D8, LC.

30. By 1914 advertising rates had reached 12 cents an inch for a minimum of 1,000 inches; in 1915–16 the basic charge was 14 cents an inch, minimum of 1,000 inches, with extra charges for composition and specified position. In early 1917 rates were raised to 20 cents, with lower rates for larger contracts, down to 9 cents an inch for contracts of 8,000 inches or more. See *Gazette* to George H. Lee, Feb. 11, 1914, LB 48; to There's a Reason Co., Feb. 2, 1915, LB 26, and Dec. 15,

1916, D8; and standard contract form [Feb. 1917], D8; all LC. For other reports of increased advertising in 1917, see *Gazette* to Fort Scott *Tribune-Monitor*, Apr. 18, 1917, D8, LC.

31. For evidence of his extensive involvement in planning and financing Hamer's campaign, see White to Frank Kenney, Jan. 7, 1914, LB 23, and Feb. 18, 1914, LB 24; circular letters of Mar. 18 and 31, 1914, LB 24; White to Hamer, Apr. 24, 1914, LB 24; all LC; EG, Mar. 14, 1914; White to William C. Harris, Jan. 19, 1915, LB 26, LC. He also warned attorney Owen Samuel against taking "these bootlegger cases." White to Owen Samuel, Jan. 30, 1915, LB 26, and Samuel to White, Feb. 1, 1915, C33, both LC.

32. Howe to White [ca. 1910]; White to Amos H. Plumb, Jan. 8, 1912, LB 19; both LC; EG, Jan. 16, 1907; Laura M. French, *History of Emporia and Lyon County* (Emporia: Emporia Gazette Print, 1929), p. 83. During the Progressive Era middle-class Americans responded to the disappearance of conditions that provided more "natural" forms of play by creating organizations to channel youth's anarchic energies in socially acceptable ways without stifling them completely. A recent study of boys' work in the YMCA and Boy Scouts emphasizes the social-control aspect of the movements but also points out their efforts to foster an acceptable masculinity. David I. Macleod, *Building Character in the American Boy: The Boy Scouts, YMCA, and Their Forerunners, 1870–1920* (Madison: University of Wisconsin Press, 1983). Jeffrey P. Hantover emphasizes the problem of masculinity as a motivation in the advent of the Boy Scouts, in "The Boy Scouts and the Validation of Masculinity," *Journal of Social Issues* 34 (1978): 184–95.

33. EG, Apr. 9, 1903, May 20, 1907, Aug. 7 and 15, 1907; White to James R. Paul, Feb. 17, 1915, LB 26, LC. The Electric Theater arrived in 1909, and the Elite in 1911. The Royal, called the first "modern" motion picture house, opened in 1915. EG, Oct. 1, 1929.

34. EG, Dec. 9, 1913. For similar attacks upon vaudeville programs in movie houses at this time, see Daniel J. Czitrom, *Media and the American Mind: From Morse to McLuhan* (Chapel Hill: University of North Carolina Press, 1982), pp. 46–48.

35. French, *History of Emporia*, p. 103. Similarities between Emporia and the fictional River City of Meredith Willson's *Music Man* are not coincidental. Willson, a native of Mason City, Iowa, set his story in 1912, when he was ten years old.

36. White to Nau, Mar. 20, 1914, LB 24, LC. On previous efforts, see White to A. A. Hyde, Oct. 14, 1911, LB 19; Hyde to White, Oct. 16, 1911, C9; White to Amos H. Plumb, Jan. 8, 1912, LB 19; all LC.

37. For details of the organizational technique of the drive, see EG, May 14 and 19, 1914. According to Macleod, *Building Character*, p. 202, the YMCA pioneered this fund-raising technique.

38. On arrangements for speakers see White to George Hodges, W. Y. Morgan, Henry J. Allen, Arthur Capper, and William Kelley, May 14, 1914, LB 24, LC.

39. EG, May 20, 21, and 26, 1914.

40. Ibid., May 23, 1914.

41. Ibid., May 21, 1914.

42. Ibid., May 22 and 26, 1914. See also ibid., May 21, 1914.

43. Ibid., May 28, 1914.

44. Ibid., May 29, 1914.

45. White to Thomas O'Connor, May 20, 1914; to Irene Pemberton, May 20, 1914; and to Robert L. Jones, May 22, 1914; all LB 24, LC.

46. White to E. W. Rankin, Feb. 5, 1915, LB 26; to A. O. Rorabaugh, June 3, 1914, LB 24; both LC.

47. EG, May 30, 1914.

48. White to Roosevelt, Dec. 15, 1914, in Walter Johnson, ed., *Selected Letters of William Allen White* (New York: Henry Holt and Company, 1947), pp. 157–58; Phillips to White, Sept. 21, 1915, C30, LC. Although the Kansas party did not disband officially until 1916, it ceased to function after the 1914 elections. LaForte, *Leaders of Reform*, pp. 256–57.

49. White to Norman Hapgood, Nov. 18, 1914; to W. R. Stubbs, Nov. 28, 1914; to Edward B. Lyman, Nov. 30, 1914; and to J. B. Adams, Nov. 21, 1914; all LB 25, LC; EG, Feb. 13, 1915.

50. Richard W. Resh discusses the connections between White's search for a unified national community and the self-sacrificing spirit called forth in wartime in his article "A Vision in Emporia: William Allen White's Search for Community," *American Studies* 10 (Fall 1969): 19–35. He does not, however, connect this with White's longstanding booster leadership in Emporia.

51. Because AP did not require members to identify its news until April 1917, it is not always possible to tell which agencies provided particular news stories. From internal evidence it is clear that the *Gazette* used a variety of sources, such as clippings, boiler plate, publicity releases, and agencies such as Reuters, but AP material predominated. On AP war coverage see Oliver Gramling, *AP: The Story of News* (New York: Farrar and Rinehart, 1940), pp. 259–70. On White's refusal to "spend my good money for newspaper cuts" see White to Charles H. Trapp, Apr. 25, 1914, LB 24, LC.

52. EG, June 10, 1915, Jan. 11, 1916, Jan. 18, 1915, Mar. 27, 1915, Jan. 15, 1916.

53. Ibid., Jan. 1 and Mar. 27, 1917. On the development of White's thinking, see Walter Johnson, *William Allen White's America* (New York: Henry Holt and Company, 1947), pp. 254–57, 268–73.

54. EG, Mar. 31, 1917; Resh, "Vision in Emporia." For discussions of other progressives' similar hopes, see Kennedy, *Over Here*, Ch. 1, and Stephen L. Vaughn, *Holding Fast the Inner Lines: Democracy, Nationalism, and the Committee on Public Information* (Chapel Hill: University of North Carolina Press, 1980), especially Ch. 2.

55. EG, June 26, 1918; see also June 21, Sept. 6, and Oct. 12, 1918.

56. In addition to the various departments of the Committee on Public Information, there were at the beginning of the war as many as fifty publicity bureaus in the various departments. It was said that every newspaper in California—and, presumably, Kansas—received from the government each day enough material to fill 1,200 columns. Vaughn, *Holding Fast*, p. 194.

57. EG, June 26, 1918. On the division's work and its use of emotional appeals, see Vaughn, *Holding Fast*, Ch. 8.

58. Kennedy, *Over Here*, pp. 116, 136.

59. White, "Early Draft of Autobiography" (ca. 1927–28), Ch. 12, pp. 8–9, ESU; EG, Apr. 6, 1918.

60. Quoted in Kennedy, *Over Here*, p. 152; EG, June 4, 1917.

61. Sallie White to Fay Clawer, Feb. 17, 1918, LB 36; White to Charles A. Singler, Nov. 14, 1918, LB 36; and Thomas Yearout to White, Nov. 24, 1918, D9; all LC. "Authors and Artists as 'Vigilantes'," *Literary Digest* 54 (Apr. 14, 1917): 1061–62; Resh, "Vision in Emporia," p. 24; EG, Mar. 15 and June 11, 1918.

62. French, *History of Emporia*, 107–12; Sehl Advertising Agency to *Gazette*, Nov. 24, 1917, D9, LC; EG, Nov. 6, 1917; see also EG, Mar. 15, 1918.

63. EG, Aug. 1, May 23, and June 26, 1918.

64. Conversation with Mrs. William L. White; White to Charles Curtis, Dec. 5, 1917, in Johnson, *Selected Letters*, pp. 184–85; George Creel, *Rebel at Large: Recollections of Fifty Crowded Years* (New York: G. P. Putnam's Sons, 1947), p. 169; White to Lippmann, Nov. 20, 1917, in Johnson, *Selected Letters*, p. 184; Johnson, *White's America*, p. 283; Resh, "Vision in Emporia," p. 25.

65. White to Dudley Doolittle, May 15, 1917, quoted in Resh, "Vision in Emporia," p. 24.

66. EG, Apr. , 1918.

67. Ibid., Nov. 16, 1918. On the similar attitudes of other midwestern newspapers, see John D. Stevens, "Press and Community Toleration: Wisconsin in World War I," *Journalism Quarterly* (Summer 1969): 255–59; and Martha Pinder, "Aggressive Americanism: The Conduct of *The Grinnell Herald* in the War to End All Wars," in possession of the author.

68. EG, Jan. 4, 1917, and Mar. 13, 1918; White to Rodney Eward, June 8, 1917, in Johnson, *Selected Letters*, pp. 180–81; to R. M. McClintock, Feb. 23, 1918, quoted in Resh, "Vision in Emporia," p. 25.

69. EG, Jan. 10, Oct. 19, and May 27, 1918.

70. Ibid., June 11 and May 23, 1918.

71. Ibid., June 10 and Aug. 12, 1918, Oct. 27, 1917.

72. Ibid., Aug 1 and 7, 1918.

73. On the experience of the German-American community of Olpe, in southern Lyon County, see Anna Markowitz Conklin, interview, Flint Hills Oral History Project, LCHM. John Higham, *Strangers in the Land* (New York: Atheneum, 1973), p. 205, notes the powerful blending during World War I of a longstanding American "urge for conformity" with the wartime "spirit of nationalism." David M. Kennedy, *Over Here*, p. 137, blames the administration's "inability or unwillingness to invoke formal authority" for the war effort's paradoxical weaknesses and excesses.

9. Mass Media Come to the Small Town

1. William Allen White, *The Autobiography of William Allen White* (New York: Macmillan Company, 1946), pp. 617–18.

2. Sallie White to W. P. Smith, Feb. 26, 1919, LB 36; White to Charles Vernon, LB 38; Laura French to White, Apr. 27, 1920, C51; all LC; C. H. Lambert, "Reminiscences," in *The Emporia Gazette's Album of Memories* (Emporia: Emporia Gazette, [1976]), n.p.

3. White, *Autobiography*, p. 625. Statements about advertising volume are based on measurement of the column inches of advertising contained in 252 randomly selected issues of the *Gazette* from 1895 to 1927. For full details see Sally F. Griffith, "Home Town News: William Allen White and the Emporia *Gazette*, 1895–1930" (Ph.D. dissertation, Johns Hopkins University, 1985), pp. 547–51.

4. After years of resistance from small-town retailers and express companies, the post office had instituted parcel post delivery in 1913. Wayne D. Fuller, *RFD: The Changing Face of Rural America* (Bloomington: Indiana University Press, 1964), Ch. 9.

5. Average size calculated from sample for the advertising study described in note 3, above; Walter Hughes to Mrs. Severance, Apr. 22, 1919, D10; to Arthur Wilson, July 23, 1919, D10; and to Elbert Severance, July 21, 1919, D10; all LC.

6. [Laura M. French], "History of the Emporia Gazette," p. 34. Installing the press again required enlarging the *Gazette* building. White to William Lindsay White, Feb. 4, 1924, A4, LC.

7. EG, Jan. 8, 1919; White to Charles F. Scott, Apr. 27, 1914, LB 24, and Scott to White, Apr. 30, 1914, C29; both LC.

8. White to William Lindsay White, Apr. 9, 1924, A4, LC; Everett Rich, *William Allen White: The Man from Emporia* (New York: Farrar & Rinehart, 1941), p. 233; and Frank C. Clough, *William Allen White of Emporia* (New York: McGraw-Hill Book Company, 1941; reprint, Greenwood Press, 1970), p. 225. Lord & Thomas listed the *Gazette*'s circulation as 5,754 in 1927. *Lord & Thomas' Pocket Directory for 1927* (New York: Lord & Thomas, 1927), p. 184. White said that it was nearly 6,600 in mid-1929. White to William L. White, July 19, 1929, A4, LC.

9. For a description of the development and use of dry mats, see George A. Kubler, *A New History of Stereotyping* (New York: privately printed, 1941).

10. Ralph M. Hower, *The History of an Advertising Agency* (Cambridge, Mass.: Harvard University Press, 1939), pp. 329–38; Roland Marchand, *Advertising the American Dream: Making Way for Modernity, 1920–1940* (Berkeley: University of California Press, 1985).

11. Marchand acknowledges that innovative advertisements emphasizing emotional appeals rather than product quality were "hardly typical of the advertising" of the twenties. Marchand, *Advertising the American Dream*, p. 22.

12. EG, Dec. 5, 1925, and May 3, 1926.

13. This process of fragmentation has continued into the present, as is described by Anthony Smith in *Goodbye Gutenberg: The Newspaper Revolution of the 1980's* (New York: Oxford University Press, 1980), especially Ch. 4.

14. White, *Autobiography*, p. 617. He explained this solution to President Harding, who had a similar problem.

15. Glenn C. Guiett and Ralph D. Casey, *Principles of Publicity* (New York: D. Appleton and Company, 1926), p. 347. On developments in the field of public relations in the 1920s, see Richard S. Tedlow, *Keeping the Corporate Image: Public Relations and Business, 1900–1950* (Greenwich, Conn: JAI Press, 1979), Ch. 2.

16. EG, Feb. 28 and June 17, 1927.

17. Ibid., Dec. 5, 1925.

18. Lambert's "Reminiscence," *Album of Memories.*

19. Richard A. Schwarzlose, *The American Wire Services: A Study of Their Development as a Social Institution* (New York: Arno Press, 1979), p. 396; Kent Cooper, *Kent Cooper and the Associated Press: An Autobiography* (New York: Random House, 1959), pp. 92–140.

20. White to Associated Press (Kent Cooper), Feb. 3, 1927, C119, LC. White had consistently denounced urban "yellow" journalism, and refused to write for any newspaper owned by William Randolph Hearst. See White to John S. Phillips, Apr. 9, 1900, in Walter Johnson, ed., *Selected Letters of William Allen White, 1899–1943* (New York: Henry Holt and Company, 1947), pp. 32–33, and White to E. S. McClure, July 22, 1919, LB 38, LC.

21. EG, Oct. 4, 1920, and Jan. 3, 1927.

22. Clough, *White of Emporia*, pp. 106–107.

23. See, for example, Nov. 30, 1925.

24. See, for example, EG, May 9, 10, and 23, 1927. Silas Bent notes that 120 reporters covered the Synder-Gray trial, not counting the celebrity commenators such as D. W. Griffith and Billy Sunday. He confessed, "this author himself was one of the 'trained seals' who helped overcrowd the press of the United States with balderdash about the Snyder-Gray trial." Bent, *Ballyhoo: The Voice of the Press* (New York: Boni and Liveright, 1927), pp. 180–98 (quotation on p. 194); Simon Bessie, *Jazz Journalism* (New York: E. P. Dutton Co., 1938); James E. Murphy, "Tabloids as an Urban Response," in Catherine L. Covert and John D. Stevens, eds., *Mass Media Between the Wars: Perceptions of Cultural Tension, 1918–1941* (Syracuse, N.Y.: Syracuse University Press, 1984), pp. 55–69.

25. EG, May 12, 1927.

26. For a sampling of the first three, see EG, Jan. 8, 1927, Dec. 5, 1925, and July 1 and 27, 1925. For the role of the tabloids in literally creating the Browning and Rhinelander sensations, see Helen MacGill Hughes, *News and the Human Interest Story* (Chicago: University of Chicago Press, 1940; reprint, Greenwood Press, 1968), pp. 237–42. On Lindbergh, see EG, May 27 and June 11, 1927.

27. Clough, *White of Emporia*, pp. 104–105.

28. EG, Feb. 7, 1927, Nov. 30 1925.

29. N. A. Huse to White, Jan. 31, 1927, C119, and William Lindsay White to Associated Press, [ca. 1928], C136; both LC. The price for the feature service was originally set at $4.00, but so many papers subscribed that it was lowered.

30. In this discussion, I am assuming that, with the occasional exception of late-breaking news and different local news, the contents of the early, regional edition and the home edition of the *Gazette* were the same. It is not possible to compare them, for only the latter have been preserved. I think it highly probable that wire service and syndicated materials, for which the *Gazette* had to pay "good money," would have been used in both editions to receive full value.

31. In her pathbreaking study of news, Helen Macgill Hughes differentiated sharply between human interest and news by arguing that the former had no actual importance in people's lives. She argued that small-town locals were news because they were related to people's lives. Such a distinction between news' symbolic and "real" uses seems extremely arbitrary. Hughes, a student of sociologist Robert Park, also argued that human interest represented an adaptation of folk culture to an urban milieu. Hughes, *News and the Human Interest Story*, pp. xxi, 103–106.

32. EG, May 7, 1898, and Oct. 12, 1916.

33. Ibid., May 17, 1926.

34. Ibid., June 15, 1926, and Nov. 30, 1925.

35. Ibid., Jan. 8, 1927.

36. Ibid., Apr. 21, 1927. David Glassberg notes an analogous emphasis upon discontinuity in civic historical pageants after World War I, in "History and the Public: Legacies of the Progressive Era," *Journal of American History* 73 (Mar. 1987): 957–80.

37. White, "The Country Newspaper," *Harper's Monthly Magazine* 132 (May 1916), p. 890.

38. White, *Autobiography*, pp. 626–27, 558.

39. Ibid., pp. 551, 587.

40. Ibid., pp. 531, 533; White to Arthur Capper, July 29, 1919, LB 38, LC.

41. Ted F. McDaniel, ed., *Our Land: A History of Lyon County Kansas* (Em-

poria: Emporia State Press, 1976), p. 176; H. C. Culbertson to White, July 28 and Nov. 5, 1917, C38, LC.

42. White to Charles F. Scott, Nov. 28, 1918, and to P. M. Hoisington, Dec. 3, 1918, both LB 36, LC.

43. White to Frederick W. Lewis, Sept. 16, 1919, LB 38, LC.

44. White to Frank Lloyd Wright, Feb. 17, 1915, LB 26; Wright to White, Feb. 25, 1915, C31; both LC; White, *Autobiography*, p. 582. Nonetheless, the house as renovated does reflect strong Prairie School influences.

45. *New Republic*, Feb. 15, 1919, 91–92, and May 17, 1919, 84–85, 88.

46. White, *Autobiography*, p. 595.

47. White to William Lindsay White, Mar. 1, 1921, and Apr. 30, 1923, A4, LC; White, *Autobiography*, p. 595. On Pemberton, see Charles R. Hill, "Brock Pemberton: Broadway Producer," *Emporia State Research Studies* 23 (Spring 1975).

48. White to William Lindsay White, Nov. 26, 1920, A4, LC.

49. White to William Lindsay White, Oct. 25, 1923, A4, LC.

50. White to William Lindsay White, Nov. 7, 1923, A4, LC.

51. W. L. White, "The Sage of Emporia," *Nieman Reports* 23 (Mar. 1969): 23–29. When a collection of White's editorials was compiled in 1937, W. L. White counted two-thirds of those published during his tenure at the *Gazette* as his own work. William Allen White, *Forty Years on Main Street*, compiled by Russell H. Fitzgibbon (New York: Farrar & Rinehart, 1937).

52. William Allen White, "Early Draft of Autobiography," (ca. 1927–28), Ch. 15, pp. 22–23, ESU. On postwar clashes in Kansas between American Legion members and unions, see Richard J. Loosbrock, *The History of the Kansas Department of the American Legion* (Topeka: Kansas Department of the American Legion, 1968), pp. 43–44, 46–47.

53. EG, July 19, 1922, reprinted in White, *Forty Years*, p. 284.

54. W. L. White, "Sage of Emporia"; Calvin Lambert, "Reminiscence," *Album of Memories;* Johnson, *White's America*, pp. 364–67.

55. EG, July 27, 1922, reprinted in White, *Forty Years*, pp. 284–85; White, *Autobiography*, pp. 613–14.

56. W. L. White, "Sage of Emporia."

57. Clough, *White of Emporia*, pp. 148–53.

58. John M. Mecklin, *The Ku Klux Klan: A Study of the American Mind* (New York: Harcourt Brace and Company, 1924), excerpted in David J. Rothman and Sheila M. Rothman, eds., *Sources of the American Social Tradition*, vol. 2 (New York: Basic Books, 1975), pp. 181–83; EG, Sept. 20, 1924, reprinted in White, *Forty Years*, pp. 93–94.

59. Anne O'Hare McCormick, "Editor White Tilts at the Kansas Klan," *New York Times*, Oct. 5, 1924, quoted in E. Jay Jernigan, *William Allen White* (Boston: Twayne Publishers, 1983). On the campaign, see Calvin Lambert, "Reminiscence," *Album of Memories;* Johnson, *White's America*, pp. 379–85; Jack W. Traylor, "William Allen White's 1924 Gubernatorial Campaign," *Kansas Historical Quarterly* 42 (Spring 1976): 180–91.

60. Charles F. Scott to White, Sept. 21, 1924, ESU; Lippmann to White, Sept. 30, 1924, ESU.

61. W. L. White, "Sage of Emporia."

62. Villard, *Some Newspapers and Newspaper-Men* (New York: Alfred A. Knopf, 1923), p. 244; Ernest Gruening, "Can Journalism Be a Profession?", *Century Magazine* 108 (Sept. 1924): 697.

63. Carroll D. Clark, "The Small Town Press Sells Out," *New Republic,* Jan. 20, 1926, 239.

64. Johnson, *White's America,* pp. 479–80. See also John DeWitt McKee, *William Allen White: Maverick on Main Street* (Westport, Conn.: Greenwood Press, 1975), and Kenneth S. Davis, "The Sage of Emporia." *American Heritage* 30 (Oct.–Nov. 1979).

65. White to C. M. Harger, Feb. 7, 1938, quoted in Johnson, *White's America,* p. 153.

66. White, *Autobiography,* p. 644; White to William Lindsay White, Aug. 1, 1929, A4, LC; Clough, *White of Emporia,* 135–37; EG, Apr. 14, 1932, reprinted in Clough, *White of Emporia,* pp. 138–41. On the role of this anticompetition strain of economic thought in the emergence of New Deal economic policy, see Ellis W. Hawley, *The New Deal and the Problem of Monopoly: A Study in Economic Ambivalence* (Princeton, N.J.: Princeton University Press, 1966).

67. White, "The Ethics of Advertising," *Atlantic Monthly* 164 (Nov. 1939): 669; White to Marco Morrow, Nov. 28, 1914, LB 25, LC.

68. Oral History with James Yearout, Flint Hills Oral History Project, LCHM.

69. White, "Early Draft of Autobiography," Ch. 17, pp. 4–5. The advent of chain stores in small Midwestern towns in this period is discussed in Lewis Atherton, *Main Street on the Middle Border* (Bloomington: Indiana University Press, 1954), pp. 240–41.

70. Laura M. French, *History of Emporia and Lyon County* (Emporia: Emporia Gazette Print, 1929), pp. 104, 105, 108, 248–49, 252; White note in Helen Ogden Mahin, *The Editor and His People* (New York: Macmillan Company, 1924), p. 21. In the early years, many farm bureau agents' salaries were underwritten by local businessmen, and both shared an interest in encouraging farmers to become more "businesslike." See David B. Danbom, *The Resisted Revolution: Urban America and the Industrialization of Agriculture, 1900–1930* (Ames: Iowa State University Press, 1979). White was a member of the board of directors of the Rotary Club. "Dear Rotarian," June 14, 1919, D9, LC. Lewis Atherton notes the rise of clubs in midwestern towns in this period, although he does not distinguish between purely local and national organizations. Atherton, *Main Street on the Middle Border,* pp. 290–93.

71. White to Burrell Engineering & Equipment Co., Sept. 17, 1919, LB 38, LC; French, *History of Emporia,* pp. 250–51; A. S. Newman to White, Sept. 16, 1910, C5; A. H. Gufler to White, Dec. 22, 1911, C9; and EG, Mar. 12 and Apr. 9, 1914.

72. C. R. Rice to White, Feb. 3, 1920, D10; Mrs. J. P. Ramseyer to *Gazette,* Aug. 19, 1921, D12; and Josephine Watson to *Gazette,* Aug. 26, 1921, D12; all LC.

73. J. S. Phillips to White, Aug. 19, 1910, C4, LC.

74. White to Herbert G. Tull, Oct. 4, 1918, ESU.

75. On the use of "facts" in Depression-era documentaries, see William Stott, *Documentary Expression and Thirties America* (New York: Oxford University Press, 1973).

76. *New Republic,* May 12, 1920, 348–49. Edward Gale Agran's study of White's ideas, focusing upon his postwar writings, emphasizes his use of Emporia as a symbol for middle-class America. Agran, " 'Too Good a Town': William Allen White and the Emerging Rhetoric of Middle America" (Ph.D. dissertation, University of Wisconsin-Madison, 1986).

77. White, "The Other Side of Main Street," *Collier's,* July 30, 1921, p. 7.

78. White, *Autobiography,* p. 605.

79. EG, May 17, 1921.

80. White, *Autobiography*, p. 605; White to William Lindsay White, May 27, 1921, A4, LC.

81. Christopher Morley to White, July 12, 1921, ESU; H. E. Hurray, July 7, 1921, D12, LC; L. W. Payne, Jr., to White, June 24, 1924, ESU. By 1947 it had appeared in over two hundred books. Johnson, *Selected Letters*, p. 216.

82. White, *Autobiography*, p. 605.

Epilogue

1. The anthologies are Helen Ogden Mahin, ed., *The Editor and His People: Editorials by William Allen White* (New York: Macmillan Company, 1924), and Russell H. Fitzgibbon, compiler, *Forty Years on Main Street* (New York: Farrar & Rinehart, 1937). Early biographies by Emporians include Frank C. Clough, *William Allen White of Emporia* (New York: McGraw-Hill Book Company, 1941); Everett Rich, *William Allen White: The Man from Emporia* (New York: Farrar & Rinehart, 1941); and David Hinshaw, *A Man From Kansas: The Story of William Allen White* (New York: G. P. Putnam's Sons, 1945). See also David Hinshaw, "Father White at Seventy," *Atlantic* (Feb. 1938); "A Great American Reaches Seventy," *Christian Century* 40 (Feb. 16, 1938): 197; "William Allen White of Emporia: An American Institution is 70," *Life* 4 (Feb. 28, 1939): 9–13; and "William Allen White: The Sage of Emporia," *Look* (Feb. 15, 1938): 9–11. Rich's biography contains a bibliography of articles about White up to 1941; three-quarters of the more than fifty articles were written after 1920.

2. For journalists this image has assumed something akin to iconic status, representing all of the stereotyped ideals of small-town journalism. A recent scholarly study that challenges the reality of these ideals is M. Salcetti, "Community Editor: Myth of the Roll-top Desk," in possession of the author.

Index